A MIGHTY CAPITAL UNDER THREAT

History of the Urban Environment

MARTIN V. MELOSI AND JOEL A. TARR, EDITORS

A
MIGHTY
CAPITAL
UNDER
THREAT

THE ENVIRONMENTAL HISTORY OF LONDON
1800–2000

Edited by Bill Luckin and Peter Thorsheim

UNIVERSITY OF PITTSBURGH PRESS

Published by the University of Pittsburgh Press, Pittsburgh, Pa., 15260
Copyright © 2020, University of Pittsburgh Press
Manufactured in the United States of America
Printed on acid-free paper
10 9 8 7 6 5 4 3 2 1

Cataloging-in-Publication data is available from the Library of Congress

ISBN 13: 978-0-8229-4610-6
ISBN 10: 0-8229-4610-6

COVER PHOTO: London skyline aerial view, iStockPhotos
COVER DESIGN: Joel W. Coggins

CONTENTS

CONTENTS

A MIGHTY CAPITAL UNDER THREAT

INTRODUCTION

ENVIRONMENT AND DAILY LIFE
IN LONDON

1800–2000

BILL LUCKIN AND PETER THORSHEIM

Two thousand years ago Rome housed close to a million inhabitants. This fact— if fact, it be—has generated an extraordinarily wide range of questions about ancient housing conditions, the provisioning of food and drink, disease patterns, the impact of the city on the rest of the empire, and vice versa, and environmental conditions in a massive city that would only be equaled in size nearly two millennia later.[1] Demographically, nineteenth-century London, or what countless proud Victorians called the "new Rome," first equaled, then superseded its ancient ancestor.[2] Already by the mid-eighteenth century the British capital had developed into a global city. Sustained by its enormous empire, between 1800 and the First World War London ballooned in population and land area. Nothing so vast had previously existed anywhere, yet the urban and economic changes that transformed London during these years were soon replicated in cities throughout many parts of Europe and North America. Then, toward the end of the twentieth century, a second revolution, shaped by globalization, made the urbanization of the entire planet seem virtually imminent.[3]

Over time the definition of London changed repeatedly as the built-up area and administrative structures expanded far beyond the boundaries of the "Square

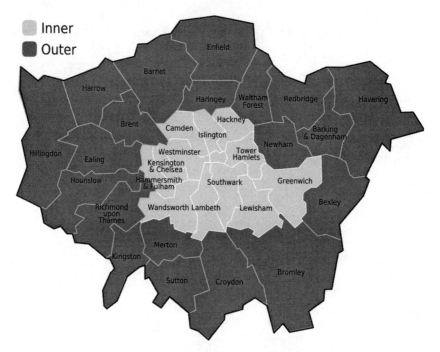

Fig. I.1. Map of Inner and Outer London, by Peter Fitzgerald, 2009. Courtesy of https://commons.wikimedia.org/wiki/File:Outer_Inner_London_Boroughs.png

Mile" situated at the center of Figure I.1. Inner London comprises the areas overseen by the London County Council (LCC) (1889–1965). With the creation of the Greater London Council (1965–1986), the boroughs shaded in dark gray in this map joined the territory governed by the former LCC to form Greater London. A Conservative Parliament abolished the Greater London Council in 1986, but following the Labour landslide of 1997, MPs voted to reestablish local control in the form of a new structure, the Greater London Authority (2000 to present).

Many of these themes provide rich fare for urban-environmental historians, practitioners of a discipline that came into being about forty years ago. In terms of origins, it is of course dangerous to trace the growth of a distinctive way of looking at the past exclusively in terms of its most significant practitioners. In the case of urban-environmental history, however, the picture is quite clear. Joel Tarr has been a seminal figure: his publications between the 1970s and the present have been central to the growth and topical diversity of the discipline.[4] Other trailblazers have included Martin Melosi, author of an important work on the development of the American "sanitary city" and numerous histories of waste disposal, water, and recycling.[5] A third pioneer, William Cronon, has probed in depth interactions between town and country. In his best-known study, Cronon illuminates the ways in which Chicago's demand for raw materials and agricultural produce transformed the city itself, its regional hinterland, and distant urban and rural communities.[6]

These historians and others have made a distinction between their way of looking at the past and longer established styles of history concerned with non-urbanized parts of the world and what remains of wilderness—or what is sometimes and somewhat problematically known as "first nature."[7] In the words of Ian Douglas, urban-environmental analysis is primarily concerned with the "impacts [of primary] nature on people in cities and the way urban people modify natural systems and change the biogeochemistry of the urban habitat."[8] Joel Tarr has filled out this definition: the discipline, he says, is "primarily [concerned with] the story of how human-built, anthropogenic structures ('built environment') and technologies shape and alter the natural environment of the urban site with consequent feedback to the city itself and its populations."[9]

Between the early 1970s and the 1990s, urban-environmental history predominantly concerned itself with structures and infrastructures, systems and ecologies. Since then its range has widened; indeed, it sometimes seems that practitioners engage with just about every aspect of cities and city life. Over the last couple of decades, the discipline has been in creative flux, and new ideas have developed at a bewildering rate. The complexities of metropolitan space and movement, and their relation to governmentality, are now much higher on the agenda.[10] So are the meanings and ramifications of nineteenth- and twentieth-century metropolitan nature and *rus in urbe*.[11] Urban green space is another growth area, as are the ideologically robust regulations that governed the ways in which urban residents were allowed to access and use parklands in cities and their hinterlands.[12] Urban-environmental scholars now also engage with historical interactions between nonhuman species and *Homo sapiens*.[13]

We can readily see that these "new" areas are directly or indirectly linked to topics first explored in the case of London between the 1960s and the 1980s. For many years historians have focused on the problems Londoners faced in obtaining a steady supply of water.[14] This has been complemented by research into the condition of the Thames and Lea and the ways in which each river generated troubling environmental dilemmas. Much is now known about the so-called Great Stink of 1858 and how this disturbing episode persuaded Parliament to fund the construction of a metropolitan main drainage system.[15] Until the recent past, historians paid far more attention to contaminated water than impure air. Recent research has done much to correct this oversight.[16] Pollution is of course intimately related to disease patterns in modern London: epidemiological and environmental history are inseparable. As early as the 1970s scholars probed the complexities of king cholera.[17] Slightly later, what the Victorians called "everyday diseases" came under scholarly scrutiny, with changing levels of infant and childhood mortality very much to the fore.[18]

Today historians are taking a fresh look at the myriad urban-environmental transformations that reshaped cities and their hinterlands between 1800 and 2000, contemporary observers' attempts to understand and cope with these changes, and the ways in which the distribution of political, social, and ideological power influenced both. Finally, the discipline of urban-environmental history is engaging with problems that are not merely local or even national, but global in character.[19]

STRUCTURES, CHRONOLOGIES, ANXIETIES

Historians once refused to consider London a manufacturing city. This was wrong. In 1850 about one in every three metropolitan adults worked in that sector.[20] Of course the capital had little in common with new industrial cities in the Midlands and North, many of which depended on a single type of productive activity. London had a more diverse portfolio. Woolwich Arsenal, which had its origins in the seventeenth century, played a central role in maintaining the nation's military might.[21] Large-scale brewing had been imbedded in the capital since the 1730s, and firms like Charrington and Bass produced huge quantities of beer.[22] Founded as two separate companies in the 1860s, Tate and Lyle later joined forces and developed into a sugar-refining giant.[23] Bryant and May, established at Bow in the East End in the mid-nineteenth century, developed into the largest match manufacturer in the world.[24]

Industry and manufacturing lived on into the twentieth century. By the 1950s, however, a different kind of London was beginning to emerge. Manufacturing jobs began to decline, in absolute and relative terms, as service industries gradually surpassed them. In the 1970s the process picked up speed, and by 2000 only about one in ten of the capital's adults was making a living in an industrial or manufacturing occupation.[25] Replicating the pace of change that had transformed the city between the 1830s and the Edwardian period, from an economic perspective London had suddenly become a quite different kind of place.

In the nineteenth century a sense of perpetual rush and change fascinated writers like Dickens and Trollope. The capital dominated every aspect of national life: it was a place you "went up to" from even the most northerly parts of the country. Population growth was abnormally high; by the mid-eighteenth century London's population had risen to seven hundred thousand. Fifty years later the capital housed a million citizens and was home to 10 percent of the population of mainland Britain.[26] By 1900 London contained six million inhabitants, a figure which grew to about eight million by 1950. The next thirty years saw a demographic pause, followed by a slight decline, and then a renewal of growth in the new millennium. The population may reach eleven million by 2050.[27] London's largest suburbs expanded in an astonishing manner after the Second World War. Districts like Battersea, Clapham, and Lewisham became as populous as cities like Birmingham, Leeds, and Liverpool. Many of them housed as many as three hundred thousand people. In the 1970s the world began to enter a wholly new demographic era. Massive conurbations like Mexico City, Tokyo, and Nairobi created a new global super-league. Nevertheless, the "greatest city the world had ever known" still retained much of its political, financial, and global power.[28]

Throughout most of its history many Londoners have experienced extremely high levels of overcrowding.[29] In the nineteenth century working-class and poverty-stricken inhabitants of regions such as the East End and squalid districts immediately to the south of the river endured catastrophically poor housing conditions. Contemporaries described the external environment transmuting into a ghastly sheet of filth, lodging houses tumbling to the ground as a result of the miserliness of landlords, and individual rooms—sometimes holding as many as ten people—spilling their meager belongings out onto stairs and landings.

The dominant ideology at this time insisted that if a working man—even a pauper—lived a moral life and resisted the temptations of drink, he might one day attain the status of lower middle-class "respectability."[30] Such expectations flew in the face of the day-to-day realities of being poor or poverty-stricken in the nineteenth- and early twentieth-century capital. In the 1840s Edwin Chadwick, briefly London's sanitary "dictator," declared that the capital must establish a new form of centralized metropolitan government that would eventually abolish the laissez-faire localism that had prevailed for longer than anyone could remember.[31] Chadwick believed that a new and more rational style of administration might make it possible, among other things, to shift ever-larger volumes of human waste away from the capital and out to rural areas where it would be sold (at a small profit) as fertilizer.[32] The scheme collapsed.

From the 1860s onward metropolitan reformers shifted their attention to what would now be called London's energy problem. In 1865, on the eve of the city's final cholera epidemic, the economist William Stanley Jevons published *The Coal Question*, a manifesto that presented an image of a capital that might soon revert to a deadly climatological regime.[33] In this terrifying new (or old) world, Londoners would either freeze to death or slip back toward a desperately primitive way of life.[34] Many believed that the only way of preventing such a disaster was to rebuild a low-energy regime in the countryside. Huge numbers of working men and their families must be persuaded—forced, some said—to migrate to rural England, thereby escaping the immorality, intemperance, and diseases of the capital, while at the same time regenerating half-forgotten pre-urban customs and trades.[35]

The malady—or multiple maladies—that threatened the capital were closely linked to the idea of pollution and a conviction that both London's civilization and rus in urbe might soon collapse in the face of urban-industrialism. In the medieval era the word pollution was synonymous with masturbation; however, by the late eighteenth and early nineteenth centuries, meanings had become less stable. Pollution still carried the connotation of what was often termed "self-abuse," but the term was also used to identify a nature and urban ecology that might imminently be befouled and perhaps destroyed by Homo sapiens acting in nonsexual ways.[36]

In 1834 John Martin, the eccentric early nineteenth-century artist of the sublime, attempted to organize a London-based campaign that would save the capital from destruction. In that year Martin told a parliamentary select committee that the government must sanction and fund the construction of two intercepting "grand receptacles" on the Regent's and Grand Surrey Canals. From these locations, what he insistently called "polluted matter" would be transported to non-urban environments. "Martin's scheme," as it was called, predated Chadwick's proposed panacea by a decade, and it revealed a more assured understanding of multiple urban and extra-urban ecological variables.[37]

For the remainder of the nineteenth century and into the Edwardian era, "pollution" continued to be used in several different though related ways, usually in the ancient context of sexual misbehavior. By the 1860s the word and idea had become institutionalized. In 1863 the government established an official body, the Alkali Inspectorate, tasked to reduce acid rain.[38] In 1866 a standing Commission on Rivers set about finding ways in which Britain's sewer-like waterways might be returned to a degree of purity.[39]

Fear of dirt spiraled during the cholera years.[40] A new breed of water scientists gradually committed themselves to a kind of bacterial theory of disease transmission. Laypeople stuck to a much simpler way of thinking about and categorizing the fetid world in which they lived. If water were visibly dirty, it would almost certainly give you a bad stomachache and sometimes lead to serious illness or death.[41] Foul supplies, "infested with insects," were contra natura. Debates raged around "matter out of place." Ideas of purity and impurity lay at the heart of the so-called Great Stink on the Thames in 1858. This anxiety-riven series of events disgusted and fascinated Londoners and constituted a moral as well as an environmental crisis.[42] A dithering Parliament eventually decided to construct a mighty intercepting sewage system, a project that reached completion in the early 1870s. Many Londoners (and some historians) assumed that this would transform the capital. In reality it was more like a promising beginning than an end. Severe and minor water crises recurred. In 1878 the steamboat Princess Alice sank on the lower Thames, with great loss of life. Horrified Londoners learned that some of the corpses had been covered in thick and disgusting sewage.[43]

How filthy was the nineteenth-century Thames? The era between 1800 and 1850 saw the river converted into a sewer-like sump. As early as the 1820s salmon fishermen were forced to find alternative employment.[44] The second half of the century saw progress in some respects. Sewage pollution became less extreme, but the volume of untreated manufacturing waste likely increased.[45] Two preventive agencies—the Metropolitan Board of Works (MBW) and the Thames Conservancy—seemed to prefer arguing with one another to getting on with the overwhelmingly complex job in hand.[46]

In the years after 1950 the Thames began to look more like a watercourse that had attained a minimal degree of genuine purity. Salmon returned, and the river was no longer officially biologically dead.[47] But this was only part of the story. As London moved through the 1990s and into the new millennium, increasingly sophisticated environmental tests pointed to the possibility of renewed regression. Thames Water, the company responsible for a privatized metropolitan supply since 1983, issued warnings about the future of the river. It claimed that nothing less than the construction of an exceptionally controversial (and expensive) Thames Tideway could protect the river from regular and dangerous episodes of sewage pollution associated with sudden outpourings of polluted storm water.[48]

What of the Lea, the capital's "second river"? In the 1860s the River Commissioners wrote a damning treatise on dangerous levels of pollution, vulnerability to manufacturing waste flowing down from the north, and the fact that waterway management was random and underfinanced.[49] Scientists and reformers kept a watchful eye on the state of the river and repeatedly warned that the Lea would soon trigger a large-scale outbreak of enteric infection.[50] In the hundred years between 1850 and 1950 the condition of this river, like that of the Thames, appeared to improve. But population growth in extra-metropolitan towns and outer suburbs posed a seemingly insoluble problem, and cooperation between these ever-larger communities rarely took place. The Local Government Board intervened, but to little effect. In the here and now, the media regularly report that the Lea is a national disgrace, as dead fish mix with ever-increasing volumes of manufacturing waste.[51]

We now know quite a bit about the history of atmospheric pollution in London.[52] In the seventeenth and eighteenth centuries its inhabitants sometimes witnessed sudden, anxiety-inducing darkening of the skies.[53] In the mid- and late nineteenth century many observers—increasing numbers of whom were versed in the science of meteorology—became convinced that the capital was about to enter a new climatological era. These fears were confirmed by recurrent smoke crises, events that triggered London "close-downs" and deprived the city's desperately poor casual laborers of work and income.

It was now widely acknowledged that death rates spiraled upward not only during dense black fogs, but also during "ordinary" ones. Between the 1870s and the Edwardian era, the passionately committed "fog expert" Francis (Rollo) Russell, Bertrand's eccentric uncle, argued that atmospheric pollution might kill as many people as a cholera epidemic.[54] Russell also stated that only a massive reduction in the numbers of people living in smoky towns would bring an end to recurrent atmospheric crises.[55] Pea-soupers, as bad episodes were called, were painted by the impressionists, written about by visitors to the capital. and editorialized (mainly by the London *Times*). The Edwardian period saw a sudden reduction in the capital's eerie black fogs. Was this because there had been a slow switch from coal to gas, or was it associated with autonomous meteorological change?[56] One thing was certain: effective metropolitan and national anti-smoke legislation was weak, contradictory and, most of the time, unenforceable. A pioneering historian of the issue noted that "Parliament passed laws giving local authorities the power to act: the local authorities, forced to confront the polluters at close quarters in the councils and courts, wavered and passed the responsibility back to the central government."[57] In 1952, when a catastrophic smoke crisis struck London, it seemed to confirm every prediction dolefully listed by Rollo Russell and his co-reformers.[58] The Clean Air Act, which came onto the statute books in 1956, was a step in the right direction. But new contaminants now threatened London's skies and health. The pressing contemporary intellectual task is to chart the development of the capital's car culture, interrogate the ambiguities of vehicular pollution data, and explore policy successes and failures between the 1960s and today.[59]

What, finally, of garbage disposal? The flawed hypothesis that there may have been a "refuse revolution" between 1870 and the early 1920s has spurred research, which has revealed that each metropolitan community followed its own hit-or-miss route toward ridding streets and houses of rubbish.[60] Depending on time and place, each area experimented with dumping outside the capital, employing "dust destructors," producing electricity from waste, tipping and burying waste on selected rural sites, and implementing weekly collection from individual homes. More efficient production processes and increases in take-home pay led to a wider range of consumer goods becoming available to the working classes; this played a central role in the expansion and changing makeup of metropolitan waste.[61] In the early twentieth century rubbish collection continued to cause citywide problems. In 1929 a report by the London County Council painted a picture of chaotic disorganization.[62] Today the capital continues to lag behind the rest of the country.[63]

The urban-environmental history of London needs to be linked to the ways in which the capital, and its component parts, were governed in the period between the early 1800s and the beginning of the new millennium. What was the "London government system"? How did it change over time? Did it possess the kinds of powers that were capable of making the capital into a better and safer place in which to live?[64] From the beginning of the nineteenth century to the 1850s, governing processes remained largely unchanged.[65] Ancient ecclesiastical parishes carried the main administrative burden and—as might be predicted—the capital avoided the kind of local governmental reform introduced in new cities in the Midlands and North by the Municipal Corporations Act in 1834. Only in the aftermath of the multiple environmental crises of the 1840s and early 1850s was London subjected to a modicum of administrative reorganization. In 1855 a Metropolis Management Act divided the capital into thirty-nine vestries or district boards and made them responsible for local sanitary management. In addition to removing nuisances and refuse, each vestry or district board had to appoint a medical officer of health and a team of sanitary inspectors, all of whom were expected to reduce the mortality rate. The measure also established a Metropolitan Board of Works, to undertake citywide improvement policies. This was a promising dimension of the act, but in 1888 the MBW collapsed amid accusations and counteraccusations of rigged building contracts.[66]

The Metropolitan Board of Works was replaced by the London County Council, a body comprising 118 directly elected councilors and 19 aldermen. The new body inherited the responsibilities—and limitations—of its predecessor and possessed London-wide powers for slum clearance, infectious disease control, main drainage, lodging houses, and animal health.[67] At the end of the century, vestries were abolished and replaced by boroughs, some of which contained as many people as large cities elsewhere in the kingdom. These administrative bodies retained the fierce independence that had characterized every part of the London government system since 1800. In outer suburban London individual district populations soared to between three and four hundred thousand, and they were even less likely than their predecessors to be dictated to by the London County Council. In addition, the council failed to gain powers to protect water quality and the purity of metropolitan air. It was also largely excluded from working with numerous long-established independent bodies charged with the reduction of infectious disease. For example, the council lacked the legal authority to collaborate with the Metropolitan Asylums Board, a capital-wide organization established in 1867 for the treatment of London's sick poor.[68] In addition, the LCC played only a minor role in the affairs of the Poor Law, the ancient voluntary hospitals, the Thames and Lea Conservancy Boards, and the Port of London Authority.

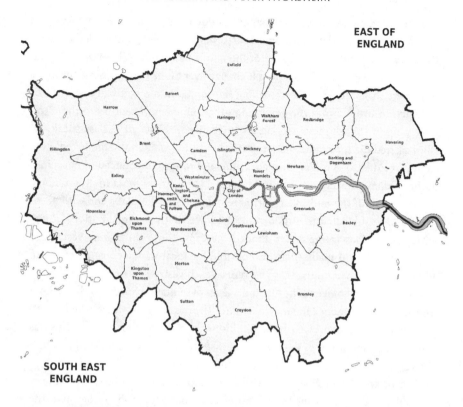

Fig. I.2. Greater London, 2000 to the present. Courtesy of https://upload.wikimedia.org
/wikipedia/commons/thumb/c/ca/Greater_London%2C_administrative_divisions
_-_de_-_monochrome.svg/1425px-Greater_London%2C_administrative_divisions
_-_de_-_monochrome.svg.png

Throughout the twentieth century and right up to the present time, the
bodies that succeeded the council lacked the kind of executive powers that
were needed to make London a less polluted and unhealthy place. Successive
would-be "governments"—the Greater London Council between 1965 and 1985,
a Whitehall-dominated "residuary" body between 1985 and 1996, and the mayoral Greater London Authority since 2000—also found it exceptionally difficult
to frame and operationalize strategies to work toward higher levels of sustainability.[69] The capital had been too administratively complex at too early a date to be
subjected to what anti-centralizers throughout our period interpreted as a wan-
ton act of constitutional and national destruction. But did the survival of localism necessarily militate against reform? We now have electronic access to the
annual reports of London's medical officers of health between the 1840s and the
1970s.[70] This material provides extraordinarily detailed accounts of how each part
of the capital dealt with its day-to-day environmental problems. What emerges is

a mixed picture. Although some areas of London ventured where no provincial urban centers of comparable size had dared to go, others—mainly smaller inner-core areas—lagged behind their neighbors and centers of comparable size outside the capital. By the 1870s Londoners had reason to feel optimistic that their city's most egregious environmental ills were gradually being addressed.

But there is an urgent need for more historians to go down to the grassroots level and report on the social and ecological dynamics of the nineteenth- and twentieth-century capital. Sometimes dismissed as antiquarianism, research of this kind can take us much closer to the "real London" and possibly to the conclusion that anti-centralizing reform played an important—perhaps decisive—role in the development of a less polluted and healthier environment.[71] Many of these local bodies worked extraordinarily hard to improve what is now known as the environment. Often they did the right thing for the wrong reasons. On other occasions they lacked the theoretical know-how and trained personnel to deal with even a tiny proportion of the nuisances they were tasked to root out. Our knowledge of this area is rapidly increasing, but we still know too little about how London's eccentrically organized local bureaucracies often went about their work.

LINES OF INQUIRY

In our first essay Jim Clifford provides a cartographically-based survey of the capital and its countless micro-localities. Clifford analyzes the growth of a capital that was once walkable, but which now occupies a staggering 1,600 square kilometers, a figure that excludes suburban development outside the boundaries of what is now defined as the greater metropolitan region. Clifford also implicitly throws light on a much-discussed nineteenth-century issue: fear on the part of reformers and planners that London would one day reach so deeply into the countryside that southern rural England would be threatened with extinction. Clifford's use of cartographic and visual evidence allows him to provide a detailed account of the ways in which the capital's forests, commons, and marshes went into gradual and then increasingly rapid decline. He links this to the issue of the ways in which the metropolitan hinterland came to be converted into inner and outer suburbs. Making powerful connections between past and present, Clifford shows how a radical reordering of metropolitan space, involving heavily built-up areas, waste, and brownfields, has given rise in our own times to "low-level" environmental risk. The current position is worryingly multifaceted. Too many impenetrable surfaces now increase the long-term possibility of serious flooding, a danger increased by the fact that global warming has given rise to a wetter climate. It goes without saying that action is urgently needed.[72] As we have seen, however, the capital's twenty-first century "constitution" makes it exceptionally difficult to translate recommendations into reality. Borough power can still stand in the way of concerted action. Too often local preoccupations obscure the larger metropolitan picture.

Where Jim Clifford focuses on the spatial complexities of the capital, Christopher Hamlin presents a cluster of interacting representations of the world's first global city, a range of different and revealing ways of seeing.[73] Beginning with a juxtaposition of Wordsworth's vision of a tranquil London and William Blake's desperate evocation of alienation and despair in his classic poem "London," Hamlin points out that the nineteenth-century capital was less "a metropolis" than simply *the* Metropolis. He touches on the extent to which the city has never been subjected to fully centralizing power and the ways in which individual boroughs continued to hold nearly absolute control until the twentieth century. Hamlin introduces a cluster of approaches to an understanding of what made London what it was (and in many respects, still is). He begins with the "experiential" city, "filled with physical and biological impedimenta," thereby providing the reader with a powerful reminder of just how profoundly "green" and "natural" so many parts of the capital continue to be—a theme developed later in the volume by Peter Thorsheim. Hamlin's second perspective is "inspectorial," a topic which, as we have seen, has now belatedly begun to be subjected to increasingly rigorous historical scrutiny.[74] Here Hamlin moves through a narrative stretching from the second decade of the nineteenth century to the 1890s, arguing that by the latter date informal and "benevolent" policing had given way to a more rigorous and punitive approach. Having probed "systemic" London, the capital as a hub of national and international science, and the extent to which it was once deemed possible to "save" the capital through analysis of large amounts of detailed data, Hamlin turns his attention to an "Anthropocene" capital. This term denotes a city that over the last sixty years or so has reached a point of absolute crisis—a phase of history driven like no other before it by human failure to reduce the rate at which *Homo sapiens* exploits and destroys first and second nature. "The Anthropocene" is a relatively novel term, but numerous late nineteenth-century commentators feared that the spatial expansion and (in their eyes) ever more polluted state of the capital might lead to nothing less than long-term global crisis.[75]

The kinds of problems with which Jim Clifford and Christopher Hamlin are concerned are explored in a demographic and epidemiological setting by Anne Hardy. Following a classically Hippocratic line of investigation, Hardy engages with maladies and causes of premature death associated with various and varying environments. Citing pioneering eighteenth-century investigations by Leonard Schwarz and John Landers, Hardy emphasizes the extent to which, even during the early Victorian period, the capital was a much healthier place than in the 1750s.[76] The eighteenth-century city was characterized by incomprehensible levels of overcrowding; the ancient core may have been as overcrowded as it had been in the late Middle Ages. In the 1730s the annual death rate was approximately fifty per one thousand population. A hundred years later, that figure had been halved. Despite recurrent epidemics of cholera, typhus, typhoid, smallpox, influenza, and the everyday but nevertheless deadly toll from what the Victorians called "the infections of childhood," the capital "survived" in a manner that astonished pessimistic contemporaries who were convinced that the greatest urban center the world had ever seen had reached a point of no return. Following the "cholera years" between the 1830s and the mid-1860s, metropolitan disease experts, like William Farr at the General Register Office, came to believe that the worst might already be over and that there would be no return to "plague-like" conditions in the capital.[77] Despite this optimism, cholera continued to appear with disturbing regularity in London through the middle decades of the century.

Hardy shows that infant mortality rates went into gradual decline, albeit with variations between and within different districts. This meant that, contrary to the belief of many contemporary experts, London fared relatively well compared to other major cities. Capital-wide infant mortality rates declined from 159 per thousand live births in 1901, to 81 in 1921, 25 in 1950, 21.5 in 1960, and 5.5 in 2000. Hardy argues that from the 1850s onward, public-health committees and their inspectorial employees gained an increasingly comprehensive understanding of the health problems of the capital. Construction of citywide infrastructure, combined with local sanitary enforcement, led to "improvements achieved against the odds" and cast doubt on the veracity of nineteenth- and early twentieth-century urban observers who assumed the capital to be the poorest, filthiest, and least salubrious city in the kingdom. It was only one step from this belief to a conviction that there was something perniciously wrong with the urban condition in all its guises and that a return to the countryside was the only solution.

Hardy's comparison of death rates in the period between the early nineteenth and the beginning of the twenty-first century is complemented by Christopher Ferguson's delineation of how what would now be called environmental specialists viewed the world in which they lived and worked between the 1770s and the 1870s. Ferguson's medical men, meteorologists, and proto-epidemiologists condemned towns and cities for the adverse impact they had on human health and resilience. Well-to-do members of the metropolitan population were warned that it was imperative either to move to the countryside or make regular visits to nonurban locations to recharge their batteries, an idea that long remained influential in a society which had industrialized and urbanized before any other, thereby losing liberating connections with a rural Eden.[78]

Obviously this therapeutic advice could be followed only by the middle and upper classes and had little meaning for the poor, who most urgently needed an escape from appalling living conditions in hugely overcrowded courts and alleys. Ferguson provides a detailed analysis of the ways in which medical experts and others viewed the urban society in which they lived and why it is unwise to project onto them bodies of thought now routinely designated "environmental." He defines "early environmentalism" as a way of making sense of discrete human and spatial subcategories, "climates, regions or cities . . . conceived of in explicitly compartmentalized terms, what contemporaries referred to as 'circumstances.'" Many experts held the optimistic position that either an individual or his or her immediate community was capable of responding to and overcoming adverse conditions. Ferguson argues that although it would be anachronistic to project our own ideas about "the environment" and "environmentalism" onto the past, people's efforts to understand the connections between themselves and their surroundings are an important aspect of every period's history.

There are strong links between Christopher Ferguson's survey and Bill Luckin and Andrea Tanner's analysis of the relationship between sanitary and "modern" environmental modes of thought and action between the 1860s and the interwar period. The authors focus on a single district (later borough)—the inner suburb of Hackney—which was transformed from a semirural community at the beginning of the nineteenth century into one of the largest districts in London, with a population that outnumbered those of all but a handful of provincial cities. Hackney had just one medical officer of public health, John Tripe, between 1856 and 1892; his voluminous reports allow us to trace the way in which typical Victorian sanitary experts conceptualized the growing range of problems that came under the purview of Hackney's Sanitary (later Public Health) Committee.

Tripe was a conservative who believed, like several of the individuals discussed by Christopher Ferguson, that even the poorest of the poor possessed the "moral" wherewithal to drag themselves out of misery and, abstaining from vice and committing themselves to temperance, find a way out of the vile conditions in which they lived. This shouldn't be interpreted as implying that Tripe lacked sympathy for the impoverished people among whom he worked. Rather, he was bound by ideas that characterized and legitimated a nearly universal and heavily class-inflected ideology emphasizing what would later come to be known as upward social mobility—an insistence that even the poverty-stricken could draw on moral means to transform the way in which they lived. In Tripe's view, there were areas in Hackney that would never attain the degree of social "decency and respectability" that prevailed in the "old town," that part of the district which had been the environmentally desirable and country-like home of merchants and bankers in the eighteenth and early nineteenth centuries and which continued to pride itself on its respectability and domestic cleanliness.

The authors unearth material that brings the reader close to the miserable day-to-day life of the unemployed and underemployed in deeply deprived sub-districts like marshy Hackney Wick. Compared with the old town, this area was characterized by appalling housing, recurrent outbreaks of disease, and one of the highest rates of infant mortality in the capital. Luckin and Tanner suggest that toward the end of their period quantitative analysis of social and epidemiological conditions contributed to the emergence of what are now considered to be "environmental" modes of thought. Yet traditional sanitary values continued to play an important role, and they would continue to do so for another couple of decades. In Hackney the discourse associated with the identification and removal of Victorian nuisances had a long and influential afterlife.

In his contribution Peter Thorsheim shows how analysis of the uses and alleged misuses of London's countryside takes the environmental historian deep into complex interactions between nature, class, gender, space, and power. At the beginning of the nineteenth century the capital's upper and middle classes claimed a near-monopoly over what should and should not be done in green places like Hyde Park, Green Park, and Kensington Gardens in the West End, and Parliament Hill Fields, Primrose Hill, and Hampstead Heath in the privileged north. Guardians of elitist values were convinced that only a tiny minority of the metropolitan working-class population knew how to behave correctly in parks and woods and benefit from socially disciplined physical and mental regeneration. They worried that countless numbers of the lower orders were far more likely to carouse themselves into oblivion and search out secret places for illicit sex. The "privatization" of magnificent squares reinforced the point: only the wealthy and privileged knew how to appreciate domesticated urban nature. Throughout the nineteenth century, however, small groups of reformers argued that working men and women, no less than members of the middle and upper classes, deserved access to green places in and immediately outside the capital. These natural oases constituted the "lungs" of the city, but they also served to reconnect urban residents with the natural world in a way that many hoped would promote social cohesion. A key proponent of this ideology, Lord Meath, the founder of the Metropolitan Public Gardens Association, insisted that if the working classes were excluded from rus in urbe, they would gradually degenerate both physically and morally.[79] Gradually green London opened its doors to the public, even though milder variants of what might be called "green moralism" lived on.

The early twentieth century witnessed the emergence of an idealistic commitment to opening nature for working people so that they could explore and enjoy parks and woods in or outside the capital. Fresh air came to be accepted as beneficial for everyone—hence the rise of the garden city movement and, following an astonishingly rapid green reconstruction of the capital in the aftermath of savage assault by German bombs, the consolidation of universal (but still orderly) access to London's green spaces. At the same time a controversial Green Belt now protected the capital and its suburbs from random development. Londoners could use the Underground—particularly the Central Line—to walk and relax in a now legislatively protected hinterland. Thorsheim, like Jim Clifford, ends his contribution with a succinct summary of early twenty-first-century threats to metropolitan sustainability.

Each of our remaining contributions is wholly or partly concerned with the nature, extent, and multiple impacts of pollution. As we have seen, economic historians once believed that in its nineteenth-century heyday the capital was a massive sink of consumption and a prolific producer of services associated with banking and finance, insurance, and the law. This made it possible to juxtapose the metropolitan economy against the supposedly quite different socioeconomic character of urban structures in the Midlands and North.

Contesting this position, Leslie Tomory surveys metropolitan industrial pollution problems between the early nineteenth century and the immediate aftermath of the First World War. He shows that, according to the census of 1851, one in three of the adult male metropolitan labor force worked in manufacturing, most notably in construction, metal production, furniture making, and woodworking. Tomory argues that the severity of the human waste problem, which peaked in the 1840s and 1850s, together with fears of diseases associated with impure water, diverted public and scientific attention away from dilemmas connected with industrial smoke. During the second half of the nineteenth century, increasing numbers of the "dirty" trades moved eastward into under-inspected areas that did next to nothing to police pollution.

From 1889 onward the London County Council and the vestries (soon to be boroughs) gained more extensive powers to combat industrial smoke nuisances. A major and lasting difficulty was that many scientists and medical men differed radically over what came to be called the "best practicable means" of reducing the smoke problem. There was a vexing legislative problem: most laws governing pollution in England and Wales did not apply to London, which had its own regulatory framework. Lawmakers tried on occasion to correct this, but with limited success. In terms of punishments that could be handed down from the end of the nineteenth century, the London County Council failed to find ways of limiting the damage committed by multiple offenders. As a final resort, a citizen or corporate body could take civil action against a gross polluter. But this route toward the improvement of the environment invariably took a long time. Suspects often employed lawyers who were adept at finding ways around the law. Judges refused to grant orders that might increase unemployment. Hearings were frequently reduced to semantic debate about the meanings of "smoke," degrees of smokiness, and the cost of rendering a chimney "less dirty."

In the early twentieth century smoke—or "smog" as it came to be called—remained a largely unsolved problem, and more research would need to be undertaken before scientific findings could be translated into preventive legislation. As Tomory shows, the problem was made more complex because of the staggering post-1850 increase in the number of domestic fires in the capital: these belched smoke into the atmosphere, where it intermixed with industrial vapors and became associated by a minority of health officials with bronchial and pneumonic disease, notably among elderly members of the metropolitan community. Decisive and meaningful action would only begin to be taken in the mid-twentieth century.

What of impure water, central to Vanessa Taylor's discussion of the nineteenth- and early twentieth-century meanings of this most crucial of utilities? Taylor's contribution is divided into three sections. The first focuses on debates surrounding the provision of a domestic supply and a primary Chadwickian obsession: the role that water should occupy in the great Victorian task of constructing a "sanitary city." Next, Taylor provides an account of relationships between water and changing conceptions of public health. Finally, she turns her attention to the "changing forms" of domestic supply in the nineteenth and early twentieth centuries and the role that they played in everyday life. Already in the 1850s and 1860s the pioneering research of John Snow and William Budd (an expert on typhoid) suggested that deadly enteric diseases were primarily transmitted by impure public water supplies. Gradually this knowledge came to the attention of metropolitan medical officers; by the mid-1860s, an increasing number of them had been converted to a kind of germ theory at least partly predicated on the "water factor." A key event was the East London Company's blatant decision in 1866 to draw on dangerous sources, leading to the deaths of more than five thousand inhabitants in eastern and northeastern parts of the capital.

In one or another form, as Taylor notes, London's "water problem" reached back to the early nineteenth century. Until the replacement in 1902 of the eight all-powerful private companies by a publicly administered Metropolitan Water Board, disputes about water supply and quality repeatedly engaged large numbers of metropolitan inhabitants. Citizens' groups adopted a position that appeared and reappeared for the rest of the century, and in a particularly intense form between the 1870s and 1900. During these years the water question became intimately intertwined with ferocious debates over the "London government problem"—a demand, as we have seen, on the part of reformers that an ancient and allegedly amateurishly administered city should finally be restructured to introduce elements of the semi-democratically elected committee systems that were believed to flourish in centers like Birmingham, Manchester, and Leeds. Taylor emphasizes that reformers repeatedly made the point that adequately treated water should be free at the point of delivery and that the poor must receive a supply under the same kind of terms as the wealthy and well-to-do. She argues that during the nineteenth and early twentieth centuries Londoners gradually became witness to the wholesale industrialization and commodification of a genuinely public supply.

In their comparison of London and New York water in the long period between the beginning of the nineteenth century and the near-present, Bill Luckin and Joel Tarr engage, like Vanessa Taylor, with the issue of the public good in relation to supply. They probe the extent to which the Empire City and the British capital have defined and served the interests of their respective populations, and they address the question of whether predominantly public or private control has more efficiently delivered an adequate per capita supply to ever-growing populations.

The authors emphasize that as early as the 1830s New York developed a much better water service than London. Instead of relying, as did London, on an adjacent river, the Empire City shifted from the pollution-prone Hudson River to a much purer source located far from the city. At times this decision gave rise to problems; intermittently throughout our period conflicts occurred with watershed communities, which complained that the urban giant had failed to acknowledge the severity of the problems that its policies had generated. Upstate villages were radically affected by waterworks developments. So too were farmers and hunters.

In the mid-twentieth century New York water and planning authorities set about finally resolving these difficulties, with the result that cumulative waves of environment- and employment-related compensation minimized mistrust between the Empire City and its water-rich hinterland. Finally, in 1995 a Watershed Memorandum of Agreement was signed between New York City and upstate communal, farming, and sporting interests. In addition, creative steps have been taken to convince city-dwellers that it is imperative to save water and acclimatize themselves to significantly lower per capita levels of consumption in an increasingly water-stressed world.

The story of nineteenth-century London water revolved around the dangers associated with inner city supplies, pollution crises, and interactions between the London government problem and the way in which water should be delivered by the capital's intensely unpopular private companies. In 1902 the latter were finally and belatedly taken over by a publicly administered Metropolitan Water Board. The MWB improved the outreach and purity of metropolitan supply. In 1973 it was replaced by the Thames Water Authority, with basin-wide responsibility for water quality, supply, and sewerage. Sixteen years later, in the full flush of Thatcher's privatization drive, the authority was handed over to an internationally owned corporation, Thames Water. Very few customers could be convinced that the new body had a genuine commitment to the public good. Consumers disliked the fact that Thames Water seemed to be repeatedly involved in business and operational deals with invisible investors. Prices rose, and the company failed to reduce its scandalously high leakage rate. As in the nineteenth century, the capital now finds itself in a position in which water supply is only distantly related to most inhabitants' conception of the public good.

The essays in this volume suggest a provisional framework for future forays into the modern urban-environmental history of the British capital. In doing so, each acknowledges the complexities of successive London government systems and the ways in which mainstream political and social history can be linked to and enriched by detailed knowledge of the development of infrastructure and public utilities. The essays also demonstrate that urban-environmental analysis can add depth to the study of epidemiological, medical, and urban history, and the histories of housing and overcrowding. Of course, each of these areas has a rich historiography of its own, but each would nevertheless be strengthened through closer scrutiny of ecological variables and systems. In addition, several of our contributions seek to reconstruct environmental conditions and experiences at the micro level. This is an exceptionally demanding task, but it is nearly impossible for a historian to understand the essence of London as a totality without having a grasp of its component parts. As the Victorians well knew, the capital consisted of a cluster of urban villages, gradually linked together by the sense that they formed part of London, a place that countless observers have described as the world's first global city. Putting the bits back together again will be a demanding historical task, but London's history can only be enriched by nuanced local and regional accounts of water and water supply, waste and waste disposal, housing, the construction of infrastructure, and fevered debates about issues that we now see as environmental.

As several of the chapters in this volume make clear, the British capital constituted a gigantic experimental laboratory in which the ideas of urban nature, pollution, and environment were defined and debated by individuals operating within scientific, medical, meteorological, and epidemiological communities. Collectively these essays indicate the multiplicity of ways in which urban-environmental history has changed over the last thirty years. Classic topics such as the dynamics of water supply and the construction of a main drainage system have been joined by complex debates about nature and rus in urbe, the construction and control of metropolitan space, the numerous meanings of pollution, and the many and seemingly contradictory ways in which London has been represented and decoded over the past two centuries.

ONE

GREATER LONDON'S RAPID GROWTH
1800–2000

JIM CLIFFORD

Greater London grew at a remarkable pace during the nineteenth century, beginning with a little under 1 million people in 1801 and ending with over 6.5 million in 1901. Population growth in Greater London plateaued after reaching 8 million in the mid-twentieth century, but the wider conurbation continued to expand, and a recent estimate places the population at more than 14 million.[1] Much of the growth in the past two centuries took place in an expanding ring of suburbs, beyond the control of London's government, and this resulted in haphazard and fractured urban development. Suburban governments were left to manage much of the expansion of the Metropolis.

London began a global trend as the first city to exceed five million people in the 1880s. Urbanization and the growth of cities with millions of people became a defining feature in the global environmental history of the twentieth century.[2] In 1900 London alone had more than six million people; a century later, thirty-six cities, spread across all the inhabited continents, reached or exceeded this level. This makes London's history unique, not only because it grew first, but also because it has maintained a population consistently above five million longer than any other city.[3] London's early growth also meant that it had few opportunities to learn from the mistakes of others.

The social, economic, and political ramifications of London's urbanization are well covered in the city's expansive historiography,[4] but the history of sub-urban growth remains underdeveloped, despite spurts of interest since the early 1960s.[5] There is also much to be learned about the environmental history of this expansive Metropolis. There is excellent work, including other chapters in this volume, on how urban and industrial development led to significant air and water pollution problems.[6] These prominent consequences were only some of the environmental transformations that came with urbanization on this scale. Moreover, much of the environmental history remains focused on central London and the inner suburbs, with little attention to places such as Brent or Enfield in Outer London.[7]

Two centuries of rapid urbanization transformed the regional environment. Urban growth, combined with rising standards of living, required ever more water, materials, and energy. It also led to a significant rise in pollution from travel and heating, and the spread of industry, landfills, and other pollution-intensive land uses across the increasingly expansive outer districts of Greater London. Greater London also contended with the legacy of ill-conceived development on estuarial marshlands. The region's wetlands were drained and covered with facto-ries, houses, and streets. This, combined with the spread of suburbs, which were less able to absorb rainwater than the agricultural land they replaced, increased the challenge of diverting storm water through sewers.

Historical maps and census data make it possible to track Greater London's growth over two centuries. These sources record the decline of woodlands, com-mons, and marshlands in the region and the conversion of hundreds of square kilometers of rural landscape into suburbs. The maps also highlight the haphaz-ard nature of suburbanization, with considerable overlap between new dormi-tory suburbs, pockets of industry, and a few remaining farms. There were signif-icant environmental consequences of this dispersal of the population, industry, and infrastructure across the Greater London region in the twentieth century. The Metropolis is still dotted with toxic decommissioned landfills and brown-fields, which are slowly are being redeveloped through very expensive remedi-ation projects.[8] Finally, the roads and buildings that make up Greater London are themselves a low-level environmental problem. Impermeable surfaces and development on the floodplains increased the risk of floods, and this problem will only increase as climate change brings more storms and higher ocean levels.[9]

LONDON'S GROWTH

Beginning in the late eighteenth century, regions on London's urban fringe generally developed first into market gardens or dumping sites, with ribbons of development spreading along the main roads. Gradually, the land between the

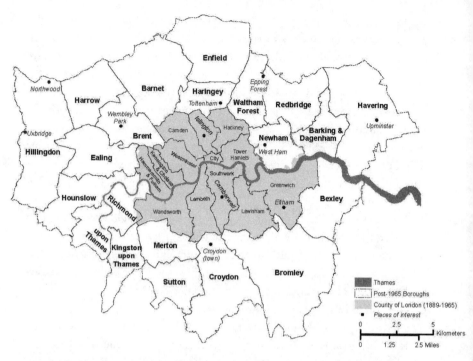

Fig. 1.1. Reference map of modern boroughs. In 1965 reforms amalgamated smaller local districts into these boroughs and in many cases kept the name of one of the former districts. Created by Jim Clifford, based on "Statistical GIS Boundary Files for London," London Datastore, 2013, http://data.london.gov.uk/dataset/statistical-gis-boundary -files-london.

thoroughfares filled in with suburban streets and row houses, or a cluster of factories.[10] This process repeated over time as new regions on the outskirts formed into suburbs, and the older districts became inner suburbs or a part of London.[11] Hackney, for example, transformed from a rural hinterland in 1800 to a growing suburb in the second half of the nineteenth century, and it was increasingly absorbed into London proper during the twentieth century. Preexisting towns, villages, and hamlets also transformed into suburbs as London's sphere of influence and transportation networks expanded. This resulted in satellite suburbs growing in Outer London, beyond the limits of the continuous built-up area. Croydon is the best early example; it started as an independent town south of London in Surrey, but increasingly became a major commuter suburb during the nineteenth century.

London grew in every direction, unrestrained by walls, large rivers, or other geographical features.[12] Thus it was less dense than most major nineteenth-century cities, and it dispersed farther with each major transportation innovation. Greater London spread from its walkable early nineteenth-century core to

1,569 square kilometers in the second half of the twentieth century, not counting suburban growth outside of Greater London's current official limits. Its continuous expansion makes London a difficult city to define, as the official boundaries never encompassed the whole of the Metropolis. It regularly spilled beyond its existing administrative borders, and the multitiered governments of Greater London were reformed and reorganized on several occasions. This has posed problems for historians who have made observations based on what happened within the census definition of London and ignored developments just across the border. For example, London continued to industrialize during the second half of the nineteenth century, but much of this happened in the Essex suburbs and was not recorded in the London census tables.[13] Historical maps of the Greater London region and regional census data provide a better measure of the city's limits than do jurisdictional boundaries. Comparing maps also makes it possible to see how the landscape transformed as the population increased by millions.

The distinction between London and the City of London further complicates the history of the Metropolis. The City of London was a walled city founded by the Romans as Londinium. The City's independent government dates to the Anglo-Saxon period. Southwark and Westminster, incorporated in the Middle Ages, grew significantly during the early modern period. Whitechapel and Stepney, the early suburbs on the eastern edge of the City, were well established by the sixteenth century, and the East End continued to grow through the seventeenth and eighteenth centuries. Yet the City of London did not absorb these suburbs, and by the mid-nineteenth century the City made up only about a fortieth of the total population. The suburbs around the City were in reality the expanding core of metropolitan London.

In 1847 the General Register Office developed a new and significantly expanded definition of London to collect weekly mortality statistics, and the 1851 census used this boundary, creating an official definition that lasted until the County of London was dissolved in 1965. This new boundary expanded official London to roughly three hundred square kilometers.[14] Although the new limits absorbed large tracks of rural land, they did not include two of the fastest growing suburbs: West Ham in Essex and Croydon in Surrey. Suburbanization continued, and the increasingly populous communities located outside of official London were designated as Outer London for statistical purposes in the early 1880s. By the end of the nineteenth century most of the population growth shifted to Outer London. In 1965 a major reorganization of London's government finally absorbed Outer London and created an amalgamated Greater London. These reforms also redrew the borders of the lower-tier governments, creating a smaller number of boroughs governing larger areas and more people. A Green Belt, established in 1947, encircled the new official border, which limited the continued spread of the city in most directions. Nonetheless, suburban growth continued to spill beyond Greater London with commuters contributing to the growth of both old cities like Reading and new towns created in the postwar era, such as Crawley.

Suburbanization was not a uniform process, and each region developed differently with distinct social, economic, and environmental results. Maps provide snapshots of Greater London's diverse development. Starting in the late eighteenth century, these maps became increasingly detailed.[15] Comparing maps produced between the end of the eighteenth century with those surveyed in the decades that followed make the scale of urban growth immediately apparent. The maps also make it possible to examine the piecemeal transformation of the rural landscape as suburban growth approached and eventually encompassed a region.

From 1792 to 1795 Richard Horwood surveyed London and produced a series of thirty-two maps, which together made up the *Plan of the Cities of London and Westminster, the Borough of Southwark, and Parts Adjoining, Shewing Every House.*[16] The complete map extends from "Mary Le Bone" in the northwest to Walworth in the south and Bethnal Green in the northeast. Even with this limited coverage, the map includes significant undeveloped lands made up of market gardens and fields in Pimlico, Mile End, and Bloomsbury. The excerpt (fig. 1.2) shows the edge of the city south of St. Saviour's Dock in Bermondsey, where rows of housing, rope walks, felt mongers, tan yards, timber yards, and paper manufactories existed alongside market gardens and fields. A little farther west there were market gardens less than a mile from central London on the recently drained Lambeth Marsh. Urban development did extend beyond central London, particularly along major roads, but the countryside was never more than a few miles from any point in the city. As it approached a million inhabitants, London remained a compact city, as the population relied on walking and horses for transportation.

Benjamin Tees Davis's 1841 map of *London and Its Environs* captures the city a few years after the first railways began to revolutionize transportation.[17] These lines, completed between 1836 and 1840, were too recent to have had much influence on suburban development. The population had recently passed two million, but London remained relatively compact. In the north the city was starting to extend beyond Regent's Park, and in the east it was spreading into Poplar and Hackney. South of the Thames, Southwark had filled in considerably since the turn of the century, with a continuous built-up area extending in a radius of at least a mile and half from Southwark Bridge, and ribbons of development extended along a growing network of roads.

Davis also included London's environs: the towns, villages, and crossroads that dotted the predominantly rural landscape around London. Kentish Town, for example, was little more than a crossroads north of Camden Town, and

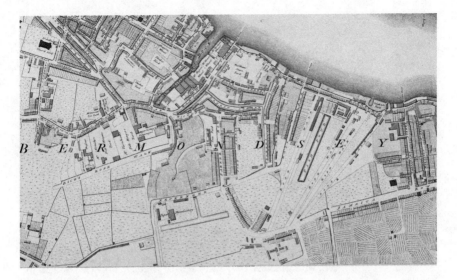

Fig. 1.2. Excerpt showing Bermondsey, from Richard Horwood, *Plan of the Cities of London and Westminster, the Borough of Southwark, and Parts Adjoining, Shewing Every House,* 1799. Courtesy of the Carl H. Pforzheimer Collection of Shelley and His Circle, the New York Public Library, http://digitalcollections.nypl.org/items/c6c5fde5-e72d-4bbc-e040-e00a 18067bd1. Free to use without restriction.

Hampstead remained a small village well removed from the edge of London. The map is also interesting for what it excludes; it extends from Ealing to Ilford, encompassing rural landscape between scattered environs, but major twentieth-century London suburbs such as Hounslow, Ruislip, Barnet, Croydon, and Sutton are all located off the map and miles beyond London's limits in the 1840s. On the eve of significant industrial development, Davis's map prominently features the Brent, Wandle, Lea, and Ravensbourne rivers, along with the extensive marshlands in the Thames Estuary, commons, and forests.[18] Roads, railroads, and buildings dominated Greater London's landscape in maps created at the end of the nineteenth century. Most of the marshlands, along with some of the forests and commons, had been drained or cleared and transformed into suburban landscapes.[19]

Draining Greater London's marshes was one of the most significant and long-lasting environmental consequences of nineteenth-century urban growth. The marshlands in the Thames Estuary and Lea Valley were very prominent in the early maps of the region, but were mostly gone in maps from the second half of the nineteenth century onward. The first Ordnance Survey (fig. 1.3), completed in 1805, captures the Thames Estuary from the Tower of London to the mouth of the Thames at Southend. It records continuous marshlands starting with the Redriff Marsh (Rotherhithe Peninsula) on the south side of the river through the Isle of

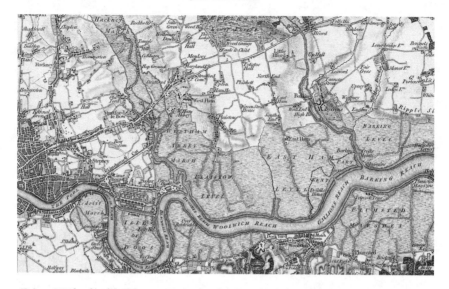

Fig. 1.3. Wetlands of the Thames Estuary in the east of London. Excerpt from William Mudge, "Ordnance Survey, Sheet 1," First Series (England and Wales, 1805). Courtesy of http://visionofbritain.org.uk/maps/sheet/first_edition/sheet1. This work is based on data provided through www.VisionofBritain.org.uk and uses historical material which is under copyright of the Great Britain Historical GIS Project and the University of Portsmouth. This work is licensed under the Creative Commons Attribution 4.0 International License: http://creativecommons.org/licenses/by-sa/4.0/.

Dogs to the Greenwich Peninsula and the Plaistow and Barking Levels. In the full map the marshlands continue along both sides of the river most of the way to its mouth.[20] The above excerpt of the 1805 map also identified marshlands in the Lea Valley. With the exception of the recently built West India Docks, some calico printers at West Ham Abbey, and a few buildings along the London to Colchester road as it crossed the Lower Lea, the map records very little urban development on the marshlands. Without steam power it was difficult to fully drain these lowlands, which were associated with ague fevers.[21] There was enough higher ground for London to grow away from the estuary and river valleys. Marshlands were not wilderness at the start of the nineteenth century. They were partly drained for gardening or pasture, and flood defenses and mills altered the flow of many of the rivers. Nonetheless, the human influence on an early nineteenth-century marsh, like those flanking the Lower Lea River, that were drained with ditches and used to fatten cattle, remained considerably more environmentally benign than the densely populated industrial suburbs that developed on these marshes in the nineteenth century.[22]

By the end of the century, thousands of homes, an intense network of streets, factories, railway embankments, sewers, and docks replaced the wetlands with polluted and flood-prone urban landscapes.[23] Factories and docks were drawn to marshlands, as both needed access to the rivers. This in turn drew workers to new marshland districts to live within walking distance from their employers. The 1893–1895 revised Ordnance Survey of London identified a few remaining pockets of marshlands in Greenwich, Plaistow, Stratford, and Hackney, but the landscape had been transformed. The undeveloped marshlands were now near gasworks, chemical factories, and suburbs with hundreds of thousands of people.[24] The significant reduction in the scale of Greater London's marshlands created an ongoing problem with urban and suburban flooding. The marshes no longer absorbed rainwater, they did not provide a buffer against storm surges, and hundreds of thousands of people lived on low-lying former wetlands. Rain regularly inundated these areas, and storm surges caused major floods in 1897, 1904, 1928, and 1953.[25]

The forests remaining at the start of the nineteenth century, like the marshes, were not untouched wilderness. They were preserved long after much of the region had been cleared for agriculture and were managed as royal hunting grounds and to supply raw materials, including wood, charcoal, and tanners' bark. Epping Forest was among the largest in the region. Large sections of this forest in northeast London, once protected as a royal hunting ground, were enclosed during the early nineteenth century. The land was first cleared for farming before later transforming into residential suburbs. Enclosure and the fences that sectioned land into private property became a major political issue in the mid-nineteenth century, as radicals demanded customary access to the forest. Protesters started visiting the remaining forest in 1866, which then developed into mass-trespass protests and organized fence breaking in 1870. In response to the popular opposition to further enclosure, the Corporation of the City of London acquired the remaining forest from the crown and preserved it for recreation in 1875. This did not fully appease the protestors, as turning the forest into a park for Londoners to visit did not reestablish local customary rights to collect and lop wood.[26]

The campaigns to preserve Epping Forest paralleled efforts to preserve common lands around London. John de Morgan, an Irish activist and lecturer who spent the 1870s in London, led plebeian radicals in an effort to maintain access to open land. He started his campaign in 1872, when the police prevented Fenian protesters from accessing Hyde Park in West London, and he continued it across Greater London by resisting enclosure in Hackney Downs (northeast), Wimbledon Common (southwest), and Plumstead Marsh (southeast). The Commons Preservation Society, led by prominent middle-class Liberals including Octavia Hill, J. S. Mill, George Shaw-Lefevre, and Henry Fawcett, shared similar goals and sought to preserve open space in Greater London, but they generally did not support the direct actions taken by de Morgan's followers and were hostile to the "traditional pastimes and recreations" that the plebeian radicals defended.[27]

The growth of Greater London in the past two centuries has significantly reduced the size of the forests and commons in the region. Starting in the 1860s political activism, not government planning, helped prevent sprawling suburban expansion from clearing them all. The result of this political activity is evident in the maps. Forests and commons shrank during the first half of the nineteenth century, and were mostly safeguarded from further development starting in the second half of the nineteenth century through to the twenty-first century.[28] This was not universally true, as suburban development, particularly in southern Outer London, did clear a few significant woodlands decades after Epping Forest and some commons were preserved. The late nineteenth-century Ordnance Survey records Petts Wood, a sizable forest adjacent to Bromley Common, which developed into a commuter suburb during the first half of the twentieth century, resulting in a significant reduction in the scale of the woodlands. Nonetheless Epping Forest, Wimbledon Common, and many other small forests and green spaces stand as important legacies of the activism of mass-trespassers, de Morgan, and the Commons Preservation Society.

The forests, commons, marshlands, and agricultural land around London came under threat of development because the Metropolis spread miles beyond its ancient walls. The expansive city stood in contrast with Paris, Europe's second largest city, which remained confined by the *octroi* wall until 1861 and by fortifications built by Louis Philippe until the First World War.[29] As a result, London covered almost ten times the land area of Paris in the second half of the nineteenth century. Camberwell and Islington (see fig. 1.1) were particularly good examples of this phenomenon. Camberwell's population grew by a quarter million to 259,339 between 1801 and 1901, and Islington grew from 10,212 to 334,991.[30] Both suburbs extended from the early nineteenth-century limits of urban development out to the new limits of London established in 1847. As their populations grew, they spread north and south, significantly increasing the geographic scope of London compared with other nineteenth-century capital cities. The five-foot-to-the-mile (1:1,056) Ordnance Survey from the 1860s and 1870s, and a revised series from the 1890s, provides a high-resolution record of the landscape down to the individual buildings in the second half of the nineteenth century.[31] This makes it possible to identify different types of urban development, ranging from predominantly residential districts on the higher ground in the northeast and south to the patchwork of factories, docks, railway yards, and residences found on the reclaimed marshlands in Bermondsey, Poplar, and West Ham.

The revised Ordnance Survey maps captured London in the mid-1890s, a little more than half a century after the first railways. The city was spreading out in every direction and increasingly shaped by the networks of omnibuses, trams, and railways, both on the surface and underground. The continuous built-up area extended from Hammersmith to East Ham, and it was encircled by growing satellite suburbs including Croyden, Wimbledon, Richmond, Twickenham, and Ealing, all connected to London by commuter railways. The revised maps also show the intensification of industry in the Thames Estuary, on the eastern edge of the Metropolis, with a significant number of new large factories in Silvertown and Beckton. In contrast, the maps record the extensive open spaces remaining within the County of London, from North Kensington and West Hampstead in the north to large sections of southern London. The revised survey did not include Eltham in the southeast (see fig. 1.1), which remained a small town surrounded by countryside with a population under ten thousand, decades after it was officially absorbed into London.[32]

The railway suburbs and scattered industrial centers created a patchwork landscape across suburban London. Farms, market gardens, and marshlands coexisted with pockets of housing or factories. The extensive detail in the Ordnance Survey maps from the 1890s record these suburbs in transition. Read alongside the census statistics that record the constant and rapid grown in the late nineteenth and early twentieth centuries, the maps allow us to explore the slow retreat of the rural landscape under the onslaught of development. For example, the Ordnance Survey shows that in the early 1890s a traveler on a District Railway train from central London to Ealing Broadway, a rapidly growing suburb with thirty-three thousand people, would have passed through Hammersmith and Acton with occasional views of farms and parklands stretching out to the west.[33] Alternatively, a trip on the Great Western line from Paddington to Ealing took a more northern route through the extensive farmlands that remained undeveloped as far east as the Wormwood Scrubs commons in Hammersmith and traveled along the edge of the suburban growth in Acton.

From Ealing it was possible to walk to the west along Uxbridge Road through the new housing and commercial development, with views of farms, nurseries, and scattered small industry to the south. At the River Brent walkers could continue along the tow path to the Grand Union Canal. Following the path west, it was possible to see new settlements that were only just starting to grow, such as Southall Green and Heston. There were brickworks, gravel pits, mills, a creosoting works, and a varnish works along the way to Yiewsley, but the landscape remained predominantly rural. From Yiewsley the urban development intensified on the approach to the long-established commercial center at Uxbridge, but the south remained rural all the way to Shepperton on the Thames. These western suburbs were centers of rapid urbanization in the late nineteenth and early twentieth centuries. The communities that would eventually form into the modern Borough of Ealing experienced nearly a sevenfold population increase from 1851 to 1901, and the population would more than triple again to more than three hundred thousand in the fifty years that followed.[34] By the mid-twentieth century London extended all the way to Uxbridge, with most of the open space recorded in the 1890s maps replaced by a sea of suburban development.

The growth was equally remarkable north of Ealing along the path of the Metropolitan Railway. During the early 1890s the Metropolitan left the built-up city in Kilburn and passed scattered new streets and housing in Willesden before reaching the countryside as it crossed the River Brent and traveled alongside Wembley Park. It next reached Harrow on the Hill with a population of thirteen thousand in 1891. From there it continued northwest through mostly rural landscapes to Penner and Northwood, where it left Outer London.[35] By the early 1950s the Metropolitan Line traveled through continuous suburbs all the way to Northwood.[36] Although it passed alongside a few large parks, it did not reach the edge of the countryside until it crossed into the Green Belt. The population of modern Brent quadrupled from 31,000 to 120,000 between 1881 and 1901, and then more than doubled again to a quarter of a million residents by 1931. The northwestern suburbs that combined in 1965 to make Harrow followed a similar pattern, growing steadily from 13,000 in 1881 to 96,000 in 1931, before doubling to 190,000 by 1939. Between 1951 and 2011 the western suburbs located north of the Thames in Outer London maintained a relatively steady combined population of about 1.2 million, up from 350,000 in 1901 and only 36,000 in 1801.[37]

In the east, heavy industrialization, sewers, and extensive marshlands limited suburban expansion on the same scale as in the west. The eastern suburbs north of the Thames that combined into the modern boroughs of Barking and Dagenham, Redbridge and Havering grew from a little under 50,000 in 1881 to 120,000 in 1901. Significant growth started after the First World War, with the combined population reaching almost 400,000 in 1931 and then stabilizing, fluctuating around 600,000 in the second half of the twentieth century.[38] In the 1890s the London, Tilbury and Southend Railway traveled from Fenchurch Street Station, through the East End and West Ham to the edge of Outer London at Upminster station. During a dry summer, it was possible to walk all the way from Upminster to East Ham through farms and marshlands, passing the small suburbs of Hornchurch and Romford in the distance, before passing through Barking to cross the River Roding. From there it was feasible to avoid East Ham and walk all the way to Canning Town on the Plaistow Level marsh, although one would have needed to pass the Beckton Gasworks, one of the largest industrial sites in the Metropolis.[39]

The marshlands of the eastern Thames Estuary developed slowly. Ford built its large factory in Dagenham in 1931, but open marshlands stretched most of the way from Canning Town to Thurrock until the mid-twentieth century. Away from the river, however, suburban development transformed the region, and a continuous network of streets and housing stretched from East Ham to Upminster in the east and up to Brentwood in the northeast. Ordnance Survey maps published in 1960 confirm the extensive growth in Ilford, Barking, Dagenham, Romford, and Hornchurch.[40] This included the Becontree Housing Estate, built during the interwar period by the London County Council, even though it was located outside the County of London. By 1939 the population of the estate exceeded one hundred thousand people, making it the largest public housing development in the world.[41]

Southern Outer London, including Croydon and the suburbs that later combined into Bromley, Sutton, Merton and Kingston upon Thames, grew steadily from 150,000 in 1881 to a quarter million in 1901, before doubling to a half million in the first three decades of the twentieth century. This region kept growing to the 1950s, after which it stabilized with 790,000 in the decades after the Second World War.[42] The Ordnance Survey maps from 1898 show large pockets of undeveloped land throughout southern London, with ribbon development continuing along major roads and commuter suburbs developing around railway hubs. The railway started a period of rapid growth in Croydon, and the city transformed into a commuter suburb as its population reached 100,000 during the 1880s, even as it remained mostly encircled by the countryside and struggled to find a means of safely disposing of its sewage.[43] The survival of contiguous green space in south London allowed walkers to return to London through Mitcham Common and Clapham Park, avoiding suburban development most of the way. The population of the south London suburbs located within the County of London continued to grow until the mid-twentieth century as these large undeveloped regions filled in with suburban streets and homes. Postwar maps show a patchwork of residential suburbs, industry, and significant pockets of open land in southern Greater London in the decades after the population finally stabilized.[44]

Population dispersion was the defining feature of London's urban development in the twentieth century and a major driver of environmental transformations. Londoners spread out across the region as transportation and economic changes allowed people to move out of the overcrowded and polluted core districts to a diverse collection of suburbs.[45] Smaller-scale dispersal started in the mid-nineteenth century, with the population decline in the City of London and other core districts, where railways and commercial buildings displaced the residential population. The total population of County of London continued to grow until 1901, long after the core regions started to decline, as people moved into the vast rural areas in the south. For example, Lewisham in the southeast grew from 51,557 in 1871 to 134,721 in 1901. Eventually the number of people leav-

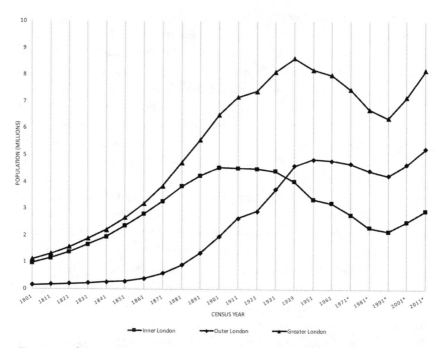

Fig. 1.4. London population, 1801–2011. For consistency, this chart uses the nineteenth-century definition of Inner and Outer London. This was reorganized in 1965, and there are alternative numbers using the modern boundaries for Inner and Outer London. Source: "Historical Census Population," London Datastore, http://data.london.gov.uk/dataset /historic-census-population. Courtesy of the Greater London Authority, which cannot warrant the quality or accuracy of the data. License: https://data.london.gov.uk/about /terms-and-conditions/

ing the crowded districts in central London started to outpace suburban growth in the south, and the population of the County of London began a decline that continued until the 1980s. Outer London grew from under 1 million in 1881 to nearly 5 million in 1939, at which point it accounted for over half the population of Greater London. Dispersal was actively encouraged by local and national governments. The London County Council, which built numerous public housing estates like Becontree in Outer London, moved hundreds of thousands of people out of the core districts during the interwar period.[46] After the Second World War, Clement Attlee's Labour government created the planned New Towns in conjunction with new limits on the expansion of Greater London. This moved some people out of crowded Greater London into smaller cities just beyond or even within the Green Belt.[47] Greater London's population peaked at 8.6 million in 1939, then dropped to 6.4 million by 1991, when a new period of rapid growth began.

The London Government Act of 1963 redefined London to better reflect the

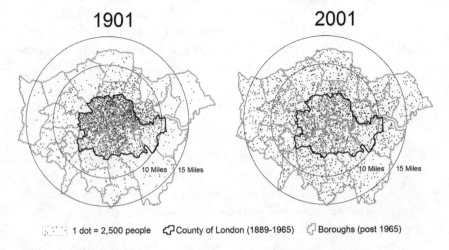

Fig. 1.5. Dot distribution population maps of Greater London, 1901 and 2001. Created by Jim Clifford, based on "Historical Census Population"; "Statistical GIS Boundary Files for London," London Datastore, 2013, http://data.london.gov.uk/dataset/statistical -gis-boundary-files-london. Courtesy of the Greater London Authority, which cannot warrant the quality or accuracy of the data. License: https://data.london.gov.uk/about /terms-and-conditions/

new dispersed population and in the process absorbed the fractured suburbs of Outer London into London's two-tier government system. Politics drove this reform, as the Labour Party dominated London County Council elections and the Conservatives recognized they could not win "as long as 'London' was confined to the inner working-class districts."[48] But population dispersal into Bromley, Ealing, and Ilford also led to demands for reform from below, as the Middlesex, Essex, and Kent county councils still controlled education and public health in these large suburbs.[49] In 1957 a Royal Commission was established to recommend reforms to local government in Greater London. The Herbert Commission report, published in 1960, recommended an expanded two-tier system of local government for Greater London. The Labour Party resisted an expanded definition of London on political grounds, but given that the 1847 boundaries never had properly defined the extent of the Metropolis, they were ineffective in defending it as the true extent of London after more than a century of further suburban expansion.[50] The 1963 act, which came into effect in 1965, reorganized local government into thirty-two boroughs, with the Greater London Council as the new top-tier regional government.

The population difference between 1901 and 2001 in Figure 1.5 is a little under seven hundred thousand people, but the dot distribution maps show a dramatic transformation during the twentieth century. The 1901 map shows the dense concentrations of people in the northern inner suburbs and across the rest of the

County of London aside from the southeast. It also shows considerable population in the Essex suburbs in the northeast. This map captures Essex suburbs, including West Ham, East Ham, and Leyton, near their peak. By the mid-twentieth century this region and most other inner suburbs experienced significant population decline.[51]

At the turn of the twentieth-first century Londoners lived in significantly less crowded homes spread across the whole region. Many had fled the crowded districts in East London and northern districts such as St. Pancras or Islington. This long-term process of dispersal significantly increased the amount of land used for housing, while also expanding the transportation network further and increasing the distances people traveled for work and recreation. The dramatic increase in the number and use of automobiles in Greater London during the twentieth century facilitated dispersal at this scale.

Automobiles, and the independent mobility they enabled, started to transform suburban Greater London during the 1930s. From the mid-nineteenth century to the early twentieth century, the railway had created a radial transportation network, with suburbs linked to central London but not with each other. Automobiles began creating more opportunities for travel between suburbs, which reduced the dominance of central London. The pace of life increased and "became more family-centric, more consumerist, more distanced from community life, less in thrall to the domination of the public transport timetable."[52] The entry-level Ford Y, built in Dagenham on the marshlands of the Thames Estuary, sold for £100 between 1935 and 1937. This car, along with several other small cheap vehicles, significantly reduced the cost of ownership and increased the number of automobiles in Greater London to about 348,000 by 1938.[53]

With all the new cars creating more traffic, 266 miles of new arterial roads were constructed during the interwar period. These roads were intended to alleviate the congestion created when automobiles confronted unplanned nineteenth-century development. Suburbs had been built along all the major roads leaving London, creating major choke points and endless traffic jams as the chaotic mix of horse-drawn carts, omnibuses, taxis, bicycles, trams, and cars needed to pass through the center of Stratford, Kilburn, or Peckham. After traffic cleared the inner suburbs, it needed to pass through the centers of growing suburbs in Outer London such as Bromley, Kingston, and Ealing.[54] Arterial roads bypassed these congested centers, but they also spurred a new phase of ribbon development along these new roads in Outer London and were "at once lined with factories and thus became more congested than the roads which they had been designed to relieve."[55] The rush to build semidetached homes on farmlands alongside the new roads led to the Ribbon Development Act in 1935, which finally stopped this form of unplanned suburban development.[56]

Car ownership continued to increase after the Second World War. By 1958 there were a million cars in London and traffic congestion, particularly in central London, developed into a major challenge. A 1959 report on London's roads warned that car adoption rates remained lower in London when compared with the national average and that building more roads would not significantly reduce traffic, as congestion was the main factor preventing even more people from switching to cars.[57] An annual census conducted by the Metropolitan and City of London Police tracked an increase in cars from 34 percent of all vehicles on the road in 1938 to 49 percent in 1962.[58] A survey of cars entering the center of the Metropolis between seven and ten in the morning recorded an increase from 37,000 private cars in 1954 to 73,500 in 1968.[59] By 1990 cars traveled over 25 billion kilometers in London each year. Outer boroughs, such as Hillingdon, Hounslow, Bromley, Croydon, and Enfield, recorded the highest number of kilometers traveled. A congestion fee in central London was introduced in 2003, and the total number of kilometers traveled since has declined to about 23 billion a year.[60]

A clear correlation exists between the increase in automobile ownership starting in the 1930s and the dispersion of Greater London's population in the twentieth century seen in Figures 1.4 and 1.5. During the 1930s the population of Outer London surpassed the declining population in the County of London (Inner London). The automobile made it possible for residential housing to extend beyond the walking distance from train stations. The road network built for automobiles also allowed the economy to diversify across the Metropolis, with new factories clustered along arterial roads instead of railways, canals, or rivers.[61] Auto emissions created a new source of air pollution during the twentieth century, eventually surpassing industrial and domestic coal smoke.[62] Car emissions, like domestic fires before them, were difficult to curtail, as millions of Londoners, rather than a smaller number of large factories, contributed to the problem.[63] Just as Londoners were deeply attached to an open hearth in the middle decades of the twentieth century, they were very devoted to the freedom and convenience a personal automobile provided at the end of the century.[64]

Automobile emissions aside, the population dispersion trend was in many ways positive, as overcrowding had had significant social and environmental consequences. The population of Tower Hamlets, at nearly six hundred thousand in 1901, created challenges to the effective disposal of sewage and solid waste, along with tens of thousands of domestic coal fires that contributed to air pollution. Because of the haphazard nature of eighteenth- and early nineteenth-century urbanization, central London also lacked adequate green space for this dense population. In the older regions of London reformers campaigned in the second half of the nineteenth century to convert graveyards to small urban parks to provide some green space for children.[65] Moving to the suburbs significantly increased access to parks and other green space for recreation. In West Ham the population peaked at more than three hundred thousand people in 1921, and many of those people lived in crowded low-quality housing built on the inadequately drained marshlands of the Lower Lea Valley and the Thames Estuary.[66] Each house in the suburb held an average of 6.2 people, and many homes near the factories and docks housed two or more families.[67] Four decades later the average number of people per house had declined to 3.6. Although authors such as J. B. Priestley and George Orwell derided suburban architecture and consumer-focused society, Figures 1.4 and 1.5 confirm that large numbers of Londoners voted with their feet and left the crowded inner city.[68] Moving to the less crowded, less polluted, and cheaper suburbs increased many people's quality of life, though it often came with some social dislocation.[69]

VARIED AND IMPERVIOUS GREATER LONDON

Population dispersal transformed the social and physical geography of Outer London. This created new environmental challenges with the spread of industry and landfills, and increased problems with storm water management as suburban development transformed the hydrology of the region. There were no simple concentric rings of different types of urban and suburban land uses and economic activities. The outer districts were a mix of dormitory suburbs with diverse socioeconomic characteristics, along with industrial centers and major transportation hubs. Water reservoirs clustered in the Thames and Lea Valleys, and landfills were located on the edges of Greater London. Metro-land, the collection of dormitory suburbs that grew around the Metropolitan Railway in northwest London, was built for the middle class to retreat from the pollution and crowds of the core districts. Major industrial parks developed in the early twentieth century near some of the Metro-land suburbs, increasing their economic and social diversity. Moreover, by the end of the nineteenth century commuter suburbs were no longer exclusively middle class; those serviced by the Great Eastern Railway, including Edmonton and East Ham, attracted large working-class populations drawn to the lower cost of housing and the affordable workmen's trains run by the railways outside of peak hours.[70] In the case of Edmonton and the middle Lea Valley more generally, it appears that industry might have followed the workers instead of the more common situation where factories and jobs drew working-class people to an area.

London's industry and logistical infrastructure dispersed along with its population during the twentieth century. An immense network of landfills had developed to dispose of the solid waste of millions of people over hundreds of years. Thirty-four landfills opened between 1860 and 1914, according to open government data, but this does not include all the nineteenth-century dumping sites.[71] More than 1,200 additional historical landfills and 104 active landfills are recorded in the "Current and Historic Landfills" database, an indication of the expanding quantities of solid waste produced in the Metropolis during much of the twentieth century. In addition to problems with toxic contamination, these landfills transformed the topography of Greater London, filling marshlands, leveling ground, and creating hills.[72]

London had significantly more industry at the turn of the twentieth century than it did a century later, but it was geographically concentrated along the Thames and Lea Rivers. In the 1890s there were a number of major railway engine works, a large shipyard, underwater telegraph works, dozens of chemical factories, numerous breweries and distilleries, large wheat mills, sugar refineries, tanneries, tar and cresol works, soap and candle works, potters, and more than thirty coal gas plants, in addition to hundreds of smaller workshops.[73] Electricity allowed industry to move away from the Thames and Lower Lea during the interwar period to cheap land near railways and major roads in the region.[74] Industry migrated north up the Lea Valley and particularly into the northwest. These Outer London industrial parks did not experience the same rapid deindustrialization during the Second World War as the older industrial districts in Inner London and West Ham. Instead, German bombers chased even more industry from central London into the suburbs.[75] Park Royal (labeled on fig. 1.6), located to the west of Willesden Junction and south of the Grand Union Canal, was the largest industrial park in London. It developed during the 1920s and attracted a wide range of industries, including the Guinness brewery, cardboard and paper bag factories, engineering works, and a metal refinery.[76] Dozens of smaller industrial parks also developed in the mid-twentieth century, such as the Beddington Industrial Estate in Croydon (labeled on fig. 1.6). Most of this industrial development in Outer London was already in place before the Ordnance Survey completed a new series of maps between 1947 and 1964.[77]

Deindustrialization eventually expanded beyond Inner London, and by the mid-1980s factories started to close at Park Royal and in the Lea Valley. The industrial workforce in Greater London dropped from 1.43 million in 1961 to 274,000 in 1997.[78] By 2011 manufacturing accounted for a mere 2 percent of the jobs.[79] The vast majority of London's factories were gone by the early twenty-first century. A few chemical works and the Tate and Lyle sugar refinery survive in Silvertown, and Ford still assembles engines in Dagenham, but these factories are anomalies after decades of industrial decline. Energy production has also largely left the Metropolis, with the National Grid transmitting electricity from power plants located outside of London.[80] In contrast to the interwar period, when London's suburbs were home to the most dynamic industrial sector in Britain, Greater London is now the least industrial region in the country.[81] Figure 1.6 suggests that

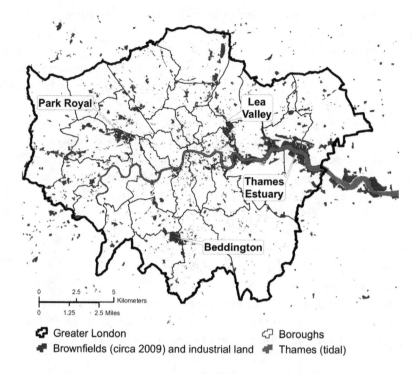

Fig. 1.6. Brownfields and industrial land in the London region, ca. 2009. This map uses Open Government data for brownfields and OpenStreetMap data for the industry. Created by Jim Clifford, based on "London Brownfield Sites Review"; "Tidal Water," OS VectorMap OpenData (Ordnance Survey, 2014), https://www.ordnancesurvey.co.uk /business-and-government/products/vectormap-district.html; "London Open Street Map Data," *Metro Extracts · Mapzen*, 2016, https://mapzen.com/data/metro-extracts /metro/london_england/.

the environmental legacy of the industrial economy remains decades after most of the industrial jobs have disappeared. Industrial buildings and whole industrial parks have been transformed to other uses, while other industrial sites languish as brownfields awaiting costly reclamation projects.[82]

The spread of Greater London had environmental consequences beyond those created by industrialization and landfills. Suburban development, including predominantly residential districts, consumed rural land, increased the threat of flooding, and reduced biodiversity. Paved roads, sidewalks, and thousands of new buildings significantly increased the area covered by impervious surfaces. Roofs and compressed clay soil in back gardens do not absorb rainwater.[83] Flooding developed into a regular and major problem by the late nineteenth century. As rural land, marshes, and floodplains gave way to suburbs, rainwater rushed down the Lea, Brent, and Wandle to flood low-lying districts. This was a partic-

ular problem in the Lea Valley, where development in Tottenham and Walthamstow significantly increased the threat of flooding in Hackney, Poplar, and West
Ham.[84] Rain also overwhelmed the combined sewer system and dumped a
mixture of urban runoff and raw sewage into the Thames, Lea, and other rivers.
Furthermore, the impervious landscape created more opportunities for storm
water to carry localized or distributed contaminants to the rivers. The low-
concentration pollutants that settled on roads, roofs, and parking lots became
more concentrated as they were flushed into the sewers and rivers.[85] Asphalt
roads, brick buildings, and small fenced gardens also significantly reduced the
land available for wild flora and fauna. Urban trees and parks provided some habitat, but this remained a significant reduction compared to the rural landscapes
that these suburbs had replaced.

London may have been less crowded than Paris, but much of the suburban
growth remained dense compared with the sprawling car-centric suburbs that
grew around North American cities in the second half of the twentieth century.
London's row and semidetached houses with small backyards extended imper-
meable landscapes well beyond the densely populated core. A few suburbs with
ample parklands, such as Wimbledon and Hampstead, retain some of the green
space and natural habitat of the rural landscape. The dense row housing in Camberwell, in contrast, completely transformed the ecosystem in the district, while
creating new challenges for storm water management.

A few districts, such as the Lea Valley and the Thames Estuary, developed
into a patchwork of housing, factories, farms, marshlands, and streams during the
late nineteenth century. These regions retained more open land in the twentieth
century than other areas in Greater London, but they also contained some of
the largest factories and landfills. The streams and marshlands in these alluvial
landscapes were heavily polluted after decades of rapid industrial and population
growth, but corridors for wildlife and space for wild plants remained alongside
new allotment gardens.[86] Maps suggest that these hybrid landscapes were in a
minority compared with the dense residential neighborhoods that spread across
much of London.

Figure 1.7 shows the 14,843 kilometers (9,223 miles) of roads within Greater
London and the clusters of roads in the satellite suburbs in Greater London's
periphery. The road network provides a good approximation of the extent of the
built environment and shows the amount of land transformed by urban, suburban, and exurban development in the past two hundred years. The absence of
roads in Richmond Park and the Lea Valley stand out, along with smaller parks
and some areas on the edge of Greater London that are protected by the Green
Belt. These open landscapes are very small when compared with the extent
of the road network. Most of these roads service buildings, which extend the

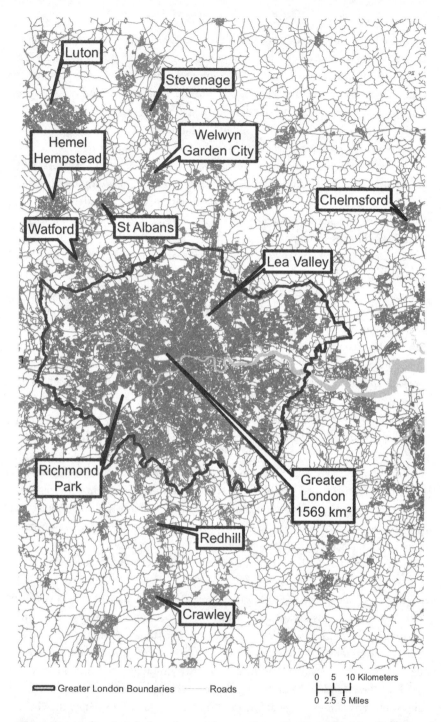

Luton

Stevenage

Hemel
Hempstead

Welwyn
Garden City

Chelmsford

Watford

St Albans

Lea Valley

Richmond
Park

Greater
London
1569 km²

Redhill

Crawley

Greater London Boundaries ━━━ Roads

0   5   10 Kilometers

0   2.5   5 Miles

Fig. 1.7. Metropolitan London's road network, 2014. Created by Jim Clifford, based on "Road Layer," OS VectorMap OpenData (Ordnance Survey, 2014), https://www.ord-nancesurvey.co.uk/business-and-government/products/vectormap-district.html. Free to use for any purpose: see https://www.ordnancesurvey.co.uk/business-and-government/products/opendata.html

impervious surface beyond the edge of the road and create additional barriers for wildlife. Beyond Greater London's border the density of the road network decreases significantly, but there are a significant number of exurban commuter towns. These suburban satellites extend metropolitan London well beyond its 1,569 square kilometers.[87]

CONCLUSION: CLIMATE CHANGE AND SUSTAINABLE DRAINAGE

Comparing the late eighteenth-century maps with Ordnance Surveys from the late 1890s and twenty-first–century satellite images highlights the growth in the intervening two centuries.[88] In contrast with the short walks out of town available from any location in London in the 1790s, it is now possible to walk or perhaps cycle 20 miles (32 km) from Enfield to Croydon or 32 miles (51 km) from Uxbridge to Upminster through a continuous mix of urban and suburban landscapes. Urban development now extends significantly beyond the modern limits of Greater London. The Office for National Statistics has a more inclusive definition called the Greater London Built-up Area that includes suburbs that are not governed by the mayor of London. This region comprised over 1,700 square kilometers in 2011, nearly six times more than the County of London's 300 square kilometers. This definition still does not include satellite urban centers such as Luton, Reading, Tilbury, or Slough. Slough, an industrial town outside the M25 on the western edge, occupies roughly the same amount of space as the land in the City, Westminster, and Southwark that Horwood surveyed at the end of the eighteenth century. Eurostat includes Slough and other towns within London's orbit and estimates that the population of the London metropolitan region surpassed fourteen million in 2014, making it the largest in Europe west of Moscow.[89]

During the second half of the twentieth and early decades of the twenty-first centuries, tighter government regulation, the shift from coal to natural gas, and congestion fees for vehicles helped improve London's air and water quality, but many of the other environmental legacies of urban development remain. A small portion of the East India Docks was converted into a wildlife refuge, and the old East London Waterworks' filter beds in Walthamstow are another sanctuary for water fowl; but small parks like these pale in comparison to the marshlands lost during the past two hundred years. The forests cleared in the early nineteenth century have not returned, and suburban houses are still spread across hundreds of square kilometers of former agricultural lands.

The impervious landscape and inadequate storm water sewers, when combined with the growing problem of climate change, will significantly increase the future threat of flooding in Greater London. There are half a million properties on floodplains in Greater London, with about thirty thousand facing a significant risk of flooding.[90] Some areas of Greater London, including the Lower Brent Valley, the Lower Lea Valley, and parts of the Thames Estuary, will face damaging flooding on an annual basis by the 2050s unless the city improves its ability to absorb water.[91] In 2015 the mayor of London released a draft Sustainable Drainage Action Plan with the goal of using, absorbing, or delaying rainwater instead of treating it as a waste product. This will require a conversion of the impervious landscape created over the past two centuries to reduce the increased risk of flooding that climate change will bring to Greater London. The alternative is to spend huge sums of money to further improve the storm sewer system, an option that would not end the flow of pollution into the rivers or reduce the demand for potable water.[92] The plan seeks to reduce the flow of rainwater into the sewers by one percent each year until 2040. The report acknowledges London's significant challenges due to the density of impervious surfaces throughout much of Inner London and the region's clay soils that further reduce absorption. Nonetheless, the Greater London Authority has little option—given the legacy of two centuries of urban development without adequate consideration of the future—than to find ways to increase the resiliency of the Metropolis. This attention to the impervious city is just one major initiative to address the inadequate environmental infrastructure developed over the past two centuries; London is also working to divert more waste from landfills, increase the production of green energy, and reduce the pollution from transportation.[93]

London's rapid growth in the nineteenth and early twentieth centuries provides a few advantages for building resilience in the face of climate change. Much of the city was not designed with the automobile as the central mode of transportation, and it is relatively easy to travel around much of Greater London by public transport, bicycle, and on foot. This gives London a significant advantage over cities that experienced rapid growth in the second half of the twentieth century, where suburban densities remain very low and the design of the residential road network actively discourages public transportation, walking, and cycling. On the other hand, much of London's industrial development preceded the stronger environmental regulations of the second half of the twentieth century, and the cost of soil remediation in brownfield developments remains challenging. The city is also committed to urban development in the Thames Estuary and river valleys throughout Greater London. Decreasing rainwater flows by one percent a year is a good step to help reduce the threat of flooding, but no mayor of London is likely to propose a radical and expensive program to clear large sections of the Isle of Dogs, Canning Town, Greenwich, and Thamesmead to restore some of the lost marshlands in the Thames Estuary or suggest renaturalizing entire suburbs so that Epping Forest can be replanted and returned to its eighteenth-century extent. The urban-environmental history of the rapid growth and dispersal of Greater London, engraved in the landscape through the road network, landfill hills, embanked rivers, and former industrial parks rebranded as business parks, will continue to constrain efforts to improve the resiliency of London for the foreseeable future.

TWO

IMAGINING THE
METROPOLITAN ENVIRONMENT
IN THE MODERN PERIOD

CHRISTOPHER HAMLIN

How to imagine London environmentally? At the beginning we are struck, perhaps surprisingly, by an expression of beauty. Standing on Westminster Bridge at sunrise on September 3, 1802, William Wordsworth declared that "Earth has not anything to show more fair." Yet William Blake found it hideous. More prosaically one may think of the metabolism of any great city—food, air, water, and energy enter, are distributed and utilized, and waste and by-products somehow leave. Yet London has been especially a magnet and transformer of money, power, and culture: for parts of the past two centuries (perhaps from 1870 to 1940), decisions made there probably had greater biospheric impact than those in any other world capital.

For much of those centuries London was singular too in size and in diffuseness. Its million plus in 1800 (seven million by 1900) was unprecedented for modern Europe. Within Britain it was "the," not "a," "Metropolis." But much more than many other cities, it lacked a single center, being an agglomeration of quite different kinds of places with the name of one of them. There were seams—not only one wide river, but large chunks of green land. Metropolitan government began only in 1829 with the establishment of a metropolitan (and quasi-national) police and then of a great sewer-building institution, the Metropolitan Board of Works, in 1855. Since then tensions between metropolitan and local units of government have persisted; there have been repeated reformulations of responsibilities, and repeated head-scratchings about what the outer boundaries of the Metropolis should be.[1] The motley group of (significantly London-based) social reformers and urban planners who struggled to define the urban at the end of the nineteenth century often imagined distinct domains of city and countryside. Yet as one of their inventions, the "garden suburb," suggests, they were of many minds as to what that distinction should mean, and yet more than many cities, huge London seems to work. Notwithstanding rough patches, often it has been a model city, a pioneering one.

Imagining this amorphous mass is a matter of standpoint; I order this chapter around six layered standpoints. Each is trans-temporal and has a complex political and cultural history. I hope only that my few examples (mainly from the nineteenth century) will be analogically fertile.

The first section combines experiential London, filled with physical and biological impedimenta, through which one walks, rides, or floats, and which one breathes, smells, and hears, with communitarian London, the imaginary of neighborhood complicity in creating and maintaining environments. The second section treats inspectorial London, the imaginary of a benevolent environmental police that brings amenity and health to every street and domicile. The third section considers systemic and dynamic London, a London ordered by circulations and feedbacks, which are both local and global, and both physical and conceptual. For London has been the *Weltstadt* not only of environmental sciences, but of imperial technosciences. I conclude with a consideration of modern London in relation to deep time, before and after this brief human era. London, a product of the postglacial Gulf Stream, was for a time a great wen. As sea levels rise, it will perhaps become a new Atlantis.

PRIVATE AND COMMUNAL LONDONS

In Wordsworth's beauteous London—"silent, bare, . . . / . . . bright and glittering in the smokeless air"—nothing is happening: "the very houses seem asleep."[2] Perhaps, but most accounts emphasize London's busyness (and its smoke).[3] For the experiential imaginary we should look to walkers. It is they who sense London's noises and smells, heat, cold, and wetness; its many forms of dirt; its air that may be neither very transparent nor very breathable. They experience too the physical discomfort of rough pavements on poorly shod feet, of maneuvering among obstacles and crowds, even of the lack of ready sites of excretion. Even at Wordsworth's dawn, many were likely already out to work or to look for work. They were experiencing, utilizing, and transforming London's environment, and even, sometimes, enjoying it. Images of sweatshops deflect our attention from Londoners' outdoor experience—particularly of those who walked to work, or to seek work, or for whom the streets were work sites. Some pedestrian commutes must have been long. Street vendors needed to visit the markets in the wee hours to buy stock and then get to their patch. Tradespeople serving the villas and crescents of the expanding northwestern suburbs might not live nearby.[4] Even after the transportation revolution around 1890, trams and buses still exposed one to outdoor London: the semi-open tram or the much-missed AEC Routemaster buses (in widespread service from 1956 to 2005) allowed one to step on or off, to feel the rush of air.

Especially in the century after 1750, accounts of walking in London are often tainted with menace. London is huge and anonymous. The standpoint is of the newcomer who quickly loses physical and moral compass, falling victim to false friends.[5] But pedestrianism held many valences for Londoners. Walkways were not only crowded, but coded for class and gender, and by time.[6] One of the two great social investigators of nineteenth-century London, Henry Mayhew, writing in the 1850s, concentrated on outdoor workers: not only hawkers and performers, but many forms of scavengers who were not only exposed to London's environment but who affected its quality. Over several hundred pages Mayhew discusses both those employed by householders or local authorities to sanitize and beautify, and those resisters of urban entropy who found markets for discarded objects—wood, bones, cigar ends, and ashes (collected by Dickens's famous dustman for brick making). Hardly anything in mid-Victorian London was not reused.

Most evocative are the collectors of "puer": dog's droppings, sold to Bermondsey's tanners to be rubbed into kid leather or fine book bindings, in order to draw moisture from the leather. Though puer still sometimes commanded more than a shilling per bucket, competition was driving down prices as Mayhew wrote. Collectors (some gloved, some not) roamed farther with their covered baskets. There was product differentiation (not all dog dung is equal; the best is "dry" and "limy-looking"). Some sold blends; others adulterated. Mayhew's informant—a well-educated sixty-year-old woman—had on the previous day gone "round Aldgate, Whitechapel, St. George's East, Stepney, Bow, and Bromley," and then delivered her load to Bermondsey, for 6d.[7] Asked why she still plied this trade, although being too frail to compete successfully against children and young men pushed into it by a poor-law guardian, she replied that she was "so used to the air," and preferred to die in the street rather be confined in a workhouse. From our standpoint that air was not very good, but contrasted with under-ventilated London interiors, the difference was probably striking. The hovel that was her home was well ventilated—the windows had been broken.[8]

Surely even on fine summer days not all gloried in the outdoors. The irregular dockers, anxious each day as to whether their labor would be needed, might not welcome the outdoors; nor would day laborers trudging from work site to work site; nor prostitutes, forced to work the streets after having been rejected by brothels. But Mayhew and later Gareth Stedman Jones remind us that the seasonality of much London work did take many out of the city for parts of the year. Costermongers used the railroads to extend the range of Billingsgate; others flocked to Kent for the August hop-picking, which, notes Orwell, was a kind of holiday.[9]

We know much more about the cramped flats many late nineteenth-century Londoners lived in—for example, families in one or two nine-foot-square rooms—than about how much time persons actually spent in those rooms.[10] But increasingly outdoor leisure, including interaction with plants and animals, was an attractive option even in nonelite parts of London. For East Enders the new Victoria Park in Tower Hamlets (completed as Mayhew wrote) and the nearby Hackney Marshes offered not only green space, but possibilities for gardening— excess bedding plants were given to residents in the terraced blocks that rose across northeast London for cultivation in their back gardens.[11]

Writing in the midst of the Second World War, almost a century after Mayhew, R. S. R. Fitter described the fascination with metropolitan nature of amateur (and occasionally, professional) naturalists who roamed London with an eye out for its plants and animals. Everywhere, even in bomb sites with their invasive species, was habitat. Local natural history had become a middle-class pursuit in England, for few town dwellers could take off for salmon fishing, deer stalking, or exotic destinations. In the north one could escape the smoky textile towns to the peaks. But the sheer expanse of London, the many parklands within it, and the relative inaccessibility of dramatically different landscapes—a matter equally of distance and ownership—encouraged the nature lover to look within the great city. Fitter found innumerable artificial sites of remarkable flora and fauna. Anywhere in which the earth had been turned over or water had stagnated would be interesting—for example, the brick-making pits at the northern edge of London. So too with reservoirs and sewage farms. Fitter saw gardening as habitat creation: turning over earth exposed bugs to birds, invited weeds, and encouraged other bugs to establish residence. Shrubs and walls were microhabitats. He noted too Londoners' immense enjoyment of the life around them, evident in the hand-feeding, by persons of all classes, of what now would be regarded as nuisance birds: gulls, pigeons, house sparrows.[12]

Coexisting with private Londons have been the many public Londons. Crowded spaces generate conventions over environmental use; for better or worse, these solidify as structures of accommodation that guide practice and expectation, demarcating both normality and decency.[13] Often such conventions exist reciprocally with statutory law; they may be habitual enactment of statute or custom reified as statute. Whatever their origins, they constituted environmental communities. The most common local government unit was the parish. Though they had extra-environmental obligations as well, the Middlesex, Surrey, and Essex parishes, absorbed by the Metropolis, and the intra-City or intra-Westminster parishes had long been responsible for maintaining and draining roads and, incidentally, for cleansing public spaces. Beginning conspicuously in the mid-eighteenth century, technological possibilities and changed sensibilities had engendered new forms of official communities, known as improvement commissions, usually concerned with better lighting, paving, and draining.[14] Parts of Greater London's environment had also been regulated by commissions or courts of sewers since the later Middle Ages, whose jurisdictions were hydrological rather than parochial.[15]

One should include too as environmental communities the co-owners of elite Georgian squares or unofficial civil society groups or "subscriber democracies"— like the "friends" of some green place, for example, Highgate Cemetery or Victoria Park. (One might add the shareholder democracies of London's gas and water companies or some of its transport services, but unlike many northern shareholder endeavors, these were more commercial than communal.)

Whether it arose from mere residence or from chosen cause, communal participation constituted a mode of self-expression and self-government. The absorbed villages had each been unique, vibrant places even as London was engulfing them. Each could celebrate a historical identity, even as its character was being transformed in environmental terms, such as population density, land use, and industry, and in social ones as well, for example, class, race, ethnicity.

Ideally, the communal "we" that regulated the environment had been a face-to-face "we": the mutual accountability of neighborliness had generated moral authority. The swelling of parish populations into the tens of thousands in the early nineteenth century challenged that, yet, notes Francis Sheppard, in the furniture-making district of St. Leonard's Shoreditch, direct democracy through the involvement of hundreds of parishioners addressing the minutiae of parish administration in biweekly meetings prevailed into the mid-nineteenth century.[16] But even where parish vestries were oligarchies operating through powerful standing committees and filling vacancies through co-optation, a sense of "we" might persist, with their local identity being more important to Londoners than any metropolitan one.

Created over centuries, London's public bodies operated under a welter of complicated and conflicting statutes and precedents. While their concern with environmental quality is often plain, they had not been conceived as institutions for managing a giant city, and it would be wrong to expect anything approaching a coherent system of environmental services. From the mid-nineteenth century administrative reformers would struggle to find the right set of institutions for efficient delivery of environmental services. Districts would be redrawn and responsibilities retooled, repeatedly. Yet even as parishes were superseded, their successors, district boards and boroughs, were often built on parish boundaries: most of London's modern localities can claim to descend from places that were historically distinct. Metropolitanism (concentration/coordination) with its efficiencies of scale would alternate with resurgent communitarianism, with the London County Council (1889–1965) and Greater London Council (1966–1985) as high-water marks of the former, and the 1985 Thatcherian devolution as that of the latter.[17]

For most of the twentieth century historians would dismiss "parish-pump" localism. Amateur local governments were surely too complacent, corrupt, or incompetent to deliver urban services. Their very existence constituted an inertial mass impeding the needed apotheosis of state-based rationality.[18] If we have recently given them more sympathy and respect, it is a Dickensian admiration for the simple, decent folks who, neck deep in a morass of institutional absurdity, occasionally overcame it. But while their activism, even heroism, is sometimes clear, the character of their environmental policing has been less so.

Consider the struggles in what may be London's tiniest local government entity, the Manor and Liberty of the Savoy, 6.6 acres running along the Thames inward to the Strand, population 320 in 1801. A part of the sovereign Duchy of Lancaster, it was in England (and London) without wholly being of England.[19] Its governing body was a leet court, an obscure and archaic institution of manorial administration/adjudication. (Manchester's leet was its main administrative body prior to incorporation in 1838; most others disappeared in the many rationalizations of local government in succeeding decades.)[20] Presentments to the court were made by large juries, embodying the views of the responsible (male) public. Their chief concern was the use of common space—which might include physical, social, visual, auditory, and olfactory space. A 1789 *Digest* of the Savoy leet's responsibilities prepared by its high bailiff, Joseph Ritson, outlined the leet's environmental concerns.[21] It acted against disgusting privies and piles of filth and rubbish, was concerned with dangerous structures (decrepit buildings, flooding, or unsafe fires), with encroachment into the streets by those seeking better light or more room, with barrels or carts left in streets, with street repair, and with traffic jams.

Was the Savoy an ideal community in which universal participation (even if limited to adult males) and respect for the fairness and wisdom of ancient institutions created environmental harmony through moral suasion? Ritson's cases stretched back over a century. While we see the leet acting against a variety of transgressions of public spaces, we cannot know how many such transgressions occurred and hence how consistently it maintained standards. And were the outrages obvious, or was someone alerting the Savoy jury to egregious trespass? And why? Was this community policing being co-opted by rivals wanting to exploit the same commons, or grudge-settling neighbors invoking some assumed standard of decency to redress a perceived slight? We do not know the backstories of cases, yet if communal standards were so clear to a community so tiny and intimate, it seems unlikely that they would be very often violated. Among the fines the leet levied were for refusal to serve as juror. Was the job so onerous? Or were neighbors hesitant to discipline transgressors when they too transgressed? We cannot say, but concern that amateurs could not remedy what they were complicit in creating would lead statist sanitary reformers, notably Edwin Chadwick in the 1840s, to pursue external modes of enforcing universal, not merely communal, environmental standards.

That groups of (bourgeois) citizens in Georgian London and elsewhere were, at considerable cost, busily forming public bodies to transform urban environments suggests that it would be wrong to undervalue citizen activism in environmental enforcement.[22] But it will be important to keep in mind too that the citizens in question were often significantly differentiated in their ways of living. The Savoy records betray no sense of class difference—conflict concerned environmental functions; it arose within domestic-commercial-artisanal settings. By contrast, much of the environmental transformation of Georgian and early Victorian London was the manifestation of class differentiation, the carving up of great estates in surrounding parishes into elite crescents, or into more modest blocks of tawny brick. Transformation (and subsequent protection of new environments) would be neighborhood-specific. The massive parish of St. Pancras, notes David Owen, included nineteen separate citizen-created paving and lighting boards. Their districts did not exhaust the entire area of the parish; they represented class-based neighborhood consciousness in certain areas.[23]

POLICED LONDONS

If we stand back from large-scale transformations, much of London's environmental history from the mid-nineteenth to the mid-twentieth century may be seen as the imposition of a common set of environmental standards. Whether the issue is sanitation, air quality, streets and green spaces, or the tidiness of domiciles, one finds much the same standards evidently in place. But who created and enforced these?

Like the Savoyards, paying fines in lieu of spending their days scoping neighbors' cesspools, the creators of the "improvement" boards were not themselves the executors/enforcers of the clean streets they desired. Where the market for refuse did not freely operate, they hired sweepers or scavengers, but the most general functionary for maintaining amenity was the "inspector of nuisances." These were paid perambulators of the streets, licensed to snoop, be repelled, and to criminalize whatever they found disgusting—for unpleasantnesses certainly existed, but it was better to use someone else's nose to smell them close up. After mid-century nuisance inspection and most other environmental enforcement would come under the mantle of "public health." While inspectors would ulti-mately become the foot soldiers of medical officers carrying out routine exam-inations of particular sites of epidemic threat, for much of the nineteenth century health-related concerns were intermixed with class-based disgust. While inspec-tors did oversee a profound revolution in household plumbing, mainly their work was tutelary: by reviling, they reinforced some (bourgeois) environmental sensibilities and behaviors.[24]

London's first nuisance inspector may well have been a Mr. Dean, appointed by the Committee on Paving of the giant Westminster Parish of St. George's Hanover Square (which included Mayfair and Belgravia) in August 1813 from a pool of sixty applicants. For £80 a year he was to "detect offenders who cause[d] annoyances or obstructions in the streets." The chief "nuisances" were Mayhew's barrow sellers, though Dean was also to act against loitering coachmen and to supervise the scavengers who had contracted for the horse dung on the streets. It is hard to miss the structural contradiction implicit in Dean's mission. Sen-sibility was a badge of class; environmental enforcement was a denial of the biological services—with respect to food, wastes, and transport—that the city (and its wealthy seasonal inhabitants) needed but did not want to confront too closely. Dean's fines (and the bribes he expected to quash a summons) did not stop street-selling; they did raise the costs of doing business and anger the street sellers, for whom Dean was the nuisance, and a costly one—he was beaten by fishwives and by coachmen. His employers too were rarely satisfied. Within two decades the experiment had failed, with the committee deciding to rely on the new Metropolitan constabulary, the Peelers.[25]

That by the late 1840s similar experiments were being made in London's par-ishes is testament equally to the power of sanitarian consciousness/paranoia and the initial experience and anticipated return of cholera. Under the Metrop-olis Management Act of 1855, which created the Metropolitan Board of Works, London's first metropolitan government and an entity preoccupied with envi-ronment, each subordinate sanitary district—large parishes and amalgamations of smaller ones—was required to appoint an inspector of nuisances. Like Dean, they were concerned with environmental quality, but their chief focus was not mainly on human uses of clean well-lighted spaces (Dean's concern), but with the ordering of those spaces in the first place—and with the mix of physical, infra-structural, economic, social, and behavioral circumstances that resisted order. The depth of sanitary paranoia would allow them to move easily from public to domestic spaces, and even to behaviors. Their remit included not only filthy run-off from yards, but also both the passive (neglect) and active (depositing filth, breaking sanitary appliances) behaviors that generated such conditions. They too were imposers of bourgeois standards on the front lines of class conflict, but their roles were more ambivalent than Dean's had been. They were mediators as well as partisans, compelling landlords to install and maintain water closets, traps, or sash windows. By the end of the century the Mansion House Council was calling the inspectors "friendly but persistent observers" and seeing them as advocates for the poor.[26]

Inspectors did sometimes intercede with landlords on behalf of tenants, but often they hectored tenants too, for allowing obstructing matters to go down drains, for example. To the degree that they became advocates for the poor by the end of the century, this probably reflected their success in changing relations of class and domesticity. That their relentless adult toilet-training—repeated accusations of "dirty," "dirty," "dirty"—eventually succeeded in creating broadly shared environmental standards among house-proud terrace dwellers (and led to the abandonment of in-home production) is remarkable. Mayhew's London-ers, moving often with the shifting rhythms of casual work in overstocked and under-skilled occupations, had been more concerned with finding dry places to sleep than with long-term sanitary security. To them the inspectors, agents of gentrification-fixated borough bureaucracies who seemed to presume stability in life course as much as in life place, were the nuisances, state minions one had to deal with even if one had avoided attention from the regular police.[27] If in parts of London these changes were well under way by 1900, their culmination would come in the interwar years.

Inspectors' daybooks show the press of gentrification on all fronts. In 1859 the inspector in the Docklands parish of St. George's in the East writes of "nuisance caused by boys and company assembling and the deposit and accumulation of filth." Another writes that all the houses on a street have been de-cesspooled, but are "dirty being occupied by the lowest class—the yards are all filthy from the imperfect drainage being drained by 4 inch pipes." Bad infrastructure mingled with problematic persons. Consider the ambiguity of "dilapidated dirty filthy house unfit for human habitation." Is this about the structure or its tenants?[28]

By 1890 routine code enforcement dominated inspectors' workdays, but in earlier decades that work had been significantly driven by citizen complaints. Under the 1855 act each inspector was to keep a Complaint Book. That mandate reflected the traditional legal meaning of "nuisance," not as an unhealthy condition but as an accusation of an "annoyance" (to property and occasionally health) of a condition or activity. To cry "nuisance" was to appeal for public confirmation of that annoyance.

It would be wrong to limit the culture of complaint to Dean's posh West End. Fifty Bow Common petitioners in 1856 complained about the Great Central Gas Company's gasworks and other establishments: "The air of the neighbourhood is contaminated with gas products, which are notorious for their offensive effluvia:—but worse, even, than that annoyance, is the nausea . . . which imperils the health and destroys the comfort of ourselves and our families." A few years later such pressure would be successful in protecting the Victoria Park neighborhood from a giant new gasworks.[29]

As with the Savoy juries and with Dean, trade was a key site of contestation. In greater or lesser concentrations, most London districts had been home to small-scale artisanal production involving unpleasant decomposing animal matters—bladder blowing, for example. If such industries were often geographically concentrated, they could also be conspicuous sites of environmental differentiation: residents complained not of the general features of the insalubrious environment they shared but about some particularly foul business a neighbor was conducting. Responding to a complaint about "effluvia from [a] sausage factory," an inspector found a "house and premises small and close for the manufacturing of sausages, etc." Pigs were the chief concern. "Pigs kept in outhouse next to complainants' kitchen" might be problematic, but mitigatable by altering the acceptable pig perimeter or the number of pigs kept.[30] Until century's end the urban pig was not usually a nuisance per se, as inspectors tried to balance precapitalist domestic production with the bourgeois ideal of a wholly domestic neighborhood.

Nuisance policing also addressed capitalist industry. In Hackney Dr. John Tripe, long-serving medical officer and the inspectors' supervisor, was so vigilant in regulating nuisance trades that industrialists *approached* him to make sure their processes would be admissible. How much his enforcement led to industrial migration to suburbs like West Ham would be interesting to know.[31]

Often it is difficult to disentangle sensed nuisances from imagined or potential nuisances. Inspectors policed potentially transgressive sites. London's mortuaries were not significant environmental problems, but the idea that their matters might get out of place—in Douglasian terms—is vivid. Slaughterhouses threatened at many levels. Beyond concern with general cleanliness and appropriate disposal of waste and by-products and belated concern with meat quality was horror at the very idea. Regular slaughterhouse inspections represented a compromise: operators acquiesced; the community transferred its disgust to the designated gaze of an official, who was guarantor that unspeakable deeds were not more disgusting than necessary. In better neighborhoods such unpleasantnesses were not to be tolerated at all, but at least the rest need not look.[32]

The single entity that gave Victorian nuisance inspectors the bulk of their authority over the vexed interface between pubic to private was sewer gas. Already in 1856 one finds East Enders complaining of an untrapped sewer grating: "We beg . . . you to trap the same forthwith or some fatal disease may be the result."[33] The objectionable character of rotting excreta was hardly new. Yet notwithstanding jokes about the "jakes" (the privy) and admonitions of plague-tract writers, it had rarely been seen as a major health threat until the early nineteenth century, when the coming of the water closet, coupled with chemical/physiological research demonstrating the deadliness of decomposition (products and process), generated both hope and paranoia.

Fear of sewer gas would be particularly acute in London: the Metropolis was the first great city to be systematically water-closeted, with sewage conveyed to downstream outfalls on the north and the south banks of the Thames. But even as they touted the superiority of the cleanly flushed over the bucket-based defecation technologies of northern cities like Birmingham, Manchester, and Glasgow, Londoners were confronting a techno-existential crisis of the first order: backdrafts. The sanitarians of the 1840s who had declared that all smell was disease had assured the public that their small-bore sewers would draw air down and away, ventilating and deodorizing the city in the process of draining it. They had been wrong.[34] As everyone knew, when the air was right, the street gullies stank, presumably with the reek of that far-off feculent vat where the great city's filth collected. But surely the gases might be rising even if one did not smell them. That people sickened and died without ever having noted bad smells was surely proof. During the sewer gas heyday around 1880, it was the lowly inspector who protected Londoners. At first this was via the U-bend. One assumed that deadly gas would not cross the water barrier of an adequate drain trap. And yet water dissolved (and sometimes emitted) gases. Hence the next retrofit was to disconnect.[35] Domestic integrity required a physical gap between house drain and public sewer (see fig. 2.1). In 1879 the doughty Florence Nightingale, used to commanding every aspect of her existence, noted a "queer smell" (unperceivable to her housemaid) and decided that her drains were compromised. She panicked, preparing to spend hundreds of pounds on an emergency retrofit of plumbing retrofitted only a year earlier.[36]

Even the coming of bacteriology did not dent concern: if it were not itself a disease agent, sewer gas might be a germ transfer medium.[37] That too proved false. Why, one may ask, was sewer gas so much more worrisome than the familiar smell of familial bowels? The fear-mongering of the sanitarians, the horrors

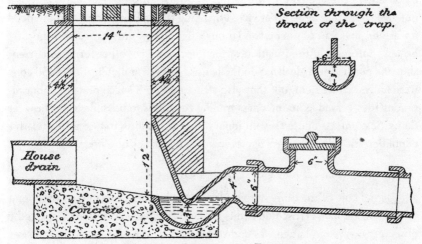

FIG. 237.—Disconnecting Traps, etc.

Fig. 2.1. Trap between house and sewer, 1890s. The technologies of traps are the best indicator of both of the depth of a sense of vulnerability to the metropolitan environment and of the profundity of retrofitting. Where the first generation of sanitarians had insisted on connection to sewers, their successors, terrified by backdrafts, insisted on disconnection to isolate the dwelling from the city. This is one of many designs. Source: E. C. S. Moore, *Sanitary Engineering: A Practical Treatise* (London: Longmans 1898), 295. This image is believed to be out of copyright.

of cholera, and the new water closets and intercepting sewers all contributed, but more than unpleasant smell or facile epidemiology, sewer gas fear reflected anxiety about individual identity in a giant, teeming, out-of-control city. Unease with the extraordinary social and ethnic changes of a rapidly growing city registered as concern with dangerous excremental promiscuity—for surely in some great sump in Barking the categories on which society depended were being undone as one's own honest English shit mixed and fermented with the foulest products of every variety of foul persons. And equally surely those fermentation products were percolating back through the pipes to violate the good burgher's happy hearth and to kill as impersonally as Chesterton's anarchists (who likewise gathered in subterranean places).[38]

In retrospect, the under-recognized Victorian and Edwardian nuisance inspectors were givers of a great environmental gift to all Londoners: a common citizenship grounded in minimal standards of habitable housing. There should be drains, water, ventilation, and sound roofs. Leaving aside occasional grousing about "dirty" occupiers, inspectors rarely said much about persons. They did not indulge in eugenicist analyses, hector the Irish or the Jews, or pretend to be social workers (that would change later). Usually an invasion of the domestic environment predicated on twin tenets of sanitarianism—that one was where one lived, and that people were fixed by fixing their places—obviated the need for greater invasion of the person (though that too would change as inspectors became enforcers of the isolation of the infected). Like other forms of citizenship, the purified and idealized domicile was both gift and obligation. Mod cons were indeed convenient, but they also structured both social practice and aspiration. They served as an interclass trading zone. It is impossible to say how far domestic comforts diluted revolutionary transformations, but London's relative depoliticization during an era of class conflict has struck observers.[39]

SYSTEMIC AND IMPERIAL LONDONS

The policing of the domestic environment occupies one (microscopic) end of a spectrum. Its macroscopic end is London as integrated system. Repeatedly observers marvel: What creates and sustains the vast metropolis? They answer differently. Optimists tout a laissez-faire London, product of interacting natural laws, a vast organic machine which has and is developing as it must. To others natural London is dysfunctional and monstrous but fixable if we can only learn its systems equations from mountains of data and iterative model-building.[40] Actually, the ideologies coexist, each drawing from the other, respectively, for dynamism and for rationality. Is London success or disaster? Can it be managed and how? The disputes persist.

The systemic view of London is a mid-nineteenth century creation, offshoot of the emergence of the social sciences in both their aprioristic and empirical forms. One may compare the grand social survey orchestrated by Charles Booth in the mid-1880s with Mayhew's writings a generation earlier. Both studied London's society, economy, and public order, but where Mayhew saw his informants as fascinating individuals, for Booth they were data points to be digested into class-specific street blocks, assignable to one of eight social classes on a great class map. Knowing how many people, of what sorts, lived by what means in what places would help to solve the "social question" of remediating misery/discontent during an age of alienation.[41]

To many systematists, London represented a set of optimality problems. Analogous data might solve the system equations for each of the environmental services needed by so vast a human population—humans might signify as mobile masses, as breathers, eaters, fuel consumers, excreters, not yet buried bodies, and so on.

If the sectors often were addressed separately, at a deeper—economic, demographic, spatial, chemical, and physical—level, they could not be. For the sectors interacted; resources and spaces were used one way rather than another; hence some master equation must integrate all. Beginning in the 1880s some utopians began conspicuously to problematize London. It had gotten out of control, they believed; some way must be found to equilibrate metropolis and world. London could not work without massive rethinking and transformation. Some, for example, William Morris and Hilaire Belloc, challenged urbanism itself, while others, such as Ebenezer Howard, Patrick Geddes, and Raymond Unwin, sought better integration of town with country, including green belts to relieve jaded spirits or to reoxygenate the vitiated atmosphere. Their interwar and postwar successors would go far to implement those principles.[42]

To an earlier generation of political economists, however, London, as the composite product of natural laws of human concentration, was a necessary entity. Therefore any moral evaluation of the conditions of that equilibrium was effectively moot: London was what it must be. Thus crowdedness produced a "silent, though certain, destruction of life," noted T. R. Malthus, hardly the first to see cities as population sinks.[43] Since markets distributed all things, including human existence, London's great size, both manifestation of and solution to overpopulation, would limit itself. In fact, the champions of inevitable equilibration never pushed their views as far as they might have. Equally, the planners who succeeded them invariably appealed to presumed natural dynamisms in thinking about what London could be: What utopian aspirations were realistic? Many of London's environmental amenities were commons in some manner; when used by all they cease to be so. That happened with London's air in an age when domestic hearths supplied warmth and comfort; more recently it has happened with vehicular traffic on Inner London's streets.[44] Custom, negotiation, and statute have operated more often than market or master plan.

Here I shall focus on discrete systems and on the problem, especially troublesome for under-defined London, of system boundaries. For self-regulating systems one may cite the fuel (and particularly coal) market, and Mayhew's scavengers, who live on in Dickens's thrifty dustman. But perhaps the classic is George Dodd's 1856 The Food of London. No one manages it, yet all eat, or so he claims, and the gourmand may sup on peacock's brains or stewed hummingbirds. No state could do this, Dodd insists, only the market.[45]

The classic case of a designed system is London's main drainage—water, gas, and electricity were more ambiguous. Over long ages building and paving had distorted the hydrology of what had once been a self-draining valley, with its several streams running off ridges north and south and into Wordsworth's river that "glideth at his own sweet will"—in fact an estuary, subject to floods and tides. Courts or commissions of sewers, communal endeavors to manage conflictual aspects of water, had arisen over time, gaining legal sanction under the 1532 Statute of Sewers. By 1800 the eight commissions that reigned over Greater London had begun to conceive sewerage as a technical (and juridical) problem of long-distance artificial drainage—sewers in the modern sense. In the 1840s Edwin Chadwick would chastise them as corrupt, incompetent, and insufficiently systemic. But they were communal institutions, more akin to the Savoy leet than to the metropolitan institutions that followed: beyond maintaining and occasionally expanding works, they oversaw the delicate matter of adjudicating fairly the benefits, damages, and costs of the works. They understood benefits narrowly: a sewer on one's own street benefited one; sewering a district did not. Sewerage would be the route to the integration of London's governance, but a prior key, as James Hanley has recognized, was a judge's decision that rating for sewers should be general rather than street-specific, which transformed a private matter requiring public coordination into a matter that was as fully public as any piece of parish business. His rationale was health: drainage was a public matter because it benefited everyone by removing noxious, air-vitiating matters.[46] In the half century after 1847 that philosophy would lead first to the consolidation of the Commissions of Sewers, and ultimately to their replacement in 1855 by a single Metropolitan Board of Works.

The greatest of its works, Joseph Bazalgette's main drainage system, built between 1858 and 1867, has more commonly been seen as an engineering achievement to solve a public health problem than as a reordering of London's environmental systems. Bazalgette's great trunk sewers north and south of the Thames intercepted local flow and conveyed it to holding stations at Barking and Crossness, where it was to be discharged into the ebbing tide. A by-product was the wide walking boulevards of the Thames Embankment, an environmental amenity that fostered riverside recreation and perhaps led to greater concern with the river's quality: systemic approaches allowed multifunction works.[47]

But more importantly, cleansing and draining the Metropolis involved the ignoring of externalities, which, to their credit, most of Bazalgette's rivals had tried to include. For in the decade before an environmental crisis—a "Great Stink" in the dry summer of 1858—triggered action, many engineers had put forth plans for sanitizing London. Almost all had been concerned with cyclicity, with the congruence of built systems with natural processes, following solution criteria outlined by Edwin Chadwick, the most advanced systemic thinker of the day. In 1848 he had called for provision of ample soft water drawn from "gathering grounds" in surrounding rural lands via agricultural under-drainage technologies. Constant high-pressure water together with universal water closets would allow the spiriting away of dangerous wastes through small (4-inch drains) into small-bore, self-scouring sewers. Their contents could then be sprayed on market gardens as fertilizer, perhaps distributed far into the countryside through networks of ramifying pipes. Sales would not only recoup capital costs but also return for reuse the nutrients and water that were the city's lifeblood. In this "arterial-venous" concept, the Metropolis was a living, circulating (and even pulsing) being. Early schemes imagined pumping the sewage to a single great tower of fertility (known as a "heart").[48]

Ambitiousness and complexity had hampered adoption of any such scheme. Bazalgette's was conceptually simple, but also open-ended: the great intercepting sewerage scheme was adopted without any specific plan for recycling. In 1855 this was defensible. Recycling technologies were in flux, a focus of intense research by the state, by capitalists, and by scientific organizations like the British Association for the Advancement of Science. And yet concentration of all metropolitan sewage downstream represented a step back from the ideal of cyclicity. The sewage would need treatment. Possibly irrigation or some other mode of partial recovery might be viable, but many were recognizing trade-offs between purification and recycling. So great a metropolis could not assume adequate demand for its sewage in its hinterlands, nor would it undertake to cultivate a market through investment in a network to distribute that renewable resource. Many entrepreneurs nonetheless believed that they could make a profit at the outfalls. Yet the Metropolitan and Essex Sewage Reclamation Company, which at great cost won the Barking sewage concession, quickly failed. Despite the Metropolitan Board of Works' efforts to clarify the sewage and to discharge effluent with the outgoing tide, by the mid-1880s the London Thames was a great de-oxygenated sewage sump. Soon thereafter, the Barking works would become a site of pioneering experiments in biological modes of sewage treatment, but the London County Council (LCC) would take greatest pride in its purification solution of barging sludge into the channel, where it was dumped in an area known as "Black Deep."[49] This, some would declare, was the cyclicity long sought: something would consume whatever went into the Deep; sooner or later it would reappear as fish biomass. People would eat the fish, perpetuating the circle of life.

Chadwick's ideal system failed in other ways too; system-thinking required control of variables. While London was largely water-closeted by 1870, failure to gain public control of the water supply until 1902 (it would be reprivatized by the Thatcher government in 1988) led sometimes to water closets without water—no one had paid the high rates, or perhaps tenants had pawned plumbing fixtures. Nor had the Chadwickians planned adequately for contingencies. Equations of ideal flow were no match for the many factors affecting sediment transport, among them the motley of objects Londoners sent down their drains.[50]

Failure in 1852 of Chadwick's gathering-grounds plan, which would have decentralized London's water supply, and later failures of plans to draw London's water from distant watersheds brought increasing attention to the quality of the (upstream) Thames (and Lea) water on which the eight water companies serving the metropolis largely relied. Failure to complete the cycle of purifying what the city had sullied led to a common riparian hypocrisy: those who befouled the river below them having the audacity to object to upstream users doing the same thing. For upstream Thames towns had heard the sanitary message too; they sought to flush their wastes into the river only to encounter opposition from the Thames Conservancy (empowered to govern the whole watershed but dominated by the London water companies and the City Corporation).[51] In response these towns sought land for sewage irrigation, the most reliable contemporary treatment technology. But here they met intransigent opposition from owners of the great estates that girdled London (and which, especially on the north and west, would later make up much of its Green Belt). Perhaps one consolidated sewage farm might be better. But no, the new Lower Thames Joint Sewerage Board founded in 1873 merely concentrated opposition. It quickly found itself, in effect, at hazard both for putting sewage in the Thames and for not putting it in the Thames. One obvious solution—to add the sewage of upstream suburbs into Bazalgette's interceptors—was quickly rejected.[52]

Among many morals of this fiasco is the arbitrariness of London's boundaries. The Chadwickians' approach to waters and wastes—imagined as veins, arteries, and linking capillaries—had been truly circulatory, impressively regional. But the systems that were built ruthlessly relied on artificial system boundaries to externalize environmental costs, creating corridors of order by exporting disorder. A few visionaries saw that water matters required watershed management, but politics in conjunction with changing transport technologies, rather than natural features of landscape, would determine greater London's boundaries.

Ironically, the most prominent linguistic remnant of Edwin Chadwick's far-reaching vision of hydrostatic equilibration has nothing to do with sanitation. The "Tube" continuously re-disperses Londoners to appropriate loci of social and economic concentration. Moving "underground" was an ingenious solution to intersystem conflicts that had become acute by the end of the nineteenth century. The chief conflict was between living and moving. Needing to move freely in any direction, casual workers had crowded into central areas. At the same time, efforts to lubricate metropolitan movement through new streets, such as Shaftesbury Avenue, or through railroad tracks and termini required sacrifice of domiciliary space, forcing workers farther from workplaces, exacerbating the need for transport.

Adding dimensions—either by moving transportation underground or by making living and working spaces vertical—were other ways to relieve pressure. And yet, as is so often the case, individual interest hampered equilibration. Recognizing that transport costs and times should not dampen the labor market, governments took steps to augment movement by mandating workmen's trains or special low fares. Owners of transport resisted efforts to make them internalize externalities. In housing too, high-rise projects were often located opportunistically, where land was available rather than where housing was needed. The LCC's showcase estate ten miles downstream at Becontree (opened in 1935) was ideally situated for sewer- or gas-workers, but hardly a signature investment in socioeconomic mobility.[53]

Central to the great sewage-recycling anxieties of the last third of the nineteenth century had been an insular sensibility: the prospect of Britain's slow suicide through loss of its fixed nitrogen, irreplaceable fertility, to the sea.[54] But not to worry, said some: the systems of an empire, unlike those of an island, were global. South American guano would compensate. London, the capital of capitals, world commander of finance, shipping, and insurance, could complete any cycle.

Thus one further way to think systemically about environmental London is to conceive all those other places whose environments it transformed, a domain bounded not only by the extent of empire, but congruent with the circulation of capital. That domain is too vast for this essay, but if one were to think only of railroads and mines over the century from 1850 to 1950, one can glimpse it. A more finite proxy is the circulation of London-based environmental expertise. It allows us also to raise the question of the ambiguous application of that expertise to London itself.

The age of imperialism was an age of new techno-scientific institutions. For a century and a half, the Royal Society (of London) had been a clearinghouse for data and objects from correspondents around the world, its members learnedly dictating what these were and meant. After 1800 London-based specialist societies arose. Many had environmental concerns—for example, the Geological Society, the Royal Geographical Society, the Anthropological Society, the Linnaean Society, the Chemical Society, and the Meteorological Society. From the Royal Society of Arts (1756) blossomed specialist engineering societies, beginning with the Institution of Civil Engineers (1818), followed by the breakaway Mechanical Engineers (1847). Notably, "of London" was rarely needed in these appellations: their territory was global. They were elite social organizations. Many savants were members of multiple societies, spending their evenings at sessions and post-session dinners. Caricatures abound of clubby gents hatching schemes to transform some distant corner of the world.

Increasingly society-empire links were tight. It was no accident that the Institutions of Civil and of Mechanical Engineers were side by side within shouting distance of Whitehall. The Imperial Treasury subsidized the Royal Geographical Society's great map collection: the would-be mine- or railroad-builder could check the best maps before embarking.[55] Their members roamed the world. Charles Blacker Vignoles, "the romantic engineer," bridged the raging Dnieper after the Tsar's engineers had failed, and then went off to build a railroad into the interior of Brazil.[56] Indeed one could speak of a global technocratic Anglicization.[57]

But no less remarkable is the relative uninterest of returning scientific travelers in rethinking London's environment. They had been exposed to environments very different from London's, to the dynamic integration of plants and animals, climate and soil, institutions and cultures. Yet few directed their insights toward asking how London worked, or became much involved with its social and environmental affairs; Darwin, disturbed by social injustices in Bahia and Montevideo, seemed oblivious to Mayhew's issues. But we might similarly interrogate Thomas Huxley, who had explored in northern Australia and New Guinea; Roderick Murchison, who had geologized in Siberia; and Joseph Hooker, ruler of Kew, who had traveled to the Antarctic, the Himalayas, the Levant, North Africa, and the American West.

For all these naturalists, London was a relatively unproblematic home. The disorder and unintelligibility they saw around the world could be appreciated only from a standpoint of order. For many, that order was eponymous with "South Kensington," with its great Natural History Museum and *Imperial* College. No mere place on a London map, it was the world's center of specialized authority. Darwin's post-*Beagle* London sojourn (1836–1839) was to allow specialists to examine specimens. Yet invariably the approaches to knowledge that South Kensington embodied required de-contextualization of the objects studied—to do otherwise was to surrender the hope for order.

Still, we should not miss the irony: shrewd and critical observers of otherness and complexity became naive and complacent at home. The young naturalist who read Malthus on his return to London and famously applied Malthusian population dynamics to nonhuman nature seemed oblivious to the dynamics of metropolitan poverty so evident to other readers of that text—for example, Francis Place and John Stuart Mill—who were endorsing contraception as a way to remediate a dysfunctional human ecosystem.[58] But quite quickly this apostle of flux left fractious Bloomsbury for peaceable Down, there to view obstreperous, confusing London at arm's length. The contrast with early twentieth-century Chicago is striking. There sociology and ecology intermingled; the city was itself an ecosystem, exhibiting the same laws of succession being worked out on the nearby Lake Michigan sand dunes.[59] When such perspectives—a union of life and social sciences—began to take hold in Britain in the new century, they were not conspicuously London-centered and did not derive directly from the social phenomena of that mass metropolis.

CONCLUSION: ANTHROPOCENE LONDONS

"Ne'er saw I, never felt, a calm so deep!" Wordsworth's silent, smokeless metropolis anticipates the Anthropocene imaginary. It emphasizes human happenstance. We are recent, and perhaps transitory, inhabitants of a lower Thames valley that is itself relatively recent.

Extending one's gaze in time (and possibility) is not new, but often the Anthropocene view is not that of the geologist but of the tragedian. R. S. R. Fitter began *London's Natural History* by contrasting the region's pre-human geological setting with its mid-1940s status as the "largest aggregation of human beings ever recorded" and went on to chart the "devastating changes in . . . natural communities" which that congregation must cause.[60] But preoccupied with the exigencies of the war itself, he did not contemplate future Londons. Yet even before the current agony of self as carbon converter, others had done so. I can think of three specific scientific contexts for highlighting London's transitoriness by imagining its environment as radically different. But behind these, and doubtless affecting their reception, is a fixation on sin, judgment, and apocalypse that is deeply rooted in English Protestant culture.

By the mid-nineteenth century the youth of Britain's islandhood, hypothesized by the first generation of geologists on lithological and paleontological grounds and explained in terms of postglacial sea-level rise, was unproblematic—just another event in the quiet, peacefully evolving uniformitarian earth. It registered sometimes as providential strategic advantage and protector of cultural/racial purity—without the melt of the ice, the dreaded masses of mongrel Europe would be marching down Pall Mall.[61] That this change had occurred in human, not geological, time has only recently begun to signify. We are now invited to contemplate the drowned communities of the North Sea, now dubbed Doggerland, and the tsunami-induced bursting of an ice dam that swept away the inhabitants of the cross-Weald valley that would become the Channel.[62]

Tsunamis, however, are not regular features of English nature, components of a happy Anglican cosmos. One need not believe in divine judgment to sense that a BBC reporter's reference to the "*moment*" that "Britain became an island" invokes an apocalyptic imaginary.[63] Recent fascination with such matters reflects a new sense of the fragility of the southeast, but it marks also an emerging universalism in which persons in apparently stable regions (keep in mind here that the doctrine of geological uniformitarianism was conceived in the Geological Society of regency *London*) begin to recognize how much and how dangerously the supposed bedrocks of land, sea, and weather have never been very reliable for many people in many places.

Other contemplations of London before and after have been more gradual—whimper rather than bang apocalypses. I have noted already the great nitrogen crisis and the temporizing market solution of guano importation. Generic concern with recycling had evolved by the 1880s into preoccupation with fixed nitrogen. Like the physicists' new concept of entropy, the nitrogen crisis seemed to represent a relentless falling apart, an erosion of the concentrated resources of life into dead randomness. London's sewage was the world's greatest offender. That loss could (and must) be slowed, insisted the chemist William Crookes in his 1898 presidential address to the British Association for the Advancement of Science.[64] Yet Crookes faced a now-familiar disjunction, between enormous and immediate environmental problems and tentative, distractible political institutions. Few denied the problem, but even for the forward-looking LCC, serious, yet soluble local problems took precedence over grand and global environmental problems. That Crookes himself was chairman of a proprietary sewage recycling scheme didn't help. In fact, the nitrogen crisis would soon succumb to a technical fix—artificial nitrogen via catalysts, physical chemistry, and cheap electricity. Faith in such technical creativity would go far to dispel future recycling concerns.

Third is the fickleness of the Gulf Stream, the source of London's (and of northwestern Europe's) habitability and relative balminess. Until recently the Gulf Stream's contribution was seen as a stable (even providential) fact of geography. In the last half century, as interest arose in its role as an on-off switch in Pleistocene glacial advances and retreats, it has become more common to emphasize its contingency—a matter not only of winds, waves, and sun, but of the reflectiveness of landmasses, impeding ice masses, and even the shapes of coastlines. Recognition of warming seas and melting Greenland ice has further complicated models of what is called the thermohaline circulation. Since the early 2000s it has been clear that this northward river of warmth has been slowing.[65] London as Labrador?

Environmental instability does not automatically generate cultural anxiety, but it often has in London. Today the end-days Jeremiahs are serious science journalists, legatees of England's and London's heritage for authoritative journalism—a city built on investment and insurance required searching and honest appraisal. But local reception of such concerns reflects too the ongoing vitality of secularized Evangelicalism. Taking itself seriously as the world's command center, ruled by a sharp-eyed elect, London also took on the burden of world guilt. We still hear echoes of the seventeenth century and the nineteenth; in anxiety about carbon footprints, physical and moral unsustainability are still linked.

From Mary Shelley's 1818 *Last Man* on, London has probably been the site of more postapocalyptic fantasies than any other city. Plagues, toxins, bombs, radiation, and deadly fog—same result: nature wins; rats rule St. Paul's.[66] Usually, however, the genre is not about no humans, but about a redeemed few—survivors bemoan the sins of their culture and get on with utopia. If sometimes sanctimonious, the genre is often fun, edgy—shock to make a point.

The theology is Calvinist. Neither London nor humans, we animated clumps of dust, deserve to be. In a sermon on "The Nothingness of Life," the Evangelical Edward Bickersteth (1786–1850) had asked, "Where are the myriads that have inhabited this busy and crowded metropolis from century to century?" and replied, "They are mouldering in the dust, and they are mingled with the earth." Bickersteth did not calculate the probability of a molecule of London dust having once belonged to a Londoner's body, but others had—a morbid application of the concept of urban metabolism.[67] That Anthropocene imaginary could be secular too, as in the hideous London of James Thomson's *The City of Dreadful Night* (1874). Thomson's world "rolls round for ever like a mill; / It grinds out death and life and good and ill; / It has no purpose, heart or mind or will. // Man might know . . . were his sight less dim; / That it whirls not to suit his petty whim, / That it is quite indifferent to him."[68]

William Cobbett's labeling of London as a great "wen" reflected its transgression of cosmic order—moral and physical. Others have kept the term: Sheppard for a history of nineteenth-century London (*London 1808–1870: The Infernal Wen*); Fitter for historical chapters—"The Wen Swells," "The Wen Bursts"—in his *Natural History*. Yet as Fitter wrote, that wen was still swelling along commuter rail lines. Worrying that London might grow forever, interwar and postwar governments, of London and of the nation, sought to check it with the Green Belt, and later with new towns like Milton Keynes.[69] Yet the M25, the closest thing to a modern wall, is daily breached.

A current (and ongoing) antigrowth touchstone is the Heathrow third runway. Business groups support it—new jobs and cheaper flights. Nonpartisan experts endorse it, yet Tories and Labour denounce. Teddingtonians object to greater noise; the shadow chancellor declares that they are being poisoned. While in fact the squabble may be whether it is Heathrow or Gatwick that gets a new runway, some reject the growth-stimulating effects of airport expansion generally. Capacity will increase demand; a runway will accelerate runaway climate change.[70]

The carbon Golem appears also in the threat of rising seas and worsening storms. Even before the age of climate change awareness, sea-level changes were evident in northern Europe, a product of uneven rebound from melting glacial ice. For three decades the Thames Barrier and the network of hydraulic checks and balances has stopped the barbarians of the sea. London's great bar was designed to protect the city until 2030, and though some think it can serve a half century beyond, it will likely be soon supplemented by a greater bar farther down the estuary. Yet will it prevent or only postpone? The culture undertaking this grand dam celebrates also Canute's warning: only fools hope to block the sea. The need for a Thames barrier reflects the tipping table of the British island. Postglacial rebound has been uneven—a rise in the north and west coupled with the sink of the south and east. Hence a last image: the Metropolis sliding slowly over a friction-free Essex and into the Black Deep, following its sludge.

THREE

DEATH AND THE ENVIRONMENT IN LONDON

1800–2000

ANNE HARDY

Health, and by extension death, have been associated with the environment since antiquity, when Hippocrates outlined the connection between human well-being and airs, waters, and places. Like all cities, London has since time immemorial probably been afflicted with relatively high levels of environmentally associated mortality, but it was only in the nineteenth century that its demographic patterns became subject to statistical evaluation and the concern of public health reformers and London government. Already in the eighteenth century, the city's death tolls were falling: Leonard Schwarz has calculated that whereas the London death rate stood at 50 per 1,000 population per annum in 1730–1739, it had fallen to 23 in 1838–1844.[1] In the early nineteenth century, however, London experienced a period of rapid population growth, which presented an environmental challenge that the city administration signally failed to tackle in terms of housing supply and regulation of the urban environment generally, until after the half century. London's population stood at some 1 million at the first census in 1801, and it reached 6.25 million by 1901. Its population was never again to rise so fast. During the twentieth century, with fluctuations, a peak of 8.16 million was reached in 1951, falling to 6.6 million in 1981, and rising again to 7.17 million in 2001 (Greater London).

Death in London during the nineteenth century was closely associated with environmental conditions of dirt and poverty; and from the 1830s, and by the 1850s with increasing specificity, with airs, waters, and places.[2] Thus Charles Mason, surveyor to the vestry of St. Martin-in-the-Fields, noted in 1895, "The health of a community depends chiefly upon the purity of air, soil, and water supply."[3] Even in 1900 London was not fully secure in these respects. Yet despite the condition of the urban environment, the city's death rates continued to fall—to 21 per 1,000 in 1881 and 17 by 1901. Developments from the 1890s onward secured an increasingly clean urban environment, in which tangible pollution—notable by sight and smell—was eventually replaced by the invisible, rarely tangible pollution of air, food, and surfaces. Death rates, meanwhile, continued their downward trend: by 1945 London's standard mortality rate had reached 14.1 per 1,000; in 1964 it was just 11.[4] During the period of London's management by the London County Council (LCC) (1889–1964), the city's annual death rates were below those for England and Wales as a whole. The replacement of standard mortality rates by standard mortality ratios in the late twentieth century makes ongoing comparisons difficult for the late 1900s.[5] In 1989–1994 London's standard mortality ratio averaged 96:100 for England and Wales.[6] The transformation of the city's environment began with the mid-Victorian impetus to administrative and environmental reform, which was spurred by outbreaks of epidemic disease which, from circa 1830 onward, suggested deadly developments in the general London environment. The continuing downward trend of the general death rate did little to discourage the impetus to clean up London and keep it clean.

AIRS

The most visible, most tangible, evidence of environmental deterioration in nineteenth-century London was in air quality. Where William Wordsworth was able in 1801 to sing of the city's early morning "smokeless air," by 1850 "a solemn grey canopy of vapour" was "sitting like an incubus" over the whole town.[7] Although the concept of miasma—the noxious vapors given off by rotting organic materials—was prominent among contemporary ideas on disease causation until at least the 1860s and prompted much of the urban cleanup which took place across the nation in the late 1800s, such vapors do not of themselves cause disease, however unpleasant to the senses.[8] The darkening skies over Victorian London were a different matter. Coal, which had fueled London fires for centuries, was used in ever greater quantities as the city's industries and population expanded, and by the 1840s coal smoke had become the subject of bills in Parliament.[9] Compounded by the products of factories, steam railway engines, steamboats, and machinery, these fogs contained such various elements as carbon soot, oily hydrocarbons, and sulfur oxides—a potent and dangerous mix.[10]

The darkening of the city's skies had other consequences than the dimming daylight. "The blacks" which, according to Charles Dickens, fell in fat flakes from skies across the city, led households to batten down hatches, sealing window frames with list (strips of material) and hanging heavy curtains in the effort to keep them out.[11] Domestic atmospheres could be stifling with heat and stale air— the re-breathed air which many contemporaries believed to be the real cause of respiratory tuberculosis. Dr. Charles Bateson credited "closed doors, closed windows, fire board, list and sandbags" with thousands of deaths, while his colleague Charles Lord considered indoor life to be "the great calamity of our wives, sisters and children, in all walks of life."[12] While such conditions undoubtedly favored the transmission of tuberculosis within families and work spaces, their effects were enhanced by domestic overcrowding. In the parish of St. James's Westminster, for example, which comprised three districts and had high mortality from tuberculosis, the district level data bore mute witness to the evils of airless homes and domestic overcrowding. In St. James's district, with an average of 1.5 families per house and a density of 134 persons per acre, there were 18 tuberculosis fatalities in every 100 deaths in 1861–1870; in Golden Square, with 5 families per house and 262 persons to the acre, there were 28 tuberculosis deaths per 100; and in Berwick Street, with 3 families per house and 432 people per acre, tuberculosis accounted for 29 in every 100 deaths. Deaths from bronchitis and pneumonia followed the same pattern.[13]

It was not, however, the quotidian domestic lack of air quality, or even the city's permanently smoky skies, that attracted the most comment and concern over air quality in the late nineteenth century. Situated as it is along a river valley, London had always been prone to mists and fogs, but as the nineteenth century advanced the nature and character of London fog changed. It became denser and darker. The dirty white fogs characteristic of the earlier years of the century were dangerous enough—as Bill Luckin has noted, accident rates rose at these times—but soon became something altogether more sinister.[14] Fogs became an increasingly frequent, and by the 1860s dirty white had become yellow-gray— the "pea-soupers" of London legend. By the 1870s the yellow-gray developed by midday into something black and choking, which cloaked visibility and so impaired breathing that even the strongest and healthiest choked to death if overexposed.[15] The most dramatic evidence of this evil is perhaps that of the calamity which overtook the Smithfield (Livestock) Show in December 1873, when prized fat cattle slumped to the ground and died and ninety-two had to be removed from the show hall and slaughtered.[16]

The fog of 1873 marked a turning point, the beginning of a "series of great crises": Christmas Day 1879 to February 7, 1880, January 1882, winter and spring 1886–1887, December 1891, December 1892, and January 1903.[17] Between 1871 and

1881 there were fifty-five fog crises, and sixty-nine between 1882 and 1892. The peak years of 1886 and 1887 had eighty-six and eighty-three episodes, respectively.[18] As the *Lancet* pointed out in 1880, there was little doubt this phenomenon was increasing: "As the population increases chimneys increase also . . . the smut-producing area is being increased."[19] The meteorologist Rollo Russell calculated in 1880 that the great fog at the beginning of that year, which started on Christmas Day 1879, and whose effects were felt until February 7, 1880, had raised London's death rate from 27.1 per 1,000 in the week ending January 24 to 48.1 in that ending February 7.[20] Yet by the end of the century the menace of smoke was fading: by 1900 coal gas and coal were gradually being replaced as fuels by electricity, while changes to London's weather pattern, bringing more wind and less moisture, may have contributed alongside the new fuels and smoke control measures to significantly reduce the incidence of fog as the twentieth century advanced.[21]

It was not until the 1960s that London finally escaped from the intermittent tyranny of fog. The Great Fog of 1952, which began on Friday, December 5 and lasted four days, killed an estimated 4,000 Londoners during the following two weeks and caused perhaps some 12,000 deaths in the longer term. There was a considerable increase in deaths even on the first day of the fog, and recorded deaths from bronchitis increased eightfold and from pneumonia threefold in one week.[22] This incident was the trigger for the Clean Air Act of 1956, which brought about a steady reduction in pollution levels already by 1960, when smoke concentrations were some 30 percent below those for 1955 and 1956. Nonetheless, John Scott, the county medical officer, noted that a succession of mild winters had contributed to this record, and wondered how far the situation would revert in the event of a hard winter.[23] Fogs in January 1956 and December 1957 again brought raised mortalities, and from December 3, 1962, fog blanketed London for five days, raising hospital admissions and causing an estimated excess of 340 deaths. This lower fatality came about because, although the concentrations of sulfur were similar to those of 1952, the concentration of smoke was much lower.[24] Yet the disappearance of the legendary London fogs after 1962 was offset, in terms of death, by the rising tide of invisible air pollution from the motor vehicles which became the country's most desired form of transport during the 1960s. By the 1990s traffic fumes were being associated with increased risk of death, but this was linked to preexisting cardiorespiratory disease; estimates of the likely number of deaths were not given. London's air quality continued to deteriorate into the twenty-first century: in 2018 air pollution was reported to be a public health disaster in the city.[25]

The advent of the motor car may, on the other hand, have been beneficial to infants born in London, whose death rates began to fall substantially in line with increased car use and a rapidly diminishing horse population in the city from circa 1900. The enjoyment of summer air in nineteenth-century London was much impaired by the urban fly nuisance, the inevitable consequence of a flawed system of domestic refuse disposal, and of a horse-dependent transport system. Environmentally speaking, Victorian London was fly paradise. During the summer months and into September, flies were to be found everywhere in the city, too often fouling exposed food-stuffs and kitchen and other surfaces with their feet and evacuations, spreading gastroenteric bacteria and stomach upsets as they went. Londoners had traditionally tossed all domestic rubbish into fixed dust-bins, which, emptied once or twice a week, became feasting-grounds for flies in these months. From the 1860s the vestries gradually began to introduce pail and other systems, but dust remained noisome and a public nuisance for many years. When the new-fangled galvanized iron dustbins with removable lids were introduced from France in the 1880s, Londoners long resisted them as replacements for the dust-holes.[26] Meanwhile mountains of stable manure, cleared from stables and mews, were stored in depots before being sold as fertilizer in country districts; these depots provided splendid breeding grounds for flies.[27] The advent of the railways in the 1840s only compounded the problem, since ever-greater numbers of horses were needed for the onward transport of railway passengers and goods.[28] Methods for dealing with stable manure varied; Newington Vestry, for example, had a large depot at Walworth where human "slops" (excrement) were mixed with stable straw and allowed to decompose thoroughly. This mass was then mixed up and carted away to the country, where it found a ready sale to farmers as fertilizer. As many as thirty railway trucks a day were said to be engaged in this traffic.[29] The fly populations which this practice engendered were a cause of great concern locally, and probably helped to maintain infant deaths below "summer diarrhoea" at a high level. Britain's horse population peaked in 1902, and Nigel Morgan has linked a sharp rise in deaths from infant diarrhea in the 1890s to this increase.[30]

By the early twentieth century horse numbers were already falling. In 1909 London County Medical Officer of Health (MOH) Shirley Murphy recorded a constant decrease in the amount of stable manure produced in the city, as motor vehicles replaced horse traction.[31] This transition was speeded up by the insatiable demand for horses generated by army needs during the Great War. These developments may or may not be connected to the fall in London's infant mortality rates, which began in 1902. William Hamer of the LCC, investigating the London fly nuisance in 1907 and aware of Manchester MOH James Niven's views on the causal relationship between flies and infant diarrhea, concluded that the relationship was very likely, but that observations fell short of absolute proof.[32] Nonetheless, London's infant mortality rate continued to fall, from 159 per 1,000 births in 1901 to 129 by 1911, to 81 in 1921. By 1940 it stood at 48, in 1950 at 25, and in 1960 at 21.5. In the interwar years, however, George Stuart Graham-Smith, a Cambridge pathologist whose core interest was in flies as vectors of disease, produced detailed analyses of the coincidental declines of horses, flies, and summer diarrhea in Britain, suggestive of a causal relationship between them.[33] Many medical observers were convinced—in 1935, for example, it was pointed out that in cities where horse transport continued to be prominent, as in Liverpool and Glasgow, the "true epidemic diarrhoea of infants" still persisted.[34]

Succeeding soot and flies as a pollutant, particularly of internal air space, the spread of tobacco smoking in the 1900s contributed to a dramatic rise in deaths from lung cancer during the twentieth century, in London as elsewhere. Cigarette smoking became popular following controls on alcohol consumption during the First World War. Propelled by images of cultural sophistication and determined marketing, it became a near-universal habit during the interwar period.[35] Smoking was broadly culturally acceptable, so that smokers were free to indulge the habit in homes, offices, theatres, cinemas, and on public transport, so also exposing nonsmokers to cigarette smoke. Death rates from lung cancer in London began to rise. In 1921 the stomach had been the main site (22 percent) involved in cancer deaths in Shoreditch; by the 1960s lung cancer had become one of the main causes of death for males, and it was increasing among women.[36] By the early 1990s standard mortality ratios (SMRs) of one hundred or more for lung cancer were spread in a belt across the city. To the north of the river, boroughs from Ealing and Hounslow in the west, through Kensington, Chelsea, Westminster, Camden, Islington, East London, and the City, to Havering in the east, had SMRs of over one hundred. South of the river, the same was true for Merton, Sutton, Wandsworth, Lambeth, Southwark, Lewisham, Bexley, and Greenwich.[37]

The relationship between death and air in London changed over the years between 1800 and 2000, as the nature of the materials providing domestic and industrial power, and the character of their means of transport, changed. The visible, tangible airborne causes of death—smoke pollution, lethal winter fogs, and summer flies—disappeared, to be replaced by the invisible, intangible pollution of automobile engines, and modern domestic appliances.[38] By the end of the century new measures against cigarette smoking in public spaces and workplaces were beginning to take effect, and levels of cigarette consumption were falling. If leaded gas disappeared as the fuel of internal combustion engines in the 1990s, it was replaced by diesel, which produces large quantities of particulates, especially when vehicles are heavily loaded.[39] King Fog of the mid-nineteenth century had been replaced by King Car and King Tobacco in the late twentieth, with less evident but perhaps as fatal consequences for the survival of individual Londoners.

If the tobacco smoke menace was radically reduced in the twenty-first century, vehicle pollution remained as an enduring, invisible pollutant and health risk.

WATERS

London's rivers, the Thames and its tributaries—the Lea, the Fleet, the West-bourne, Tyburn, Walbrook, and many others—were among the reasons for the original siting of the settlement. With time, however, most were built over and disappeared, leaving their memory in street names and legend.[40] By 1800, although piped water supplies were available to the wealthy, most residents were dependent on well water, which became increasingly liable to pollution through soakage from neighboring cesspits as population densities climbed. By the 1820s, when concerns about the condition of the Thames first arose, piped water sup-plies had also become liable to contamination, as upriver settlements poured effluent into the rivers, and locals tipped any unwanted items, from dead dogs to domestic refuse, into the passing tide. By this date the Thames fisheries were in sharp decline, and the river "horribly turgid."[41] Water was not yet associated with death, but it had become associated with illness. When the Grand Junc-tion Company was charged with delivering polluted supplies in 1828, evidence was provided to that end from a local milliner whose women employees drank their water and suffered regular stomach upsets, while their male colleagues, who drank beer, did not.[42] At this period, and for much of the nineteenth century, water quality was assessed on appearance, taste and smell, and while brackish waters might be suspect, clear and sweet-tasting waters were not.[43] The classic waterborne death dealers, typhoid and cholera, were effectively newcomers to the British medical scene, typhoid having been conflated with typhus (which is transmitted in the feces via the bites of infected human body lice) in the gen-eral designation of "fever." It was suggested by Charles Creighton that typhoid appeared in England only in 1826, after the "driest and hottest summer of the century," and was then identified as a new fever, but that its identity was sub-merged in that of the then-dominant typhus.[44] In 1848, however, William Jenner, physician to the London Fever Hospital (LFH), differentiated the two infections on the basis of clinical characteristics.[45] From that date the LFH's statistics were accepted by the registrar-general as reliably indicating the relative prevalence of the two diseases in London.[46] It was not until 1869, however, that the General Register Office separated the two infections in its own statistical accounts.

Assuming typhoid was a newcomer circa 1825, it remained a constant pres-ence in the city for the rest of the century, with death rates significantly below those for England and Wales. Yet water is not the sole means of typhoid transmis-sion, and the safeguards against water pollution which were put in place to com-ply with the law after the Metropolis Water Act of 1852 were long in becoming reliably effective.[47] The natural habitat of typhoid is in the gut of healthy human carriers, whose excreta pass on the infection through various channels, whether water, milk, or foodstuffs.[48] Explosive outbreaks, indicative of a widespread common food or drink source, were rare. Ernest Hart, who published details of 205 typhoid outbreaks occurring in Britain and Ireland between 1858 and 1893, recorded just three in London—all caused by milk contaminated with infected water.[49] Explosive outbreaks of typhoid were more commonly caused by milk that was infected by unhygienic practices among dairy workers; Hart listed five such occurring in London between 1882 and 1895, the most fatal of which (in St. Pancras) caused thirty deaths.[50] By this date most typhoid deaths in London occurred singly or in small groups, and only rarely could the source of infection be traced—a fact which suggests continuing small infringements of good food hygiene by individual convalescents and carriers, rather than significant sources of wider environmental contamination.

Recorded typhoid deaths fell across London with improved filtration technology and the expansion of piped water services after 1870.[51] In 1871–1880 the London typhoid death rate stood at 0.24 per 1,000; in 1881–1890 it was 0.19; in 1891–1900, 0.13.[52] Yet problems with water were not a thing of the past. In 1894 exceptional typhoid mortalities were recorded in the first three weeks of December over a large area of the county, which investigation showed to be common to all water company areas except those of the East London and Kent Companies. It was found that "notable" flooding of the source rivers in November had changed the condition of the waters, complicating the filtration processes, at a time when the authorities had reason to suppose that a new factor in the causation of typhoid must have entered London's water ecology.[53] By the early 1900s, however, company water was fast fading as a component in London's typhoid mortality. With the realization of the role of healthy human carriers in the distribution of the disease, concerns shifted from the environment to people.

If typhoid was the indigenous infection transmitted by London's water supplies for much of the nineteenth century, the blockbuster water contaminant of that century was, of course, cholera. Imported, rather than indigenous, the national effort at exclusion, effective from 1872, limited the country's encounters to just four, occurring in 1832, 1849, 1854, and 1866.[54] London suffered in all of these, the aggregate death rates in each being closely associated with levels of water pollution.[55] In 1832 the water was said to be very polluted, with death rates at 31.4 per 10,000 population; in 1849 the water was "very much polluted," and the death rates stood at 61.8 per 10,000 population. In 1854 the water was less polluted, with death rates at 42.9, and by 1866 much less polluted, with death rates at 18.4.[56] In 1832 the worst-affected districts were those south of the river—Southwark

(616 reported cases and 295 deaths), Lambeth (116 cases, 85 deaths), Bermondsey (116 cases, 22 deaths), and "Afloat on the river" (83 cases, 35 deaths).[57] Between February 10 and March 27 a total of 1,574 cases, 836 deaths, 426 recoveries, and 312 still under treatment had been recorded.[58] The cholera pandemics of 1848–1849 and 1853–1854 left London relatively unscarred, although the 1850s, more than any other decade, were haunted by cholera. These last epidemics, the one following hard on the other, roused fears that the disease might become indigenous, or at least that the intervals between epidemics would shorten still further, and in 1857 a small outbreak at West Ham was regarded as a warning to expect a full-blown epidemic in 1858.[59] No epidemic materialized, perhaps because the great heat and drought of that summer—it was the year of the Great Stink—caused cholera to retreat from the southern Baltic seaboard to ravage Stockholm and St. Petersburg instead.[60] The 1866 outbreak occurred in the territory of the East London Water Company, whose reservoir arrangements, despite the rules laid down under the 1852 act, had allowed contamination of the supply. It was this outbreak that finally convinced a wider public of the evils of polluted water.[61] The apparent broad effectiveness of recent sanitary provisions also spurred the Medical Department of the Privy Council to further preventive action. When cholera became epidemic in Eastern Europe in 1871, the Department's inspectors advised the forty-eight leading port authorities on necessary preventive measures to such good effect that a system of Port Sanitary Authorities was implemented the following year.[62]

If London's mortality pattern ceased to be disturbed by epidemic cholera after 1866, its shadow still lurked, and typhoid proved an enduring problem. As the security of drinking water supplies progressed, albeit unevenly, broader environmental water hazards began to attract attention in the 1890s.[63] It had become national practice to shoot raw sewage effluent into the sea, in the case of coastal towns, and in the case of London to ship sewage wastes out beyond the outfalls at Crossness, to be dumped in deeper waters.[64] In 1888 a Board of Trade fisheries inspector found oyster beds in the Thames badly affected by untreated sewage, and oyster mortalities of up to 50 percent were being recorded in beds in the lower reaches of the river.[65] In the years that followed, typhoid caused by sewage-polluted shellfish became an issue across London and Essex. Typhoid cases were being linked to the consumption of sewage-contaminated oysters in the early 1890s, and in 1893 a trail of cholera cases across the east of England was traced to shellfish taken from estuarial waters at Cleethorpes and Grimsby.[66] By 1895 typhoid cases caused by oyster consumption were being recorded in London, and in the early twentieth century cockles and mussels, very popular working-class luxuries, were also indicted. In 1900 George Millson, MOH for Newington, noting that shellfish were "pretty universally eaten" in his district in the autumn months, printed and hung placards of warning, and suggested to local fishmongers that they not stock mussels in October.[67]

London's typhoid death rates had been well below the average for England and Wales since 1871–1880, and in 1891–1900 averaged fourteen per one hundred thousand population, falling again to seven in 1901–1910.[68] Within the bounds, however, they varied considerably, from thirty-two in the City and twenty-five in Poplar and Stepney, to eight in Greenwich and nine in Camberwell.[69] Scattered cases were frequent, but outbreaks and deaths did still occur.[70] In 1903 the chief seasonal incidence of typhoid in London occurred in November and December, whereas in the rest of the country the typhoid season happened between August and October; London's shellfish consumption chiefly occurred in those later months, while for the rest of the country it took place in early autumn.[71] Food scares associated with oyster consumption in 1902–1903 induced greater public wariness around shellfish. In 1902 Shirley Murphy noted that the subject most frequently referred to by MOHs in connection with enteric fever was shellfish, especially cockles from Southend.[72] The local authorities and the Fishmongers' Company took action. From the beginning of 1902 the latter refused to allow cockles from Leigh-on-Sea in Essex to be sold in the London market; in the six months to June 30, 1903, London typhoid incidence was "materially less" than during any previous year on record.[73]

Death-dealing shellfish taken from the estuarial waters of the Thames were promptly dealt with by the Fishmongers' Company in the early 1900s, but in these years another piscatorial source of typhoid infection manifested itself. In 1900 the MOH for St. George-the-Martyr became aware of a typhoid outbreak which had tallied up 102 cases and 2 deaths since September 14 and the eighth of the month in which he wrote his annual report (January 1901?), mostly among schoolchildren and all aged under twenty, in the northwestern ward of the parish.[74] An inquiry by William Hamer of the LCC suggested that the cause of this outbreak had been fried fish; and in 1902 further cases in Finsbury, Woolwich, and Greenwich were thought to be due to this cause.[75] The year 1903 saw a thoroughgoing investigation into the connection between fried fish and enteric disease, making use of Charles Booth's poverty maps to assess the extent to which such cases were occurring in poor areas (black and dark blue on the maps) of the city.[76] In concluding his remarks, Murphy observed that the common phenomena in these food outbreaks (multiple cases and abnormal age incidence) were found by Hamer to be "always associated with the two conditions—poverty and fried fish eating"—in fact, it was impossible to find an area of London where the two circumstances existed independently of each other.[77] Typhoid associated with the eating of fried fish was due to the consumption of small (and therefore cheap), immature fish which were difficult to clean, and by 1912, due to a clampdown on the trawling of these creatures in the interests of long-term fish stocks, had disappeared as a public health problem.[78]

By 1920 death by fresh- or saltwater had virtually disappeared from London health concerns. A major component of the city's deaths half a century previously, waterborne diseases had effectively been vanquished by the sanitary surveillance of shipping, the treatment of drinking water supplies, the "cutting off" of grossly polluted fish and shellfish supplies after 1910, and the energetic dissemination of preventive advice. If cholera was defeated by a national campaign of exclusion, the disappearance of typhoid from London was due to sanitary management from within. "The behaviour of typhoid fever in the years preceding the war and subsequently, is one of the most noteworthy epidemiological phenomena of the time," wrote Hamer in 1920.[79] It was also one of the clearest instances of environmentally caused death defeated by public health endeavor.

PLACES: HOME, SCHOOL, WORK, WAR, AND DEPRIVATION

Like all great cities, London contained areas of great wealth and great poverty, which in many cases retained their character over time. The identity of London fragments on the ground into east and west, north and south; the City; into areas governed by civil vestries in the nineteenth century, and by boroughs in the twentieth; into homes, workplaces, schools, shops, hospitals and asylums, recreational spaces. As an international port and the heart of empire, Victorian London lay exposed to imported pathogens from abroad such as cholera and smallpox, while diphtheria became naturalized in the country after being introduced from France in 1855–1856. A severe strain of smallpox introduced from France resulted in the ferocious 1871–1872 epidemic, and the 1881 epidemic, beginning in the East End close to the docklands, was probably also introduced from abroad. The disease was repeatedly introduced into the city from abroad in the 1880s, but once the City of London was constituted sole sanitary authority for the Port of London under the Public Health Act of 1872, outbreaks of any significance became rare.[80] Harry Leach, the new port medical officer, conducted his own investigations into disease prevention procedures in the likely European ports of disease embarkation in 1874, concluding that preventive measures in Belgium and Holland were sufficiently reliable for preventive purposes, but that shipping from France should always be treated with caution.[81] Across the writings of London's health personnel, however, the classic Hippocratic influences on place-related disease occurrence—climate, soil (excepting always specifically polluted ground), and topography—received little attention, perhaps because these factors were considered common to the city's experience as a whole.

Although vulnerable to the introduction of infections from abroad and elsewhere in the country, much of London's fatal disease was homebred. Already by 1800, even before death registration became mandatory, some of the city's spaces were specifically associated with death and disease. The city's great fever specialist, Charles Murchison, noted in 1858 that certain small courts in the area of Gray's Inn Lane and other central parts had long justly been regarded as hot-beds of fever, and had been noticed as such already in 1818.[82] This part of London was still very subject to relapsing fever—of a total of 441 cases received by the LFH in 1857, half had come from the central district and more than a third from Holborn.[83] Murchison provides a very clear picture of fever distribution in London circa 1860, the three distinct types carefully described and differentiated: typhus and relapsing fever prevailed to any extent only in certain districts, the poorest and most overcrowded; typhoid was everywhere, including the areas thought to be the city's most favored.[84]

Over and above which airs they were exposed to and what waters they were supplied with, homes were a critical determinant of death. As Shirley Murphy pointed out in 1902, there was a distinct relationship between overcrowding and mortality. Taking as his measure the proportion of total population living at more than two to a room, in tenements of five rooms or less, Murphy calculated that deaths from all causes in 1885–1892 stood at 17.51 for districts with under 15 percent so housed, rising to 25.07 for those with over 35 percent so housed.[85] Yet this picture is not uncomplicated: persons living in these conditions were also likely to be poorly nourished and exposed to a variety of other life pressures. In 1920 Hamer noted that, regarding tuberculosis, the war and its aftermath clearly demonstrated that lowered resistance, such as from poor feeding, was a "far more important influence for harm than increased exposure to infection."[86] Commenting on the epidemiologist Major Greenwood's analyses of London tuberculosis mortality, Hamer exclaimed, "What a unity of opposites London is . . . a witches' cauldron of ingredients," where age, sex, employment, daily travel, immigration, emigration, housing, and local history all had bearing on tuberculosis mortality.[87]

Employment-related deaths, while evidently present in London in the nineteenth century, cannot be precisely sited, since deaths took place at home or in a hospital, usually remote from the site of the problem. As noted by Charles Booth, "The localization of trade does not involve a corresponding localization of the homes of those engaged in it."[88] Booth's researchers made note of ill health (as leading to eventual death) as it related to particular trades: white lead poisoning in the chemical industries; phossy jaw among match-girls; anemia and gastric troubles in the clothing trades; exposure and alcoholism among omnibus drivers, bus conductors, and tramcar men ("men rarely grow old in this service"); consumption and rheumatism in laundresses; scrotal cancer in chimney sweeps.[89] The latter, at least, was said to be rapidly disappearing: "In the old days not only was a daily wash a rare occurrence, but some apparently never washed at all, while the boys habitually slept on bags of soot which they collected during the day."[90] Anthrax was a rare cause of death in the leather and shaving brush trades, and glanders an occasional one among stablemen.[91] Tuberculosis was also equally likely to be communicated in the indoor trades, while rabies could be contracted by anyone crossing the city on foot. If the Metropolitan Police Act of 1839 was successful in remedying a situation in which "herds of Dogs . . . infest every avenue in London," rabies deaths were not uncommon in the city, and London dog-bite victims were making the trip to Louis Pasteur in Paris for treatment against rabies into the 1890s.[92]

These various environmental sources of death notwithstanding, London's general death rate had fallen to 14.2 per 1,000 in 1913, and death rates in London continued to fall after the First World War. In 1935 the city's death rate stood at 11.4 per 1,000, and the infant mortality rate (IMR) at 58 per 1,000 live births— the lowest IMR ever recorded in London. Measles deaths had fallen from 3.4 in 1911–1914 to 0. 07; tuberculosis from 3.4 to 0.56; bronchitis from 6.41 to 1.9; and diarrhea from 24.28 to 10.61.[93] Reviewing the progress of public health in London since 1889, William Hamer in 1925 emphasized several factors: the various housing acts and building regulations; the code of bylaws regulating house drainage and the disposal of offensive refuse; the supervision of offensive trades. The licensing of common lodging houses since 1902 had banished smallpox from the city, while "steady work," assisted by doss-house staff, and later the Salvation Army, had improved conditions in the common lodging houses beyond measure.[94] Preventive measures taken in schools and local communities had been effective in reducing measles death rates.[95] Hamer also emphasized the importance of the LCC's role as Education Authority in improving personal hygiene—"now generally recognised as forming such an important part of preventive medicine"— thereby reducing death rates and sickness among school children. "Any observer who is old enough to recall the appearance of poorer London children of half a century ago," he recorded, "in the days of unregulated child labour, of boy bootblacks and child crossing-sweepers; the days of 'ragged schools,' when bare feet were the rule, and frostbite, ophthalmia, running ears, enlarged glands . . . skin infestations, malnutrition and deformities were only too common," now seeing scholars trooping to school, could not fail to realize that the improved health of London children was due to the heightened sense of parental responsibility which existed among a generation of parents who had themselves passed through the schools.[96] Hamer considered this to be an environmental issue. "Compulsory elementary education," he wrote, "is now considered so much a part of our environment that its manifold effects on all the affairs of life pass almost unnoticed and unrecorded." For Hamer the single example which overwhelmingly demonstrated the indirect beneficial effects of the education system was the remarkable fall in infant mortality as the beneficiaries of the new education system became parents themselves.[97]

The steadily improving trajectory of London's death statistics in the 1920s and 1930s was rudely disrupted by the outbreak of war in 1939. In his first post-war report, Allen Daley ascribed this to two factors: first, the registrar-general's acceptance in 1940 of the principal cause of death listed on a death certificate as the sole cause; and second, the war itself, as a result of which a young and healthy section of the populace was removed from the mortality statistics.[98] The death rate from all causes rose sharply in 1940, partly as a result of these factors, but also as the outcome of a new environmental hazard: air raids. Air raids exacted a heavy toll. In 1940 alone casualties stood at 2.59 per 1,000 population. As late as 1945, Daley noted, V-bomb fatalities stood at 0.34, but for which the general death rate would have been 13.8.[99] The journal *Medical Officer* added a gloss to this account: "During the war, according to the waxing and waning of enemy activity, there were alternate outgoings and incomings on a large scale, so the vital statistics of the war years relate to a shifting population of varying and generally unknown composition." The damage done to London by bombardment was "terrific": the journal cited a total of 17, 811 deaths, with roughly half the properties in the city suffering some damage; the hospitals suffered very badly.[100]

The most significant mortality indicator of the Second World War's impact on London lay in the city's tuberculosis death rates. The continuous decline in these death rates experienced since 1919 was "arrested," with an increase in deaths preceding an increase in new cases. Existing patients died earlier deaths; in 1941 London's tuberculosis death rate was 72 percent higher than in 1938.[101] The aerial bombardment of 1940–1941 took its toll in physical and psychological strain and overcrowding; and following Dunkirk, heavy demands on war industries staffed by less physically fit personnel were thought to have activated latent infections. There were more new cases of pulmonary tuberculosis among adults than of non-pulmonary tuberculosis, which suggested that contact and droplet infection had been important. The pasteurization of London's milk had limited bovine infections; the principal infecting source was human.[102] Daley did not think this rise ominous, pointing out that even in the worst years of the war, morbidity and mortality were much below the level experienced thirty years previously. By contrast with the rise in tuberculosis deaths, those from measles fell dramatically, from 0.8 per 1,000 in 1931–1935 to 0.2 in 1941–1945, partly because of the evacuation of children, but also through reduction in case mortality. Here again, Daley considered, environmental factors were responsible: improved nutrition together with "widely operating hygienic advancements."[103]

After the Second World War, however, the structure of London's public health management began to change, partly because of political developments, partly in reflection of the changes in death and disease patterns and the improvements in public hygiene. The Public Health Act of 1946 transferred the functions of maternal and child welfare, vaccination and immunization, and the care and after-care of tuberculosis from the boroughs to the county. The LCC, meanwhile, created nine county divisions for the decentralized functions of child welfare and school medicine, thus ignoring the metropolitan boroughs.[104] The journal *Medical Officer* noted, presciently, that this step had probably been taken "with the remote objective of suppressing the health departments of the metropolitan boroughs altogether," further observing that such a step had many advocates.[105] It was in these years that the health responsibilities of the London boroughs shifted decisively from environmental health concerns to the provision of social services. In 1951, for example, the medical officer for Shoreditch was still recording the good work of the Rodent Section and the effectiveness of "Gammexane" in killing fly maggots and suppressing refuse odors from dustbins.[106] By 1960 he was detailing the services provided for old people and families, including the Holidays and Rest Home at Copthorne near Crowley, Sussex, a large Victorian house set in nine acres of grounds where Shoreditch inhabitants could vacation at minimal cost.[107] By the early 1970s, with the department on the verge of abolition, his successor's annual report (borough of Hackney) covered social services such as health education, personal health services, health visiting, and health centers at somewhat greater length than environmentally related services such as housing and rodent control. Recording the anxieties of departmental staff who did not know what would happen after April 1, 1974, and the current report as his last, the MOH noted, "It is not known in what form, if any, reports of this nature will take place in the future."[108]

This pessimism was justified. In the administrative shake-up of 1974, the MOHs were replaced by community physicians, attached at various levels to the National Health Service. As a measure of the depressing effect of this change, the journal *Medical Officer*, a lively publication for local government officers, became *Community Medicine* in 1971 and ceased publication in 1973. The sanitary inspectors, meanwhile, became environmental health officers under the local authorities, and likewise lost their historic sense of identity.[109] While environmental health services survived into the twenty-first century, no documents akin to the tradition of the MOH reports appeared under succeeding London government regimes, and London's health history since 1970 is much the poorer for it.

The abolition of the London County Council in 1964, and its replacement by the Greater London Council, prefigured the abolition of the borough medical officers in the 1974 reorganization. Daley's successor, John Scott, was the last LCC medical officer, and with his retirement and the abolition of his post in 1964, published annual surveys of death and disease in the city vanished.[110] By the mid-1960s, however, it was already clear that the pattern of death in London had changed dramatically since the mid-nineteenth century. The infectious diseases had all but disappeared as a cause of death, even tuberculosis death rates being reduced to less than 1 per 1,000 population.[111] Instead, heart disease, cancer (mainly lung cancer), and bronchitis had risen to dominate the death statistics. In 1964 deaths from heart disease stood at 3.27 per 1,000, cancer at 2.5, and bronchitis and pneumonia at 1.37.[112] Both lung cancer and bronchitis were associated by the MOH with cigarette smoking, but commenting on the bronchitis figure in 1962, Daley noted that although there was known to be an urbanization gradient in mortality, the striking difference between London and the rates for England and Wales deserved further investigation.[113] Bronchitis was, however, also associated with specific localities within the city. All London boroughs had high bronchitis death rates in the early 1960s, except those in a "wedge" running from Hampstead, Paddington, and Kensington through St. Pancras, Chelsea, Westminster, and the City to the Thames. South of the river, there were comparatively low rates in Wandsworth, Lewisham, Greenwich, and Woolwich. Daley also noted a steeply rising gradient of male mortality from bronchitis as social class descended from Class I to Class V. Social class and "born in London" were, according to Daley, both "highly significant" to these high death rates.[114]

While environment was still a factor in London's local death rates, local specificity was becoming more opaque as the obvious local environmental problems—slum housing, filthy neighborhoods, overcrowded and under-ventilated working conditions—disappeared, while more generalized contaminants such as cigarette smoke and traffic-related air pollution remained.[115] Geographically speaking, environmental factors detrimental to health became less site specific, less within the control of local authorities at the borough level. Despite concerns around air pollution initially from industrial and domestic coal smoke, and following the Clean Air Acts of 1956 and 1968, increasingly from traffic fumes, London's death rates remained, as they had historically done, below the average of the country as a whole. In 1989–1994, the city's all-cause all-age mortality ratio stood at ninety-six against the standard of one hundred for England and Wales. Death rates from coronary heart disease were below those for the rest of England, as were those for stroke in the sixty-five to seventy-four age group. Stroke under age sixty-five, and lung cancer deaths were slightly above the average for the rest of England.[116] At District Health Authority (DHA) level, all-cause standard mortality ratios were above one hundred only in Camden and Islington (102), East London and the City (109), and Lambeth, Southwark, and Lewisham (105).[117] All three of these groups were noted to be "part of inner-deprived London"—those areas of Inner London still harboring poor and socially deprived populations.[118] Environmental influences were especially clear in the case of lung cancer, whether from exposure to tobacco smoke, radon, traffic fumes, or a combination: all the DHAs with riverside frontages had SMRs above one hundred, with the sole exception of Richmond and Kingston.[119] Radon, a naturally occurring gas which seeps from the ground, began causing health concerns around 1990, being more especially associated with lung cancer.[120] Radon levels in London are, however, nonexistent or low, with southeast London and some areas of northwest London being only slightly affected.[121]

The complexity of the relationship between death and the environment in London by the 1990s was well brought out in a study published in 1999 under the auspices of the King's Fund.[122] This study found inner and east London to have the highest death rates, but pointed out that they also had more unemployment and social deprivation. With the exceptions of the City, Westminster, and Kensington and Chelsea, most of the inner ring of boroughs had SMRs of 102–108 (Barking, Newham, Tower Hamlets, Greenwich, and Lewisham), with some outliers, like Camden, in the range 89–93.[123] Lung cancer death rates were, however, well below those for the rest of the country, the worst rates (60–80) being in Barking, Tower Hamlets, Islington, Hammersmith, Greenwich, and Southwark.[124] Fires caused eight-two deaths in the city in 1997, and two hundred people, mostly pedestrians, were killed on the roads.[125] The worst SMRs for heart disease (81–112) were to be found in Barking, Newham, Tower Hamlets, Hackney, Hounslow, Greenwich, and Lambeth; in a very similar pattern, the worst general rates of cancer, per one hundred thousand population, were in Barking, Newham, Tower Hamlets, Hammersmith, Greenwich, Lewisham, and Southwark (215–240). The worst concentration of high cancer rates ran eastward from the City, on both sides of the river.[126] Unusually in such literature, Mark McCarthy and Jake Ferguson also drew attention to London's excess winter deaths at ages seventy-five and over, for the years 1993–1995. The worst rates (975–1,060 per 100,000 population) were found in a belt running southeast from Enfield to Waltham Forest, Harringay, Redbridge, Hackney, Newham, Tower Hamlets, Bexley, and Greenwich. "It is of interest," they noted, "that some countries such as Finland, with very cold winters, did not register increased winter death rates. Londoners, they suggested, perhaps took inadequate precautions to protect themselves.[127]

CONCLUSION

Between 1800 and 2000 death rates in London probably first swung sharply upward to circa 1850, to be followed by a slow, long-term decline. Environmental causes of death played the commanding role in this trajectory, even as the nature of those causes changed over time. One environmental component not followed here is the evolving pattern of food retailing and consumption in the city, which has recently been shown to play a significant part in obesity-related deaths, which tend to cluster in the most deprived neighborhoods.[128] Across London's modern history, deprivation has instead been a constant feature in environmentally related death.

Yet despite its reputation among contemporary observers and later historians as an environmental death trap, especially for the poor, London's record on environmentally associated deaths was from the mid-nineteenth century onward substantially better than those of many large English cities and Continental capitals. One reason for this misleading judgment of London's health performance may lie in the structure of its government, which from the point of its reform in the mid-1850s privileged the smallest administrative units against the totality of the city. From the civil vestries of 1855 to the boroughs of 1889, real power over local environments lay with the rate-payer electors and vestry local authorities. It was only with the establishment of the London County Council, and of the post of medical officer for London, that citywide surveillance was achieved. Local studies of London's health history have often, perforce, focused on a handful of vestries or boroughs for scrutiny, rather than on the diverse and sprawling whole; the history of the LCC medical officership and its successive incumbents from 1889 to 1964 remains unexplored. The absence of "London context" from most accounts allows for the privileging of local problems over the experience of the city as a whole.

It is clear, however, from Shirley Murphy's reports that from the beginning he conceived of the city as a unit, one whose performance should be ranked against others. From 1895 a section of his annual report was devoted to such comparisons: to London's standing on the death rates from the principal "zymotic" (infectious) diseases as against those of English towns of over two hundred thousand inhabitants, and those of various foreign capitals.[129] Thus in 1885–1894 London had a higher death rate from these diseases than any of the other great English cities except for Manchester, Liverpool, West Ham, and Salford; in 1895 only Bristol, Nottingham, and Bradford fared better.[130] In 1885–1894 Copenhagen, Stockholm, Brussels, Amsterdam, Paris, St. Petersburg, Berlin, Rome, Vienna, and New York had all fared better than London; in 1895 London's rates were better than all except St. Petersburg and New York.[131] In the years that followed London retained the good standing of 1895 in these annual comparisons. The principal infectious diseases were, by the 1890s, by no longer a leading cause of death in England, but historically they stood as the diseases most closely associated with unsanitary environments. Murphy also reflected on mortality comparisons within his city. In 1902, for example, he noted that life expectancy in poor Whitechapel was then nearly that of the rich in St. George Hanover Square sixty years previously.[132] Yet the continuing wide range of death rates between poorer and wealthier districts was still reflected in the comparative rates for the various boroughs: the death rate in Finsbury was 32 percent above the London average; that for Hampstead 33 percent below.[133]

Throughout the nineteenth and twentieth centuries London remained a city composed of multiple local authority areas contained within the unifying identity of Britain's capital. Even today, London is composed of 31 boroughs, 2 cities (the ancient City of London survives as a distinct administrative unit within Greater London), and numerous unofficial villages, as in, for example, Dulwich Village, Little Venice and Primrose Hill.[134] Each of these units had its own character, its areas of comparative or real wealth and comparative or real poverty; areas with better health, areas with worse; neighborhoods more or less salubrious. In the 1990s "inner deprived London" still existed, if of a markedly different character from the unsanitary slums of the 1850s. London was from the 1850s a pioneer of environmental improvements directed at improving the lives and health of its inhabitants, and although the trajectory of improvement was variable, the downward curve of the city's death rates bears witness to the steady and enduring nature of environmental improvements achieved against many odds.

FOUR

LONDON AND EARLY
ENVIRONMENTALISM IN BRITAIN

1770–1870

CHRISTOPHER FERGUSON

If the "environment" has a history, so do "environmentalism" and the "environmentalist." Though there are obvious points of intersection between them, thinking about the "environment" is not necessarily the same as thinking like an "environmentalist," either today or in the past.[1] In chapter 2 of this book, Christopher Hamlin examines the history of London as an environment, identifying a number of ways Britons conceptualized the city as a distinctive physical and social milieu during the modern era. This chapter, in contrast, analyzes British ideas about the ways the metropolitan environment was believed to influence the lives of its inhabitants. In doing so, it examines the place of London in a larger body of thought we might retrospectively define as "environmentalist," one that coalesced in the 1770s and exerted considerable influence throughout much of the subsequent century before evolving in new and different directions in the 1870s.

As the editors of this volume observe, terms like "environmentalism" possess their own complex histories. Thus, it must be stressed at the outset what the phrase "early environmentalism" is—and is *not*—intended to convey in the historical context of the first three-quarters of Britain's long nineteenth century examined here. As the late Clarence J. Glacken demonstrated in his classic study *Traces on the Rhodian Shore*, theories of "environmental influences" have represented a recurring component of the intellectual heritage of Western civilization since at least the ancient Greeks.[2] Yet most of these earlier theories focused exclusively on understanding the way specific environmental conditions—Hippocrates's "airs, waters, and places"—shaped the health and cultural character of human societies.[3] For most of Western history, theories of "environmental influences," therefore, represented a consistently anthropocentric mode of thought. These earlier notions of "environmentalism" lacked the belief in an interconnected "web of life" uniting the world into a single ecosystem that is often assumed in twenty-first-century definitions of "environmentalism."[4]

This type of response to the environment was not unknown in the nineteenth century, especially in its final decades, when a number of British individuals and organizations sought to protect and preserve aspects of the natural world— rivers, wildlife, forests, or "open spaces"—from the destructive actions or incursions of other humans.[5] In fact, scholars argue that the destruction, pollution, and upheaval created by British industrialization and imperial expansion played a leading role in giving birth to the concepts of "conservation" and "resource management" that have come to be routinely associated with environmentalism today.[6]

The worldview that will be labeled "environmentalist" here, in contrast, shared far more in common with the ancient, medieval, and early-modern forms of environmental thinking than with those that would subsequently develop in the twentieth and twenty-first centuries. First, it remained focused on understanding the influence of discrete "environments"—climates, regions, or cities— conceived of in explicitly compartmentalized terms. For most of the nineteenth century the primary interest of British "environmentalism" was interpreting the implications of inhabiting "distinct physical settings"—what James Winter calls "environs," and what contemporaries often referred to as "circumstances."[7] It likewise retained the anthropocentric tendencies associated with earlier theories of environmental influence. Nineteenth-century "environmentalists" sought to understand the impact of different environments on humans with the goal of protecting, preserving, and promoting human life and human interests. This anthropocentrism not only manifested in an exclusive focus on examining the impact specific environments exerted over humans, but also in a faith in human agency to adequately respond to these conditions, thereby improving the quality of human existence. Thus, while much of "early environmentalist" writing sought to identify "circumstances" that were detrimental to the human condition, these writings were nevertheless undergirded by an optimistic belief that humans could respond to these dangerous influences effectively either as individuals or collectively as communities.[8]

As Vladimir Jankovic notes, these ideas—and the personal practices and public reforms they promoted—were not called "environmentalism" or "environmentalist" in the nineteenth century. Instead, this designation was applied later: first by adherents and critics of this mode of thought at the turn of the twentieth century, and then subsequently by scholars, above all those working in the history of medicine.[9] Nevertheless these earlier ideas made important contributions to those we equate with environmentalism today.[10] Indeed, this inheritance helps to explain why, while many aspects of nineteenth-century "environmentalism" seem strange to the inhabitant of the twenty-first century, others feel remarkably familiar.[11] Thus, the terms "environmentalist" and "environmentalism" will be applied to this earlier mode of thinking in this chapter (hereafter without quotation marks) as a useful shorthand for a body of thought that, though different from the environmentalism of the late twentieth and twenty-first centuries, was nevertheless deeply engaged in thinking about the relationship between human beings and their surroundings, and thus constituted an important precursor to present-day environmentalism.

London occupied a central place in early environmentalist discourse as a discrete topic of inquiry and as a ready example illustrating specific environmental influences. The author of one particularly exhaustive environmentalist account of London in the 1830s aspired to demarcate those "circumstances which are either prejudicial or conducive to the health and happiness of the people," in order to offer recommendations about how to improve the "physical and moral health" of those Britons inhabiting the Metropolis. In the same work, however, he simultaneously sought to illustrate the "difference between not only the classes of maladies prevalent in London and the country, but also between the physical conditions and dispositions of the people." To this end, he made frequent comparisons between "the town and the country" and "between London and foreign countries, and cities," with an eye toward improving the overall quality of British life.[12] In doing so, he engaged in a habit of thought practiced by a wide swathe of the national populace during the first three-quarters of the long nineteenth century.

EARLY ENVIRONMENTALISM IN LONDON: A CASE STUDY

To understand the distinct set of ideas and assumptions undergirding early environmentalist thought, and how these related to and were inflected by contemporary perceptions of the Metropolis, we might begin by examining how they were applied to understanding one specific set of London "circumstances": a neighborhood in Southwark during the cholera epidemic of 1853–1854.

Early in the epidemic, the surgeon John K. Wakem was called to give evidence at an inquest occasioned by the death of the metalworker John Hickie. Hickie had lived in a row of ten houses known as Mason's-buildings, in a neighborhood notable for many "noxious trades," including "knacker's yards, bone boilers, and catgut makers."[13] Wakem was well acquainted with Mason's-buildings, having already "administered" to several children in the same houses "attacked with cholera," including a "child of the deceased." Thus, when asked to report "on the state of the premises," the surgeon extensively described the "unwholesome" state of the dwellings, concluding that they were "totally unfit for human habitations."[14]

Having heard Wakem's evidence, the coroner charged the jury with the task of determining whether Hickie's death could be fixed on the actions of "any particular individual." The conclusion was negative. All the jurors concurred with Wakem that there was likely some connection between the "unwholesome trades carried on in the neighbourhood" and Hickie's illness and death. They likewise agreed with the surgeon that "with all these nuisances" concentrated in a single place, it was impossible to identify "any particular one . . . that caused the man's death." They thus returned the verdict: "Deceased died from Asiatic cholera, induced by the unwholesome trades."[15] In other words, the surgeon and jurymen alike concluded that the environment of Mason's-buildings, rather than cholera, was primarily responsible for Hickie's death.

The ideas of Wakem and his contemporaries illustrate several features of the mode of environmentalist thought that had coalesced during the final decades of the eighteenth century. Drawing on an older Hippocratic tradition interested in examining the relationship between health and "airs, waters, and places," late-Enlightenment thinkers placed a new emphasis on the relationship between the human body and its immediate surroundings—on comprehending and cataloging the influences of different types of "circumstances"—including not only the climate and built landscape, but also the habits, customs, and bodies of the inhabitants of these varied environments.[16] The primary emphasis of early environmentalism involved understanding the consequences of humans' movements between different milieus and, above all, the way individuals' periodic or permanent migrations between topographies resulted in their being exposed to specific effects for good or (more often) for ill.[17]

It was this belief in the direct correlation between physical health and an individual's immediate surroundings that informed the 1853 inquest's seemingly contradictory verdict that Hickie had died from *Asiatic* cholera induced by the "unwholesome" state of his *Southwark* dwelling. Observable in the statements of all the inquest's participants—the surgeon, coroner, jury members, and other witnesses from the neighborhood—was the foundational assumption that Hickie's exposure to specific environmental conditions had resulted in his death. Rather than attributing cholera to a specific pathogen, the laborer's illness was understood as the ultimate outcome of the conditions prevailing in his home— from the "stench emitted" by the neighboring factories, to the contents of nearby privies "pouring into the adjoining houses," to the "intolerable" smell of "decomposing animal matter" and the "dampness exuded through the ceiling down the walls" from the bone boiler's shop above. It was the sum of these individual, "offensive" environmental elements that made Mason's-buildings "unfit" for human habitation. Hickie's wife confessed that while there were "very bad smells in the house," she herself "could not tell whence they came."[18] Her husband's death, therefore, like those of other cholera victims, according to the eminent physician Dr. John Charles Hall, was the unfortunate consequence of inhabiting "low, dirty, crowded, and badly ventilated localities."[19]

In fact, when cholera arrived in Britain in 1831, this understanding of the environmental origins of disease was so deeply ingrained among large numbers of the country's medical profession that they consistently attributed cholera to local environmental factors, even though it was a "new" disease never previously recorded on British soil (as the designation "Asiatic" cholera implied). A treatise about the disease intended for the country's laboring classes in 1832 repeatedly emphasized the necessity of understanding that cholera—like every other disease, whether measles, scarlet fever, or whooping cough—was a condition "excited" by specific "circumstances."[20] Indeed the word "circumstances" appeared twenty-eight times throughout the treatise's more than two hundred pages, while "Asiatic" appeared merely twice, exemplifying the work's consistent argument that cholera was a disease caused by local "influences," rather than some unknown, transferable contagion.[21]

Despite cholera's well-documented identity as the nineteenth century's sinister tourist—its oft-recorded tendency to appear and disappear from different localities, and to travel the globe in periodic pandemics—with the exception of a small minority (the "*avant-garde* of epidemiology," in the words of Bill Luckin), most British physicians continued to emphasize the role of environmental factors in explaining outbreaks of the disease into the 1870s, arguing that these influences either caused cholera to arise spontaneously, or predisposed inhabitants to infection.[22] Michael Zeheter rightly notes that although throughout the century "questions about cholera's causes and transmission were among the most bitterly argued among medical experts," the only point of consensus among them was the belief that cholera was caused "by some combination of environmental factors."[23]

The evidence Wakem provided at the Southwark inquest reflected this thinking. In fact, his testimony suggested that while cholera had literally killed Hickie, the laborer had really been slain by his unfortunate choice of dwelling, which also had "destroyed" a "great number of families" previously. Mason's-buildings, the surgeon reported, had witnessed "frightful ravages" during the preceding cholera epidemic of 1848–1849. Furthermore, Wakem insisted that the houses "were never without fever, if not attended by cholera." Fever and cholera, he implied, were merely two different manifestations of a single environment, and prevailing medical opinion at mid-century consistently posited a similarly generalized relationship between diseases and environmental factors.[24]

If Wakem's evidence exemplified contemporary medical professionals' belief in the existence of an intimate connection between individuals' health and their immediate milieu, the testimony provided by other participants in the inquest demonstrates that much of the British populace also embraced such assumptions. The *Times* reported that in attributing Hickie's death to the district's "unwholesome" industries, the members of the jury had confirmed the "common opinion" prevailing in the neighborhood. Many of the previous inhabitants of Mason's-buildings had expressed concerns to the authorities regarding the state of the district. The chief officer of the nearby Queen's Prison likewise reported that the prisoners frequently complained about the smells that "arose from places in the neighborhood." Even the coroner noted that "he knew from his experience in his public office for 25 years that this was a neighbourhood he was at all times anxious to avoid, and it was only by extreme necessity he passed through it at any time."[25]

The coroner's stated desire to avoid Mason's-buildings whenever possible illustrates a second foundational component of early environmentalist thought: the importance of human agency, in this case, the agency of movement. Since contemporaries understood health and disease as the end products of exposure to specific "circumstances," human susceptibility to disease was dependent on human choices regarding travel and lodgings.[26] Disease, in contrast, did not move; it manifested because of specific environmental conditions, appearing in the same "old haunts," in the words of one anonymous Briton, as "dried up springs flow anew after long rains."[27]

Again, the danger individuals or populations faced from disease, argued Dr. Hall, depended on "circumstances"; some of these "invited pestilence," while others did not.[28] In this way, the early environmentalist worldview united an older meaning of "circumstance"—as indicative of the totality of one's surroundings—with the word's newer, more limited sense of contingency or context, of the prevailing "condition or state of affairs."[29] In the nineteenth century "circumstances" could be understood as referring to both a milieu and an individual's inhabiting or encountering this milieu at a specific moment in time; and for some individuals, environmentalists warned, certain circumstances could prove deadly. Why was this the case? Why did some environments cause certain individuals to sicken and die while leaving others apparently unscathed? What of Hickie's wife? She also inhabited Mason's-buildings. Yet amid the very same "circumstances," she remained healthy, while her child fell ill, and her husband died.[30] How did early environmentalists explain this inconsistency?

Early environmentalists addressed the relationship between the onset of illness and specific "circumstances" by arguing that individual constitutions responded differently to similar environmental influences. Thus, although they often focused on the same environmental dangers—the stench produced by rotting garbage and overflowing cesspools, for example—early environmentalists posited a very different model of health and disease than the narrower explanations provided by contemporary miasmatic theories, especially those articulated by Thomas Southwood Smith, and his most vocal propagandist Edwin Chadwick. Smith contended that disease arose directly because of exposure to "poisons" ("miasmas") produced by decomposing "organic matter." Illness was the "immediate" outcome of encountering a single "exciting cause." This claim, that disease represented the consistent, predictable result of exposure to miasmas, in turn allowed public health reformers like Chadwick to argue that simply removing the sources of miasmas (via improved sewers, for example) would ensure the physical health of the populace.[31]

Environmentalists, in contrast, offered far less simple explanations or solutions, arguing that varying degrees of health and illness depended not only on discrete environmental circumstances, but also on the specific individuals exposed to these influences at a given moment in time. Differences between individual "dispositions" explained why in certain circumstances some men or women remained healthy, while others sickened and died. Individual dispositions in turn varied according to the previous chain of different circumstances a given individual had encountered.[32] The physician Thomas Bateman, for example, argued that "London constitutions" responded differently to specific types of treatments than those of individuals situated elsewhere in the British Isles.[33] Early accounts of airborne allergies in the 1820s likewise posited that "Summer Catarrh" ("Hay Fever") was a condition not only found more commonly among city- than country-dwellers, but also one that manifested with far greater frequency among "brain-workers" (clergy, doctors, and lawyers) than physical laborers.[34] While most medical men contended that differences between individual dispositions merely explained the speed with which detrimental environmental influences manifested in individual bodies, some went as far as to argue that each individual constitution was unique, and thus could be expected to respond to the influences of different environmental conditions with an equal degree of diversity.

Writing in the 1850s, the physician Thomas Bartlett described the case of a "robust and hearty" country child, who after two months in London was transformed "from a healthy child to an exceedingly delicate one." When his family returned to the country, however, his health "rapidly improved." Bartlett nevertheless argued that one should not conclude from this example that London was always less healthy than the countryside, because of the inherent "idiosyncrasy" of all human constitutions. He claimed there were "many cases" of "persons who breathe comfortably and enjoy health in cloudy London," but whose "respiration is laborious" when "residing in the country."[35] The point, Bartlett argued, was not that the London environment was inherently dangerous, but that migrations between environments were dangerous. That one reviewer dismissed Bartlett's volume as "devoid of the least novelty or original idea from beginning to end," indicates how widespread these types of assumptions about the potential risks (or benefits) of individual humans' movements between different environments had become by mid-century.[36] It was this same faith in the potent influence of a "change of air"—whether for good or ill—that allowed the tailor James Carter to claim in 1845 that moving from Colchester to London had improved his asthma, despite the fact that this opinion went against most contemporary medical thinking about the influence of London's sooty atmosphere on respiratory conditions and diseases.[37]

Admittedly claims regarding the role of constitutional idiosyncrasies appeared more frequently in discussions of consumption (pulmonary tuberculosis) than those of fever or cholera, because of consumption's long-standing perception as a disease of "individuals" (rather than as a disease of "the masses," like cholera), and because many physicians continued to argue that it passed between generations as a "hereditary" illness.[38] Such differences of opinion were also indicative of divisions within the medical community. The mission of public health reformers required the claim that certain environmental conditions could be expected to produce illness in every individual exposed to them. The professional survival of private physicians, in contrast, required them to negotiate treatments with individuals, and to assure them that the treatments might prove effective.[39]

Beneath these professional differences, however, remained a common faith in the potent influences different environments exerted over the human frame. In fact, by the second quarter of the century, prominent British medical theorists of consumption had begun to de-emphasize the importance of heredity in explaining the onset of the disease, placing a far greater emphasis on the role of environmental factors.[40] Both prior to and after the public health "revolution" of the 1840s, a large swathe of the medical profession—including many of Chadwick's allies—embraced a more ecumenical vision of environmental disease causation, wherein illness was understood as arising from a combination of immediate and predisposing "circumstances" rather than a single "exciting cause"—including architecture, ventilation, and sewage disposal, but also diet and modes of employment.[41]

As Charles Rosenberg asserts, many contemporary medical thinkers claimed that diseases as different as cholera, fever, or tuberculosis (or even "hysteria") ought to be understood as merely one possible outcome of the "body's unending transactions with its environment"—the final chapter in a lengthy story of "wear and tear," in the words of one influential contemporary physician.[42] Disease, it was argued, as often as not arose as the end result of prolonged exposure to unhealthy influences, what the public health reformer Hector Gavin labeled "deteriorating agents."[43] In 1853 a different inquest concluded that the death of another cholera victim, the servant Carolyn Lloyd, had been "accelerated by the effluvia arising from foul water emptied daily from a cesspool" behind her residence.[44] Hickie's death might likewise have been attributed to a similar ongoing process, since his wife noted that the "smells" in their home had made it almost impossible for the laborer to "eat his dinner," undermining his constitutional strength and depressing his spirits long before his death.[45]

Early environmentalist doctrines articulated a vision of the human body that was malleable and permeable, continually subject to, and potentially under attack from, exterior influences of the surrounding milieu, including "miasmas" but also a range of other factors that conditioned individuals' physical and mental well-being.[46] The implications of this environmental worldview arguably became most pressing in the imperial context—above all in Britons' encounters with tropical climates in India, Africa, and the Caribbean.[47] Yet for much of the nineteenth century similar environmentalist theories informing medical practice and state policy in colonial settings were applied on a smaller scale within the specific micro-geography of the British Isles. The same ideas that discouraged long-term British settlement in the Caribbean or prompted the development of hill stations in India, for example, also informed the recommendations of metropolitan physicians who encouraged affluent Britons to periodically vacate the national capital to protect their health.[48]

Metropolitan Britons regularly invoked environmentalist ideas when explaining differentials of health and well-being among the population of the British Isles. In particular, many physicians, journalists, and reformers emphasized how internal migration or periodic movements between the country and the city (or vice versa) exposed individuals to the influences of specific environmental "circumstances," whether in the form of "nuisances" like cesspools or overcrowded burial grounds; physical surroundings like poorly ventilated bedrooms, workshops, or ballrooms; or specific local practices, like long (or late) hours, unhealthy diets, or heavy drinking.[49] The London landscape, contemporaries warned, abounded in a wide range of these types of "deteriorating agents," exposing migrants to the capital to a multitude of threats. Indeed, in 1848 Charles Dickens described newcomers to the Metropolis as destined to become "food for the hospitals, the churchyards, the prisons, the river, fever, madness, vice, and death."[50]

MEDICAL AND MORAL INFLUENCES IN THE LONDON ENVIRONMENT

Dickens's summary of the range of negative fates potentially awaiting migrants to London illustrates the contemporary perception that metropolitan influences threatened not only the physical health of migrants, but their morality as well. If the early environmentalist worldview assumed a permeable human body perpetually besieged by external influences, it likewise posited an equally porous understanding of the dangers these influences posed to individuals' physical and moral health. The words "unwholesome" and "offensive" that witnesses employed when describing the conditions of Mason's-buildings exemplified this tendency to unite moral and physical dangers. These terms routinely were used by contemporary Britons to describe influences detrimental to health and morality alike.[51] Exposure to "offensive" sights and smells, Dr. Gavin maintained, could result in "physical ailments," but also might produce an "infinite extent of demoralization," reducing persons forced to inhabit such surroundings to a state of "brutality." Living amid such "circumstances," he contended, was a "kind of training" for "degradation and profligacy."[52] Thus, as Dickens claimed, contemporaries believed exposure to London not only carried the risk of "fever" and "death," but also of "vice"—of a descent into criminality (becoming "food" for the "prisons") and even self-murder. Suicide remained a felony in Britain throughout the nineteenth century, and most contemporaries viewed the act as a potent expression of "moral failure"—and "the river" (i.e., the Thames) was the canonical location for metropolitan suicides.[53]

Furthermore, as Dr. Gavin's comments regarding "demoralization" and "training" suggest, the moral damage caused by exposure to noxious environmental influences was likewise understood to function primarily as an incremental process. The favorite contemporary model for the deterioration of an individual's sense of morality under the influence of debasing external factors was "habituation."[54] The shoemaker James Devlin argued, for example, that in most metropolitan lodging-houses, the laborer became "familiar with vice, and imperceptibly fell into its snare," such that "at length he is reckoned in the same class as those with whom he lives."[55] As in the case of physical disease, contemporaries did not rule out the possibility that exposure to "unwholesome" environmental influences—what one clergyman labeled "moral miasmas"—might result in rapid, if not spontaneous transformations of the human character.[56] The anonymous working-class author of an 1853 prize essay contended that in the worst London dwellings, "Angels from heaven would not remain angels for a single night."[57]

One achieves a particularly rich sense of how this mode of environmental thinking inflected life far beyond the realms of medicine and public health by examining the role of the London environment in the spiritual autobiography of the Quaker minister Thomas Shillitoe (1754–1836). The contents of Shillitoe's autobiography serve as an exemplary indication of the degree to which early environmentalist ideas had expanded far beyond the ranks of the contemporary medical profession. Shillitoe frequently addressed threats he believed the London environment had posed to his physical well-being. He recalled how, at the age of twenty-four he had moved from Westminster to a place of business in the City, and his health immediately began to decline. "I concluded I had no alternative," but "leaving London altogether ... After a few months my health improved." The older Shillitoe writing in the 1830s ultimately interpreted this series of events in providential terms—as an incident of divine "favour," that allowed him to later pursue his life as a minister. In narrating this act of providence, he nevertheless also asserted the early environmentalists' faith in the benefits of a "change of air."[58]

If the contents of Shillitoe's autobiography illustrate one contemporary mind alive to the dangers the London environment could present to physical health, the author's focus was the threats that same environment posed to the soul. Like many nineteenth-century spiritual and secular autobiographers, Shillitoe sought to "afford lessons of instruction and encouragement," especially those "appertaining to salvation," and the early portion of Shillitoe's narrative focused heavily on the spiritual dangers and moral failures of his early years.[59] Shillitoe lived most of these years in London, and his narrative repeatedly emphasized the role metropolitan environments had played in contributing to his dissolute youth.

Again, the primary moral threat was conceived of in terms of "exposure." The words "exposed" and "exposure" appeared repeatedly in the early portion of the autobiography (ten times in half as many pages in the first chapter alone).[60] Shillitoe argued that different types of London "exposures" threatened his moral health via three separate vectors: first, by subjecting him to new temptations he had not encountered previously; second, by presenting him with negative examples of behaviors that he was encouraged to imitate; and third, by placing him in physical and social circumstances whose overall influence threatened to deaden his moral sense through a process of habituation.

By his own account, Shillitoe was frequently subjected to the influence of these threefold dangers by locations in London. When his family was forced to take up "residence in [a] public house" at Islington, his "exposed situation" opened him to "almost every vice," presented "great temptations" (including addiction to "vanity"), placed him under the influence of the "artifices of such evil-disposed persons," and "nearly affected my ruin." In like manner, his apprenticeship to a grocer in Wapping entailed similar moral threats, not only because his master was "given to much liquor and company," but also because "the examples of wickedness exhibited in the neighbourhood . . . rendered my new situation every way a dangerous one." Nor was a later position as a banking clerk in Lombard Street free from dangers, as his "new companions" were "much given up to the world, and its delusive pleasures," and thus he was "near made shipwreck of faith again." It was only by being "mercifully preserved within the holy enclosure" of "pure love and fear of the Lord," that Shillitoe argued he was able to weather the moral hazards of the Metropolis.[61] His account once again presents us with the internal/external division—and the dangers of influences moving through the permeable barriers between them—already observed as central hallmarks of early environmentalist thought, albeit here reworked within a religious paradigm of divine faith exposed and threatened by worldly influences.

If Britons outside the ranks of the medical community like Shillitoe tended to conflate London's moral and physical dangers into a single miasmatic mixture, members of the medical community did much the same.[62] In the early months of the 1853–1854 cholera epidemic, a group of physicians wrote to the *Medical Times and Gazette*, not to alert their fellow medical practitioners to the host of environmental threats spreading physical disease in London, but about the moral dangers metropolitan medical education posed to young men—especially those hailing from outside the capital. The authors argued that there were "some circumstances which place the Medical student in a more precarious position than other classes of pupils." The fact that "the exigencies of the Profession require that Medicine should be learned in large cities," they warned, ensured that young students of the field had to be educated "in these great centres of civilisation, with their attendant luxuries and vices," and too often these proved a "severe trial to the firmest principles and to the most rigid morality," causing many young men to "forsake the straight and narrow path of rectitude, and deviate into the byways of dissipation." They thus argued that the administrators of London medical schools had a "paternal" responsibility to not only educate their students in the knowledge of medicine, but also to protect them from contracting vices by continually reminding them of the "punishments which are attendant upon indolence and folly."[63] In an era when physicians still regularly attributed physical disease to moral failings like envy or rage, the members of the medical profession likewise saw little reason to differentiate between moral and physical environmental threats.[64]

Consider, for example, the role excessive drinking played in early environmentalist accounts of the Metropolis. For most of the nineteenth century Britons portrayed drinking and drunkenness as moral failings. Yet many reformers contended that the tendency toward heavy drinking was as much attributable to the influence of environmental circumstances as to personal choice or addiction.

Dr. Gavin asserted that London workers' insobriety was directly related to the "moral depression" resulting from dwelling constantly amid "filth and . . . foul air." Furthermore, like many contemporary medical thinkers, Gavin argued that drinking in turn damaged the physical constitution, increasing individuals' susceptibility to disease. Thus, he and other public health reformers claimed that negative environmental influences promoted "drunkenness, immorality, and crime," while simultaneously undermining "health and longevity."[65]

"It is most assuredly a truth," Gavin concluded, that the physical, social, and moral "condition of the people" was collectively determined by the environment they inhabited. The mid-century authority on tropical medicine, James Ranald Martin, agreed, asserting that there was a direct correlation between individuals' moral and physical health, observing that "a slothful, squalid-looking population invariably characterises an unhealthy country." In making such claims, he was mostly parroting the ideas of his equally influential predecessor, Dr. James Johnson, who had made an almost identical assertion in 1818, arguing that fevers arose among the "squalid dregs" of society, because the "brain labours merely through sympathy with the stomach and other . . . organs." Furthermore, Johnson contended, such effects were intensified in the constitutions of individuals subjected to "artificial life," above all those inhabiting "a crowded and high-viced [sic] metropolis."[66]

LONDON ENVIRONMENTS OR THE LONDON ENVIRONMENT?

James Johnson's claims regarding the relationship between physical and moral decline and the "vice" of the Metropolis functions as a useful reminder that the focus of early environmentalist ideas regarding London involved not only the identification of individual, isolated threats to body and soul lurking in its streets and alleys, but a systematic effort to understand how the metropolitan environment affected its populace, and that of the entire British nation. As the eminent physician's general claim regarding the detrimental bodily and moral influences present in the "artificial" life of large cities exemplified, for many nineteenth-century Britons there was a tendency to slip from discussing the influences of individual, discrete metropolitan "environments" to discussing the influences of *the* London "environment." Much as early environmentalists posited a permeable human frame and a blurry distinction between the sources of physical disease and moral degradation, so they also articulated a vision of the Metropolis in which discrete environmental hazards within the city accumulated to create a single unhealthy urban milieu.

Dr. Johnson had much to say about the London environment, and none of it was good. In 1831 the physician devoted the first part of his treatise examining the medical benefits of travel, *A Change of Air*, to demonstrating how life in the capital presented individuals with a "unique" collection of circumstantial threats. These included "over-strenuous exertion," "unnatural hours," "anxiety of mind," and "bad air." Johnson warned that the overall effect of these accumulated factors was a relentless deterioration of "the living machine," one "daily and hourly felt by tens of thousands in this metropolis," making "much work for the doctors . . . if not for the undertakers." As his book's title implied, Johnson argued the best way to avoid the detrimental effects of the London environment was to minimize one's exposure to it, either by obtaining suburban dwellings or breaking up sustained periods of residence in the Metropolis with prolonged sojourns in the countryside. Many other contemporary physicians advocated similar preventive strategies.[67]

Later in the same decade another London surgeon, John Hogg, expanded on Johnson's claims, producing arguably the most exhaustive description of London informed by early environmentalist doctrines. Hogg's *London as It Is* (1837) sought to catalog all of those "circumstances . . . prejudicial or conducive to the health and happiness of the people," from diet, late hours, gin drinking, fashionable clothing, and leisure activities, to housing, street widths, sewage disposal, and atmospheric conditions like "smoke and fog." By doing so the surgeon hoped not only to illustrate the dangers of metropolitan life, but also to suggest improvements that might "promote the physical and moral health of the metropolis," measures he argued ought to be embraced by both "private individuals" and the "various offices of the executive government." Hogg asserted that he was especially well suited to undertake such an examination because he was not a native Londoner, having lived the "earlier part" of his life "in the country," and thus "could not but observe the difference between not only the classes of maladies prevalent in London and the country, but also between the physical conditions and dispositions of the people.[68]

Hogg thus invoked all the ideas we have come to identify with early environmental thinking. He emphasized the totality of physical and social "circumstances" attached to a specific milieu, and he deployed a permeable definition of environmental hazards as applying equally to physical and moral health. Hogg likewise placed a central importance on the geographic situation of individuals and their movement in and out of (and thus their exposure to) different environments, and the necessity of defending against these negative environmental influences, either by personal decisions or public reforms. He placed human agency at the center of his account, arguing that Britons had the choice to encounter or avoid many of the dangers lurking in the metropolitan environment, and that they also could decide to act individually or collectively to remove those threats to physical and moral health that could not be merely avoided. In framing these arguments, Hogg also exemplified early environmentalists' emphasis on habituation and deterioration—on "wear and tear" (an image he borrowed from Johnson)—arguing that individuals in London suffered from a greater susceptibility to physical and mental illnesses (everything from smallpox and cholera to headaches and hysteria) but also recovered from these disorders more slowly. The health trajectory of the Londoner, Hogg warned, did not involve existing on a spectrum between wellness and illness, but instead represented one continual "train of ills."[69]

In making these claims, Hogg, like Johnson and many other early environmentalist thinkers, deployed a vision of London as an inherently unnatural, "artificial" environment. Indeed, one reviewer argued that Hogg was especially adept at portraying the "artificial modes of living" said to prevail in the nation's capital—in the form of the longer and later hours Londoners worked and socialized, for example.[70] In doing so, Hogg invoked another favorite concern of early environmentalists—"artificial" or "unnatural" modes of life.[71] For the Britons of the first half of the long nineteenth century, it was a veritable axiom that cities represented the greatest manifestations of unnatural human activity. "God made the country, and man made the town," proclaimed the poet William Cowper in 1785, and his claim became an oft-cited shorthand for encapsulating the inherently "unnatural" character of the urban environment throughout the subsequent century. The same Britons who quoted Cowper shared the poet's belief that no city was more "artificial" than London, the "Modern Babylon."[72]

Furthermore, Britons warned that the many-faceted artificiality of London existence endangered all the city's inhabitants—young and old, male and female, rich and poor. Hogg, for example, repeatedly emphasized the way the concentrated population of the enormous city had the tendency to democratize environmental threats—to endanger the physical and moral health of rich and poor alike (albeit sometimes in different ways)—on account of its "artificial," manmade atmosphere, built environment, pastimes, and customary observances.[73] For the surgeon nothing exemplified this tendency of the London environment to impact the lives of all of the city's inhabitants equally more than the perpetual "firmament" of smoke that "enveloped" the Metropolis, imposing a barrier between the Londoner and the sun and the heavens, regardless of social class. Londoners were literally but also symbolically united as the inhabitants of a single environment by being collectively situated "*in nubibus.*"[74]

Other contemporary authors agreed. It was not just isolated nuisances, buildings, neighborhoods, or districts of London that potentially threatened individuals' survival, they warned, but the entirety of the city itself. If for the early environmentalist a myriad of local influences might present potential dangers to health, London, contemporary reformers argued, concentrated an especially large number of these different "foes to human life" into a single, densely populated zone of existence.[75] Close quarters and population pressure ensured that it was much more difficult for inhabitants of the Metropolis to protect themselves from the influences of environmental threats than those inhabiting other parts of the British Isles. Warning of the dangers invited by continuing the "unsanitary" practice of intramural burials in London in the 1830s, the surgeon George Walker noted that the capital's "vast number of burying places" represented "foci of infection—generating constantly the dreadful effluvia of human putrefaction— acting according to the circumstances of locality . . . and the power of resistance in those subjected to its influence—(and who is not?)—as a slow or an energetic poison."[76]

"And who is not?" Walker's rhetorical question summed up the emerging consensus among medical practitioners in the second quarter of the century about the peculiar threat posed by the London environment. The concentration of London's population and the density of its built landscape seemed to negate most of those prophylactic measures (choice of dwelling, the use of ventilators, or closed stoves, for example) available to individuals elsewhere in the British Isles, placing rich and poor alike at the mercy of the miasmatic disease mists. Environmental theories thus de-emphasized class differences when explaining the incidence of disease and death among the city's inhabitants, by foregrounding physical proximity over differentials in wealth.[77] In the capital, observed the working-class writer Thomas Miller, the "self-same breeze" that "uplifts the dark ringlets" of the duchess, "a few seconds ago swept over the poisonous avenues of . . . St. Giles's."[78] Total insulation or isolation, mid-century public health reformers warned, was not a possibility in the Metropolis.[79]

This contemporary vision of the Metropolis as a single, all-encompassing environment, however, extended far beyond the ranks of the public health movement, and informed the metaphors Britons employed in general when describing life in the capital. The favorite image for describing the "total" influence London exerted over the minds and bodies of its inhabitants was aquatic. An author in *Chambers's Journal* observed in the 1840s that at one time the prevailing metaphor used to describe London was the "microcosm"—"a world" with many different nations and customs. Beginning in the 1770s the writer noted, this global metropolitan metaphor was joined and steadily supplanted by the vision of London as "ocean," with individual men and women mere droplets collectively contributing to, while simultaneously being immersed within, its massiveness.[80]

It seems far from coincidental that the same cultural moment that witnessed an increased willingness to conceive of London as a single environment produced a parallel shift in prevailing metropolitan metaphors, from one emphasizing compartmentalized differences, to one that focused instead on the experience of immersion. Dr. Johnson himself began his description of London's environment with an autobiographical account of his own first exposure to the "ocean of London." Johnson recalled how as a young man when he had first "mingled" with this "tide of human existence," his "heart sunk." "I felt," he recalled, "as it were, annihilated—lost, like a drop of water in the ocean," and the physician asserted his was not an uncommon experience. "I believe there are few who do not experience this feeling of abasement on first mixing with the crowd in the streets," Johnson asserted. The prevalence of the image of the individual in London as a "drop of water in the ocean" in the literature, life-writing, and journalism of the 1830s and 1840s suggests he was correct. Many contemporary Britons also described the "depressive effect" occasioned by mingling with the London crowds—the "realization of one's utter insignificance," in the words of Thomas De Quincey—and argued that it represented yet another metropolitan "circumstance" eroding Londoners' fragile fabric of health.[81]

If many nineteenth-century Britons believed that London represented a single environment alive with dangerous influences on mind, body, and soul, there was less consensus about the degree to which these "offensive influences" associated with the metropolitan milieu represented a unique amalgamation or merely a notable example of those conditions said to characterize all urban environments. Given the porousness observable in other aspects of early environmentalist thought, it should not surprise us that it was only a short step from positing "London" conditions to reimagining these characteristics of metropolitan life as generalized urban conditions, especially in an era of unprecedented, rapid urbanization.

While at the end of the eighteenth century London still appeared like an exceptional, if monstrous, milieu in the national landscape, by the middle of the nineteenth century in the eyes of many Britons the Metropolis looked far less anomalous and more like the largest example of a broader type: the country's rapidly proliferating "large towns and populous districts."[82] Dr. Johnson's observations about "artificial life" in a "high-viced metropolis," for example, gestured as much to the generic as to the specific, and many of his other observations did the same. The introduction to *A Change of Air* was couched in these imprecise terms, noting that his observations about the "wear and tear of mind and body" applied to "civilized life, and especially in large cities."[83] Hogg made similarly ambiguous claims, moving from discussing the differences between the compromised frame of the Londoner and the "vigorous health" of the country-dweller, to observing that "children reared in large towns and cities never acquired the sinewy strength and robust vigour of children born and bred in the country."[84] At this and other points of his analysis of "London as it is," Hogg frequently shifted from examining differences between Cockneys and provincials, to those of the city and the country conceived in generic terms.[85]

A similar slippage appeared in claims made by many other early environmentalist writers during the first half of the century. Throughout this period, for example, many Britons remained convinced that the "London fog" (the celebrated "pea-souper") represented a unique atmospheric phenomenon. In an era of expanding air pollution, however, many others wondered if the "London Particular" was actually "particular" to London at all, or if it merely represented the largest cloud of smoke overhanging the nation's towns. The inability to answer this question definitively in either the affirmative or the negative consistently undermined both local and national efforts at improving air quality throughout the century.[86]

A similar history characterized the relationship between ideas about the representativeness of the London environment and the mid-century public health movement. In 1845, for example, Dr. Martin informed a Parliamentary committee that, "what is socially true of London, is so in [the] great part of all provincial towns."[87] Such a mode of thought was ideally suited to a public health movement that sought to centralize power in the national government. Furthermore, as both Christopher Hamlin and John Pickstone observe, this public health vision adopted by early British reformers was not only overwhelmingly indebted to early environmentalist ideas, but to their articulation in the metropolitan context. The aspirations of 1840s public health reformers, therefore, represented a particularly strong instance of early environmentalist thinking concerning the Metropolis influencing thinking about the entirety of life in the British Isles—or at the very least, life in the country's rapidly expanding cities.[88]

The reformist vision articulated by Chadwick and his disciples—and the resistance they provoked—likewise indicate the problems involved in uniting environmentalist ideas with large-scale public health reforms, and the 1853 Southwark inquest exemplifies why this was the case. Recall the inability of the members of the jury to "fix the man's death on any particular individual." Each of the "unwholesome" trades in the neighborhood presumably belonged to some person (as did Mason's-buildings themselves), yet the totalizing framework articulated by environmentalist thinkers—the emphasis placed on the collective influence of "circumstances," rather than in identifying "causes" of disease—made it difficult to separate one "unwholesome" influence from all the others, and thereby assign responsibility and accountability. In fact, John Rush, the owner of the bone-boiler above Hickie's dwelling, informed the jury that he "did not discover anything offensive" in his place of business; "the smell" did not come "from his premises. He believed it came from the houses in Green-street."[89]

The permeability of early environmentalist thinking—its ability to identify a range of potentially dangerous influences operating in a single milieu—thus ironically allowed individuals to escape public censure for polluting the community. Hickie's death was viewed as the product of the collective influence of these "unwholesome trades," and thus future illness and death could be avoided only by removing all of them from the district. Such a transformation, however, could be accomplished only when, as the coroner regretted, "a stringent law was passed to remedy this state of things," and in the age of laissez-faire governance, this was not easily accomplished.[90] Furthermore, the application of these environmentalist ideas to the question of urban health produced pages upon pages of public investigations throughout the 1840s, detailing a seemingly endless succession of London streets, each as "filthy" as the next. The result was a voluminous literature identifying a seemingly insurmountable mass of discrete environmental threats.[91] If, as Asa Briggs observed, "Victorian cities were places where problems often overwhelmed people," the application of early environmentalist theories to the life and landscapes of these cities played a prominent role in helping to make them seem this way.[92]

Thus, the history of public health during the second quarter of the nineteenth century is indicative of the broader way in which thinking about London could very quickly become thinking about "the city" as an abstract, replicable category of physical and social existence. An author in *The Builder* noted in 1846 that while it was "said with justice, that London is not England[,] [i]ntelligence, wealth, and power, dwelling in fine cities . . . are to be found in every quarter of our island, and make up an extraordinary aggregate." The writer thus concluded, "In a very short time it seems certain, that all England will be a London," and that the "advantages possessed at one time exclusively by the latter will become universal."[93] Yet with the good came the bad, and in the case of the Metropolis, early environmentalists suggested there was much to be feared at the prospect of a nation transformed into a single enormous London.

CONCLUSION

By the 1870s the era of early environmentalism was ending, and with it the belief that London "circumstances" ever could become national ones. During the final decades of the century, this earlier environmentalist vision—and its understanding of, and application to, life in London and beyond—began to lose much of its coherence as a medical-moral worldview among physicians, reformers, politicians, and average Britons alike. This loss of consensus occasioned a parallel decline in influence, as new ideas also brought with them new programs for personal and public reform and improvement.

Understanding how and why this came about requires that we return to where this chapter began: London during the cholera epidemic of 1853–1854. Today this epidemic is usually remembered, not for the more than 10,700 Londoners like Hickie who died from the disease, but for the actions of another metropolitan surgeon, John Snow. During the previous epidemic of 1848–1849, Snow had become convinced that the specific symptomatology of cholera suggested that the disease arose as the result of "something that acts directly on the alimentary canal . . . being accidentally swallowed," and that cholera epidemics began when this infectious agent made its way into the "drinking water of the community."[94] Snow had published this theory in 1849, but it was largely ignored by a medical establishment committed to more diffuse environmentalist explanations of disease.

The return of cholera in 1853 provided Snow an opportunity to prove his theories. Using data supplied by the Registrar General's Office, Snow collected the addresses of every metropolitan cholera victim, elaborately mapping the correlation between specific London water sources and deaths from the disease. Snow's most memorable example concerned the pump in Broad Street, Golden Square, whose "contaminated" drinking water Snow linked to "upwards of five hundred fatal attacks of cholera in ten days"—attacks that quickly abated after Snow had the handle on the pump removed.[95] Thus had Snow—like his fellow surgeon Wakem—been asked about the likely reason for Hickie's death, the surgeon also would have contended that the metalworker's illness was directly related to his place of residence, but not because Mason's-buildings were surrounded by "unwholesome" trades, but because "the greater part of Southwark . . . was supplied with worse water than any other part of the metropolis."[96]

Though Snow's theories continued to be ignored by much of the medical profession throughout the 1850s and 1860s (with tragic results in 1866, when thousands more Londoners perished in yet another cholera epidemic), the subsequent bacteriological revolution ultimately demonstrated the truth of his theory, while simultaneously invalidating early environmentalist medical doctrines. Thus Snow—a radical outlier among the medical men of the 1850s—is often portrayed today as a heroic agent of medical progress.[97] Though historians of medicine have demonstrated that late nineteenth-century discoveries linking microorganisms with specific diseases were far less "revolutionary" among the British medical profession than once believed, the interaction of these new ideas alongside miasmatic and zymotic theories of disease nevertheless tended to narrow the range of factors the medical profession identified as responsible for spreading illnesses. They likewise promoted a medical worldview increasingly inclined to view the human body as either "sick" (infected) or "well," rather than as existing on some perpetually shifting trajectory between the two.[98] Indeed, as Gregg Mitman observes, from the 1880s onward the medical profession increasingly situated the causes of infection within the human body itself, rather than the environment it inhabited.[99]

In this new era, prevention and containment—whether through vaccination, hygiene, or the elimination of "epidemic streets"—became the order of the day in London, as in other Western cities.[100] Ironically, this shift to a medical world-view informed by the idea of "cause-specific mortality," meant that government policies aimed at protecting public health by eliminating environmental dangers tended to focus on a single type of threat at a time—and "no more than one," as Luckin notes—for the remainder of the nineteenth century, and during much of the century to come.[101]

In such a climate, it made little sense to continue to articulate a vision of London as a single environment, and after mid-century such an understanding of the Metropolis as a physical and social space became equally untenable for a wide range of other Britons as well. By the final decades of the century, it had become clear that despite the fact that the majority of the nation's populace now inhabited cities, life in the country's other "large towns and populous districts" differed considerably from life in London.[102] It was likewise no longer possible to ignore the vast gulf separating the city's rich and poor.[103] The accounts of travel writers, journalists, and social investigators from the 1870s onward routinely described the city as a unique entity, noting not only London's monstrous size when compared with other British cities, but also that this size allowed the capital to accommodate drastically different conditions of life within the confines of a single urban geography. Thus these writers again favored the earlier metaphor of London as a miniature world, while the vision of the city as an ocean went into decline. Whether emphasizing the East End–West End dichotomy, or producing more detailed spatial or statistical demarcations, such as Charles Booth's minutely specific maps of London poverty, the prevailing vision of the Metropolis at the century's close had become one of a city of many compartments, rather than that of a single united environment.[104]

The rising influence of evolutionary theories and the application of these theories to understanding human societies in the final decades of the century further worked to undermine the influence of early environmentalist ideas. In an era when politicians, reformers, physicians, and social scientists increasingly focused on the threat of racial degeneration, the movement that mattered most in human populations was vertical rather than horizontal—between generations, rather than between different environments. In this context, the primacy early environmentalists attributed to local "circumstances" in explaining individuals' moral and physical health looked increasingly outdated and naive. At the turn of the century the term "environmentalist" was often employed as a disparaging label, indicative of persons who clung to older, discredited theories in an era increasingly dominated by a faith in biological determinism.[105]

Vestiges of early environmentalism nevertheless continued to linger in British society. While germ theory allowed physicians to ignore environmental factors when treating diseases, they never found it entirely possible to do so when treating allergies, which retained their character as situationally specific conditions of "circumstances."[106] Experts likewise continued to warn that air pollution threatened the public health not only by promoting respiratory disorders but also mental depression and alcoholism.[107] Medical professionals and the general populace alike continued to articulate a faith in the value of "fresh air." Indeed, it was often claimed that the appreciation of "fresh air" was a unique attribute of the English people.[108]

Social and moral aspects of early environmentalism also persisted. Assumptions about the relationship between individuals' immediate surroundings and their moral development continued to inform the efforts of reformers who sought to improve the lives of children among the London poor. "Rescuing" children from the baneful influence of their urban surroundings by physically removing them either permanently or temporarily featured prominently in the activities of several late nineteenth-century children's reform programs, whether in the form of the homes operated by Dr. Thomas Barnardo, or in the annual excursions to the countryside organized by groups like the Children's Holiday Fund.[109]

In the 1940s similar ideas reemerged in response to the wartime evacuations of metropolitan children into the countryside. Lady Sanderson observed of the evacuations, that there "could have been no better proof of the belief that the country is a child's spiritual home."[110] Other Britons made similar claims repeatedly throughout the war, even though the recorded experiences of both the evacuees and their hosts offered a far more varied and ambivalent picture of London childhoods interrupted by wartime sojourns in the countryside. A study conducted by the London County Council after the war found no evidence that the development of children who had spent the war years in the countryside "showed any significant difference" from that of children who had grown up in London either before or during the war.[111] The very existence of such a study, however, is itself indicative of the persistence of discrete elements of early environmentalist thinking in British life.

Though in the twentieth century environmentalist thinking would become a more encompassing worldview concerned with understanding and protecting a single global "environment," the early environmentalist focus on individual, compartmentalized "environments"—and their influences—continues to inform social, medical, and ecological politics and policies today. Comprehending and responding to the threats of "exposure" to specific circumstantial influences, like industrial pollutants, radiation, or waste, for example, has reemerged in the twenty-first century as a pressing public concern.[112]

Where the history of the Metropolis is concerned, perhaps nothing better illustrates the persistence of early environmentalist thinking in British culture than the perennial claim that individuals need to "get away from London."[113] The idea that time away from the Metropolis is necessary to preserve the health and happiness of the city's inhabitants is very much akin to the early environmentalists' concern with "wear and tear" and the necessity for a regular "change of air." In this, as in other respects, British life continued—and continues—to be informed by the assumptions of early environmentalism.

FIVE

GREEN SPACE IN LONDON

Social and Environmental Perspectives

PETER THORSHEIM

London is famous for its green space, which encompasses a wide range of forms, including churchyards, gardens, playgrounds, squares, heaths, municipal parks, and royal parks. Although the latter remain the hereditary property of the monarch, they have long been enjoyed by millions of people each year for rest, recreation, and special events. Today, over a hundred different bodies oversee parks and gardens in the metropolis.[1] Although Londoners are justifiably proud of the amount of publicly accessible green space in their city, its distribution is uneven, with much of it located in the most expensive neighborhoods to the west and north of Trafalgar Square.

Two centuries ago things were far worse. "From Regent's Park in the north to Limehouse in the east," notes Susan Lasdun, "there was not a single place preserved as a park or public walk; and south of the river there was only one, near Lambeth Palace."[2] The population of London, already the greatest of any European city in 1800, ballooned by a factor of six over the next hundred years. This tremendous demographic growth fueled an enormous wave of construction, which expanded the boundaries of the built-up area at the same time as it intensified land use. The same processes that diminished the overall amount of green space in the Metropolis prompted campaigns to preserve and widen access to it.

Such struggles have played a significant role in the social, cultural, and political history of modern London.

Although green space may appear to be natural and unchanging, it is no less dynamic, nor as shaped by human beings, as are streets, architecture, and technological systems. Over time the ways that people have thought about and interacted with green space have changed in fundamental ways. This chapter begins by examining how class, age, gender, and other social categories influenced decisions about whether to preserve green space in particular places, who had access to it, and how they used it. Next, it uses the history of green space in London as a window into the history of ideas and practices concerning the relationship between nature and the body. Finally, it focuses on how the Second World War and subsequent reconstruction transformed green space in London in ways that had a profound and lasting impact on the city and its people.

LAND AND POWER

Rules about who can access green space and what sorts of behavior can occur within it are inherently political—as are attempts to redefine or resist such prescriptions. During the eighteenth and nineteenth centuries, landowners across Britain enlarged their holdings by depriving ordinary people of their customary rights to use commons. This process of privatization, known as enclosure, took a particularly early and heavy toll in London, which had the highest land values in the kingdom. By the middle of the eighteenth century, many of London's most famous squares—including St. James's Square, Lincoln's Inn Fields, and Grosvenor Square—had been enclosed. Although this action preserved them from being built upon, it also excluded many of their former users, as only those who lived in the houses that faced these squares could set foot within them. Enclosure was both a legal process, sanctioned by acts of Parliament, and a physical one, often demarcated by walls or railings.[3]

Regent's Park served as a particularly significant flash point for concerns about the continued disappearance of public green space in London, for its creation in 1811 marked it as a place of social exclusion. As one contemporary complained, "It was formerly an open field, in which thousands found recreation and health."[4] Despite initial promises that it would remain accessible to everyone, officials soon decided to allow access only to the wealthy residents who lived nearby. They claimed that this was needed to prevent "immoral" activities in the park and to protect saplings from damage, but their primary motivation was economic: they wished to maximize the property values of the surrounding houses by making the park an elite space.[5] By the time the Prince Regent was crowned George IV in 1820, Hyde Park was the only large park in the Metropolis that remained open to all. Nearby St. James's Park and Kensington Gardens, however, admitted only those who were "well-behaved and properly dressed": a standard that served to exclude many poor and working-class Londoners.[6]

During the 1830s and 1840s demands for a more democratic political system coincided with discontent about lack of access to green space in Britain's rapidly growing towns and cities. Prior to the Reform Act of 1832, only 5 percent of the total population of the United Kingdom had the right to vote in national elections, and several of the nation's fastest growing urban areas lacked any parliamentary representation. The 1832 act was quite limited in scope, but it nonetheless expanded the number of middle-class voters and redrew the electoral map.[7] Following years of protest, Regent's Park opened to the public in 1838, the same year that Victoria was formally crowned. Two years later, thirty thousand residents of the East End petitioned the new queen for a park in their part of London. Although many of those who signed this petition owned insufficient property to vote in parliamentary elections, their plea succeeded. Victoria Park, built between 1842 and 1845, proved immediately successful, and it has remained a popular site of recreation ever since. On one particularly crowded day in 1892, Victoria Park attracted over three hundred thousand visitors.[8] Despite the creation of this and other parks in the East End, many residents lacked green space within convenient walking distance, as well as adequate public transport that would have taken them to more distant parks.

To promote deference to authority, park designers sought to create public spaces where the lower classes would observe, and emulate, the respectable conventions of the middle and upper classes. Strolling, sitting on benches, and gazing at trees and flowers, elites believed, would tame and civilize the urban masses. These social benefits might accrue not only to those who entered parks, but even those who passed near them. The possibility of this happening seemed more likely as owners began to replace the opaque brick or stone walls that surrounded many green spaces with iron railings, which allowed people to see into them even if they could not set foot in them. Susan Lasdun suggests that this change marked an advance of democratic ideals and "an increasing appropriation of the parks by the public."[9] In contrast to her interpretation, contemporaries often decried railings as a symbol of class privilege and social exclusion: tangible proof that the authorities did not trust the people to act responsibly.

Many people found ways to use parks and gardens that differed from, and sometimes overtly rejected, the notions that their designers had sought to inscribe. One of the most significant ways in which users of green space challenged these ideas involved sexuality. Unlike most middle- and upper-class individuals, whose sex lives generally took place behind closed doors, working-class people, as well as sexual minorities, frequently lacked this means of discretion. Instead they often sought anonymity, if not privacy, in parks and other open spaces. Lasdun describes St. James's Park as having had "a notorious reputation after nightfall" during the nineteenth century, and David Reeder uses the same language in reference to Hyde Park.[10] Officials raised similar concerns about Kensington Gardens, where they responded by uprooting "ancient and over-grown yews and hollies . . . in the name of public decency."[11]

Landscaping was not the only means by which the authorities sought to regulate behavior; they also relied on policing. As Antony Taylor puts it, "The urban parks of the 1840s and 1850s were . . . scrupulously maintained, and patrolled and policed by the hated park-keepers, who became a part of working-class demonology in their own right, co-operated with the police, dressed like them, and used fences, gates and padlocks to exclude" those whom they deemed unfit to enter.[12] These keepers cracked down not only on sexual activity, but also trespass after hours, gambling, and other offenses. Parks became even more restrictive on Sundays.[13] During the 1850s moralists succeeded in banishing games, the sale of refreshments, and even music from parks on the "Lord's Day," even though this was the only day of the week when many Londoners could visit a park.[14] Philanthropic groups often proved at least as dictatorial as the vestry committees that governed at the parish level. As Taylor notes, "The Commons Preservation Society was more enthusiastic than the vestries in attempting to clear away traditional pastimes and recreations from the open ground."[15]

In addition to providing a venue for a wide range of leisure activities, both licit and illicit, London's green spaces played an important role as sites of working-class protest and activism.[16] In April 1848 tens of thousands gathered in Kennington Common to hear the Chartist leader Feargus O'Connor speak. Four years later the common was enclosed and turned into a park, and protests and political meetings were prohibited within its confines. Hyde Park became the next epicenter of mass politics in London. On two successive Sundays in the summer of 1855, more than one hundred thousand people demonstrated there after Lord Robert Grosvenor introduced a bill that would have closed shops and public transport on Sundays. When the police attempted to halt the demonstration, the protestors expanded their list of demands to include the right of free assembly.[17] Hyde Park again became a political stage in July 1866 when demonstrators pushed over some of its railings during protests in favor of the Second Reform Act. This action carried important symbolic significance. The destruction of railings was not only an act of vandalism against crown property, but also an attack on the inequality and exclusion that railings helped to sustain. Tearing down railings thus became associated in the public mind with a host of radical ideas, ranging from republicanism and socialism to electoral reform.[18] Further mass protests rocked Hyde

Park in subsequent years. Gareth Stedman Jones asserts that more than one hundred thousand protestors occupied it in May 1867, and he notes that rioters overturned upper-class carriages there in 1886.[19]

Even after parks became open to the working class, officials sought to exclude certain groups of people because of who they were. Nan Dreher argues that a "moral panic" infected much of the British public at the end of the nineteenth century. In a move disturbingly similar to policies that the Nazis would later pursue, they imagined "antisocial" behavior as originating in a dirty or diseased other. In 1892 the London County Council (LCC) established a policy that barred "gipsies [sic], hawkers . . . beggars, and rogues and vagabonds" from its parks. In line with Linda Colley's arguments that Britons formed their national identity in opposition to the French, Dreher suggests that park regulations helped to establish middle-class identity: "Discrimination against verminous persons, like opposition to indecent behavior in parks, made the respectable citizenry seem purer, cleaner, and healthier in comparison."[20]

Although the initial expansion of public green space in London occurred under the auspices of central government, municipal bodies and philanthropic groups soon took the lead in making such places more accessible and preserving them for future generations to enjoy. In the 1850s Parliament empowered the Metropolitan Board of Works (the closest thing London then had to centralized and coordinated governance) to establish its own parks. The board soon used these powers to purchase land for the creation of Finsbury Park and Battersea Park. Further legislation in 1866 and 1878 made it possible for the board to protect commons, including Blackheath, Clapham Common, and Wimbledon Common.[21] In 1870 the Metropolitan Board of Works, aided by private donors, purchased Hampstead Heath, a large piece of land located six kilometers north of the center of London.[22] The Corporation of the City of London played an even greater role, not only helping to preserve places such as this that lay relatively close at hand, but also using some of its enormous wealth to purchase large tracts of land farther afield. By the end of the nineteenth century it had acquired 6,500 acres of green space in the London region, and it had saved other areas, including Epping Forest—the largest public green space near London—by bringing lawsuits that halted enclosure. The historian Jerry White suggests that "the preservation for Londoners in perpetuity of open space wrenched from landlord enclosure and the house-builder" may have been the "greatest achievement" of the City Corporation.[23]

Historians disagree about why public access to green space grew so substantially during Victoria's reign. David Reeder suggests that those in power experienced a change of outlook, which led them to accept "a more democratic version of the value of open spaces as necessary to the health and quality of life of Londoners as a whole."[24] In contrast to Reeder's claims that altruistic considerations predominated, other scholars argue that efforts to expand access to green space stemmed from upper-class fears that poor people and workers posed threats of violence and possibly even revolution. Jeremy Burchardt attributes the change to a growing literary appreciation for nature, coupled with a new consensus among the governing elite "that the physical and moral dangers of urbanism needed to be tempered by rural elements. Providing rural 'lungs' in which city dwellers could breathe the restorative fresh air of the countryside was therefore the means to ensure not only public health but also social order."[25]

Several important pressure groups, all established between the mid-1860s and the mid-1880s, focused on expanding access to green space as a means of promoting social cohesion and, later, health.[26] The first was the Commons Preservation Society, begun in 1865, which sought to abolish enclosure in and near London.[27] The founder and longtime chairman of this group, George John Shaw-Lefevre (later Lord Eversley), argued that green space promoted national unity by instilling in everyone "something of the sense and beauty of nature."[28] A decade later two sisters, Miranda and Octavia Hill, established the Kyrle Society, the principal aim of which was to create accessible green space, including playgrounds, for working-class Londoners.[29] Both sisters had long been involved in efforts to provide affordable housing, and they believed that rich and poor alike deserved contact with art and nature. Writing in the *Fortnightly Review* in 1877, Octavia Hill argued that far from being a luxury, the preservation of green space was essential to national identity: "The love of being connected with the land is innate; it deepens a man's attachment to his native country, and adds dignity and simplicity to his character."[30]

The development of railways, the most advanced technology of the nineteenth century, made it possible for large numbers of urban residents to access the countryside quickly and relatively cheaply. In 1850 the Great Western Railway began to offer discounted rates for Sunday travel, and many other companies soon followed its lead. The cost of such trips, as well as the time required, made it impossible for everyone to benefit, but thousands of people took advantage of increasingly affordable rail fares to leave the city on weekends.[31] The possibility of doing so expanded further in the early twentieth century, when, as Reeder puts it, "The bicycle, green line (country) buses and extended metropolitan railways enabled more people to enjoy the countryside and its historic amenities and beauty spots."[32] One advantage of rail excursions, which walking enthusiasts continue to make use of today, was the possibility of buying a return ticket to one station, spending the day "rambling" in the countryside, and returning home from another station closer to London on the same rail line.[33] Some who took part in such walks viewed them simply as recreation, but others saw them as a form of direct political action. The Marxist historian Raphael Samuel, for example, considered his youthful acts of trespass on privately owned land as a conscious rejection of capitalist property relations.[34] "Walking the countryside," notes Patrick Joyce, "became closely involved with British ideas about freedom itself."[35] Railways, trams, and the growing Tube network allowed relatively speedy and convenient access to places such as Parliament Hill Fields, Highbury Fields, Primrose Hill, and Epping Forest.

NATURE AND THE BODY

During the nineteenth century the United Kingdom experienced unprecedented urban growth. As London and other large towns and cities expanded, an increasing proportion of Britons lived in cities. By the middle of the century half of the nation's population was urban, a first in European history. Not surprisingly, numerous commentators expressed concerns about the dire consequences that this would have for the nation's health. Statisticians had long observed higher mortality rates in cities than in rural places, and many medical experts attributed this disparity to impure air.[36]

In contrast to today, when urban air quality is most often associated with the combustion of hydrocarbons in motor vehicles, other sources of bad air existed in nineteenth-century cities, including sewage, horse manure, garbage, animal processing, industry, and coal fires. As the miasmatic theory lost support during the final decades of the nineteenth century, people increasingly focused on soot, smoke, and depleted concentrations of oxygen as detriments to health.[37] Using the body as a metaphor, public health reformers sought to increase the circulation and respiration of the city. The best way to improve urban air quality, they argued, was to assist the cleansing powers of nature by building new sewers, creating wider and straighter roads, and cultivating more plants and trees.[38]

Following the "Great Stink" of 1858, when unusually high temperatures and drought caused an overpowering stench to emanate from the sewage-filled Thames, the Metropolitan Board of Works embarked on one of the most ambitious engineering projects of the Victorian age: the construction of a series of intercepting sewers that prevented waste from pouring into the river in central London. Designed by the engineer Joseph Bazalgette, the new system conveyed wastes several miles downstream from the city before discharging them into the Thames twice a day with the outgoing tide. Bazalgette's plans called for the largest of these intercepting sewers to run parallel to the river along its north bank through the heart of London. Rather than tear up the existing streets and buildings situated along the river, he came up with an ingenious, albeit costly, alternative. On mud flats that extended right up to the buildings along the river, and which flooded with each high tide, thousands of laborers constructed elegant stone embankments, within which were hidden a new intercepting sewer and an underground train line. Aboveground the embankment provided space for a new road, as well as gardens.[39]

Most of the South Bank, however, long remained inaccessible to those who wished to walk along the river. Perpetuating class and geographical stereotypes, the *Times* asserted in 1914 that the embankments on the north side of the river "are there to prove how rich and orderly we are; on the other side the fascinating tumble of lines and masses tells the secret of our wealth. It speaks of men at work, of the homely needs of the body, of fetching and carrying, of making and buying and selling, of the ten thousand common duties, faithfully carried out, by which London has grown through immemorial ages to be the queen of all great cities of all time."[40]

At the 1879 meeting of the National Association for the Promotion of Social Science, members of its health section endorsed a resolution that called on local authorities to plant trees in cities. This action was important, they argued, because trees "have a valuable bearing not only on the beauty of towns, but on the health of communities."[41] Vegetation trapped soot and smoke particles, and it produced oxygen, but it could also be harmed by the intense air pollution found in London. Conifers found it nearly impossible to thrive there, as did many deciduous species. But the London plane tree, which periodically shed layers from its bark, proved unusually capable of withstanding London's smoke and soot.[42] Although many experts advocated frequent and close contact with trees and plants, others maintained that urban green spaces benefited everyone, even those who never set foot in them. Robert Angus Smith, who led the world's first environmental protection agency, the Alkali Inspectorate, from its inception in 1864 until his retirement two decades later, declared that parks "allow the wind to blow around us during the day, and . . . supply us [with fresh air] also during the night."[43]

Circulation, whether of oxygen, people, or disease, was a key obsession for many experts who sought to manage the Victorian environment. From the ocean-going schooners of the age of discovery to jet planes today, developments in transportation have resulted in the movement not only of goods and human beings, but also unintended passengers such as plants, animals, and microbes. In the nineteenth century British railways functioned as "green arteries" that brought plants and animals into London. Foxes and other mammals used them to migrate between the country and the city, and they also acted as corridors for seeds and pollen to travel. Oxford ragwort, which initially existed in Britain solely as a specimen at the botanic gardens in Oxford, gradually spread along the railway lines that passed near the university. In the 1860s it reached all the way to London, along a route of some fifty miles.[44]

In 1882 Lord Reginald Brabazon (who became the twelfth earl of Meath five years later) founded the Metropolitan Public Gardens Association.[45] This influential group enjoyed support from the highest levels, including the Prince of Wales and the Duke of York. Its goal was straightforward: "to supply one of the most pressing wants of the poorer districts of London by providing breathing and resting-places for the old, and playgrounds for the young, in the midst of densely populated localities."[46] As Meath put it in 1892, "London is for the moment well enough supplied with large parks; her more immediate needs are a large number of small gardens and playgrounds in the heart of the crowded districts, and more cricket and football fields accessible to her youthful population in the suburbs."[47] At the same time Meath believed that private gardens also performed a public benefit, for in his view such places "gladden the eyes of all by the sight of nature, materially increase the number of cubic feet of pure air which each citizen may breathe, assist in the production of oxygen and the consumption of carbonic acid gas [carbon dioxide], and give pleasure and health to a large majority of the inhabitants of towns in which they are situated."[48] Building on the small-scale work that the Kyrle Society had already begun, Meath's group embarked on a major program of converting disused burial grounds and other derelict property in crowded parts of London into gardens and playgrounds.[49]

Shortly after he established the Metropolitan Public Gardens Association, Meath emerged as one of the leading proponents in Britain of the idea of physical degeneration. Writing in 1892, he decried "how short of stature, how narrow-chested, how physically weak is the average town-bred lad." City residents, he argued, were declining in health because of insufficient exposure to sunlight, fresh air, and outdoor exercise.[50] Meath and many of his contemporaries viewed physical exercise as essential to the health of both the individual and the nation. Yet most parks in nineteenth-century Britain were designed for strolling and sitting, not for vigorous exercise, and they often displayed notices that ordered people to keep off the grass. Over time a growing number of park users objected to such limitations. The reasons were many: the physical expansion of cities meant that rural areas were ever-more distant; the popularity of football and other team sports was increasing; the amount of leisure time was expanding; and increasingly congested streets made them ill-suited as places for games. To push for change, in 1890 a small group of reformers established the London Playing Fields Society, which they hoped would "encourage the love of those manly games which had done so much to make England and Englishmen what they were, and to afford facilities for joining in them." The *Times* supported the new group's efforts to provide more opportunities for physical exercise, but it criticized the group's exclusive focus on providing playing fields for men. "The juvenile and feminine portions of the community," it asserted in an 1890 editorial, "have rights which cannot be overlooked even in a laudable enthusiasm for manly games. . . . Probably the best thing the ladies can do is to start an association of their own, otherwise they will find every available space monopolized both near and far by masculine enterprise and selfishness."[51] Chauvinism made it difficult for females to exercise not only on land, but also in the water. Women were not permitted to swim in any of the ponds at Hampstead Heath until 1902, and then only one day a week.[52]

At a time when many people attributed an individual's physical characteristics to heredity, experts often asserted that urban residents whose parents and grandparents also hailed from the city were particularly at risk of degeneration. These medical and environmental ideas combined with heightened anxieties about Britain's place in the world to create a sense that something had to be done.[53] Britain's difficulties in the Second Anglo-Boer War, which it fought in South Africa at the turn of the century, intensified concerns about national decline, and they grew even more in the decade that preceded the Great War. Arguing that the nation's strength required much more than just state-of-the-art naval hardware, the Manchester reformer Thomas Horsfall insisted that Britain's continued preeminence required a healthy environment. Speaking at an urban planning conference in 1910, he asked, "Does the nation ever ask itself where it is going to get the men for those Dreadnoughts?"[54] Many others, including Lord Meath, argued that playgrounds and playing fields would help to counteract the physical deterioration that appeared to be afflicting Britain's increasingly urbanized population.

While higher wages, more free time, and a growing interest in physical fitness were stimulating greater demand for outdoor recreation, the supply was shrinking as urban growth and rising property values made it extremely expensive to secure new places for adults and children to exercise. In 1912 a new group, the London Society, emerged. Among the many proposals that it put forth was its goal that no child in London would have to travel more than half a mile to reach a playground.[55] The First World War interrupted these plans and instead prompted the authorities to use some of London's green space for military drills and the growing of crops. Two decades later, during the Great Depression, the LCC sought to increase the number and distribution of playgrounds for children— largely on land made available through slum clearance. One reason for this was a recognition that the streets were becoming more dangerous for play because of growing motor vehicle traffic.[56] Another group, known as the National Playing Fields Association, began in 1925. In its first eight years alone, it purchased six thousand acres of land and established more than a thousand recreation areas around Britain.[57] During the mid-1920s, in response to growing scientific and popular support for exercise, the Ministry of Health declared that London required more playing fields to foster the development of strong and healthy male citizens. Prompted by this pressure, the LCC surveyed the distribution of playing fields, which it found to be extremely uneven. In response, it argued for the creation of many more playing fields in underserved parts of the capital.[58] Despite the growing number of women and girls engaged in sports like tennis and swimming, however, the authorities continued to pay little attention to their needs—perhaps because of their focus on the physical fitness of potential (male) soldiers.

Restrictions on the use of green space on Sundays had served as another point of contention since the early Victorian period, and they faced ever-more challenges in the increasingly secular and democratic twentieth century. In the 1920s the LCC began to allow boating and paddling in ponds all day on Sundays, and the playing of amateur games on Sunday afternoons. In 1932 it further liberalized its rules to allow professional football matches on Sundays.[59] Many other restrictions remained, however. Although the LCC allowed men to play football, hockey, netball, and cricket on Sunday afternoons, it made no similar provisions for women or young people.[60] Restrictions on Sunday play had a particularly negative effect on Jewish children, many of whom could not play sports on Saturdays for religious reasons. In June 1934 a representative of the Association for Jewish Youth asked the LCC to allow Victoria Park to be made available for track events on Sunday afternoons.[61] This modest request faced substantial opposition. As one critic testified to the Parks Committee, "It would be injudicious . . . of the London County Council to yield to a demand made on behalf of a few anonymous Jews, which would outrage the Christian convictions of this nation regarding the holy character of Sunday." Another critic, the Marquis of Aberdeen, insisted that although he had no problem with allowing people to visit LCC properties on Sunday afternoons, athletic competition would be inappropriate. "Rest," he insisted, "consists in quiet recreation, and in enjoying, especially in summer, the open-air and the beauties of nature."[62]

WAR AND RECONSTRUCTION

Of the many forces that shaped London during the nineteenth and twentieth centuries, none was as abrupt, arbitrary, or consequential as the Second World War, when the capital's green space became a vital element in the nation's defense. The military used large parks for training, and it set up searchlights, barrage balloons, and antiaircraft guns in many smaller ones. Civilians used London's green space to grow food and as a place of refuge when bombs fell. In addition to providing land for shelters, military requirements, and agriculture, London's parks and gardens served as a valuable source of raw materials for the war effort. Within weeks of the war's start, workers began excavating tons of sand from Hampstead Heath to fill the sandbags used to protect buildings and defense posts.[63]

Even before fighting broke out, the digging of shelters caused dramatic changes to the surface of many parks. In 1938, as tensions with Nazi Germany increased, British officials began a crash program to excavate shallow air-raid shelters in many of London's open spaces. One such place was Spa Fields, in Clerkenwell, which reformers had transformed in the late nineteenth century from a notoriously overcrowded burial ground into a children's playground.[64] To dispose of the tons of clay that they excavated to build underground shelters, officials from the Ministry of Home Security obtained permission to dump it in Regent's Park.

The authorities also converted many high-profile spots, such as flower beds in parks and the moat of the Tower of London, to agricultural production. Much of Richmond Park became a hayfield. By May 1941 over two hundred acres of royal parks in London had been converted to food production. The London County Council took matters even further by granting allotments in its parks and open spaces to thousands of individuals who grew vegetables in them. Over the course of the war, the LCC released at least 1,800 acres of green space for emergency uses ranging from vegetable gardens to antiaircraft emplacements. Even some cemeteries became temporary vegetable gardens.[65]

In September 1940, just over a year after the Second World War began in Europe, Germany and Britain began large-scale bombing attacks against each other's capital cities. The resulting devastation was enormous. Over the course of the war, German bombers and rockets killed thirty thousand Londoners, most of them civilians, and left far larger numbers of people injured or homeless. Damage was especially severe within the City of London, where bombs flattened 164 of its 677 acres.[66] To increase food production, many bombed-out sites in the capital were soon planted with vegetables. In 1944 the *Illustrated London News* published photographs that showed firefighters raising vegetables, apples, chickens, and pigs in the heart of the City of London, with St. Paul's Cathedral in the background.[67] Others became temporary playgrounds, pending a decision about how to rebuild.

As officials cleared streets and bombed-out properties, they faced a challenge of what to do with the vast amount of debris that remained. Initially workers transported the bulk of this material to Regent's Park and Hampstead Heath, where it was sorted for use in building repairs, conversion into hardcore or concrete, or as landfill. The rubble from destroyed buildings added to the large quantities of clay from shelter excavations that these parks already contained. All this raised the level of the ground substantially and led the bailiff of the royal parks to ask civil defense officials for assurances that such places would be restored after the war. He pointed out that this clay and debris had been placed on "one of the finest sports fields in London" and warned that they would face "serious and justifiable criticism if . . . we did not take every possible step to restore it to its former condition."[68] Facing criticism for the damage they were doing to centrally located parks, officials turned increasingly to disused canals and wetlands as a place to dispose of rubble. Over the course of the war, they used 2.9 million cubic yards of debris to fill in wetland areas of Hackney Marshes. By the time they finished, the ground level had risen by ten feet.[69]

As the war transformed land use within London's green spaces, it also prompted the removal of the iron railings that surrounded them. As noted above, railings carried a great deal of political as well as physical weight in British culture. Many viewed them as tools of class privilege that functioned to exclude working people and the poor from spaces that ought to be open to all. Others disliked them for aesthetic reasons, suggesting that they represented a fusty Victorianism that was not only out of fashion, but which hid parks and squares from public thoroughfares. Debates about the future of railings had simmered for years, but the war brought them to a boil for an entirely new reason: as a source of scrap iron in the war effort. Despite the efforts of some officials, property owners, and historic preservationists, in 1941 the government ordered the removal of virtu- ally all railings in Britain—including those that separated most parks and play- grounds from surrounding streets—to be melted down for use in the war effort.[70] During and after the war officials complained about an increase in vandalism and sexual activity in London's green spaces, most notably in Hyde Park.[71] Striking an elitist tone, a writer in *Country Life* noted in 1942 that "total war has swept the railings into the smelting furnaces for conversion into guns and tanks, and what were enclosed and protected spaces now lie open to all and sundry. . . . Grass . . . is now being worn away . . . and here and there may be seen loungers of an objec- tionable type."[72]

Although the war expanded many people's access to parks, it simultaneously reduced the number of playing fields. Field-Marshal Lord Cavan, president of the National Playing Fields Association, warned in 1940 that the push to plant crops on every uncultivated piece of land threatened to reverse decades of work to provide playing fields. He argued that these places served an essential role in wartime as well as peace, and if they were dug up, the high cost of restoring them to playable condition might result in their permanent disappearance.[73] The asso- ciation petitioned the government to ensure that all open spaces and recreation grounds that had been converted to wartime functions be restored within a year of the war's end, but this goal proved impossible to achieve.[74] Three years after the fighting stopped, London possessed fewer than half as many football pitches as had existed when the war began.[75]

The upheaval of the Second World War prompted many people to question traditional ways of doing things, including the proper use of Sundays. Numerous pressure groups resisted such reforms, however, including the London Free Church Federation, the Imperial Alliance for the Defence of Sunday, and the Lord's Day Observance Society. The secretary of the latter group asserted that allowing children to use playgrounds on the Sabbath "would necessarily attract many boys and girls from Sunday Schools and Bible Classes, and the young people would consequently lose the benefits of moral and spiritual instruction so necessary in these critical days in the history of our Country."[76] Despite this opposition, the Parks Committee decided in 1942 to open its "children's gymnasia" from 10 a.m. on Sundays.[77] In contrast to its liberalization of the rules involving playgrounds, the LCC maintained its ban on Sunday sports prior to 2 p.m. In 1943 one resident complained that she was "ashamed and indignant" when she witnessed "four Canadian airmen apply to play" tennis at Battersea Park on a Sunday morning. She argued that it was inhospitable for the LCC to bar men who were risking their lives for the people of Britain from enjoying the use of public facilities during their rare free time, and she expressed the wish "that this mean-spirited and purposeless rule will be abolished as quickly as possible."[78] The LCC rebuffed such pleas, however, and the ban remained, even for members of the armed forces.[79]

One of the great paradoxes of the Blitz was the way in which it heightened people's awareness of London as a natural as well as man-made landscape. As the eminent photographer Emil Otto Hoppé put it, "the hot blasts of war" had made London "more dignified and countrified . . . and open to the winds of heaven."[80] In contrast to the fragility of buildings and human bodies in wartime, nature proved remarkably resilient. The ability of nonhuman life to survive and even flourish in places ravaged by war inspired many with the realization that humanity's most destructive powers paled in comparison to nature's ability to heal and survive. Even plants and animals that had long been absent from London soon appeared on sites leveled by bombs. Some observers urged their compatriots to pause and appreciate the temporary resurgence of wildness before human beings had a chance to regain control. Reflecting on the temporary nature of this situation, one journalist noted: "Wild flowers in the city, a stone's throw from Fleet Street, with bees hovering among them and the black redstart flitting to and fro—it will all be, one day, just a memory of London in war-time."[81] Defying such predictions, however, some of the species that established themselves in the "green oasis" that bombing had created in London remain there today.[82] For although the war caused enormous damage to London's natural and built environment, it also created the possibility for a new relationship between people and their surroundings. One example of this was the decision, suggested almost immediately after an extremely destructive raid on the City of London in December 1940, to transform the sites of many of its ruined churches into gardens.[83]

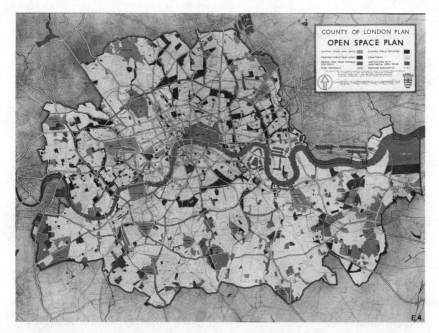

Fig. 5.1. "Open Space Plan," in J. H. Forshaw and Patrick Abercrombie, *County of London Plan* (London: Macmillan, 1944). This image is believed to be out of copyright.

Long after the war ended, London remained deeply scarred. New buildings were being erected on many sites, but thousands of other places remained in limbo. Coordinated planning seemed essential to reconstruction, just as it had been vital to the economic and military effort needed to win the war. The architect and urban planner Patrick Abercrombie, who in the 1920s had helped to establish the Council for the Preservation of Rural England (later called the Council for the Protection of Rural England), played a key role in articulating a broad vision of how London might be rebuilt in ways that would improve people's relationship with the natural environment.[84] In 1943 the London County Council paid Abercrombie 3,000 guineas (equivalent in 2018 to over $200,000) to assist its architect, J. H. Forshaw, in the creation of the *County of London Plan* (see fig. 5.1).[85] One year later Sir John Reith, who led the Ministry of Town and Country Planning, commissioned Abercrombie to create an even broader document, the *Greater London Plan, 1944.*[86]

In their *County of London Plan*, Forshaw and Abercrombie criticized London as a garden that had not been tended. Using organic terms such as hypertrophy, overgrowth, and decay, they argued that careful management, in the form of urban planning, was needed to prune the unnecessary and diseased parts of the city and to reconcile its inhabitants with the natural world. Treating planning as horticulture writ large, they described their task as "the grafting of a new, vigor-

ous growth upon the old stock of London."[87] Along with the enormous suffering and loss of life that the Blitz had brought, it also provided an unprecedented
opportunity to take the bold, even revolutionary, steps needed to make access to
green space in London more spatially distributed and socially equitable. In many
places, observed Forshaw and Abercrombie, bombs had "removed property that
cried aloud for redevelopment, or . . . [had] opened up hidden beauties which
we hope will not be needlessly obliterated." Conveniently they believed that the
best antidote to the "maldistribution of open spaces" was the creation of a large
number of small parks and playgrounds.[88] They insisted that urban green spaces
should not only be scattered widely throughout the Metropolis, but that they be
linked to one another, to the Green Belt, and to the countryside beyond. Parks,
they argued, could never substitute for the countryside as an antidote to urban
life. Somewhat surprisingly, they looked to the automobile as the ideal means of
transport. In their view, "radial open spaces," which some now refer to as "green
wedges," would allow people to experience nature from the windows of their cars
while traveling between urban, suburban, and rural areas.[89]

In contrast to many leading architects of the period, such as Le Corbusier
and Gropius, Abercrombie rejected high-rise residential architecture, not for
aesthetic or social reasons, but because he followed the nineteenth-century epidemiologist and senior government statistician William Farr in believing that a
direct correlation existed between population density and disease.[90] Abercrombie simultaneously opposed the construction of new housing on greenfield sites
near London, for he believed that every acre of unbuilt land that remained there
should be preserved for recreational uses. In his view London was simply too big,
and he advocated policies that would move both people and jobs to new settlements at a distance from the capital.

Many of Abercrombie's recommendations soon became embodied in law.
The Town and Country Planning Act of 1944 gave local government extraordinary powers to acquire war-damaged properties for conversion into green space.
Subsequent legislation, particularly the Town and Country Planning Act of 1947,
did even more to fulfill Abercrombie's goals. By nationalizing development values and placing heavy restrictions on new construction in rural areas, the 1947
law sought to protect the countryside from becoming more urban in appearance.[91] Between 1945 and 1965 the government approved every single application for compulsory purchase made under this act, and municipalities were not
required to pay market prices for these acquisitions until 1959.[92]

Perhaps the most significant legacy of Abercrombie's labors was the establishment of a comprehensive Green Belt around London, which he and his support-
ers hoped would finally put an end to London's "march of bricks and mortar" (a
phrase made famous by the caricaturist George Cruikshank in an 1829 engrav-

ing). The idea for the Green Belt had emerged at the dawn of the twentieth century as a response to fears that London's suburban expansion would destroy all the countryside that remained in southeastern England. In 1901 two men, William Bull, MP, and Reginald Brabazon, twelfth earl of Meath, suggested that a "green girdle" around London would be an ideal memorial to Queen Victoria, who had died in January of that year.[93] Support remained small at first, but it gained strength in the interwar period, due in part to the efforts of the Council for the Preservation of Rural England, founded in 1926. Although the population of London grew by less than 20 percent between the wars, its area doubled to 610 square miles. To arrest this expansion and protect land that was still rural in character, Parliament enacted the Green Belt (London and Home Counties Act) of 1938, which preserved slightly more than 100 square miles of land.[94] Although this was an enormous area, it failed to encircle London fully. In 1942, just two years after the fall of France, the *Daily Mail* had decried the incomplete nature of London's existing Green Belt as another "'Maginot Line,' which protects only a part of the fringe from building development."[95]

Due in large part to Abercrombie's determined efforts, an enormous quantity of land became part of London's Green Belt after the Second World War. Popular support for the Green Belt remains strong, but scholars disagree about its social and environmental consequences. Some, such as Camilla Ween, see it as an unmitigated success. In contrast to many of the world's other large cities, she notes, London "is still surrounded by relatively undeveloped countryside.... Development within the greenbelt is very restrictive, and any proposals must demonstrate a real benefit that outweighs the loss of greenbelt land. As a result, much of Outer London remains a patchwork of countryside and small villages."[96] Others, who focus more on its social impact, offer a more critical assessment. Much of the enthusiasm for the creation of the Green Belt, suggest the historians Marco Amati and Makoto Yokohari, stemmed from a desire to prevent a blending of urban and rural landscapes.[97] They argue that it is simplistic to view the politics that created the Green Belt exclusively in terms of "a demand from the public for leisure, amenity, or agricultural production." In contrast to Ween's positive assessment of the Green Belt's impact, Amati and Yokohari blame it for contributing to the inadequate supply and high cost of housing in the London region.[98]

David Matless and Patricia Garside each take the argument further by suggesting that this aim derived from a larger set of profoundly conservative, if not reactionary, ideas. In Matless's view, preservationists disliked suburban development primarily because it threatened to undermine sharp moral dichotomies that they sought to maintain involving "land use, class and gender."[99] Garside notes that "the ferocity of local communities opposed to any possible development of the

Green Belt" stemmed not from arguments about the opportunities that it offered to all in terms of beauty, health, or relaxation, but something far more selfish: "They saw defending the Green Belt against new housing as a means of protecting existing property investments and amenity interests."[100] More broadly, Bill Luckin suggests that much of the impetus for the Green Belt derived from feelings of hostility toward cities in general and London in particular.[101] He criticizes planners for being so obsessed with maintaining a strict urban-rural dichotomy that they failed to recognize the existence of, much less the reasons for, the rise of suburbia. Strangely, even some proponents of the garden city seemed oblivious to the ways in which the suburb, without their intervention, came to embody the fusion of urban and rural elements that they championed.[102]

Attitudes, policies, and people's use of green space in London continued to evolve during the closing decades of the twentieth century. These changes included a rise in running and other individual forms of exercise, growing affluence, and transformations in municipal governance. By far the most influential, however, was the development of a host of interrelated concerns about the natural environment at both the local and global scales. In contrast to their immediate predecessors' focus on green space as a site of aesthetic refinement or rational recreation, a new breed of environmental activists and policy experts began in the 1970s to emphasize the important role of green space in sustaining biodiversity, lowering summertime temperatures, filtering particulate pollution from the air, and helping Londoners to connect with the natural world. Recent studies have shown that London's parks are often cooler by up to two degrees Celsius than surrounding places in summertime.[103]

During the late twentieth century many Londoners expressed a renewed interest in allotment gardening, and others took matters into their own hands to turn unused patches of land into "guerrilla gardens."[104] Echoing the transformation of burial grounds into gardens a century earlier, in the 1970s borough councils sought to halt the deteriorating condition of Nunhead Cemetery in Southwark and Highgate Cemetery by turning parts of them into nature reserves.[105] Other new uses of green space also became popular, such as nature trails, environmental education centers, adventure playgrounds, and green chains that connect open spaces with walking trails.[106] One such place was the North Camberwell Open Space, created by the Greater London Council in the 1970s. Part of the land for this site, which was renamed Burgess Park, came from filling in the former Surrey Canal.[107]

Throughout most of the period under consideration in this chapter, people considered the draining of marshes and the embankment of streams and rivers as unmixed blessings. By the late twentieth century, however, a new understanding of the ecological value of wetlands led officials to seek other sources of land for reclamation. The obvious choice, both for parks and for building purposes, were brownfield sites, places once occupied by industrial activities or even rubbish dumps. As part of the redevelopment of the Docklands area in the 1990s, expensive pollution mitigation efforts took place in connection with the construction of Beckton Park and the Millennium Dome (both of which are situated on land where large coal gasification plants once operated).[108] More recently the 2012 Olympics took place on another long-neglected brownfield site in Stratford, East London.

EPILOGUE

Today 46 percent of London consists of green space, most of which is open to the public. These areas include 600 squares, 142 parks and gardens, and nearly 900 conservation areas.[109] "Few cities of a comparable size," asserts John Burton, "can boast as many parks, commons, woods and gardens."[110] The existence of so much green space in a city as crowded and expensive as London is remarkable, yet the work of creating and sustaining it is often forgotten by residents and visitors alike.

Green space offers many benefits to London, including relaxation, contact with the natural world, fresh air, exercise, and a place for athletic events, political protests, and concerts. The preservation of green space is unquestionably a public good, but its benefits continue to accrue to some people more than to others. In a neoliberal property market, proximity to green space is itself a form of capital. London has some of the highest rents in the world, and the most expensive areas continue to be concentrated around the royal parks, Hampstead Heath, and fashionable squares, while the zones of greatest poverty are generally far from such green spaces.[111] Kensington, one of the wealthiest districts in London, contains no fewer than seventy-nine squares within its borders. Many of its squares, and those elsewhere in the capital, are gated and off-limits to all but those who live in the buildings that face them. In some cases their owners grant provisional access to visitors during a limited number of hours each day, but public as well as private squares and gardens continue to impose significant restrictions on the activities allowed in them. They often prohibit even informal games, and it is not unusual to find signs demanding that people keep off the grass.

A well-worn aphorism states that land is the most valuable investment because nobody is making any more of it. It might be easy to assume that the same is true of green space—that once a place contains a building, it will never again contain plants or trees. Yet this is not always the case, as evidenced by the small gardens that can be found on the sites of churches destroyed during the Second World War. Today architects are finding new ways to incorporate plants and even trees into their creations, for a range of reasons that often blur ecol-

Fig. 5.2. Rooftops in the City of London, as seen from the Sky Garden, 2019. A number of large buildings in London now possess roofs containing vegetation, but few are accessible to those who work in them, much less to the public. Photo by Peter Thorsheim.

ogy, public relations, and the generation of profits. In 2015 a publicly accessible "park," the Sky Garden, opened on the thirty-fifth floor of 20 Fenchurch Street, a new building that Londoners quickly nicknamed the Walkie Talkie. Although anyone can enter the Sky Garden's greenhouse and observation deck without charge, doing so requires a timed reservation booked well in advance. Visitors are allowed only sixty minutes at the top unless they dine at one of the property's pricy restaurants, and they may not bring outside food or drink to have lunch in this park—something that many Londoners enjoy doing elsewhere in the city.[112] Although the Sky Garden is covered and occupies only part of its building's footprint, some buildings in London, both new and old, are now topped with green roofs containing living plants and even trees (see fig. 5.2). According to one proponent of the green roof, it "not only helps reduce flooding, urban heat-island effects, and air and noise pollution but also provides wildlife habitat and tranquility." Although few green roofs have been created in London as of this writing, their potential benefits are substantial as the city develops strategies to cope with the growing problems of climate change. Roofs cover approximately twenty-four thousand hectares of Greater London, or 16 percent of its surface area.[113]

The concept of sustainability—which holds that environmental, social, and economic questions are interrelated and must be considered in concert with one another—has much to offer those who seek to make sense of the past. In a reciprocal fashion, historical analysis may deepen theoretical discussions of sustainability by demonstrating the significant ways in which temporal, geographical, and cultural contexts have influenced people's interactions with and understandings of the urban environment.[114] In contrast to critics who once decried London as a cancerous growth that was destroying the natural world, proponents of sustainability have argued persuasively in recent years that its residents require far less land and energy, and generate less pollution, than an equivalent number of people living in rural areas or suburbs. Investments in public transportation, cleaner technology, and new bike paths have in recent years made London much more environmentally sustainable than it once was, as have efforts to rejuvenate parks and gardens that long suffered from neglect and decline. Londoners can feel justifiably proud of their green space, yet many factors continue to limit some people's enjoyment of this resource. Over the past two centuries social, political, and economic forces have done much to shape where green space was located, who could access it, and what they could do once they got there. Far from being the antithesis of culture, London's green space always has been—and will continue to be—an inextricable part of it.

SIX

MOVING EAST

Industrial Pollution in London, 1800–1920

LESLIE TOMORY

In the nineteenth century London experienced significant industrial pollution caused by the large industrial base found in the city. The most important sectors of London's economy were associated with its traditional strengths in law, politics, trade, finance, and insurance, together with trades that supported its vast population, such as food retailing and construction. It had, however, long been home to many manufacturing and productive industries that caused pollution, such as silk weaving in Spitalfields and brewing in many parts of the city. The ongoing industrialization of nineteenth-century Britain also touched the Metropolis as new industries were established and old ones, including brewing, evolved. Despite the large literature about pollution in London, relatively little is known about industrial pollution over the long nineteenth century. Most researchers have concentrated on areas that most concerned the Victorians themselves, namely sewage and smoke, both of which were chiefly domestic in origin.[1] The public health acts and the epidemics that prompted them were primarily related to pollution from domestic sources. To the extent that parliamentary action seriously addressed industrial pollution beginning in the middle of the nineteenth century, it was directed at the predominantly rural alkali industry, which had no presence in London.[2] Nevertheless industrial pollution weighed heavily on the city's inhabitants, but unevenly, as industries tended to cluster in certain areas.

This essay offers a sketch of industrial pollution in London during the long nineteenth century. The first part gives an overview of London's geography and the legal and administrative responses to industrial pollution. The activities that faced specific regulation from mid-century on, the organic trades and smoke emitters, are then discussed. The last section explores other polluting industries, especially those using the largest plants, specifically gasworks, fertilizer manufactures, and later, engineering factories. The pattern that emerges from this overview shows that, from their earlier bases within the historic core of the city, industries and their pollution tended to move east to the Lea Valley and along the Thames in West Ham, where there was little effective control from institutions, notably boards of health, that had managed to exert some pressure on polluters in the City.

GEOGRAPHICAL, INDUSTRIAL, AND LEGAL CONTEXTS

From the early modern period onward, London had an expanding industrial base, including brewers, sugar refiners, iron founders, and chemical manufacturers. By the early years of the nineteenth century the presence of industry and its pollution had become significant. The 1851 census revealed that manufacturing accounted for about 34 percent of the city's workforce. A finer analysis of the figures reveals that the largest manufacturing sectors, employing at least 9,000 workers, included building materials, iron and steel production, other metal trades, furniture making, woodworking, textiles, carriage and harness making, dressmaking, and watch- and instrument making.[3] Furthermore, the vast majority of businesses in the city were small. The same census reported that 86 percent of firms had fewer than 10 workers, and only 80 had over 100, although this figure underestimated the total.[4] At mid-century whatever industrial pollution existed was secondary to domestic sources within the context of the entire Metropolis. This situation was quite different from the new industrial towns of the Midlands and North, such as Birmingham and Manchester. Due to London's size, however, even a proportionately secondary industry could be a significant source of pollution. With 468,000 people employed in London's manufacturing sector in 1861, it represented 15 percent of all workers in this class in England and Wales.[5]

The intensity of pollution was exacerbated locally by the clustering of industries, leaving some urban areas largely free of industrial pollution while others were engulfed by it. Locals were often powerless to act or resigned to their lot. One particularly dense cluster composed of tanneries and related leather trades was found in Southwark, especially in its Bermondsey district. All told, one third of England's production in these trades was located there. By contrast, the City of London, Westminster, and the West End had relatively few concentrated polluting industries, but even they were not exempt; for example, some large gasworks were in Westminster and many individual workshops and factories were scattered throughout these areas. In the early part of the century, before the Metropolis had expanded greatly toward the east and to the south of the river, many industries were in the central zone, partly due to the high cost of transporting both goods and people. Most goods were consumed close to where they were produced.[6] As London grew, an inner industrial belt formed, based on older manufacturing sites. It ran from Holborn and Clerkenwell west and north of the City, to Stratford and the Isle of Dogs in the east. The belt continued on the south bank between Deptford and Lambeth.[7] As the nineteenth century wore on, larger industrial sites gathered along the banks of waterways. Most were located along the Thames, but they increasingly concentrated in the Lea Valley in the east after 1840 and farther east later in the century. They were also found along canals, notably the Grand Union and Regent's Canals in the north and the Surrey Canal in the south. The lower cost of water transport and land, and the easy disposal of waste into the water, made such sites attractive to large-scale industry. The inner industrial core of mostly small operations remained, however, concentrated on the south side of the Thames.[8] Larger peripheral industrial sites were also found along the upper Thames, such as plants at Fulham, notably the Imperial Gas Company gasworks, and in Lambeth, where pottery manufactures were concentrated.

The East End, stretching to the Lea, along with more recently established locations farther east in Essex, suffered especially from industrial pollution as it became the densest industrial area of the Metropolis. The poor, with little political or social clout, had long occupied lands east of the Tower of London.[9] Several factors pushed industry toward the east in the nineteenth century: Easy access to water along the Lea and Lower Thames constituted an advantage that grew as the great docks were built there and coal could be received on the Thames in great quantities. The availability of cheap land outside of the metropolitan core also attracted industrialists, especially as they built plants much larger than had previously existed.[10] Finally, London's fractured political map encouraged industrialists to hunt for jurisdictions where the hand of public health authorities lay limp.

As weak as environmental regulation and enforcement mechanisms were for most of the nineteenth century, what little existed tended to be stronger within the older areas of the city. These included regulations from 1848 on nuisance businesses within the City, and in other districts in London in 1855. Regulations expanded to cover Greater London, the area under the Metropolitan Board of Works' (MBW) jurisdiction in 1874, later transferred to the London County Council (LCC) in 1889.[11] These regulations had an effect, especially in closing many nuisance-causing businesses as described below. The Lea, being the boundary of West Ham in Essex, marked the MBW/LCC border. Officials on the other side lacked the financial means to pursue the expensive prosecutions that challenged even the City's authorities. Although each of these factors individually could not prevent cases of even the foulest pollution being produced farther west, they collectively made the eastern half of the Metropolis much more attractive for nuisance-causing trades. As a result, heavy industry clustered north of the Thames in the Lea Valley, around its conjunction with the Thames, and farther east along the Thames into Silvertown.[12] A smaller industrial cluster also formed on the Greenwich Peninsula opposite the Lea's mouth. Some of London's largest industrial sites were located in the east, such as the Royal Arsenal at Woolwich, where the manufacture of munitions had begun in the late seventeenth century; the Great Eastern Railway works, established in Stratford in the 1840s; and Beckton Gasworks, opened at Barking in 1870.[13] In addition, the direction of the prevailing winds, blowing from the west and southwest, as well as the flow of the Thames toward the east, added further to the east's misery. While the east became ever more blighted, most areas within the MBW/LCC saw improved conditions in the 1870s and beyond.[14] The exception was areas to the south of the Thames, which housed organic trades, railway yards, and chemical factories.[15]

The effects of the move east become apparent with time. A commission investigating the state of the Lea observed in 1867 that "the district immediately bordering the tidal portion of the Lee [sic] has become a nuisance district, the seat of trades expelled beyond the limits of the better parts of the metropolis."[16] *Engineering* reported in 1874 that compared to twenty years earlier, the Thames was much cleaner above London Bridge. This was due in large part to the construction of the MBW's sewer system, which brought the city's sewage to the east, but it was also because many manufacturers had relocated to Greenwich, West Ham, and other areas downriver.[17] The politician J. J. Terrett described an East London scene in 1902: "The industrial district of Silvertown [is a] collection of immense factories and wharves fronting on the River Thames—a more desolate region, contrasted with which St. Helens or Widnes seem beautiful townships by comparison. The atmosphere is blackened with the noxious fumes of chemicals, and the stench of bone manure and soapworks, and the only sounds are the shriek of railway engines and the mournful foghorn toots of the steamboats coming up the river."[18] The woeful state of East London also affected neighboring areas, as its industrial pollution frequently overflowed. For example, the wealthier Blackheath Heights to the south of Silvertown suffered from smoke and vapors blown in by the northerly winds common during winter months.[19]

The control of pollution in London evolved significantly over the course of the nineteenth century. Although regulation of specific industries is discussed in the following sections, an overview of the broader evolution of English environmental law is presented here. Initially mechanisms available to local authorities were limited to nuisance prosecution. This procedure dated back to the Middle Ages and was used to control actions that were deemed to impinge on another person's welfare. Nuisances were private when they harmed an individual, or public when a common good, such as a river, was affected. In the latter cases, local authorities brought charges. Nuisance procedures could work for limited cases such as slaughterhouses aggravating their neighbors, but they were not designed to deal with systemic problems that came with industry-wide issues, let alone with the difficulties in identifying damages arising from new forms of industrial activity, such as gaseous emissions. Nevertheless Ben Pontin has shown that courts sometimes ordered polluters to pay substantial damage awards and to take remedial actions.[20] On occasion such rulings forced offending firms into bankruptcy. In other cases nuisance suits may have played a part in driving pollution eastward, but it is not evident how important they were in this respect.[21]

The intensification of industrial pollution and reactions to it eventually forced significant changes to environmental law in three ways relevant to London. The first legal innovation came when the public health movement achieved a decisive momentum with the sanitary reformer Edwin Chadwick in the 1840s. The sanitary movement aimed to foster cleanliness and eliminate visible malodorous waste, especially in the domestic context. To this end, reformers persuaded Parliament in the late 1840s to create boards of health with medical officers of health (MOH) with powers of inspection and nuisance abatement. Although their work was not primarily concerned with industrial pollution, they had powers to bring suits beginning in 1855, especially against slaughterhouses and other trades in the organic material process chain.[22] As described below, their powers of inspection were strengthened and extended to other industries over subsequent years. Industrial pollution, however, remained secondary for MOHs.[23]

The second change consisted of the Alkali Acts, which, beginning in the 1860s, not only created the first industry-specific standards for certain kinds of pollution (emission of acid fumes), but more importantly established a governmental bureaucracy to test and enforce the standards. Alkali inspectors also cajoled and informed producers about control mechanisms.[24] Although London had no alkali works, the regulatory model was extended in 1881 to other industries present in the city, leading to the introduction of acid condensers or scrubbers.[25]

The third legal trend was anti-smoke legislation. As air quality deteriorated, Parliament passed a series of anti-smoke laws aimed at reducing black smoke from furnaces and steam engines, such as the Smoke Nuisance Abatement (Metropolis) Act of 1853 and the Sanitary Act of 1866. Initially enacted with no enforcement mechanisms, the laws gained teeth as MOHs and nuisance inspectors became active in mid-century. The faulty wording of the legislation to cover only "black smoke," however, made evasion easy.

Legislation was one aspect of pollution control; matters of jurisdiction were another, though these two intersected. Often laws passed by Parliament applied to the whole country except London, while a second act applied only to the Metropolis, though not always. This meant that sometimes London was able to avoid national legislation. Furthermore, London's own political geography was deeply fractured. At the beginning of the century it was a complex patchwork of overlapping local entities, many dating to the Middle Ages. They had authority over sewers, roads, lighting, navigation, taxation, poor laws, and many other functions, with different sources of authority, including elections by property-owning ratepayers or perpetuation by self-appointment. At the metropolitan core lay the City of London, guarding its privileges and resisting attempts at amalgamation, even as Parliament reformed municipal governance elsewhere in the country from the 1830s.[26] Change did, however, come to the City with the sanitary movement. This began with the formation of the Metropolitan Commission of Sewers in 1847, which was replaced and extended by the MBW in 1855. Twenty-three vestries and fifteen newly formed district boards appointed members of the MBW's governing council. The MBW survived until its abolition in 1889, when scandals over bribery and the sale of lands to insiders prompted an investigation by a Royal Commission and the creation of the LCC.[27] Besides taking over the MBW's functions, the LCC had a much wider mandate, including health. It began to receive yearly public health reports that integrated the local MOH reports. Nevertheless the LCC's powers to act against pollution were still largely restricted to what the Board of Health and the MBW had possessed before it: nuisance inspections with the power to order abatements and initiate prosecutions in accordance with the LCC's own bylaws relating to specific industries.[28]

TARGETING POLLUTING INDUSTRIES: THE "OFFENSIVE TRADES" AND SMOKE

Generic nuisance law provided a mechanism that could in principle be used against any industry. Some types of industries were, however, specifically targeted for regulation, usually because of their pervasiveness. These were smoke-producing industries and trades specifically designated as "offensive," meaning the organic trades. These were found at many sites throughout the Metropolis. Slaughterhouses especially numbered in the thousands, but fertilizer manufacturers also stood out for their size and pollution.

The processing of animal substances in all their forms and by-products constituted one of the most polluting industrial sectors of London. These "blood and guts industries," as Peter Atkins has called them, mostly began with the preparation of meat, but also included knackers, who disposed of horses. In addition, imported processed materials, such as dried hides, should be included among these trades. The process chain from butchering onward was long, as carcasses were separated into their many components for a multitude of end products. These processes had many chemical inputs, such as acids. Many of these businesses were located close to each other as the source materials were passed on from slaughterhouses.[29] The blood and guts industries created "effluvium" pollutants: these were the malodorous organic vapors that poured from putrefying materials as they were stored, processed, and transported. Moreover, the organic trades often dumped liquids into sewers and rivers.

The organic industries were enormous. In 1842, 175,000 cows and 1.4 million sheep were sold at Smithfield, London's primary meat market. They were also diffuse: even as many other British cities erected large public slaughterhouses, London butchered its meat mostly in small private shops until well into the twentieth century.[30] Smithfield itself was so vile and crowded that Parliament, after repeated inquiries, finally forced its removal to larger and more distant grounds in Islington in 1855, although leaving a smaller poultry and meat market in place. This coincided with the decisive weakening of the old Butchers Company that had regulated butchery in the City since the Middle Ages. As a result, private butchers scattered far and wide throughout the Metropolis.[31]

Pollution in the organic industries began at the slaughterhouses. Many animal parts were simply discarded by butchers into sewers or ditches, and blood could sometimes be seen running freely from city shambles.[32] A London butcher described the situation in 1847: "The filth, garbage, and impurities of every description generally to be found in slaughter-houses, in almost every stage of decomposition, contribute their quantum of deadly exhalations to the atmosphere of the slaughter-house, and then, after having impregnated the neighbourhood with offensive and unwholesome effluvia, are consigned to the sewers, by which they are ultimately conveyed to the Thames, to increase the noxious exhalations from its banks, or, detained in their progress through those notoriously defective channels, to breathe forth at every loophole putrescence and disease."[33] Because there were so many slaughterhouses—well over a thousand until the 1880s—they were the subject of higher levels of regulation. The number of knackers, by contrast, was much smaller, numbering fewer than ten by the end of the century.[34]

After slaughtering, animal parts went in different directions for further processing. Many of these trades, notably tanneries, clustered south of the Thames. This was due to early regulations dating to the Middle Ages. The City had banned them, and they moved to where civic resistance was weaker south of the river.[35]

Further regulation of the organic trades came only in the nineteenth century. Parliament passed the Act for Better Paving, Improving, and Regulating the Streets of the Metropolis in 1817, which required the abatement of nuisances from slaughterhouses and "horse boiling."[36]

The rise of the public health movement, especially in the wake of Edwin Chadwick's 1842 report on the condition of the working classes, stimulated interest in the environmental conditions affecting public health.[37] Even before the report, a parliamentary committee in 1840 on the Health of Towns had recommended moving slaughterhouses to the outskirts of cities.[38] The reformers behind this and similar efforts, such as sewer construction, were inspired by the "sanitary idea" that pushed for the removal of malodorous materials from cities.[39] The focus on organic industries was primarily but not exclusively on slaughterhouses; they were the most numerous in the cities. The first major act containing specific regulations was the 1844 Metropolitan Buildings Act. It prevented the construction of slaughterhouses and other businesses deemed offensive within fifty feet of houses or forty feet of a public street. Furthermore, it mandated that all offensive businesses within the Metropolis be closed within thirty years, with some exemptions if sufficient means were in place to restrict pollution. Finally, all offensive trades were placed under a licensing regime.[40] The businesses thus restricted were blood boilers, bone boilers, fellmongers, slaughterers (including knackers), soap makers, tallow melters, and tripe boilers. These were repeatedly listed as "offensive businesses" in subsequent laws.[41]

Means to enforce the provisions of this law did not exist until the 1848 Public Health Act created Boards of Health and MOHs. The boards were given the power to register slaughterhouses and prevent new ones from being created without permission.[42] These laws, however, failed to suppress these businesses within the Metropolis. When Parliament renewed many of their provisions in 1855, witnesses testified that they had never been used.[43] In 1873, a year prior to the thirty-year deadline for closing offensive businesses, few people even realized that such a law existed. With all slaughterhouses at least potentially threatened with legal proceedings and even closure, Parliament repealed the clause.[44]

Despite the general failure to use the acts, the suppression of offensive businesses could proceed if a local MOH acted with energy. This was the case within the City of London beginning with its first MOH, John Simon, who was in office from 1848 to 1855.[45] Relying on inspectors of nuisances, he and his successors reduced the number of slaughterhouses from 138 in 1848 to 31 in 1873.[46] However, Simon complained that his powers were limited to the City (districts outside the City lacked MOHs until 1855). Furthermore, he had no power over some of the organic trades, such as glue making and fertilizer manufacturing, which also produced significant pollution.[47] For example, blood driers and boilers processed blood from slaughterhouses, mostly for agricultural fertilizer. In addition, albumin was used as a clarifying agent in sugar manufacturing and as a fixative in the manufacture of dye. In the 1850s about eight hundred thousand gallons of blood were processed yearly.[48] The process involved allowing the blood to boil or stand under heat for many hours, after which the dried clots were disposed of, often into sewers.[49]

Another large polluting trade was that of the bone boilers, who collected bones from large slaughterhouses and taverns all over the city (domestic sources tended to be too small to be worth their while). After being sawed and crushed, bones were boiled in large vats for many hours to separate their fats, after which they were dried in heaps two or three stories high. Quicklime could be thrown on the bone heaps to speed their decomposition. They were then further ground into dust or sold for use as fertilizer (known as "manure," a term that has remained stylistically prominent until the present day), for sugar refining, paints and inks, as well as for water filters.[50] The fats were processed on-site or sold to soap boilers.[51] Bone boilers were sometimes prosecuted, as in 1854 when the government sued Hunt & Co. in Lambeth for nuisances caused to Millbank Prison.[52]

Fellmongers processed sheepskins, both fresh from butchers and imported into London from overseas. The skins were cleaned, treated with lime, bleached with sulfur, and allowed to dry, after which the wool was scraped off. The wool was sent for further processing, while the skins were made into leather or mats. This trade not only filled the air with objectionable odors, but also contaminated watercourses with lime and sulfur when the skins were washed.[53] Most fellmongers were concentrated in Bermondsey, where they carried out their work in open yards. Many other leather-related industries were also concentrated nearby, such as tanneries, curriers, leather goods makers, bark peelers, and by-product processers, such as glue makers. Peter Atkins has demonstrated from the 1851 census returns that Bermondsey represented not only a local concentration of these industries.[54] Pollution in this location was so pervasive that as late as 1885, a medical officer observed that so many offensive trades "are carried on entirely in Bermondsey, (which is closely identified with them), it is doubtful if they can be said to cause a nuisance to the locality."[55] The leather industries, however, declined after 1890 as they shifted to the north of the country and as demand for horse saddles decreased.[56]

Tanneries received "pelts" from fellmongers, and they were often part of the same business. The hides were scraped, cleaned, and left in lime for several weeks. They were then treated with a solution of "puer," a substance made from dog feces. They were later washed with sulfuric acid and brine, before finally being tanned with sumac or other agents. Tanners typically ran the puer and other washings into streams and sewers.[57] Leather from tanneries found a wide range of uses, from bookbinding to drive belts.

Glue makers took hide clippings and other soft tissues and, after treating them with lime, dried and boiled them. Depending on the type of glue produced, the tissue was also treated with chemicals such as hydrochloric acid. The by-products that remained included a substance called "scutch," left behind in the boiling pans, and piles of discarded "fleshings" in the yards. The smells from both were extremely foul and carried great distances.[58] Like the leather trades, glue makers were located in Bermondsey, but they too declined after 1900 with the introduction of vegetable glues.[59] There were many other trades processing animal parts, such as tallow chandlers and tripe boilers, which took the edible first stomachs of sheep and cattle, and scraped and boiled them, usually running waste into the sewers.[60]

Beyond the reach of the City's MOH, and facing mostly ineffective local MOHs, these organic trades continued their polluting ways in Bermondsey and elsewhere. Alfred Spencer, a sanitary officer for the MBW, observed in 1877 that except in a few cases, the original 1844 provisions had been "inoperative" for many of the offensive trades until 1874.[61] Parliament then centralized authority over the offensive trades in the hands of the MBW. This proved to be a turning point in bringing nuisance cases against many of the offensive trades. With its regulatory powers, the MBW managed to close 284 sites in 1875 alone. The Public Health Act of 1875 gave local authorities the power to pass regulations for the offensive trades, in addition to designating more of them. Over the following decade, the MBW enacted bylaws that regulated the activities of tripe boilers, knackers, catgut makers, glue manufacturers, blood driers, fat extractors, fat melters, gut scrapers, and animal charcoal manufacturers.[62]

When the LCC took over from the MBW, it passed further bylaws, which mandated the disposal of animal parts within twenty-four hours of slaughter and their removal in closed containers. The LCC also forbad the disposal of any filth into sewers or ditches.[63] In addition, slaughterhouses and knackers needed to apply for licenses yearly, some of which were not granted. In the 1890s the LCC reduced the number of slaughterhouses and knackers by rejecting some license applications each year.[64] Finally, the Public Health (London) Act of 1891 completely banned the establishment of new blood boilers, bone boilers, fertilizer manufacturers, soap boilers, tallow melters, and knackers within the Metropolis.[65]

The MBW's and LCC's bylaws allowed MOHs to prosecute businesses found violating them. The reports of MOHs from the 1890s indicated that these could be successful, even to the point of shutting down businesses. For example, in

1892–1893 a series of summons in relation to a fertilizer manufacturer in Rother-hithe led to court injunctions to cease causing nuisances. When the manufacturer failed to comply, he was fined and later ordered to shut down. The same report describes how a bone boiler in Deptford causing a serious nuisance went out of business after the MOH threatened prosecution.[66] Similarly, the LCC refused a fat melter in Shoreditch a license to operate in 1894 because of the effluvium he was producing.[67] The combination of a number of factors—greater enforcement of noxious business bylaws, the licensing regime in place since mid-century, and an increase in railway shipments of dead meat into the city from the 1870s—led to a decrease in the number of slaughterhouses in metropolitan London from about 1,500 in 1870 to 300 in 1905. Similarly, the number of offensive trades licensed to operate was 83 in 1906, a sharp decrease from the 1870s when P. L. Simmonds had counted around 336 trades that fell into this category.[68] Enforcement had brought the blood and guts industry under much tighter control.

Just as weaker enforcement in the areas outside the City allowed the offen-sive trades to thrive until the MBW brought them under tighter control, so too did its creation prompt many of these trades to flee its jurisdiction, especially to West Ham and farther east. In contrast to the MBW, West Ham had no law allowing for the designation of noxious businesses, and it became London's dumping ground for these businesses. The absence of a local authority was due to West Ham's rapid growth outpacing its minimal government. In the 1830s the parish encompassed only a few small villages, but by the 1850s it had grown by twenty thousand, with many of its residents living in slums in Canning Town and Stratford. Industry also located in Silvertown along the Thames.[69] In 1857 Henry Morley observed that Silvertown had become "quite a refuge for offensive trade establishments turned out of town; those of the oil-boilers, gut-spinners, varnish-makers, printers' ink-makers, and the like."[70] Parliament finally created a local board of health in 1856, allowing for a local medical officer. Yet corruption and weak fiscal capacity meant that the local board was crippled when faced with overwhelming health problems; the board acquired a full-time MOH only in 1898, although the department had several full-time inspectors.[71]

Even as legal means brought these trades under much tighter control, tech-nical measures also improved the worst aspects of some of the pollution they created. The trades sometimes adopted these measures voluntarily, but often they were compelled to act by the MBW and later the LCC. For example, slaugh-terhouses and other nuisance trades had to use building materials such as imper-meable stone and tile for their structures. Another commonly mandated remedy was tall chimneys, which may have relieved the immediate neighbors but also displaced the pollution elsewhere, as the inhabitants of the Blackheath Heights south of Silvertown discovered. The requirement to connect drains to sewers created the same displacement situation. Standards of cleanliness were also pre-scribed, such as washing walls with lime yearly, using disinfectants, or cleaning instruments after daily use.[72]

Other standards were specific to trades. For example, starting in 1874 bylaws obliged glue and tallow makers to use closed pans for boiling, run the fumes produced into furnace flues, and dispose of scutch (see above) as quickly as possible. As a result, nuisance complaints dropped significantly by 1885.[73] Some of voluntary technical means were adapted from the alkali industry, which had been the subject of the earliest concerted national regulations. Alkali manufac-turers had adopted Gossage towers or scrubbers to mitigate the acidic fumes they poured into the surrounding countryside. The scrubbers were filled with coke and had water running through them to condense the acid. The Alkali Act of 1863 required that 95 percent of the acid be removed from alkali vapors.[74] Par-liament extended this requirement to the fertilizer industry in 1881.[75] Variations of this scrubber using bricks were applied in fertilizer manufacturing to remove odors. Incondensable organic substances could be purified from the waste gases by burning them in a furnace.[76] Alfred Spencer, a sanitary officer for the MBW, reported in 1885 that the introduction of new technical means had reduced com-plaints greatly. Nuisance officers worked closely with offensive trades in helping them implement mitigation strategies, a practice pioneered by Angus Smith and his alkali inspectors.[77] The Alkali Inspectorate had relatively limited importance in London. In 1892, for example, the inspectorate reported that there were 204 plants under its jurisdiction, all in the southeast of the country, which included London, compared to 1,047 for the whole country.[78]

The fertilizer manufacturers that produced these acid vapors were significant polluters because they had the largest plants among the offensive trades. They were the end point of many of the materials that had begun in slaughterhouses. Fertilizer production was a significant industry, encompassing a broad range of materials and processes such as imported guano, local manure, and animal parts. In bone-fertilizer works, ground bones were mixed with sulfuric acid and mineral phosphates to produce superphosphate fertilizer. Nitrogen fertilizers were made by mixing imported guano with sulfuric acid. Other organic materials, including fish heads, blood, and leather scraps, were ground and mixed with these other fertilizers. The fertilizers were then left in the open to dry.[79]

London had many artificial fertilizer manufacturers located in the east, beginning at the Greenwich Peninsula, the spit of land formed by the Thames's northward loop opposite the Lea's mouth.[80] One of the largest in this area was Lawes's Oil of Vitriol and Manure Works, established in 1857 at Barking. It pro-duced about eighty tons of fertilizer daily.[81] In 1864 the secretary of state for war, prompted by complaints from the Woolwich Arsenal about the unbearable

stench coming from Lawes's factory, referred the matter to the MBW. Joseph
Bazalgette and Dr. Henry Letheby investigated, reporting that Lawes was the
principal cause, although none of the factories in the area made any effort to
reduce fumes.[82] Very little changed as a result of this visit. In 1873 Dr. Gordon,
the principal medical officer of the Woolwich Arsenal, and others complained
to the Local Government Board about the odors from fertilizer and other chemical works along the Lower Thames. This prompted its Medical Board to inves-
tigate their source. Edward Ballard, a physician, medical inspector for Islington,
and ubiquitous special investigator for John Simon's Medical Office of the Privy
Council, undertook many investigations there, and he found that the odors predominantly emanated from fertilizer works in the area. These were most likely
Hills's Oil of Vitriol and Manure Works on the Greenwich Peninsula and Odams'
Chemical Manure Company on the opposite side of the Thames. Lawes's factory
was still a problem, as was a "putrid sickening odour" that came from Brown's
Glue and Manure Works and Bevington's Manure Works on the Erith Marshes
along the Thames.[83] Lawes's, which had erected a scrubber at its works to condense acid fumes after its previous troubles, had also installed a bypass to allow
the venting of fumes, often at night.[84]

London was notorious for the thick black smoke by which it was frequently
enveloped in autumn, winter, and early spring from the 1850s onward. Spewed
from the ubiquitous industrial furnaces and increasingly from steam engines,
it was not specific to any one industry. John Simon, the City MOH, described
the situation at mid-century thus: "Soon after day break, the great factory shafts
beside the river begin to discharge immense volumes of smoke; their clouds soon
become confluent; the sky is overcast with a dingy veil; the house-chimneys
presently add their contributions; and by ten o'clock, as one approaches London
from any hill in the suburbs, one may observe the total result of this gigantic nuisance hanging over the City like a pall."[85] Steam engine pollution became steadily
worse as the nineteenth century wore on and the number of engines in London increased. Minimizing smoke from engines also required skilled workers to
ensure that coal was spread within furnaces carefully, with freshly loaded coal
placed toward the front. By mid-century, however, many firemen were poorly
paid laborers who lacked the skills of their peers from an earlier time when steam
engines were rare. As a result, most engines belched black smoke. There were a
few cases before 1850 of irate residents forcing emitters to switch to smokeless
anthracite coal, but this was exceptional.[86]

As a pollutant, smoke was exceptional because of the legislative attention it
received as early as the 1820s, when Parliament passed one of the first anti-smoke
acts on the instigation of the City of Durham MP Michael Angelo Taylor. The act
compelled steam engine owners to use a smoke-consuming apparatus, but lack-

ing any enforcement provision, the act was a dead letter. It was not until the mid-1840s that there were renewed attempts to pass legislation. More public pressure came to bear on politicians as it became clearer that smoke abatement was possible. Another cause for reluctance was that it was not evident just how harmful smoke pollution was; indeed, it was considered beneficial in some cases, such as for some chest conditions. This began to change in late nineteenth century as smoke was clearly identified as "pollution."[87] Moreover, furnace owners came to understand that smoke suppression could be in their interest, as black smoke represented lost fuel. Industrial interests, however, were still predominantly against legislation, and six bills went down to defeat in Parliament by 1850. Finally, in 1851 John Simon succeeded in getting a clause inserted in a City of London Sewers Act that allowed the MOH and his nuisance inspectors to prosecute offenders.[88] In the first year Simon reported that 115 offenders had been notified.[89] The Smoke Nuisance Abatement (Metropolis) Act followed in 1853, with an amendment in 1856. It allowed the Home Office to employ inspectors of nuisance working for the police to prosecute smoke nuisances and levy fines of £5 to £10. The act also established the expectation that smoke emitters use the "best practicable means" to diminish smoke, a phrase repeated often in later laws applied to other forms of pollution. The act applied to "every furnace employed or to be employed in any mill, factory, printing-house, dye-house, iron foundry, glasshouse distillery, brewhouse, sugar refinery, bakehouse, gasworks, waterworks or other buildings." Because of its loose wording, however, judges often dismissed charges.[90] About 150 convictions followed in 1854, rising to nearly 700 in 1860.[91] By 1887 there were ten full-time smoke inspectors enforcing its provisions. Despite this activity, the effectiveness of the act was marginal: the fines were too low to deter industrial polluters unless applied repeatedly, and many moved to the east, outside the inspectors' jurisdiction in the areas covered by the MBW.[92] Furthermore, the powers of nuisance inspectors were weakened in the 1870s. This occurred when a judge extended the reach of a clause from the 1855 Nuisance Removal Act that had prevented inspectors from acting against mines to all industries that used the products of mines, effectively sheltering all trades using minerals.[93] In addition, by the 1880s the fines levied by courts were often less than 10 shillings, not enough to cover the costs of the prosecution. This left little motivation for action.[94] Polluters also could defend themselves with the claim that they were applying the "best practicable means," even as terrible pollution continued.[95] For example, in 1906 an electrical generating station in Chelsea was prosecuted for producing black smoke, but the case was dismissed on these grounds.[96]

As bad as industrial smoke was in London, domestic fires constituted an even bigger problem. Londoners had switched from burning wood to coal in large numbers by the seventeenth century.[97] Domestic smoke grew far worse in the

Figure 6.1. *Royal Gun Factory, Woolwich Arsenal, London: The Factory Buildings Seen from Above.* Lithograph by G. Clausen, 1917. Courtesy of Wellcome Collection, CC BY 4.0, https://wellcomecollection.org/works/s378brxz?query=Royal%20Gun%20Factory %2C%20Woolwich%20Arsenal%2C%20London%3A%20the%20factory%20buildings %20seen%20from%20above.%20. This image is believed to be out of copyright.

nineteenth century as London's population grew. In 1892 Chelsea's MOH estimated that 95 percent of London's smoke came from domestic sources. The pea-soup fogs grew thicker and more common over the century. They reached a peak of around seventy days per year between 1870 and the early 1890s.[98] Despite this, it was industry, not domestic stoves, that Parliament continued to legislate against to abate smoke. Anti-smoke clauses were added to the Sanitary Acts passed in 1858 and 1866, as well as the Public Health Act of 1875. Political agitation in the capital led to the formation of the Smoke Abatement Committee in 1880, which put on a Smoke Abatement Exhibition in South Kensington to encourage people and companies to adopt the devices on display, such as low-smoke grates and stoves. It had little immediate legislative effect. Finally, the Public Health (London) Act of 1891 mandated that all furnaces, private ones excepted, consume their own smoke. There was, however, a fatal flaw in the wording that applied the injunction to "black smoke," without further definition. This meant that polluters could defend themselves by arguing their smoke was not black and even by mixing steam with their black smoke to make it gray, worsening the pollution but

Figure 6.2. A man covering his mouth with a handkerchief, walking through a smoggy London street. Source: *A London Fog, 1802.* Courtesy of Wellcome Collection, CC BY 4.0, https://wellcomecollection.org/works/mtjtuxwm?query=A%20man%20covering%20 his%20mouth%20with%20a%20handkerchief%2C%20walking%20through%20a%20 smoggy%20London%20street. This image is believed to be out of copyright.

evading sanction. It was not until 1926 that the word "black" was deleted from legislation.[99] To make matters worse, within London itself one of the most egregious offenders was the Woolwich Arsenal, which was exempt from anti-smoke legislation. Although residents and the Woolwich Board of Health complained bitterly, its managers made no effort to introduce smoke-abatement measures.[100]

Methods to reduce smoke had existed from the early nineteenth century, but they were slow to catch on. Johann Georg (later John George) Bodmer had patented a smoke-consuming device in 1834, which was installed by a Spitalfields brewery. The furnaces featured a rotating chain of bars within the fire chamber that carried coal forward into the heat of the flame, ensuring more complete combustion and less smoke. John Juckes designed another furnace based on this same principle in the 1850s.[101] By the 1860s the police reported that there were 8,272 furnaces in London.[102] Smoke in London did drop off after 1900 as meteorological conditions changed, gas replaced coal to a limited extent for heating and cooking, and the efficiency of both domestic and industrial furnaces improved. A definitive shift to smokeless fuels, which came only in the 1950s, finally did away with London's notorious fogs.[103]

OTHER INDUSTRIES: MANUFACTURED GAS, ENGINEERING, AND CONSTRUCTION

London was home to many other polluting industries in the nineteenth century. Probably the most important among these was manufactured gas. Although other significantly more polluting industries existed within the country, notably copper smelting and alkali production, none of these affected London. Gas, used for lighting and later in the nineteenth century for heating and cooking, was an urban industry. Many of London's largest industrial sites were gasworks. Of the sixty-six largest industrial sites, based on insurance data gathered in the 1880s, twenty-three were gasworks.[104] The industry began in the 1810s, with a few companies operating in Westminster and the City before 1820. The process of gas production involved heating coal in an oven with a low-oxygen environment to prevent combustion. The coal gave off methane, ethylene, and hydrogen, which were piped throughout the city to be burned for lighting and heating. The process also produced many toxic by-products, including hydrogen sulfide, ammonia, tar, and many other heavy hydrocarbons. The hydrogen sulfide, stinking and very poisonous, was removed from lighting gases mostly by a reaction with lime-water (calcium hydroxide), which produced sulfuric acid. The other by-products were condensed using cold water. At first little demand existed for these by-products, and gasworks simply dumped them into watercourses, all of which eventually led to the Thames. By the 1820s the river was becoming quite foul with sewage and gas effluent. Gasworks created a sheen of tar and oil on the water's surface, as well as milky slicks of foul-smelling lime, which killed fish in large numbers. City authorities brought several nuisance lawsuits against gas companies in the 1820s. This led to an oft-repeated cycle of indictments, promises of remedial action from gas companies (perhaps leading to the displacement of the effluent), and finally repeated injury, all with little overall effect. The indictments

Figure 6.3. *Gas Works, Near the Regent's Canal*, by Thomas H. Shepherd. Source: *Metropolitan Improvements, or London in the Nineteenth Century* (London: James Elmes, 1827). https://commons.wikimedia.org/wiki/File:Gas-works-near-regents-canal-1830.jpg. Reproduced under an Open Content license: https://commons.wikimedia.org/wiki /Commons:Reusing_content_outside_Wikimedia

and fines were mostly too small and easily avoided to force the companies into any effective action.[105] The failure to control gas pollution wreaked havoc on the Thames fishery. In 1827 a commission investigating the state of London's water supply revealed that the number of fishing boats had halved in just fifteen years, and salmon had disappeared from the river. The oily "gas-water" that looked like "'scum" on the river's surface, dumped by the companies at night, was the chief culprit among many suspects.[106]

Gas companies were prohibited by their incorporating acts from dumping effluent into rivers, but they had ignored this provision with impunity. The Lighting and Watching Act of 1830 gave local authorities the powers to initiate prosecutions against gas companies with penalties specified by the act, but it went no further than this. The Gasworks Clauses Act of 1847 specified a fine of £200 with an additional £20 per day that the nuisance continued.[107] None of these, however, created any sort of administrative bureaucracy as the Alkali Acts would. Nor did they make it easier for courts to find the gas companies guilty. Each case had to be tried individually through a nuisance indictment, with all the associated expense and uncertainty. The result was that gas companies continued to pollute water and air, to a large extent because the state manifested little interest in controlling its pollution.[108] What impetus there was in creating and maintaining state mechanisms for controlling pollution, especially of the Thames, was largely focused on sewage, in part because industrial interests stymied national legislation directed against their pollution in watercourses. This was true even after London's main drainage was completed in 1865.[109]

Some court judgments, however, could be harsh, such as the one against the Imperial Gas Company in 1854. A local resident, Samuel Broadbent, won £708 in compensation for damage to his fifteen acres of cropland arising from air pollution from the Chelsea gasworks. After the company expanded the gasworks the following year, he sued again, this time seeking an injunction for abatement. The Court of Chancery granted one, which was upheld on appeal, even in the House of Lords. Chemical analysis of the vegetation from the garden had shown it to be encrusted with sulfur and ammonia compounds. The company evaded the abatement order by purchasing Broadbent's land and removing the complainant. Of course, the remaining residents continued to complain of "painful difficulty of breathing, disturbed sleep, nausea, and headache."[110]

Despite the environmental horrors gasworks could produce, the worst could be mitigated. Two new methods for the purification of gas were introduced. The first relied on dry rather than wet lime, meaning that the purifier waste could be carted away rather than dumped into the river. This at least displaced the problem to where it caused fewer complaints. Alternately, the dry lime could be exposed to the air, which allowed most of the sulfur to evaporate. A second more important technical measure gas companies introduced in the 1850s was the use of iron oxide as a catalyst purifier. The iron oxide absorbed the hydrogen sulfur from the gas, and it was refreshed by exposure to air. The catalyst then gave off acid fumes. Both methods simply transformed water pollution into air pollution. Another improvement to gasworks pollution came with the introduction of scrubbers or condensers, similar to those used by the alkali industry. A new law mandated their use from 1881.[111] In addition, iron oxide purifiers could also be used to produce sulfuric acid rather than be allowed to vent their charges freely.

Gas companies came under more pressure when MOHs were created. This led in time to gas companies moving plants and pollution eastward and to adopting some forms of mitigation. For example, the City Gas Company was dumping liquid lime effluent into the Thames from its works at Whitefriars in 1847, leading the City to prosecute it for causing a nuisance.[112] When the court ordered the company to abate the nuisance, it introduced both dry lime and iron oxide purification with a 150-foot chimney to disperse the fumes. The odors about the plant, however, grew much worse, and a new complaint followed in 1856. Henry Letheby, the MOH for the City, reported on the cause of the odors to the sewers commission.[113] He stated that the company had done all it could, but the odors were terrible, causing people in the area to vomit.[114] The gasworks remained, however. It was closed only in 1873, after the Gas Light and Coke Company (GL&CC) bought it and many other gas companies, transferring gas production to the east once again. This was possible because of its massive gasworks at Beckton, which opened in 1870. This colossal site, one of the largest industrial plants in the metropolitan area, allowed the ever-expanding GL&CC to close or scale back its other plants.[115]

Another case from 1876 shows how nuisance suits could be effective and as a result drive pollution eastward. The West Ham Board of Health brought a major lawsuit against the GL&CC in 1876 for odors from its Bromley works in Canning Town. In a long and detailed trial, the judge found against the company because, although producing foul odors was part of the gas-making process, the GL&CC was doing more than this. It was bringing spent lime from other plants by barge and leaving it on the Bromley site to be aerated and buried, producing a tremendous nuisance. The court enjoined the company to abate the nuisance and pay legal costs. The company decided to dump the lime at Beckton instead.[116] As a result of its drift to the east, the GL&CC, which was the dominant gas company on the north side, was by the late 1870s making about 75 percent of its gas at three eastern sites: Bromley, Bow, and Beckton.[117]

There were several other major polluting industries, such as ammonia production. Parliament directed no specific legislative attention their way until late in the nineteenth century when some were placed under the alkali regime because they produced foul acidic emissions. In 1878 the Noxious Vapours Committee reported that fertilizer manufacturing caused the most complaints in London for vapors, followed by the potteries at Lambeth and the sulfate of ammonia works at Battersea. Hugh Wallace owned the Battersea works, and he had begun to manufacture ammonia sulfate on the site in the early 1870s. The plant had produced nitric and acetic acid for some time before that.[118] The new activities were so foul that the Wandsworth Board of Works prosecuted the company in 1877 for the "highly baleful fumes ..., not only odious and sickening to the smell, but distinctly injurious to health." Wallace & Co. would dump ammoniacal liquor mixed with hydrogen sulfide at steaming hot temperatures into the sewers whenever it received too much from a nearby gasworks, which was its regular source. There was even a pipe running directly between the two sites. The nuisance was so egregious that in response the MBW passed a bylaw in 1877 giving it powers to regulate the manufacture of ammonia.[119] Finally, Wallace was convicted in 1877 at the Croydon assizes and ordered to pay £2,000 in legal costs, and a further £3,000 should the nuisance resume. The firm soon collapsed into bankruptcy; although industrial interests sometimes evaded prosecution and influenced legislation, they could not always prevail.[120]

Another significant source of industrial pollution in London was large engineering and machine works. The largest was the huge government-owned Royal Arsenal in Woolwich, founded in the seventeenth century. It grew significantly in the nineteenth century when it contained a large munitions plant, and by 1911 it employed 3,211 people. Ironically, given its complaints about fumes from the Thames chemical plants, it too produced many emissions, mostly in the form of smoke, as described above.[121]

Other large engineering and machine production sites proliferated in the late nineteenth century, stretching to the outer reaches of the capital. North of the River Thames, the publicly owned Enfield Small Arms factory was established far up the Lea Valley in 1815, employing from 2,400 to 3,200 workers for the rest of the century. South of the Thames, Deptford, Greenwich, Lewisham, and Woolwich had larger plants concentrating on marine boilers and engines, railway equipment, armaments, and other space-hungry activities.[122] Shipbuilding contained some of London's largest enterprises, employing up to 2,000 men. The Thames Estuary dominated British shipbuilding in the early nineteenth century, but this ended before the outbreak of the Great War, as firms sought lower wages in cities such as Glasgow.[123] Like the Royal Arsenal, these sites produced large volumes of smoke from furnaces and engines. Air and water pollution received nearly almost all the attention, but these industries also contaminated workers' bodies and the environment with large quantities of asbestos, lead, and other toxic substances. Occupational health became a significant medical and political issue after 1910.[124]

Manufactures of stoneware were also substantial polluters. The largest was Doulton & Co., located in Lambeth across the river from the Houses of Parliament. Originally known as Doulton &Watts, John Doulton had established it in 1815. It grew throughout the nineteenth century, employing six hundred people by 1878. This figure reached two thousand by 1900.[125] The glazing of stone involved throwing salt onto white-hot ceramic, producing muriatic (hydrochloric) acid fumes, which were vented to the atmosphere. The plant's fumes came to be called the "Lambeth fog," which ate away at surrounding buildings and greenery. Lambeth Palace was located nearby, and in 1877 Archbishop Archibald Tait complained of the destruction of his trees, as well as his silverware and books. Trees planted in 1871 as far away as the Albert Embankment were also dead by 1878. Like other acid fume nuisances, stone glazers came under the Alkali Acts in 1881 and were forced to condense their acid fumes.[126] Ironically, Henry Doulton had been a complainant twenty years earlier against the London Gas Company's lime pollution at its Vauxhall works. When someone at the inquiry pointed out to him that his own works shrouded the neighborhood in fog, he rejoined that he merely produced smoke, not the gasworks' "foul yellow vapors."[127] Under the new regulatory regime, the company rebuilt the plant in 1882 with tall chimneys to disperse the fumes and smoke.[128] The company also reduced the quantity of salt used, diminishing the fumes further.[129] Despite this, Doulton was the subject of a lawsuit by the Church of England as a result of alleged damages to Westminster Abbey and Lambeth Palace in 1900, although it was dismissed.[130]

There were still more polluting manufacturing industries. In 1885 Alfred Spencer, who was by this time the MBW's chief officer in the sanitary division, listed among these others brick and ballast burning, cement making, tar distilling, iron galvanizing, pottery production, papermaking, India rubber making, palm oil bleaching, and varnish making. Among the worst were brick and ballast burning, which produced "nuisances consist[ing] in the pungent and irritating emanations, mostly also of a putrid character, which are given off in immense volume during the processes." "Ballast" referred to the rough material used for road construction, which was prepared by firing clay removed from building sites. The most offensive odors were produced when the bricks or clay were fired with waste in open heaps rather than in kilns. Ballast was typically made on building sites where the clay was dug.[131] In 1888 the MOH for Kensington prosecuted three brick burners. Two of them agreed to cease operations, while the third lost his appeal and was found liable for damages and forced to shut down.[132] The making of asphalt for paving also caused pollution. In 1875 Limber, an asphalt company in Poplar, was indicted for nuisances caused to its neighbors, who were forced to keep their windows shut against smoke and odors. An earlier episode had prompted Letheby to suggest modifications to enclose their cauldrons, a step that diminished the problem, but not sufficiently.[133]

CONCLUSION

Industrial pollution in London could at times be intense, and action against it could be slow. This was not unusual throughout the country. In Manchester and other northern industrial towns antipollution campaigners gained very little support, even into the twentieth century.[134] Despite the relative ineffectiveness of reform efforts, London was nevertheless the center of debate, even as the sheer size of the city meant that no industry dominated like alkali production did in a town like St. Helens near Liverpool.[135] Moreover, industrial pollution never produced as acute crises as domestic pollution in the form of smoke and sewage, notably within the context of mid-century cholera panics, the "Great Stink" on the Thames in 1858, or the London fogs. Nevertheless, in some areas industrial pollution could be overwhelmingly severe. This was emphatically the case in the eastern dumping grounds. Attempts to control industrial pollution were partly dependent on what the national government was willing to do, and partly on the ability of local authorities to use the powers given them. In many cases, they were passive. Although the City was often vigorous from the 1850s on, most other districts took little action. Improvements came only when the MBW, and later the

LCC, obtained powers to regulate offensive trades. Up to the 1870s industrial pollution was regarded as a sanitary problem creating opportunities for inspectors of nuisances to act against it. After that "pollution" increasingly formed a discrete category and was the object of scientific discourse.[136]

The local lethargy of the earlier period can be explained partly by the presence of industrialists on the local boards that were supposed to prosecute them. The difficulties in winning cases and the uncertain effectiveness of any success in court also made authorities reluctant to act. Smoke nuisance fines were a case in point: they were simply too small to be any more than a petty expense for emitters. The ineffectiveness of action was exacerbated by the uncertainty over whether chemical industries, although causing foul nuisances, were indeed harmful to health.[137] Moreover, the exemption given to London in many forms of national legislation caused delays until Parliament passed specific acts covering the city.

Despite all this, attempts to control pollution had evident effects throughout the nineteenth century. The organic trades were much reduced within the Metropolis, even if economic factors were important motivators of this change. Parliament also brought more industries under the Alkali Acts regime after 1881, including factories producing sulfuric acid, fertilizer, and sulfate of ammonia.[138] While it is not clear to what extent this was effective, more industries were in principle supposed to install scrubbers. Smoke pollution took longer to be mitigated, but it declined from a peak in the 1890s. Finally, nuisance lawsuits, although fraught with difficulty, scored a few notable victories. Much of this success, however, came at the cost of the wretchedness of eastern London, where polluters faced less scrutiny and more effective opposition.

SEVEN

WATER AND ITS MEANINGS IN LONDON

1800–1914

VANESSA TAYLOR

"Water has a nearly unlimited ability to carry metaphors," as Ivan Illich pointed out. His philosophical essay on H_2O, published in 1986, was a hymn to the richness and ambiguity of water but also a lament for its "lost . . . ability to mirror the water of dreams."[1] Though marginal within London's environmental historiography, Illich's insightful depiction of the problems of engineered water crystallizes a paradox also found in many recent narratives of the Victorian capital's changing relationship to its water. The paradox is that although London's water provision expanded massively during the nineteenth century—constant tapped supply reached much of the city by 1900—there is a pervasive sense in accounts of this period that the meaning of water became somehow narrower and that access to it was restricted in important ways. The industrialization of water supply, the rise of water expertise, and private ownership of London's water networks have all been implicated in this process of restriction. This chapter explores the complex meanings of water in London at a time of major change in the light of this tension between expansion and restriction. Though the critique of triumphalist accounts of the development of a clean water supply is crucial for understanding this period, I argue that water lost none of its richness of meaning. This is because radically different understandings of water—what it was, what it was for, who had a right to it—remained crucial to political debates over price, quality, quantity, and conditions of access during this period. Equally, it is because water is never simply abstract and cannot be stripped of meaning. Its meanings remain as variable as its material presence in people's everyday lives.

Understanding the changing meaning of water in the industrializing city is part of a wider question of cities' relationship to the natural world. Cities prove to be as metaphorical as water. Environmental historians and political ecologists in recent years have illuminated the interaction between urban and natural processes at the heart of city life. Cities depend on the inward flow of natural resources, the outward flow of waste, and the balance between them (the city is an "urban metabolism"). The "urbanization of nature" itself entails the "discursive representation of nature as a 'resource.'"[2] The idea of water as "hydro-social" conveys its "hybridity," always embodying social, economic, and political power as well as "nature."[3] Recent historical and geographical literature employs an abundance of metaphors to describe the expanding role of water in the economies and socio-technical systems of London and other major nineteenth-century cities: the "sanitary city," "hydraulic city," "state hydraulic paradigm," "networked city," "public city," "city of flows." The image of the "archipelago," referring to uneven and inequitable islands of provision today in the global South, partly captures London's variable Victorian networks, fragmented by different providers, topographies, political boundaries, economic inequalities, and competing claims on rivers and sources.[4] But no single metaphor will do. This chapter tells a story of dominant ideologies and of technological systems that "scripted" behavior, but also of water's dense entanglement in the life of the city which defied any script.[5]

London's geology, elevation, climate, and flows of resources and wastes shaped its nineteenth-century "waterscape."[6] Its rivers and water bodies formed a dynamic ecosystem, with fluctuating tides, pollutants, temperatures, and capacity to sustain life. Its networked flows could be legislated for, treated, and managed, but also could break out in disease, drought, or flood with the "lively capacities of [all] biophysical systems."[7] Water's meanings could not be contained because it saturated the city, washing through industries, everyday life, and political entitlements, and through understandings of disease and health. The same element that threatened inhabitants with changing categories of impurities also rose up through South London basements in heavy rains and surged in from the North Sea during storms. It cleaned kitchen utensils and clothes, its "hardness" using up more soap than in "soft water" cities. It was the estuary's Black Deep where London's sewage was dumped from the 1890s and came back with the tide like the return of the repressed. It cleansed the streets from local authority carts, transported world shipping, and entered the docks and markets as "virtual water" in fruit, meat, and vegetables. It was the free water from public pumps, sold by street

Fig. 7.1. Vere Street, Lambeth, and its inhabitants, 1850. Low-lying Thames-side districts were subject to annual tidal flooding. This decorous image belies the destruction caused by powerful floods from the polluted river. The late January spring tide was reported to be the highest in two decades. Source: "The High Tide—Overflow of the Thames, 1850." © Museum of London Picture Library, Image No. 010376. Reproduced with permission.

sellers of ginger beer and sherbet, and God's "living water" flowing from charitable drinking fountains. It diluted milk and the beer of unscrupulous licensed victuallers, powered steam engines and water mills, supplied the steam baths of the East End Jewish population, and watered the lawns of suburban villas. It swelled and burst household pipes in frost, and failed in standpipes and cisterns during drought. It was the River Lea, thick with dyes, sewage, and heavy metals, and the groundwater waiting in London's chalk, extolled by speculators as "inferior only to claret."[8] All these manifestations had their changing social worlds, their competing interests, political debates, their statutory frameworks or vacuums.

This multifaceted, mercurial nature of water is intrinsic to its meanings, destabilizing any single narrative. Throughout this period, it was simultaneously a natural element, a force of nature, a manufactured product, and a tool. This created the conditions for intractable debates over the rights of Londoners, despite the emergence of dominant policy frameworks. The "meanings" of water—what it was, where it flowed, its benefits and risks, and what you could do with it—all underwent dramatic changes in the capital over the nineteenth century. These changes shaped but were also shaped by the lives of those who used the water.

The mode of this chapter is predominantly thematic rather than chronological. But to help readers on their way, a brief summary is given here of the major conventional landmarks relating to water supply in the nineteenth-century capital. The narrative begins with the rapid expansion of commercial piped supplies in the early 1800s, broadly charting changing conditions of supply until the public takeover of London's water companies in the early twentieth century. A shift from highly fragmented and intermittent provision to constant supply ("on tap") in the home was a key development. The rise of public health concerns over polluted water in nineteenth-century London is most famously associated with outbreaks of epidemic disease, especially cholera (1831–1832, 1848–1849, 1853–1854, 1866) and typhoid (which was also endemic). The identification of cholera as a waterborne disease, following the discoveries of the physician John Snow and others in the 1850s, was borne out by the new science of bacteriology in the 1880s; these were part of a wider contemporary shift toward professionalized, expert knowledge about water. At the same time a more mixed group of public agitators, sanitarians, moral reformers, and urban administrators kept a fight for clean water and improved sanitation at the forefront of political debate in mid-Victorian London. Sanitary improvements were supported equally by those still wedded to "miasmatic" theories of disease (conveyed by atmosphere and smell) and by the newer "contagionists" who saw water as bearing specific "germs."[9]

The 1850s marked a turning point in the environmental governance of London. New quality regulations for London's water supply were introduced in 1852. A "Great Stink"—the sensory implosion of the sewage-laden Thames in 1858—finally created enough pressure for a new sewage system (beneath a grand Embankment) in the 1860s and 1870s. Later problems in the lower Thames were signaled by the *Princess Alice* collision of 1878: the many hundreds who died were suspected to have been poisoned rather than drowned in the effluent issuing from the new downstream pumping stations. Across the city, however, there were indications—most reliably in the falling numbers of typhoid deaths— that London was becoming healthier, its mortality rates comparing favorably with other British and European cities by the 1870s.[10] A more democratic, pan-metropolitan approach to urban management was promised by the creation of the London County Council (LCC) in 1889. The LCC sought to tackle ongoing river pollution with a fleet of barges conveying sewage sludge to the lower estuary, an arrangement that continued for one hundred years. But the efforts of LCC "Progressives" to take over the private water supply were frustrated by the government's creation in 1902 of a separate quango, the Metropolitan Water Board (MWB), to manage the supply for the whole of Greater London. The board remained in charge until the 1970s.

The following section traces the main developments in London's water and sanitary provision, and explores themes of improvement and dispossession in the historiography of London's water. The second section addresses the contested status of water as a manufactured commodity at odds with nature. The role of changing forms of domestic supply in everyday London life is the focus of the third section.

WATER AND PUBLIC HEALTH: IMPROVEMENT AND DISPOSSESSION

Eight private water companies supplied London for most of the nineteenth century. Some, such as the New River Company (1619) and Chelsea Waterworks (1723), were already well established at the start of this period. Most of the others, including the East London Waterworks Company (1807), were newcomers. By 1820, after acrimonious competition in the early 1800s, the companies operated as "natural monopolies" in separate districts.[11] (Natural monopoly, arising from the capital-intensive nature of the infrastructure, "naturally" seemed to require a single operator.) There were no new undertakings until the creation of the MWB.[12] Company water served domestic, commercial and industrial customers, and local authorities. From the early 1800s large industrial consumers such as brewers invested heavily in their own independent artesian wells.[13]

Potable company supplies were intermittent for most people until the final decades of the century, supplied for a few hours every other day or (from the 1850s) daily, excluding Sundays. Many poor households shared a single water butt or common standpipe in courts and alleys for much of the century. But there were numerous ad-hoc arrangements for getting hold of water in the age before household taps. Edwin Chadwick's 1850 report on the London supplies described poor riverside areas in Bermondsey and Lambeth where people depended on the Thames and tidal ditches for their water.[14] In Southwark in 1843 thirty thousand people occupying five thousand tenements were reported to have no company provision, relying on public "pumps or such rain-water as they can catch." Some nineteenth-century Londoners witnessed great changes. One ninety-nine-year-old Islington resident, a Mrs. Malins, looking back in 1908 to her childhood, remembered supplies collected from "water-butts, " or "filled from the New River, except in frosty weather, when the donkies [sic] brought pails round for sale."[15] "Constant supply," introduced gradually from the mid-century, brought most Londoners closer to tapped water by 1900, though there remained stark differences in provision.[16]

London's suppliers struggled to meet the requirements of a rapidly rising population during the nineteenth century. At just under a million in 1800, the population increased by around a fifth each decade up to the 1890s; the city boundaries also expanded. The capital held 6.5 million people by 1901, representing a fifth of the population of England and Wales.[17] At the time of the MWB's takeover in 1904, "Water London" (London's supply area) contained around 6.75 million people, with 1.02 million domestic, trade, and industrial customers.[18] Population expansion, new sanitary technology, and sanitary regulations had brought water supplies and human waste into damaging proximity by the early decades of the nineteenth century. Connections between water closets (WCs) and the capital's rainwater sewers were legally permitted from 1815 and were compulsory from 1847.[19] These sewers discharged directly into the tidal Thames—the city's main water source. At the same time overused cesspools from the earlier waste regime leached into neighboring water courses and shallow public wells. The impact of sewage and other effluents on water sources and human health was the focus of repeated public health scares and debate from the 1820s.[20] Over the next twenty years an increasing sanitarian focus on clean water emerged as the key to preventing zymotic diseases, such as typhoid and cholera. Londoners became increasingly separated from their water sources and sewage during the mid-nineteenth century. The 1852 Metropolis Water Act obliged companies to draw their Thames water from the river above Teddington Lock (west of London), to filter supplies, and to cover reservoirs within five miles of St. Paul's Cathedral in the heart of the City.[21] Public pumps and wells were condemned and closed in the 1850s and 1860s, increasing people's reliance on company supplies. Sewage problems in the Thames—finally deemed intolerable when the "Great Stink" descended on the riverside Parliament in the hot summer of 1858—led to a new "main drainage" system in the 1860s, conveying London's waste to pumping stations far downstream. When pollution concerns reignited in the 1870s, they focused on the Thames below London.

Were London's rivers "irrevocably polluted?"[22] Could they provide for its future needs? Despite expanding provision in the late 1800s, these questions persisted alongside widespread conflicts over prices and quantities. Water users and sanitary reformers were frequently pitted against water companies over possible links between their supply and disease. Inequalities between people living in different parts of the city's water networks became increasingly clear. Although the 1853–1854 cholera epidemic is best known for deaths in Soho linked to the Broad Street pump, it implicated the Southwark & Vauxhall Waterworks Company above all, with 3,476 dying in their district (out of a London total of 10,739).[23] The East London Waterworks Company was widely held responsible for the 1866 epidemic, with deaths from cholera in its "waterfield" (including West Ham, then in Essex) amounting to 4,286 out of a total of 5,973 for the whole of London, West Ham, and Stratford.[24] Investigations following the 1866 outbreak found that the East London company had habitually used an illegal source (an uncovered reservoir at Old Ford) as a backup when stocks were low, and that groundwater linked to the heavily polluted River Lea was leaching into the company's covered reservoirs.[25] Local property owners forming a pressure group (the East London Water Supply Association) condemned the Lea as "nothing else than an open sewer," and demanded constant supply and an official inquiry.[26] One of the reports on the 1866 cholera, by Registrar General William Farr, lent weight to calls for distant water transfers that were to persist for the rest of the century. "By a whole host of terrible diseases," Farr wrote, "God forbids the consumption of contaminated waters": "the pure waters, which are the very life-blood of cities, must be sought in the hills or river-heads."[27] A debate over whether polluted public supplies or defective domestic cisterns were to blame for disease was not resolved until "mains water" taps replaced intermittent supply cisterns.[28] The problems with privately owned supplies generated calls for public water management throughout the century, from early arguments for parish supplies to late Victorian pan-London schemes.

The sanitarian insistence on improved supplies and sewerage as the pre-eminent public health measure looks like simple common sense. Typified by centralizer Edwin Chadwick, a commissioner of the General Board of Health (1848–1854) and secretary of the Poor Law Commission, the image of clean water remains central to popular visions of the problems and solutions of Victorian cities to this day. But within the social history of medicine a different picture has emerged.[29] A 1986 history of the Thames emphasized the socially constructed nature of distinctions between clean and dirty water, and of the sense of environmental crisis that dominated debates about the mid-century river. Other studies have argued that Chadwick's obsession with pipes and sewers as the foundation of "public health" represented a new approach to poverty as much as a new medical paradigm. Destitution as an effect of dirty water and disease replaced older ideas about destitution as a cause of disease. This new public health, argues Christopher Hamlin, shaped the boundaries of "state medicine" (what the state was and was not responsible for).[30] At the same time an increasingly professionalized expert domain in the nineteenth century is seen to have supplanted the senses— sight, taste and smell—as a source of knowledge available to all. For Hamlin this process helped to complete a transformation from "waters" to "water": "Water went from a class of infinitely varied substances to a monolithic substance containing a greater or lesser concentration of adventitious ingredients, known as 'impurities.'" The identification of cholera as a waterborne disease in the 1850s further narrowed the conception of water.[31] Hamlin's interpretation of this process has an echo of Illich's story of the death of "living water." The geographer Jamie Linton too has recently characterized the rise of a hegemonic, instrumental view of water, divorced from both society and nature, as a "disenchantment" of water.[32]

A theme of dispossession also underlies historical accounts of Londoners' changing physical access to their water bodies. The new sewerage and embankments built in the 1860s and 1870s feature prominently here. In the capital's centuries-long struggle between land and water, the embankments were a win for land—for property developers, local authorities, the new underground transport system: "Some fifty-two acres of prime real estate were literally dredged out of the river," as Dale Porter puts it. In one account, the way the embankments separated London's poor Thames-side populations from the river was a process repeated in the domain of knowledge. The late nineteenth-century Thames was "transformed . . . into an object of study and simultaneously distanced . . . from everyday structures and processes."[33] For the archaeologist Hanna Steyne, writing more recently, the displacement of the poor and those engaged in marine and river trades by the embankments was a form of "enclosure of the commons," similar to the enclosing of the docks sixty years earlier. The geographer Stephen Oliver has suggested that the embankment provided something that Victorian Londoners needed psychically: the solid granite containment of the river's disorderly boundaries and the creep of disease.[34]

The idea of the Thames as a commons that became enclosed is to some extent misleading. Rivers are in many ways unsuited to private property claims. They flow across property and political boundaries, carrying "externalities" of pollution, overuse, and flooding, as well as shared benefits. There are always competing claims on a river for drainage, water supply, and navigation. But urban rivers such as the Thames have long been intimately tied to property rights. There have been some rights for the riverbank, others for the foreshore, and legal disputes over the river's uncertain relationship to nearby groundwater. Ownership of the riverbed formed the core of an argument between the Crown and the City Corporation with the longevity (if not the poetry) of a Wagnerian epic. Only the establishment of the Thames Conservancy in 1857 ended the battle. The stream of water was free for navigation but restricted for other uses, such as moorings, and abstraction for supply.[35] Nevertheless the idea of London's water, and the Thames, as a natural commons is not simply a scholarly creation. It infused nineteenth-century debates. George Shaw-Lefevre, a Liberal Progressive on the LCC, expressed a widespread view when calling for the public takeover of supply in 1898: "The day is at hand when London will . . . come into possession of the heritage from which it ought never to have been dispossessed, the supply of its own water."[36]

Critical approaches to Victorian improvements in scientific knowledge, public health, and urban infrastructure are essential to our understanding of the implications of "clean water." They tell us a great deal about how these developments created losers as well as winners, how they may have reduced popular rights and access to water even as public supplies were expanding and becoming safer. It is argued here, however, that water's meanings remained irreducibly plural in the face of pressures to surrender the capital's water to the realm of experts, policy makers, and private property. These pressures could be found in many Victorian cities. London was exceptional in having the largest body of water users concentrated in one place, in making the most voracious demands on resources, and as the center of political life. The problems of its rivers and supply took on an importance in national debates that was unmatched in any other British city in this period.

COMMODIFIED NATURE

Improvements in London's water in the nineteenth century—in both scientific expertise and infrastructure—may have been double-edged, as we have seen, in narrowing the conceptions of water and reducing public access. Contemporary voices expressed this sense of restricted access. The increased commodification of water with expanding piped networks only added to the sense among many in London that water as a natural "public good" was under threat. Equally important, I look at the sometimes contradictory ways in which Londoners perceived water as "nature" and at forces that disrupted the idea of water as a commodity.

It has not proved possible to find a fixed baseline for water in its natural state. "Perfectly pure water does not exist in nature," as the 1869 Royal Commission on Water Supply report put it. For Christopher Hamlin, the compound H_2O was already the outcome of a narrowed, eighteenth-century conception. Illich, writing in 1980s Dallas, saw H_2O as the "stuff which industrial society creates." Conversely, for the political ecologist Maria Kaika, H_2O is the "natural element" which when transformed into "potable, clean . . . water" becomes "a socially produced commodity embodying powerful cultural and social meanings." Severed from its role as "mere use value," it then supports an array of new commodities—from hygiene regimes to swimming pools.[37] This transformation is worth looking at more closely because the tension between water as nature or as something else lay at the heart of nineteenth-century debates.

Material and discursive dispossession is an important theme in political ecologists' critiques of water commodification over the past twenty years—a time of expanding marketization of water globally and of numerous struggles over the corporate acquisition of local supplies. For Kaika, this commodification is a condition of modernity. The nineteenth-century "urban sanitation conquest brought water squarely into the sphere of money, cultural capital, and power relations." Drawing on Marx's concept of commodity fetishism, she describes the process by which water's transformation into a commodity erases not only its unique natural properties but also the commodification process itself: "Blurring the socioenvironmental process of their [commodities'] production by grounding their character as universally exchangeable for anything else is an amazingly powerful ideological mechanism. . . . Acquiring exchange value, without revealing at the same time the social power relations of their production, permits commodities to be presented as exceptional, as *outside* and *over* the thing that really make them exceptional, i.e., the social metabolism of nature."[38] There are two important problems with this analysis in the case of nineteenth-century London. First, it is difficult to distinguish between water's "mere use value" and the array of other uses to which it could always be put. Suppliers and administrators trying to draw lines between basic necessities, luxuries, and waste were up against a widespread view among truculent London water consumers that needs would "naturally" expand.[39] The next section returns to this theme.

Second, Londoners challenged the social relations of the commercial networks from the outset. A well-developed market for water existed in the capital long before the great nineteenth-century expansion. For some historians this early modern market replaced a previous "moral economy of the [public] conduit." By 1804, according to one estimate, six London waterworks already supplied over 80,000 of the estimated 105,000 properties in their areas.[40] Greater reliance on piped supplies and the decline of alternatives to the market were mutually reinforcing. The increasing use of open water courses, such as the River Fleet, for (legal and illegal) waste disposal in the eighteenth century led to their condemnation as "nuisances" and subsequent culverting—a "tragedy of the commons." At the same time, as Carry van Lieshout has shown, company powers to "lock-up" more and more water in pipes over the course of the eighteenth century created a path dependency.[41] The abandonment of London's polluted tidal river as a public source and the closure of its public wells in the 1850s and 1860s sealed this process. The nineteenth century saw the decisive expansion of networks that established some form of access to piped supply as the norm for most Londoners. Writing off polluted public watercourses reflected a view by this point, at national and local levels, that supply could legitimately be consigned to the marketplace.

But many rejected this view. Arguments over public access to piped supplies returned repeatedly to the tension between water as natural and freely available, and water as a manufactured product. The Anti-Water Monopoly Association of the early 1800s followed an eighteenth-century tradition of protest against water industry price fixing. At a Parliamentary inquiry in 1821, the group's chairman called for local authority control of supplies and free provision for the poor. "Water," he said, "must be considered . . . one of the elements necessary to existence, the same as light and air, and not merely as an article of subsistence like corn, nor of convenience like coal; and therefore its artificial supply to a great city ought not to be the subject of . . . any kind of trade."[42] Over forty years later the Reverend Charles Kingsley, novelist, priest, and sanitarian, similarly called for public ownership of water—and also gas. Here the right of "the people, the Commons" to "comforts, and even luxuries" symbolized political as well as material entitlements: "We, the people, will have our fountains; if it be but to make our governments, and corporations, . . . remember that they all—save Her Majesty the Queen—are our servants, . . . and that we choose to have water, not only to wash with, but to play with, if we like."[43]

Late nineteenth-century discontent about London's provision led to political agitation for constant supply, fair prices, and public ownership as entitlements of citizenship. Progressive Liberalism in the new LCC after 1889 added a party-political voice to these demands. An important anomaly in water's status as a commodity strengthened its link to citizenship: water was charged not according to quantity supplied but as a percentage of property values, like other local rates. This set London and other British cities apart from most European and North American networked cities. Only now in the twenty-first century are Thames Water (the current supplier, private since 1989) installing meters in London households. At the end of the nineteenth century defenders of the capital's private industry were still trying to squash the idea of piped water as nature. The physician, journalist, and industry supporter Arthur Shadwell objected to a Water Consumer Defence League claim in 1898 that the East London company got their water "out of *our* rivers." The abstraction, treatment, and distribution of water changed everything, he insisted:

> Water *is* a gift of Nature, and every one *has* a moral right to it—in the river. Or it may be in the earth or in the clouds. But water laid on in the house is *not* a gift of Nature. Nor does the . . . company by cutting it off deprive any one . . . of the necessaries of life; it only deprives him of the convenience of drawing it from a tap. He can still do what he would have had to do had there been no water company. . . . He can take his bucket to the river or to some well, or he can pay some one else to do it for him.[44]

But for the six million inhabitants of Greater London by this point, access to non-piped supplies was not just inconvenient. The networked commodification of urban water represented the failure to maintain alternatives in the modern city, but it did not obscure water's transformation into a commodity.

So was water a special kind of commodity in this period? For all the talk of nature and necessities, claims to water rights were highly adaptable and tied to debates over some distinctly non-natural goods. Water activism ran parallel to campaigns over gas (manufactured from coal), which was slowly spreading through the streets and households of London and other British towns from the 1820s. As networked services became embedded in daily life for increasing numbers of Londoners, they generated similar complaints about monopoly suppliers, high prices, and quality, and their regulation took some similar forms from the 1840s. The historian Martin Daunton has pointed out that the nature of domestic gas as an "invisible commodity" (about which the consumer could not be expected to "make an informed decision") led to increasing government regulation of gas standards and pricing.[45] The transfer of water to the realm of experts—capable of identifying impurities unperceived by ordinary people—arguably brought potable water closer to gas as an "invisible commodity" over time, especially with the rise of bacteriology, though sight, smell, and taste remained important alarms for water users. For Daunton the state's backing of campaigns for fair gas prices and protection from monopolies was "a sign that the market in Victorian Britain was permeated with notions of morality." Gas, like water, promised to "moralize" public and domestic spaces: streets and homes that were lighter and cleaner could improve working-class living standards.[46] But water remained a special commodity. It was undeniably essential for life. Agitators could shift at will between its status as natural and as a potentially polluted product from which they required protection. And it retained spiritual and moralizing powers that no other product could match.

The muscle-bound reclining river gods of eighteenth- and nineteenth-century London—created by sculptors John Bacon (1780s) and Raffaelle Monti (1850s) for the Thames, and Joseph Theakston (1811) for the Lea—embodied metropolitan aspirations for prestige, sacred timelessness, and civic amenity that invoked imperial Rome.[47] In practice they were also symbols of hubris and a gift to satirists. "Old Father Thames" was a favorite with *Punch* magazine's cartoonists from the 1840s onward, which they showed dripping with pollution and recrimination against London's failing institutions, both public and private.[48]

The mid-nineteenth-century fusion between public health, cleanliness, and morality lent new layers of meaning to water. From the "water drinkers" of teetotalism to Chadwick's calls for dirty children to be driven from the streets, water was harnessed to campaigns for an improved social order. Water became a disciplinary tool in this period, as historians engaging with Foucault's work have demonstrated.[49] A "really strong caretaker," a Bethnal Green policeman told one of Charles Booth's poverty surveyors in 1898, could instill an effective "sense of orderliness" into the inhabitants of housing blocks: "Once you get these people

Fig. 7.2. Industrial riverscape, ca. 1800. This watercolor shows a river god in the making at Eleanor Coade's Artificial Stone Manufactory in South London. Note also the water pump used for the process. A Coade stone river god today sits outside Ham House, Richmond. Source: George Shepherd, "Westminster Bridge Road," ca. 1800. © London Metropolitan Archives, City of London. COLLAGE: The London Picture Archive, ref. 19373. Reproduced with permission.

driven to cleanliness for their own sakes . . . you have won half the battle . . . for they know that if they do not act up to a certain standard they will be turned out." In "The Edwardians," a major oral history project carried out in the 1970s, Whitechapel resident William East (born 1897) recalled being required to take turns with the weekly window washing and hearth-stoning of the stairs in his model Peabody Estate housing block, with the superintendent checking the work.[50] Charles Kingsley, writing in the 1870s, preferred a more voluntarist approach for a similar moral outcome. Nature itself can be seen as a tool of "self-governance" here; it drew people to the light: "every fresh drinking-fountain, . . . every fresh public bath and wash-house, . . . every fresh open window, every fresh flower in that window . . . is so much, as the old Persians would have said, conquered for Ormuzd, . . . so much taken from the causes of drunkenness and disease."[51] Over three hundred public baths had been built across British towns by 1914. But the moral promises of water could never be completely fulfilled. Every "orderly" use of water had its less visible, unscripted side, as Thomas Crook shows in his work on the "misuse and re-appropriation" of cubicles at public baths—for convenience or pleasure.⁵² East Ender Mrs. Bella Curl (born 1898), spoke in "The Edwardians" of her work from the age of fourteen in baths at Mile End, Golden Street, Beck Street, and Ratcliffe: "There's things—secrets been told to me for— lots and lots of people and there's never a word said about it," she said. "You see things, well you just keep your mouth shut."⁵³

A resurgence of the principle of free, natural, even "enchanted" water, along- side the gradual expansion of commercial piped supply, can be seen in the work of the Metropolitan Drinking Fountain and Cattle Trough Association (MDFCTA; established 1859). This nationwide phenomenon had spread from Liverpool but London's effort was characteristically grander, supported by the capital's formi- dable philanthropic networks. By the 1890s the charity had helped install over a thousand fountains and troughs, most of them within London. The fountains were intended to provide clean (company) water as a sanitary and temperance gift for the residential and itinerant poor—those left behind by the expanding net- works.⁵⁴ This gift was not always appreciated. The fountains in the poor district of Canning Town were destroyed as quickly as they were replaced. The grand open- ing in June 1893 of the Shaftesbury Memorial Fountain ("Eros") in Piccadilly Cir- cus was followed by a night of enigmatic vandalism. Only two of the fountain's eight chained drinking cups remained the next morning. A third was "carefully broken and deposited in one of the basins, . . . no doubt meant as a malicious criticism," the designer Alfred Gilbert later recalled.⁵⁵ Nevertheless the fountains and troughs were widely used, if not always as intended. The West Middlesex Waterworks Company threatened to cut off a fountain's supply in Chiswick in 1868 because "people were in the habit of carrying [away] water . . . for domestic purposes." Magistrates' courts regularly heard reports of drivers recharging their traction engines at the troughs, road sweepers washing their carts, and passersby urinating in them. But the counts carried out by the charity also indicate real demand, undermining the persistent myth that Victorian Londoners drank beer rather than water. Nearly three thousand people drank at a fountain in the Inter- national Exhibition at South Kensington on a single October day in 1862. Over a thousand drinkers were counted at a fountain on the Embankment over twenty- four hours in October 1887, and another thousand near Vauxhall Bridge on the same day. Horses were also important users in the city, until they were replaced by motor vehicles: over 1,500 horses stopped to drink at a trough in Bishops- gate on an October morning in 1903; another 800 in the Old Kent Road. These structures, an important part of the "mixed economy of welfare" in Victorian and Edwardian London, coexisted alongside calls for improved domestic supply.⁵⁶

By the end of the nineteenth century, however, water was increasingly about rights not gifts, and the right to a constant tapped supply in particular. The East London Waterworks' high-profile failure to maintain supply during summer droughts in the 1890s revealed the vulnerability of the city's fragmented networks and the extent to which people of all classes in the district had come to depend on constant provision. The poor with no facilities for storage were particularly hit at those times.[57] Much political and technical debate centered on the extent to which these "water famines" were the company's fault or natural, "unusual droughts," exempting the company from liability. The East London Waterworks Company pointed out that rainfall in the Lea Valley during the first six months of 1895 (the year of "the Great Drought") was the "smallest ever recorded," but policy debates in the 1890s and 1900s remained highly polarized over the need for new, distant sources and the reasonable entitlements or wastefulness of domestic water users.[58] Tapped water had brought new perceptions of needs and entitlements in the late nineteenth century, while long-standing ideas about natural rights had become harnessed to a new ideal of "municipal socialism" in the provision of urban services in London and elsewhere. The turn to municipal water supply and other utilities across nineteenth- and early twentieth-century British cities did not reflect a single ideology; it was the outcome of numerous technical and political debates at the local level. When it came, the public take-over of London's supply was to some extent a technocratic response to market failures demonstrated by the recent droughts.[59] The creation of the MWB, as we have seen, disappointed LCC radicals. It supplied water on similar lines to the companies and maintained regulations about plumbing, "domestic purposes," and "waste." It guarded its sources as jealously as any private company, but it also equalized water rates across the city, achieved standardized provision over time, and met expanding demand. It represented official acceptance of the idea that a public provider could best serve the public interest, defusing popular tensions around supply.[60] The board's coat of arms, incorporating symbolism from the seals of the eight private water companies—with Hygeia, Aquarius, and raindrops falling from the hand of God—continued the companies' ambiguous evocation of the sacred source of the water being processed and sold.[61]

Londoners' claims about their water rights rarely acknowledged the territorial character of water as a public good—sourced in nature, but from geographically bounded areas.[62] The subtext of these rights was the increasing infringement of the "water-fields" of neighboring rural areas. The city had depended for centuries on its hinterland. The New River Company effectively had rights to "drain the Lea Valley dry," it was reported in 1892.[63] But where water came from and its journey to the user remained an ideologically charged element of scientific, political, and popular discourse into the late nineteenth century.[64] Many still condemned the Thames and Lea as water sources. Speaking of schemes to build reservoirs in the Thames valley in the 1890s, the LCC Progressive member B. F. C. Costelloe complained that this "would only in the end give us river water after all. . . . We in London," he said, "go on being content to use river water taken below vast and populous areas of sewage pollution, only because our fore-fathers drank something still worse."[65] The LCC campaign against these reservoirs revived earlier schemes for long-distance transfers. George Shaw-Lefevre's vision for London's future possession of its heritage was based on an LCC plan to bring 210 million gallons of water a day from the Welsh hills. The battles over supply in the twentieth century were increasingly those between London and surrounding areas, as the MWB looked farther afield to meet growing demand.[66] Demand was met by ever more intensive abstraction and by storage reservoirs in the Thames and Lea catchment areas. By 1907 just over 57 percent of the 225 million gallons pumped each day (estimated at 32.84 gallons per capita) was derived from the River Thames; just under 20 percent came from the Lea; almost 23 percent came from springs and wells; and some from gravel beds and other sources.[67]

EVERYDAY LIFE

While piped commercial supplies continued to expand over the nineteenth century, this did not weaken Londoners' sense of water as their natural property. At the same time, the moralization of water—the surge in its perceived capacity as a force for good—only further undermined claims that it was a commodity like any other. This section moves beyond these debates about water as a public good to consider the implications of increasingly available amounts of it on everyday life in the home. Changing modes of domestic provision in this period gave rise both to a host of distinctions by which providers sought to define (and charge for) appropriate usage and to some very different ideas about this held by water users themselves. The question of agency is important. Did water networks and new household technologies create a new kind of water consumer? It is argued here that the multiple ways in which people used water in the home, and the highly unequal conditions of access to it, ensured that Londoners' perceptions of water at the end of this period were likely to have been, if not as variable as in the era of buckets and donkeys, still very far from homogeneous.

Changing domestic usage transformed everyday life during this period and left its mark on the meanings of water. The arrival of a constant tapped supply in particular allowed people to use more water, more flexibly, and in different ways. Tapped provision has also been seen by many historians as a driving force in the privatization of daily life, allowing WCs, baths, and washing facilities to be increasingly located within private households, instead of shared or external facilities. In Foucauldian accounts the domestic technology of this privatized sphere created new routines of hygiene and "self-rule": the self-regulating practices of "liberalism."[68] Others have seen this late-Victorian period as the moment when tapped water as socio-technical regime "trapp[ed] . . . users in a constant mode of consumption." This period undoubtedly saw a shift from water supplied in the public domain to indoor access. Constant supply also created a path dependency that has shaped water-use practices up to this day, fostering "the illusion of water as an unlimited resource."[69] But the idea that technology determined routines in a newly private sphere in this period is problematic for two important reasons. The first involves the role of consumer agency in these changes. The second relates to the incomplete nature of the water revolution in the home.

To address the first point, domestic water users in London and elsewhere did a great deal to forge the path of limitless tapped supply, both through consumer activism—with repeated demands for constant supply from mid-century onward—and through their water-use practices. While the speculative London companies had helped create demand, they had also soon found themselves pitted against customers with a vivid sense of their entitlements in relation to prices, quality, and quantity.[70] Providers in London and elsewhere struggled with the freedoms that water on tap handed to individual households. The evidence of the Balfour Commission shows that at the end of the century much was still unknown about how people were using their water or even what kinds of spaces the companies were supplying. Confusion reigned when the Commissioners and the East London Waterworks engineer tried to match supply statistics to official population figures.[71] Unmetered "domestic purposes" were hard to monitor at a household level. Domestic purposes varied from cooking to making tea, flushing the toilet, washing utensils, doing the laundry, household cleaning, and washing the body. Portable baths were increasingly joined by fixed baths in the late nineteenth century. Companies tried to limit the definition of "domestic" uses, charging for activities such as watering gardens, filling ponds and in some districts even the use of the toilet and fixed bath as "extras." By the late nineteenth century such extra charges were the focus of political agitation by groups objecting to "taxes" on domestic life. East London Waterworks employed over thirty "waste" inspectors by 1892.[72] Domestic consumers, then, had their own agency distinct from that of technology and public policy.

Alongside those who engaged in collective protests, many more people simply got on with using water as they saw fit. Usage fluctuated wildly between households according to the available supply, domestic space, and individual circumstances. Trade use was charged differently from domestic use, but blurred lines between domestic activities and informal trading in the home added to the companies' management problems: for example, many women took in washing without declaring it to their supplier. In 1895 an East London Waterworks Company inspector stationed himself outside the house of Sarah Day, watching a boy come and go with an incriminating bundle. Mrs. Day, a widowed mother of five, was later fined 10s plus £7 costs for using water "as a laundress." The magistrate did not believe her claim that one of her children, a domestic servant living elsewhere, simply "gave her a trifle weekly for doing her washing." But he did not uphold a £5 "penalty" for "having more than three children, and thus necessitating the use of an unreasonable amount of water" under company rules.[73] There must have been an array of hidden or unpredictable uses in homes and backyards across the city. Another oral history interviewee, Amelia King (born 1878), recalled her eight-room childhood home in Poplar. Like many of their neighbors, the family bathed only once a week in a portable zinc bath, but outside they had a rockery and "aquarium" stocked with "silver and gold and black" fish brought home from the Mediterranean by their ship's carpenter father. "A fountain . . . used to go round and round on top of the fish—it was so nice," she said, until one day the East London Waterworks Company turned up, threatening them with a "terrible tax" (for extras) and they had to get rid of it.[74]

Ideas about what water was *for*, then, differed radically between water suppliers and their customers. But to talk about "consumer agency" hardly does justice to the complex ways in which people used and thought about water. Gender and class were central to this complexity. While the water consumer's public face in the nineteenth century was the male "water ratepayer," there was little doubt about who was *using* most of the water, for cooking, laundry, and household cleaning. Gender distinctions governing who did what within the home were both well established and subtle. Some husbands might help by preparing the coal fire in the morning, but not with the washing-up.[75] According to contemporary wisdom on household management, water inside the home was women's responsibility. "The mistress should ascertain that the water supply is plentiful," declared Mrs. Beeton's best-selling household manual in the 1860s, "for it is on these apparent trifles that the health of households depends." Domestic water was imbued with ideals of femininity every bit as much as the naked women with water pitchers that adorned London's Victorian drinking fountains. Water and femininity already had a long-standing, if ill-defined, metaphorical association.[76] In some ways, though, water itself was nothing special. For Mrs. Beeton, water was just like the "bedroom, clothes, and other closets [that] should be kept scrupulously clean" and the curtains that must be "arranged in seemly folds."[77] The meaning of water in middle-class Victorian homes was partly shaped by long-standing traditions of "domestic economy," which enjoined a woman's orderly stewardship of her husband's property, as a public as well as private duty.[78] Water, though, could fight back in a way that curtains could not, and so required greater vigilance. As Mrs. Beeton warned, "A few hours' neglect of a drain may breed pestilence, and the *cause* of such a disaster is the mistress's neglect of sanitary precautions."[79]

Control over the household water system would have been no more than a pipe dream for most women in late nineteenth-century London, however. This brings us to the second problem with discussions of the privatized late-Victorian home. The provision of piped water and drainage to individual households was incomplete in London even by the end of this period. Constant supply (on tap) developed at different rates according to company district and household type. By the mid-1890s the East London district had transferred almost entirely to the constant system; all other company districts were still split between properties with water on tap and those—sometimes in a different part of the same street— still dependent on domestic cisterns and water supplied intermittently for any- thing between two to nine hours a day.[80] While social class did not determine the pace at which constant supply arrived in different areas, it had much to do with people's access to water within the home. Tenants especially were at the mercy of others' decisions. Landlords dodged the expense of installing and maintaining the regulation pipes and fittings for tapped supply. Equally important was the prevalence of multi-occupancy residence in houses built for single households. Water in the home remained burdensome, inconvenient, and far from private in thousands of tenements across London and other cities where people continued to share sinks, washhouses, and WCs or privies. A 1908 study of working-class housing in London and other UK towns shows the variability of domestic pro- vision at the end of this period. In Tottenham, North London, between 5s 6d and 7s 6d a week would secure a tenement occupying one floor of a suburban house; those lucky enough to have a bath and WC on their own floor paid the higher rent. There were also here "a considerable number of five-roomed houses containing baths, hot and cold water supply, . . . for the most part occupied by foremen, shop assistants, clerks, &c." (price around 12s). In the South London district of Southwark, two- and three-roomed tenements were sublet in houses with often no more than "one washhouse and water-closet for the joint use of several tenants." Nearly 10 percent of the district lived in one room, around 22 percent in two rooms, and another 22 percent in three rooms.[81]

Water use in this shared housing had routines that crossed public and private space. William East recalled that Christmas puddings in his housing block were always boiled in "the copper" in the shared washhouse, where residents also took turns to bathe, but most cooking was done inside the home on the kitchen range. Here you also "had—your—teapot— . . . that was always hot, Oh yes, always." This nostalgia for the bygone, intertwined technologies of water and energy use suggests not just how changeable these were, but how emotionally signifi- cant they were as rituals of daily life. Shared norms cut across different types of household: cleanliness no doubt meant different things to different groups of

Fig. 7.3. Boys at Aldgate Pump, 1908. This pump was located on the border between the City and the East End. The arms of the Corporation of London are displayed at the apex of the structure. It remained an important source of public water supply into the twentieth century, originally fed by groundwater and later supplied by the Metropolitan Water Board. Source: "Aldgate Pump, 1908." © London Metropolitan Archives, City of London. COLLAGE: The London Picture Archive, ref. 280698. Reproduced with permission.

people, but it did not depend on a constant flow of water in the home. Another interviewee, the daughter of a family with a hairdressing business, described their first-floor home in a house in Drury Lane. Here they shared a nearby sink on the staircase with three households on the second floor and two households on the third floor, including a family with twelve children. "You couldn't have a bath every day," she said. "You didn't use water like you do now," but "you could wash, [and] none of us children was put to bed dirty."[82]

The implications of different household provision could be profound, however, determining people's health and life chances. The role of poverty in ill health—poor diet, lack of medical care, bad housing, inadequate plumbing, and polluted water—was a complex area that local medical officers of health dealt with on a daily basis, but it was not addressed as a specific policy domain during the nineteenth century.[83] Official interest in water provision in the household increased only once it was integrated into studies of housing and urban health in the Edwardian and interwar periods. Reporting on the housing conditions and lives of 1,250 "married working women" in 1933, the Women's Health Enquiry Committee described tenement homes that were badly insulated, damp, lacking in water or sanitation, and maintained only by long days of hard physical labor alongside the rigors of child-bearing and rearing. These women were often chronically sick by their early thirties. Many poor women in London and other British cities were fetching their water from shared taps in basements several flights down each day, with washing day "the really dark day of the week."[84]

CONCLUSIONS

Increasing water provision underpinned a massive growth in London's population across an expanding urban space. By 1904, when the Metropolitan Water Board took over, its networks spanned over four hundred square miles. Second only to New York City in capacity, it was pumping an estimated thirty-six gallons per capita each day by 1914.[85] Behind these figures lay a transformed "waterscape," linking reservoirs, filtration beds, and pipelines to the domestic world of taps, sinks, coppers, and kettles.[86]

Did the nature of water itself change? Did it become merely "recirculated toilet flush," as Illich put it? This chapter has argued that water is never merely one thing. It is the "product of . . . various kinds of social processes and practices," as Jamie Linton says, and these practices were diverse and in flux during this period.[87] Water retained multiple meanings for three main reasons. First, political debate kept competing meanings alive. Second, ideas about water were tied to what different groups of people could and could not do with it. While some uses were more officially sanctioned than others, defining valid usage was not a one-way process but a matter of ongoing negotiation. Third, the plurality of water's meanings was sustained by its shape-shifting, dynamic nature, encompassing everything from the rain falling from the sky to the hundred-gallon baths of the richest Londoners to the rising damp in the homes of the poor. Water's "unruly" nature could take over in the form of drought or disease at any moment, sparking debates over causes that ensured that the circumstances of water's production remained always in view.[88]

The meanings of water were enmeshed in the often-contradictory priorities of policy-makers and the city's inhabitants. For all the debate on the Thames, the public in this period was not especially interested in the condition of London's rivers except where this affected supply or public health. Water derived from the freshwater Thames and Lea was acknowledged by many (though not all) to be improving by the late nineteenth century.[89] But the tidal Thames in London at this point was beginning a fifty-year decline toward complete deoxygenation. Though the LCC closely monitored river quality, being responsible for the main sewage discharges meant it was also the river's chief polluter. Knowledge about water did not automatically translate into political will. The tidal river's function as a drain for the city's waste outweighed any public concern about its "natural" state. Concerns about the Thames as a landscape emerged in the late nineteenth century, but the river as an "ecosystem" was still a long way off.[90]

The key constraints on the fluidity of water's meanings were embedded in London's infrastructure. While the capital's inhabitants did much to shape the conditions under which they obtained water in this period—especially through their role in the spread of water closets and constant supply—the major policy decisions about public infrastructure were taken over the heads of ordinary people. These included strategic decisions about the provision of piped commercial supply to the city and the adoption of the "combined" sewerage system—for both rainwater and sewage flows—which still shapes understandings of practicable urban drainage today (and the recent arguments over the Thames "super-sewer").[91] In nineteenth-century debates about the nature of water and conditions of access to it we see Londoners making the best of what they were given, and creatively regenerating water's potential for new meanings.

EIGHT

"A ONCE RURAL PLACE"

Environment and Society in Hackney, 1860–1920

BILL LUCKIN AND ANDREA TANNER

By the late nineteenth century London had become a vast network of increasingly heavily populated communities. Each metropolitan district (redesignated in 1900 as borough) displayed a high degree of independence and opposed the development of a centralized, capital-wide form of government.[1] Yet we have very few detailed studies of the activities, successes, and failures of these component parts of the capital; only a handful of scholars have provided us with nuanced portraits of London's basic units of government and administration. In addition, very few have engaged with the metropolitan experience of environmental change at the local level.[2]

In this contribution we focus on the northeastern inner suburb of Hackney, a once lightly populated area that went through a demographic revolution between the first third of the nineteenth century and the end of the First World War. Boasting a population of little more than 12,000 in 1801, Hackney registered over 50,000 inhabitants in 1851; by the latter date it had already outgrown several of the most rapidly expanding manufacturing centers in the Midlands and the North.[3] Thereafter the annual rate of growth, at over 4 percent between 1861 and 1880 and 2 percent between 1881 and 1900, was one of the highest in the capital. At the beginning of the twentieth century, approximately 270,000 people lived in Hackney. Only in the Edwardian era would the rate of increase finally begin to fall, before entering a period of absolute decline in the 1930s. Nevertheless, between 1900 and 1920 Hackney had one of the highest growth rates in the capital.[4] In the years with which we are concerned, parts of the district retained a semirural character. But these existed cheek by jowl with overcrowded slums, which generated a multitude of environmental problems. Marshy Hackney Wick, which will feature heavily in this chapter, was a semirural locality which was suddenly and explosively transformed into an area dogged by exceptionally serious sanitary and environmental problems. By the 1870s it had become one of London's most unhealthy areas.[5]

Daniel Defoe has left us with a vivid picture of what Hackney looked and felt like in the early eighteenth century, long before the Victorian demographic revolution. Defoe stated that Hackney was an idyllic place in which to live for the "middle sort of mankind," some of whom had grown wealthy "by trade . . . and who still taste of London." A small number of this social elite, who were immensely wealthy, had houses both in Hackney and the City of London. Defoe was also struck by the peace and quiet of the area, which differed markedly from the filth and foul air of the burgeoning inner city.[6]

The professional classes continued to dominate the way things were run in what had come to be known during the Victorian period as the "old town."[7] Bounded to the east by the River Lea (or Lee) and Hackney Marsh and to the west by Islington, the nineteenth-century administrative area contained large tracts of empty land. Throughout our period newcomers, particularly those settling in poorer parts of the district, were frequently stigmatized as "aliens." Established residents accused them of drunkenness, immorality, and raising death rates to levels associated with the East End. In more stable areas, notably "old" Hackney and Stoke Newington, social conditions rivaled some of the best in London.

The existence of a two-sector district was confirmed by Charles Booth's fin de siècle exploration of eastern and northeastern areas of the capital. He concluded that well-to-do parts of the region could probably look forward to a rosy future.[8] However, the great metropolitan investigator appears to have been unconvinced by his own analysis. Might even highly "respectable" parts of a place like Hackney hide islands of desperate poverty? A street-by-street analysis seemed to confirm that this was indeed the case: in every subdistrict Hackney contained invisible pockets of deprivation very similar to those found in the East End.[9] This remained the case for the next twenty years. As late as 1906 unemployment and underemployment caused grave concern. Hackney's Distress Committee pondered the implications of the environmental and epidemiological problems that it discovered and concluded that the existence of a large pool of "unemployables" should be attributed to the numbers of households in which poorly paid

Fig. 8.1. Hackney in 1887. This postcard shows Mare Street in Hackney decorated for the celebration of Queen Victoria's Golden Jubilee. Source: London Borough of Hackney Archives. Reproduced with permission.

women had become the major breadwinners. This, the Committee argued, was against the "best interests" of the borough because it would lead to an increase in neglected homes, higher levels of infant mortality, and children "morally, mentally and physically unable to become productive members of society."[10] Between 1860 and the First World War, low wages and uncertain employment reinforced social and environmental stress.[11]

Everywhere in nineteenth-century London, reformers sought to understand and stem the massive increase in numbers of poverty-stricken members of the metropolitan population, a vast group that comprised what was widely known as "outcast London."[12] The capital was almost certainly the wealthiest city in the world. Why, then, reformers asked, was its wealth so unevenly spread? Why were so many Londoners in Hackney and elsewhere forced to live in appallingly tight-packed areas that housed as many as fifteen thousand slum dwellers?[13] Surely something must be done to reform the capital's system of government and administration in a way that would cut through what many deemed to be selfish localism, thereby addressing the challenges of poverty, overcrowding, and disease. As we shall see, by 1920 progress had been made, but Hackney still harbored desperately deprived subdistricts and environmental problems that defied an easy solution.

London's complex governing system did little to narrow economic and environmental inequalities. As a whole the nineteenth- and early twentieth-century capital relied on a curious mix of recently created institutions and premodern bodies established in the sixteenth, seventeenth, and eighteenth centuries. This resulted in a system characterized by unparalleled complexity. For example, the Metropolitan Board of Works (MBW), which had come into being in 1855 primarily to construct a metropolis-wide sewage disposal system but which remained in place until it was replaced in 1889 by the London County Council (LCC), failed to exert significant rationalizing power over individual districts or the anciently established vestries and parishes. The board had exceptionally limited powers in relation to policing and pollution monitoring on the Thames, the functions that had lain at the root of its emergency creation in the 1850s. Later, at the end of the 1880s, the ambitious London County Council attempted to make itself into a guiding spirit for the improvement of the capital, rationalizing and centralizing what would now be called environmental and health services. As we shall see, the council's ambitious agenda had an only limited impact on the way in which an anciently established world city went about its business.

The council failed to develop a working relationship with the Metropolitan Asylums Board (MAB), a body founded in 1865 that provided medical care and later isolation for the poor, particularly those suffering from infectious diseases that might develop into citywide epidemics. The Poor Law guardians followed a path of their own, and their cooperation with other parts of the "London system" was often exceptionally limited.[14] The independent Thames and Lea Conservancy Boards had little contact with other bodies responsible for reducing pollution on the two rivers that provided the bulk of London's water. As the twentieth century dawned, eight private companies provided water for the entirety of the capital. Protection of purity rested with company engineers, the General Register Office (GRO), the Local Government Board (LGB), and semiofficial analysts, the most important of whom was the distinguished chemist Sir Edward Frankland, whose expertise in water pollution made him a distinguished member of the second Royal Commission on the Pollution of Rivers.[15] In 1902 the capital's supply finally became the responsibility of a Metropolitan Water Board (MWB), but for several years thereafter this new body found it exceptionally difficult to introduce much needed reforms.[16] In addition the London County Council, like the London mayor and his numerous bureaucracies in our own times, lacked sufficient authority and funds to convert ideas into reality. The council fought tenaciously to increase its environmental, health, and housing powers, but throughout our period this proved a long and dispiriting battle. The problem is still with us in the early twenty-first century.[17]

In what follows we offer an environmental portrait of Hackney in the late nineteenth and early twentieth centuries. This is designed to reveal the inner mechanics of vestries and boroughs as governing authorities in a decentralized capital. It is of course impossible to cover every sphere of change. However, the annual reports of successive medical officers of health, and particularly those penned by the astonishingly long-serving medical officers John Tripe (appointed in 1856) and John King Warry (who succeeded him in 1892), provide invaluable information on water supply, the pollution of the River Lea, atmospheric deterioration, housing, and the refuse problem.[18] Analysis of these issues allows us to evaluate the impact of sanitary reform in general and the kinds of activities that may have led to improvement. We also examine the ideas that shaped how health and environmental experts in Hackney addressed the dilemmas they faced. Central to this task was a gradual shift, we argue, from sanitary to environmental ways of interpreting the world. There was no sudden transition from one to the other mode of thought; however, between the 1890s and the end of the Edwardian period, increasing numbers of experts in Hackney and elsewhere began to think proto-environmentally. The discursive changes that this involved were subtly different in each of London's boroughs. On balance, elements of sanitarianism mixed with—rather than replaced—environmental visions of the urban world.

A profound paradox or puzzle lies at the heart of our essay. According to several contemporary indicators, the nineteenth- and early twentieth-century capital appears to have been one of the healthiest cities in the world. Its demographic and spatial scales were immense, however, so consequently different districts and neighborhoods experienced widely divergent patterns of environmental welfare and justice.

Throughout his career Charles Booth emphasized the sociological "invisibility" of the capital.[19] His massive output of description and analysis showed historians and social scientists that two dwellings on the same street in London could be as different as chalk and cheese. Splendor and squalor very often lived—and still live—intimately close to each other. We can of course readily see the kinds of problems that characterize Booth's style of analysis, for historians need large as well as miniature portraits of late nineteenth-century London. Nevertheless, until more work is done at the grassroots level, the history of the capital will continue to lack a crucial dimension. If microanalytic work remains as thin on the ground as is currently the case, the bigger picture will remain distorted and incomplete.

TAINTED RIVERS, DARKENING SKIES

When an appalling cholera epidemic struck London in 1866, many inhabitants of Hackney assumed that their area had been decimated by tainted water. This was not entirely accurate. The pandemic wrought havoc in the East End, but adjacent Hackney escaped relatively lightly. Like many of his colleagues, John Tripe violently castigated the East London Water Company, but he denied that impure water was the sole reason for the catastrophe.[20] Instead Tripe committed himself to a position that married a "tainted" water explanation with the long-established miasma theory.[21]

During the late nineteenth and early twentieth centuries John Tripe and his successor John King Warry advocated the development of a universal supply of water in Hackney that would fulfill one central function—an economically sustainable system that would meet the financial means of ratepayers.[22] This was easier said than done. Labyrinthine company regulations hindered the steady development of a universal service.[23] Water providers harangued rather than attempted to work in harmony with landlords and tenants as they sought to keep pipes and faucets in good repair.[24] From the late 1850s to the 1880s Tripe repeatedly criticized the lack of understanding that existed between water suppliers and consumers. Simultaneously, growing numbers of people demanded the creation of a water service superintended by a publicly owned metropolitan body; as we have seen, this would not occur until the beginning of the Edwardian era.[25] Nevertheless by the 1890s significant progress had been made in providing Hackney's working-class population with access to a constant, albeit sometimes tainted, supply of water. During the second half of the 1890s, however, a sequence of unusually hot summers revealed the inadequacies of the East London and New River companies. These so-called "water famines" became a landmark in London's supply history.[26] There was another prominent and recurring problem. When he succeeded John Tripe in 1892, John King Warry agonized that the storage facilities people relied on for water during times of interrupted service remained unsanitary. Sooner rather than later, he said, this "domestic pollution" would trigger another appalling epidemic.[27]

The Edwardian period witnessed continuing tensions on the supply front. The Metropolitan Water Board found itself confronted by numerous difficulties inherited from the private companies, so much so that it seemed unlikely that Hackney or any other borough in the East End or the northeastern suburbs would in the foreseeable future become a "well-watered" area. But in 1907 the unlikely finally began to happen. A complex and contentious Metropolitan (Charges) Act sought to ensure that the great majority of Hackney's working-class population would be promoted from intermittent to constant users. The measure sought to charge 5 percent of the ratable value of a house and abolish payments for extra fittings, which had deterred many landlords from making improvements.[28] It played a central role in improving Hackney's service. By 1920 water-transmitted infection had nearly become a thing of the past.[29]

Badly polluted sources still required urgent attention. Although the Thames was beginning to recover from its mid-century crisis, the Lea was coming to resemble a stench-ridden sewer.[30] Already in the 1860s a standing commission on river pollution had passed negative judgment on it as a watercourse that required urgent attention.[31] Tripe and King Warry repeatedly warned their Sanitary and Public Health Committees that the Lea was an environmental time bomb. In 1874 Tripe reported that the river was in a "very bad state."[32] A decade later it had developed into a "serious" nuisance.[33] In the late 1890s the Hackney Public Health Committee told the Local Government Board that the river was still "disgracefully" polluted.[34] In 1905 King Warry reported that it was in a "filthy state" as it passed through the district.[35] The problem seemed insoluble. Throughout the early twentieth century the Lea remained a disgracefully polluted river.[36] Recent assessments of the state of the river give scant cause for optimism.[37]

The Lea issue was intimately linked to the ubiquitous London government problem. Too many bodies claimed jurisdiction over the river, and too many sought exclusive control over antipollution measures. Too few saw the Lea as a watercourse that could only cumulatively deteriorate if it were to become a repository for sewage and other forms of waste attributable to exceptionally rapid upriver expansion in population and industry.

Newly expanding communities such as Tottenham, which were just outside "official" London, poured ever-increasing volumes of their filth into the massively overloaded river. The Lea Conservancy continued to operate as an independent body. Whitehall, in the form of the Local Government Board, attempted to reduce tensions, but without success. The LCC was convinced that it should be given a more powerful say on antipollution committees and measures. So too did Hackney and each of the communities upstream. Constant institutional conflict between each of these places and agencies made a mockery of anything akin to a coherent "purification" agenda.[38]

A key to an understanding of the great Lea debate is that Londoners looked upon both this river and the Thames as the rightful possessions of vestries long designated as part of Inner London. This view denied the natural and sociological elusiveness of pollution, which refused to acknowledge administrative boundaries. What was needed was a social and political acceptance of modes of cooperation between large numbers of metropolitan and nonmetropolitan communities, brought together by disciplinary action on the part of Whitehall and long-established bodies with an interest in the Lea.

If there had been notable successes on the water front in our period, the same cannot be said of Hackney and its neighbors' efforts to reduce atmospheric pollution. Compared with the water problem (or problems), Tripe and King Warry only rarely recorded major technical breakthroughs in the struggle against the age-old dilemma of "smoke."[39] Nor did they engage with mainstream ideas that were already the coinage of reform and action among anti-smoke organizations. In the 1860s little progress was made. Metropolitan medical officers were gloomily preoccupied by the thorny problem of how to implement the overoptimistic smoke clauses of the Sanitary Act which passed into law in 1866.[40] The gradual emergence of a nuisance officer with special responsibility for pollution detection did something to reveal the full seriousness of Hackney's (and its neighbors') atmospheric problems. More effective identification led to an increase in informal bargaining between John Tripe and miscreant furnace owners, some of whom agreed to invest in smoke-control technologies.[41] And yet it was the law itself that engendered the central problem: a perusal of annual reports confirms that the vestry often felt hamstrung by deeply flawed national and metropolitan statutes that provided inadequate powers of enforcement. Officials continued to encourage unscrupulous furnace-owners to reduce smoke, but polluters often ignored these suggestions with impunity. At the very end of the nineteenth century King Warry reported himself satisfied by the completion of about six hundred observations of smoke a year.[42] In 1902 a London Fog Enquiry attempted to get to the heart of the matter. Its results were incisive but had little effect on day-to-day prevention on the part of medical officers or the national government.[43] All parties remained locked into a pattern that had been validated by the Alkali Act in 1863, which made an absolute divide between industrial and domestic smoke. The former must be rapidly reduced; the latter was an untouchable fact of everyday life.[44]

In 1914 a survey appeared under the aegis of the LCC. It provided an approximate pecking order of the effectiveness with which boroughs were tackling the smoke problem. Hackney appeared about halfway down the preventive league. Disappointingly, the survey brought bad news for progressives who believed that, unless reduced, metropolitan outpourings of smoke—ever more of it now attributable to domestic sources—would take the capital back to the extreme foggy conditions of the late Victorian period and have a disastrous effect on health.[45] The survey stunned all those committed to the passing of a measure— any measure—that would underline the dangers of doing so little. Spotting one offender here and another there was a needle in the haystack affair. But that wasn't the main problem. A less poverty-stricken London was still tightly wired into a mind-set that either denied or dramatically played down the impact of domestic smoke. Organizations committed to converting urban populations to the reality that prevention measures would fail if they restricted themselves to industrial pollution struggled on, but they failed to gain any significant political support. In Manchester, as well as in London, darkening skies continued to be a depressing presence for decades rather than years to come.[46]

In that same year of 1914 each borough was asked for a table giving an indication of work undertaken in relation to the smoke issue during the preceding year. The results confirmed that many boroughs were following their own route to atmospheric salubrity, without reference to a wider metropolitan pattern. Too many allowed offenders to delay acting on "intimations" (warnings to workshop and factory owners), and too few sought magistrates' orders. The most striking statistic of all concerned recourse to the law: during the year in question only two prosecutions instigated by boroughs took place throughout the entire metropolitan area.[47] As for Hackney, it was still relying far too heavily on unenforceable "intimations" and observations, the number of which made it impossible for more than a small proportion to be visited by the desperately overworked smoke inspector. Here and elsewhere little would change in the absence of national legislation and national standards, a much deeper understanding of the scientific aspects of smoke pollution, akin to what was now definitively known about the "water route," and an effectively organized capital-wide inspection system. What kind of conclusions best capture Hackney's anti-smoke activities between the 1870s and the 1920s? Much was tabulated, much was negotiated, but little was achieved. Throughout our period, however, Hackney performed better than many of the poorer areas across the border in the East End. The central issue remained how best to make a highly imperfect set of legal sanctions bite and how to convert many more warnings into binding orders.

HOUSES, SPACES, AND REFUSE

When we address the seemingly insoluble problem of housing in London and Hackney between the 1870s and the aftermath of the First World War, it is helpful to make a number of socio-environmental distinctions. First, there was the issue of rent and relationships with landlords, particularly for those who had no option but to scrape a living outside the full-time labor market. Next, attention needs to be given to the quality of individual dwellings: the extent to which they offered minimal accommodation, structural safety, and warmth (or at least the absence of bitter cold). Third, the historian should focus on relationships between internal and external environments. The former comprised the way in which space was used for everyday routines, particularly cooking, washing, and changing babies and toddlers. The external environment was made up of filthy (or now in some places less filthy) streets, courts and alleys; the presence or relative absence of human and equine waste and refuse; and the availability of piped water systems.

Given the severity of the long-term housing crisis, many hoped that the establishment of the London County Council would bring an improvement.[48] Achievement was frequently less impressive than intent. Too often the council found itself having to deal with different kinds of opposition on the part of central government, interest groups, vestries, and boroughs. In addition, and partly because of changes in ideological orientation within its own ranks, it frequently set off in one direction, encountered obstacles, retreated, and then set off in another. From slum clearance, to house building, to the construction of large-scale and cottage estates, policies came and went.[49]

In 1891, 16 percent of the capital was badly overcrowded, with some areas—such as Finsbury at 35.2 percent—in a much worse position than others.[50] This figure is difficult to interpret, however. Density was evaluated either by numbers of houses per acre or numbers of occupants per room. The latter was the more meaningful indicator. Railway building was a disaster, with eighty thousand people displaced due to construction between 1850 and 1900.[51] These initiatives had a wholly adverse effect on sections of the urban poor, in what one historian has described as "the irony of improvement."[52] The program caused major financial distress to the very poorest, who had to remain in their old location if they were to keep up any kind of normal life with access to full- or more frequently part-time or "zero hours" employment. In 1889 the founders of the LCC had viewed slum clearance and building high-quality artisanal housing as major priorities. Opposition in the press (most notably in the *Times*) and from ratepayers' groups, as well as the impossibility of gaining permission from central government for large projects, meant that after 1900 the program was limited to building cottage estates, which consisted of individual houses rather than multistory flats.[53]

Exceptionally high levels of overcrowding peaked in Hackney in the period between the 1870s and the 1890s. It was universally acknowledged that poor neighborhoods like Lower Clapton, Homerton, Hackney Wick, Hackney Marsh, and several smaller areas may have reached a point of no return. Even those fortunate enough to experience regular employment in these deprived localities struggled in the face of paltry wages.[54] Charles Booth caught the atmosphere of economic and environmental crisis. He said that it was as if, in the "remoter" areas of the district, those "rejected from the centre" had been flung over the heads of the rest of the population. They had alighted "where no man had yet settled" and were now occupying "ill-built" houses on marshy ground that was frequently flooded by the Lea.[55] A tabulation of the decline in unoccupied properties between 1881 and 1900 revealed that about a fifth of the total population of Hackney in the latter year were living in rooms occupied by more than two people.[56] As elsewhere in the capital during the late nineteenth and early twentieth centuries, the district as a whole was characterized by spiraling rents, an increase in subletting, and consequent overcrowding. Opinions varied as to the proportion of weekly income that should be set aside for rent among the district's casual or intermittently underemployed population. Confronting this issue at the turn of the new century, John King Warry stated that a tenth of income was probably "ideal" for rent. His researches confirmed that vulnerable families were in fact paying between a sixth and a quarter.[57]

In 1910 the Hackney Social Democratic Federation set about politicizing causal connections between abject poverty, overcrowding, housing, and health within a wider environment that appeared designed to devastate communal welfare. The Public Health Department begged to differ. Structural determinants played only a minor role: "degenerated behavior" was much more important. The poor should give more attention to infant feeding and "carelessness" and make the most of their limited financial resources. Victorian ways of viewing the world of the poor survived and flourished.[58]

For almost the entirety of our period, an intense moralism dominated perceptions of the housing problem and the solutions that reformers proposed. In the 1870s and 1880s John Tripe repeatedly agonized over interactions between the impact of changes in the law, the responsibilities and failures of a nascent housing industry, the misdemeanors of landlords, and the failure of the poor to drag themselves a rung at a time up the residential ladder. In the 1870s Tripe focused on the temptations and sinfulness of "indecent" overcrowding. Some of the evidence that he presented to his Sanitary Committee defied description. Repeatedly Tripe reported on individual flats that housed well over twenty people; single beds occupied by a man, his wife, and teenage daughter; and subletting arrangements designed to prevent entire families from sleeping rough. In 1875 he wrote that he had been widely typecast as "injudicious" because he had publicly identified "dark spots" in Hackney. His bluntness was deliberate, for he used the threat of exposure on his "black list" to dissuade landlords from overcrowding their properties to such a grotesquely high degree. It seems to have been taken as given that incest thrived in the worst and darkest parts of Hackney and particularly in places like Hackney Wick.[59]

In summary, the housing issue caused John Tripe as many problems as the state of the Lea. He was torn between applying public health regulations and taking a realistic view of the plight of the casually employed poor and those who scraped together a miserable living on the streets. Therefore he adopted a compromise position, while at the same time castigating the "destructive" classes for much that was wrong and seemingly unalterable in a city that refused to stop growing. But there was also a powerful sense of guilt. If Tripe designated a house "uninhabitable" and listed everything that needed to be rectified, he would automatically trigger rises in rent resulting from the cost of bringing inferior properties up to standard. Increased weekly expenses would force the poor to leave and attempt to find accommodation in cheaper and even more overcrowded houses elsewhere. This would have two effects. First, the sanitary habits of those at the very bottom of the social ladder would further deteriorate and trigger infections among slightly better-off members of the community. Taking action of this kind would also force the poverty-stricken out of their existing accommodations and allow them to spread "destructive" behavior into larger numbers of the just-about-coping.[60] This for Tripe was the most important point of all and once again demonstrated the way in which progressive action on the part of medical officers would always be countermanded by the failure of the free market to provide affordable quality housing—a problem that has reached crisis proportions once again.

During our period, domestic dwellings also attracted attention because of the ever-expanding volumes of rubbish they generated.[61] In the early nineteenth century it had been the stench of streets that had attracted the scrutiny of urban reformers. The external environment was so foul that it was at the top of the list for every urban activist in every administrative area. When it came to household rubbish, each district (and later borough) seems to have used a slightly different method, or medley of methods. Every town or city—or in London vestry or borough—was quite different both in relation to getting to grips with the problem and the order in which different approaches were tried. In 1890 London refuse is thought to have comprised 82 percent "breeze"—small cinders and cinder-dust, and small coke and coke-dust. Vegetable, animal, and mineral refuse accounted for 5 percent, and straw, glass, metal, rags, crockery, and boxes 13 percent.[62] By the late 1870s some domestic refuse was being used as fill for the shaky foundations of working-class housing developments, but most of it was transported by cart to enormous dust heaps on the edge of London or via the Thames to surrounding counties.

What happened in Hackney? The narrative here, as in most vestries and boroughs, was exceptionally complex. Chadwick and many others had been convinced that it was possible to make a profit from every form of waste. But was this the case? What if, as contemporaries argued, Hackney was so "dispersed" a region that comprehensive collection was infeasible? In 1867 a "ticket" system was introduced. This involved the distribution of a card with a "D" on it, designed to ensure that householders, if they so wished, could have their rubbish collected. (The card was to be displayed in a downstairs window on a designated day of the week.) The task was placed in the hands of a contractor, an arrangement which was supposed to save £160 a year when compared with a direct local authority labor system.[63]

This method fell far short of expectations. Consequently in 1871 Hackney appointed a "dust inspector" who divided the district into nine areas and recruited a new contractor. Tripe was convinced that the new arrangement saved money and claimed that "we do not spend more than for the work done, as, doubtless was the case under the old contract system."[64] Although Tripe praised the "D" notice method, the LCC later condemned it for causing exceptionally large volumes of waste to remain uncollected.[65] Tripe eventually agreed with this view. Dumping had become an appalling problem. The medical officer told his

Sanitary Committee in 1881 that "when fields were near to the houses and coste-rmongers and gardeners had not far to take the refuse," they had deposited their dust and waste just about anywhere. Now, however, houses had been built on the fields and "refuse was surreptitiously shot in avenues or other places near houses."[66]

Something had gone very badly wrong. Consequently Hackney decided to solve its rubbish collection problem by burning it to generate electricity. This provided a brief respite from internal and external criticism. However, when private electricity firms began to compete, their lower prices made borough supplies less attractive.[67] Hackney was back to square one, switching and experimenting with different contractors and schemes that depended on its own employees. At the end of our period the problem was still unresolved. In 1929 the LCC castigated the borough and others for a "slapdash" and "unhygienic" approach to household rubbish disposal.[68] The problem refused to go away. Local parsimony continued to shape the way in which the metropolitan boroughs organized their dust and refuse services.

BALANCE SHEETS

By way of conclusion, we attempt to estimate what kind of sanitary progress, as the Victorians called it, had been made by the authorities in Hackney between the 1870s and the 1920s, the ways in which medical officers and nuisance inspectors identified and conceptualized the problems they confronted, and the changing language that reformers used to describe and make sense of the socially constructed world in which they lived. Finally, we describe emerging strands of environmental discourse that can be found in many medical officers' reports in the period between the 1890s and the 1920s. The importance of this changing way of defining place in London and interactions between place and the individual or family is highly significant, not least since proto-environmental modes of thought reduced the burden of responsibility and shame that was central to the doctrine of sanitarian moralizing which had dominated the Victorian period in Hackney and everywhere else in urban Britain. Only in the late Edwardian era did metropolitan medical officers of health begin to make a definitive move away from highly moralized sanitarian discourses. These rejected the idea that where you lived rather than how you lived as an individual determined your fortunes in a great city. Yet as Michel Foucault emphasized in another context, the power dynamic between "specialists" and "clients" remained profoundly one-sided, as intellectuals and sanitarian reformers shaped the lives of ordinary workingmen and -women and deprived them of their existential autonomy.[69]

How much changed in Hackney between the 1870s and the 1920s? By the first decade of the twentieth century, a minority of experts who worked for the LCC or the boroughs had become aware of the connections between ill health, urban nature, and what would later be called "infrastructure" and "systems." In terms of responsibility for making British towns and cities cleaner and safer places, the major emphasis continued to be on the morality of the individual, the state of the domestic sphere, the extent to which family units applied the "laws of hygiene," and inhabitants' willingness to cooperate with local authority officers who reported on nuisances in dwellings, streets, courts, and alleys.

From the 1890s onward medical officers began to pay increasing attention to new and predominantly quantitative markers, particularly information that could be derived from subtle spatial variations in infant mortality. By the end of Edwardian period, the overall rate for the capital was close to the national average, at around 105 infant deaths per 1,000 live births, though this hid massive differences between well-to-do areas and islands of abject poverty, many of which existed within or adjacent to them. Hackney, the "once nearly rural town," recorded an infant mortality rate of 122 per 1,000 live births in the period 1891–1895. But in Hackney Wick, it was more than twice that, at 263 deaths per 1,000 in 1895.[70] John King Warry attributed "surplus" deaths to infant diarrhea and bronchitis, and he argued that the former condition was exacerbated by hot weather, lack of access to adequate supplies of pure water, and the washing of soiled baby clothes near areas used for meals.[71]

As death rates declined in the capital as a whole, a larger proportion of aggregate mortality occurred in localities that had been "left behind." Hackney Wick, which was ridden with marshy ground, second-rate, unsafe housing, and exceptionally high levels of overcrowding attributable to poverty-stricken migrants from the heart of the East End, was one of the worst parts of London in which to be forced to live. As we have seen, it was cut off and distant from the heart of the capital. Poverty, overcrowding, an inadequate water supply, poor sewerage, and the noncollection of dustbins on a weekly basis were some of the environmental factors responsible for such a prominent degree of urban backwardness.

Progressives, including John King Warry, hoped that the London County Council would usher in a new era in the perennial battle against metropolitan environmental inequality. This didn't happen. The council could make bylaws, but their enforcement still rested with local sanitary bodies—some of which refused to act. In addition, the size of inspection staff varied wildly between authorities, as did the range of their duties.[72] The energy and commitment of individual vestries and boroughs directed everything from the provision of local libraries to the ownership of electricity plants.[73] Differences in quantity and quality of services in different districts resulted in part from differentials in ratable value per head of population.

Despite the myriad problems it faced, Hackney achieved significant progress between 1870 and 1920. By the beginning of the interwar period, it contained fewer impoverished and overcrowded dwellings, lanes, courts, and alleys than half a century earlier. However, the emphasis here is on "fewer." As our examples relating to infant mortality have shown, in several boroughs abject poverty, dirt, and disease persisted in places that were now clearly demarcated as "special areas." That was certainly the case in Hackney.[74] On balance, however, Tripe and King Warry achieved more than might have been expected. Their strategy was unapologetically to write their annual reports to persuade their employers that investment in sanitary improvement would protect the district's good name and reduce expenditure on medical services, charities, and the Poor Law. Tripe's success is demonstrated by the legacy that King Warry inherited. By 1900 Hackney's medical officer and his staff were inspecting food and water, milk sheds, markets, and abattoirs.

Tripe and King Warry did much to change the face of urban reform in Hackney in our period, which can once again be substantiated by scrutinizing the changing nature of their annual reports. They persuaded key governing figures in Hackney that the district must invest in larger numbers of nuisance inspectors. They played on the fact that the Hackney social elite had never given up idealizing an image of itself that reflected many of the rural delights of the eighteenth century. Both officers publicly and sharply differentiated the district from the East End and did everything that they could to "civilize" the hordes of "foreigners" who poured into the district from that deeply deprived region of the capital. However, both acknowledged that they could do little to bring places like Hackney Wick up to the sanitary level of more prosperous parts of the borough.

A clear impression of the ways in which medical officers changed practices and expectations can be gained by comparing Hackney's *Reports* of the late 1850s with those of the late 1870s. In the former period Tripe's remarks had much in common with the "sanitary rambles" that had been undertaken since the 1820s and 1830s.[75] Medical men in these writings clearly perceived their territory as a foreign country into which they made infrequent, anthropologically-inflected forays. Tripe's early *Reports* devoted only a limited number of pages to demographic, environmental, and epidemiological facts and figures. At the level of enumeration, annual aggregates had yet to be fully replaced by percentile rates.

Later Tripe presented calculations of deaths occurring in hospitals and workhouses outside Hackney, and he attempted to calculate how these fatalities affected cause-specific percentages for the whole district and its component parts.[76] He provided a detailed account of water and water pollution by interrogating external analytic findings in relation to the chemical composition of supplies derived from the Lea. He also played a major role in sounding the alarm about the industrialization of the Lea Valley and the ways in which this—together with sewage flowing from extra-metropolitan communities—might one day make the river too polluted to be used. As early as 1873 he assured his Sanitary Committee that Hackney had benefited greatly from "man-made" improvements. He noted the area's relative absence of "manufactories," access to open countryside, the beneficial "inclination of the ground," and the "large proportion of persons in good circumstances." The district, he claimed, was now the "third healthiest" in London. And how had this been achieved? Against all odds, "active sanitary works" had prevented Hackney from being overwhelmed by migrants from the East End and the undesirable habits they brought with them.[77] Some of this was true, some of it exaggerated.

Finally, there was the gradual emergence of a kind of environmental discourse. In 1895, Frederick Waldo, the medical officer of health for St. George the Martyr, Southwark, penned a remarkable analysis of the alcohol problem. "In the matter of drink," he wrote, "the individual responds to the influences of the environment." Bad surroundings, he went on, produced drunkards. Waldo next emphasized that, other things being equal, a good environment would act in such a way as to "neutralize quite large amounts of alcohol."[78] ("Neutralization" was held to occur in a nearly physiological manner: a good environment, the medical officer seemed to say, acted directly on a body that might otherwise succumb to a variety of "town maladies" and infections.)

To hammer home his point, Waldo made a diversion into the venerable town-country debate that obsessed so many fin de siècle intellectuals and social reformers convinced that "the machine age" had failed and had massively demeaned the industrial working classes. The only way forward, they claimed, would be to revive rural crafts and industries and encourage underemployed men to return to the hamlets and villages whence they were believed (in nearly every instance wrongly) to have had familial origins.[79] To force home his point, Waldo argued that a "hale" country dweller was capable of consuming exceptionally large volumes of drink without developing the kind of abject wretchedness that afflicted countless numbers of poverty-stricken slum dwellers. "The same amount" drunk in a city environment as in the countryside would inexorably lead to alcoholism. (Partly, Waldo cannily noted, this was because so much "town drink" was subject to so high a degree of adulteration: dangerous beverages of this kind were all that "morally depressed" slum-dwellers could afford.) Moving toward a conclusion, Waldo reiterated his conviction that a deeply deprived environment—he was now using the phrase almost routinely—acted as a direct "physiological stimulus" to alcohol use. The desperate slum-dweller, living in appallingly substandard conditions, sought relief from the "nearest stimulant at hand."[80]

Waldo believed that his argument would be clinched by a spatial factor that has recurred in this contribution, and which he correctly believed to be universally present in every urban locality, but preeminently in the "cities of cities," London. Waldo insisted that nearly every global estimate of the death rate in a town or city must be badly flawed. "All comparative figures of class mortalities bristle with fallacies."[81] A place like affluent Hampstead, he said, did indeed compare in terms of healthiness with a quiescent rural retreat. But given the way in which the registration system had evolved, its very presence in the capital "diluted, as it were," the returns for the whole metropolis.[82] Consequently, neither medical officers nor urban reformers had accurate information to hand in relation to what is best described as the distribution of good and bad environments throughout the capital.

The originality of Waldo's carefully constructed argument lay in the extent to which throughout his *Reports* between 1895 and the early 1900s he emphasized and reemphasized the relationship between "bad places" and self-destructive behavior among the very poorest of the urban poor. In so doing, he homed in on the idea that the burden of responsibility and shame that automatically flowed from the application of the main principles of sanitarianism might be reduced. This must be counted an entirely positive development. Individual and familial moral rectitude could do very little to change a physical setting shaped by so many rampantly destructive forces.[83]

What can be said of John King Warry's vision of the environment? In 1913 he analyzed the strategies that a new generation of infant health workers should follow to protect those who lived in the poorest areas of the borough. King Warry listed eighteen variables that needed to be graded as either "good" or "bad." These included the mode of baby feeding, the use or nonuse of a comforter, the "condition" of parents, the presence or absence of a reasonable degree of cleanliness, the level of "comfort," and the degree of cleanliness of people's lodgings and employment.

King Warry's mode of analysis was underwritten by the assumption that mothers must construct their own "familial environments." Clearly there are similarities here with traditional sanitarian laws of hygiene. Furthermore, although he recognized the existence of a specific form of environment in any given place, King Warry also continued to place a heavy emphasis on wives and mothers as the creators and protectors of a safe domestic haven. Although his program was by no means as original as Waldo's, it represented a significantly modified sanitarian view of what it meant to be poor and needy in the great city. Very slowly things had begun to change in "once rural" Hackney.[84]

NINE

WATER FOR THE MULTITUDES

London and New York
1800–2016

BILL LUCKIN AND JOEL A. TARR

Several chapters in this book have been directly or indirectly concerned with water and water supply in London since the beginning of the nineteenth century. We now move into comparative terrain and examine the history of this most vital of human resources in the British capital and New York City. It goes without saying that all cities have commonalities in their need for water to exist and sustain population and economic growth and diversification. Thus, as Matthew Gandy has noted, the history of cities *is* a history of water.[1] However, New York and London have had strikingly different experiences in supplying their populations. First and foremost, the British capital has had an exceptionally complex "owner-ship" history. Over the last two hundred years—and particularly in the twentieth century—it has oscillated between private and public solutions. Only one aspect has remained constant—exceptionally and excessively heavy dependence on the River Thames, and its major tributary, the River Lea, which flows down through Bedfordshire and Hertfordshire into the northeast of the capital. These sources still supply London with nearly 50 percent of its water; the remainder comes from underground deposits.[2]

In contrast to the British capital, since the 1830s New York has relied on public systems of "ownership" and distribution. Rather than drawing on the close-at-hand Hudson River, the Empire City opted for water derived from upstate New York—successively and cumulatively the Croton River, the Catskills, and the Delaware River. An attempt on the part of a private company at the end of the nineteenth century to wrest control of the city's supply went to the U.S. Supreme Court. Defeat marked the end of attempts to take New York's water system into private hands. Despite their differences, both cities have also faced many similar problems. How should the public good in relation to water be defined at a time of rapid urban change? Who could best protect the health of ever-larger numbers of inhabitants: public or private entities? How were each of the cities to cope with industrial, commercial, and fire prevention needs and increasing *per capita* demand?

Demography has lain close to the heart of the problem. By 1800 London had swollen to an enormous size: contemporaries routinely called it the largest city the world had ever known. The population grew from a million at the beginning of the nineteenth century to 2.5 million in 1850 and just over 7 million on the eve of the First World War. Despite several temporary downward dips, by the beginning of the new millennium London had a population of about 7.5 million. New York followed a quite different demographic trajectory. Compared with the British capital it was a late starter, but when it began to catch up the city grew at an extraordinarily rapid rate. In 1800 New York had a population of approximately 60,000—around the size of one of London's larger boroughs at that time. Following steady consolidation until mid-century, rates of increase spiraled between 1860 and 1910: massive levels of European immigration played an important role. Thereafter both cities followed a broadly similar path. In the early twenty-first century New York had a population of around 8 million.

Throughout the nineteenth century eight private companies supplied water to London. Following a long, drawn-out struggle, in which the London County Council (LCC) played a prominent part, the parliamentary tide finally flowed toward public ownership. In 1903 the Metropolitan Water Board (MWB) bought out company shareholders. The board survived for seventy years before being replaced by another public body, the Thames Water Authority (TWA), which held river basin responsibility for water and sewerage services. Following an initial attempt in the early 1980s, which generated wide-ranging opposition, in 1989 the Authority was privatized as part of the revolutionary Thatcherite assault on public ownership in every area of national life.

For its part New York has seen much less institutional and organizational change. However, as demand for water increased in the late nineteenth and early twentieth centuries, it found itself coming into conflict with upstate towns and villages. The displacement of entire local populations to make way for the construction of reservoirs added fuel to the flame. Tension remained at a high level until the near-present. Over the last thirty years long, drawn-out negotiations regarding environmental and recreational issues and provision of employment for residents have reduced mistrust between New York and the water-rich upstate region. An important agreement, signed in 1995, seems to have confirmed a new deal between the Empire City and communal, farming, and sporting interests. More work remains to be done, but urban-rural relations are now probably more stable than at any time since the early nineteenth century.

Throughout our period relationships between water supply authorities and national and state governments have been exceptionally important. New York has always had more autonomy and flexibility than London. Room for maneuver has of course been delimited by federal and state agencies and statutes. But once crucial requirements—relating, for example, to levels of drinking water purity— have been met, the Empire City has been well placed to make its own economic, environmental, and infrastructural policy decisions. London is quite different. For more than 150 years, rancorous debate has revolved around whether the capital should become self-governing, the kinds of responsibilities that should remain in the hands of London's component boroughs, and the degree of influence that the national executive should wield over metropolitan affairs. The introduction of a mayoral system at the beginning of the new millennium might seem to suggest that the capital's independence has significantly increased, but that is not the case. The mayor's unfettered executive responsibilities are surprisingly limited, and the incumbent's role is predominantly strategic and advisory. As Tony Travers has pointed out, London's new seemingly self-governing body has very few powers compared with those of New York, Berlin, and Tokyo.[3] In the present context, the Mayor's Office cannot in any way interrogate the day-to-day activities of Thames Water, the gigantic private company that now provides the capital and large swathes of the neighboring extra-metropolitan region with water supply and sewerage services.

In what follows we provide a broadly chronological survey of London's and New York's water supply (and wastewater) problems in the long period between the beginning of the nineteenth century and the near-present. At first sight the presence of radically divergent cultural traditions and political structures might seem to confirm that developments in one city will throw only limited light on what was happening (or not happening) in the other. In some areas, however, this very difference allows us to ask important questions about urban water supply systems in general, difficulties associated with dependence on urban as opposed to extra-urban sources, the private-public debate, and most important of all, conflicts between human needs and the extent to which nature can be indefinitely manipulated and engineered to satisfy them. Many major cities in Europe and the United States are now beginning to work toward environmentally sustainable solutions to reduce the severity of climate change–associated water stress. How have London and New York reacted to these developments? As we shall see, the Empire City appears to have achieved a relatively high degree of environmentally forward-looking stability. For its part, the British capital remains enmeshed in irreconcilable differences over the ever-controversial public-private divide, and the related issue of how and by whom it should be governed.

LONDON: THE DEAD WEIGHT OF POLLUTION

Already by the late medieval period London was beginning to display characteristics associated with a contemporary world city. By the early nineteenth century, it had become desperately polluted. The Thames, the "legendary imperial stream," intermittently stank to high heaven. By the 1820s the river had become biologically dead: eels survived, but not salmon or most other fish species.[4] By the 1810s wealthier inhabitants had begun to use flush toilets.[5] Domestic hygiene improved, but the Thames and seepage-prone surface wells were rendered more dangerous. Cholera struck in 1832, 1848–1849, 1853–1854, and 1866. The final outbreak was triggered by the gross inefficiency and irresponsibility of the East London Water Company, which took its supplies from the River Lea and supplied the poverty-stricken East End and several better-off suburbs in the northeast of the capital. Following this outbreak, it became more widely acknowledged that the Lea had developed into a dangerously polluted source.[6] In the 1890s many thousands of inhabitants in the east and northeast of the capital, customers of the East London Company, had their water cut off or greatly reduced during a cluster of notorious "water famines."[7] Both in terms of available volumes of treatable water and ever-rising levels of pollution, the Lea had become environmentally and epidemiologically unreliable.

Water company regulations played into the hands of house owners or those holding a secure lease. Multi-occupancy dwellings inhabited by the poor and poverty-stricken were excluded. So were upper stories.[8] Every year the "autumn fever," typhoid—only designated a separate disease by the General Register Office in the late 1850s—struck down exceptionally large numbers of inhabitants. The infection was spread in many ways—via milk, shellfish, ice cream, and "invisible" human carriers—but between the distant past and the early twentieth century its main mode of transmission had been through the consumption of polluted water.[9] Finally in this array of infections, by the 1850s and 1860s it had already been quite widely thought that polluted rivers and supplies played an important role in the dissemination of summer diarrhea, a killer of massive numbers of infants right up until the end of the First World War.[10]

Already by the 1850s public health reformers were depicting London's greatly expanded water supply system as a deadly circular transmitter of disease, but most experts believed that miasmas and an "epidemic atmosphere" constituted the main route of disease transmission. Contaminated rivers and water played only an indirect role: filth-impregnated watercourses triggered atmospheric deterioration, and the vapors rising from this fetid water intermixed with a disease-generating atmosphere, greatly increasing the possibility of fever.[11]

We should not assume from this dismal picture of the first half of the nineteenth century that company engineers knew nothing about the slowly emerging water sciences. Chemical and then bacteriological knowledge gradually made it possible to render supplies less dangerous.[12] The appointment of an informal metropolitan water examiner—the distinguished chemist Sir Edward Frankland—led to the circulation of ever more detailed information on the state of the Thames and Lea and the techniques that the companies should adopt to ensure rising levels of purity.[13] From the 1870s onward there was steady though uneven improvement in the effectiveness of storage and filtration procedures.[14]

The so-called Great Stink of 1858, the event that persuaded Parliament that the capital should be financially assisted to construct the world's first large-scale intercepting sewage system, marked an important turning point.[15] There is strong evidence to suggest that, following its completion in the early 1870s, pollution levels in the Thames significantly declined within London. A key indicator, dysentery, began to move in the right direction.[16] Far downstream, however, raw sewage still poured into the "imperial stream." In a truly ghastly tragedy, in 1878 a pleasure steamer, the *Princess Alice*, sank in a vilely polluted part of the river. Over six hundred people died, their recovered corpses horribly shrouded in a thick coating of human waste.[17] River pollution prevention remained a hit-and-miss affair. The Metropolitan Board of Works (MBW) had been responsible for kick-starting the construction of the intercepting sewer, master-minded by the engineer Sir Joseph Bazalgette, but had no powers of inspection. In 1857 this became the responsibility of the gentlemanly and amateurish Thames Conservancy.[18] Progress was slow.

During the final third of the nineteenth century demand increased for the creation of a public supply authority. Many water reformers were also intent on modernizing London's system of government, an aspiration that has survived in one form or another until the present day.[19] Critics of the status quo were convinced that supply should be municipalized in a style that was now becoming increasingly prominent in younger industrial and commercial centers in the Midlands and the North. For another full generation, the reformers were outflanked. The private companies hung on until the beginning of the Edwardian era. Finally, in 1903 shareholders, pressured by the London County Council, were made an offer that even they found hard to refuse.

A new body, the Metropolitan Water Board, was created and set about extend-

Fig. 9.1. Crossness Pumping Station, 2019. Completed in 1865 and restored in the early twenty-first century, this ornate monument to the ambitions of Victorian sewerage is now a museum. Photo by Peter Thorsheim.

ing constant supply. As late as the 1890s the percentage of the London population with a full service probably hovered somewhere between 30 and 50 percent.[20] From the early twentieth century onward, this figure began to rise. In the longer term the board made a reputation for itself as a constructor of reservoirs, the creator of a world-famous bacteriological research center, and an innovator in the fields of subsidence, filtration, and, controversially, chlorination.[21] On balance Londoners had good reason to be proud of the MWB and its achievements. We should not overlook the fact that metropolitan supply had already begun to improve during the final thirty years of the nineteenth century. The board built on rather than discarded London's existing private water supply system.[22] There was no need to reinvent the wheel. London entered the new century in a greatly improved environmental state. Problems remained. The MWB labored hard to provide the capital with water supplies that were much less likely to encourage the transmission of disease than had been the case in the second half of the nineteenth century.

PRIVATIZATION AND ITS MULTIPLE PROBLEMS

The Metropolitan Water Board controlled London water supply for seventy years. In 1973 it was replaced by the Thames Water Authority, one of ten such bodies in a national system with basin-wide responsibility for water quality, supply, and sewerage.[23] Sixteen years later the authorities were privatized. Throughout their existence they had been underfunded and hesitant in confronting the short-comings of water and sewage systems constructed in the nineteenth century.[24] The privatizing measure was part of the Thatcherite revolution that transformed British economy and society between the end of the 1970s and the early 1990s. Her governments were driven by a determination radically to reduce the size and influence of the "big" postwar Labour state and a conviction that by their very nature markets always deliver goods and services more cheaply and efficiently than the public sector. Thatcher was also committed to the populist creation of a "share-owning democracy," and the belief that it was wise to sell off large quantities of what the ex-premier Harold Macmillan memorably called the "family silver" to help fund ever-more-demanding public borrowing requirements.[25]

Post-privatization Thames Water found itself confronted by massively complex problems, as "underground London" was creaking at the joints. To make its task more complex, the new company found itself subject to increasingly stringent European antipollution targets.[26] From the very beginning, it played its cards badly. This has continued to be the case for more than twenty-five years. As with all Thatcherite privatizations, small investors were rapidly brushed aside. From 2001 onward Thames Water was owned by RWE, the German utility giant. Partly because of a bad metropolitan and national press, in 2006 RWE auctioned off the company to Kemble Water Limited, which was itself owned by Kemble Water Holdings, a corporation dominated by Australian investors. At this point the Australian bank Macquarie developed into a commanding presence: its European Infrastructure Funds 1 and 2 attracted the keen interest of pension funds and worldwide institutional investors. Then in 2011 Infinity Investments S.A., a subsidiary of the Abu Dhabi Investment Fund, bought 10 percent of Kemble Water Holdings. In the same year, a further 9 percent went to an unnamed subsidiary of the Chinese Wealth Fund. Little wonder Londoners became increasingly confused. Who owned what? In the words of a skeptical financial commentator, the capital's water now belonged to "the Chinese people, the people of the UEA, and assorted Europeans and Canadians controlled by Australians."[27]

Critics were also convinced that Thames Water was repeatedly playing fast and loose with the five-yearly price targets set by the Water Services Regulation Authority (Ofwat), a body that works alongside the Environment Agency (EA), the Drinking Water Inspectorate (DWI), the Department for Environment, Food and Rural Affairs (Defra), and the Consumer Council for Water (CCW). The proliferation of supervisory and control agencies illustrates the lengths to which post-Thatcherite governments have had to go to soften the edges of what is the most fully monopolistic water-associated company in the economically developed world. "Reregulation" has become the order of the day, but often to little effect.[28] Thames Water remains a "hidden" company unlisted on the London Stock Exchange.

Ofwat is the most important and potentially powerful of the controlling bodies. It has had a mixed history. Ofwat sets prices for five-year periods and bases them on operating costs, capital needs, and rates of return. Estimates are made in relation to efficiency gains: a company performing more effectively than the industry as a whole can increase profitability above an agreed rate. In the case of failure, profits will be lower. During the first five years companies exceeded expectations, allowing them to make exceptionally high profits. In due course Ofwat tightened the screws, and in 2000 the rate of profit declined. This sparked company complaints that vital projects and maintenance tasks were being perilously delayed. Consequently in 2005 financial disciplines were relaxed, but they had to be retightened in 2014.[29]

Anti-privatization critics have attacked Ofwat for allowing the companies to use the security of a massive assured flow of funds derived from consumer bills to boost profits and share prices, and build up ever-increasing levels of debt. Heavy reported losses have then been used to justify the payment of minimal levels of corporate tax.[30] In 2013 Thames Water stumbled into a severe postrecession financial crisis. Excessively high levels of debt had undermined corporate stability. To deal with the problem, the company demanded that its customers pay a onetime £29 levy.[31] The 2013 drama also highlighted the extent to which indebtedness has been used to gain deadline extensions for a reduction of London's litany of water delivery problems—above all, its monumentally high leakage rate. An astonishing 27 percent of the capital's piped water supplies never reach their destination.[32] In addition, London has always been a profligate water user: the average is still around 160 liters per capita per day, a much higher figure than in New York and other major European cities.[33]

On the financial front, the political and economic commentator Will Hutton has made a compelling case for much tougher "balance sheet" powers.[34] Ofwat has also been accused of mistakenly exaggerating company costs and allowing Thames Water to make excessive profits. Other critics insist that Britain's private water companies have not yet been brought under meaningful and transparent regulatory control.[35] By 2016 it was widely agreed that something had gone badly wrong both with London's water and sewage services and with Ofwat. In a scathing attack the parliamentary Public Accounts Committee concluded that since 2010 the regulatory body had greatly overestimated company financing and tax costs when setting price limits. Thus, in the aggregate, the privatized water concerns had made windfall gains of at least £1.2 billion between 2010 and 2015, while annual customer bills had been much higher than they should have been. Ofwat was told to go away and find out what had gone wrong.[36]

By far the most important of Thames Water's investment projects is the Tideway Tunnel. This massive west–east under-river project ranks as the largest ever European undertaking of its kind. The aim is to drain polluted storm water out of the Thames and channel it from the far west to the far east of the capital.[37] The Tunnel has been attacked by environmental specialists who favor a less costly phase-by-phase green runoff reduction solution rather than what is now widely depicted as an outmoded form of engineering muscle flexing. Critics have also argued that Tideway is a way of "marching backwards to the future" and that levels of pollution are too small to justify the construction of so gargantuan a scheme.[38]

Professor Chris Binnie, a onetime supporter of the project, now argues that the company itself has admitted that supply will decline by 10 percent by 2030 and that "with less water in the system, the spill frequency and volume will be less than it was in 2006—even without the Tunnel."[39] Thames Water has also been criticized for announcing that it will partly fund the project out of proceeds derived from a substantial one-off customer price rise.[40] However, the company's confidence has been greatly strengthened by being designated part of the National Infrastructure Plan: this gives it a government-backed safety net.[41] The Tunnel is too vast an undertaking for any government to allow itself to be seen standing idle while an internationally trumpeted scheme hits the sidings. "Failure" is out of the question: memories of the deeply embarrassing Channel Tunnel project are still vividly alive among ministers and senior civil servants.

Much rests on the monumental Tideway project. Success—and an end to levies and sudden price hikes—might do something to reduce suspicion of the way in which Thames Water has gone about its business. Failure and another period of passing around the begging-bowl to dig the company out of a self-created debt hole will reinforce an image of a massive multinational corporation that has only rarely placed the interests of its customers above profits and dividends. Thames Water and the currently discredited Ofwat will need to come up with a rapid response to the problems and mistakes that its critics have so clearly identified.

NEW YORK: THE BUILDING OF A PUBLIC SUPPLY SYSTEM

In late eighteenth-century New York, originally Manhattan Island only, had drawn water for its residents and businesses from several local public sources, including the Fresh Water Pond, the Tea Water pump, and private and public wells. Hollow logs laid in the streets distributed water from these wells. Over time, as population and various urban activities proliferated around them, these sources became increasingly polluted. The city was driven to transporting large casks of clean water from suburban springs to meet its inhabitants' needs.[42] Epidemics of yellow fever in the 1790s increased concerns about the relationship between water quality and the disease—and the necessity of improving it to prevent future epidemics. In this context, the possibility of securing supplies from a private company appeared more attractive than the sources provided by the city.

In 1799 Aaron Burr, a politically connected New Yorker and later vice president, gathered a group of businessmen to organize the Manhattan Company to provide clean water to the city. Alexander Hamilton, another major player in both New York and national politics, had been instrumental in pushing the New York City Council to approve a private water company. Burr proceeded to refocus Hamilton's plan to combine control over water supply with a charter providing banking privileges in the city. For Burr, however, provision of clean water was a secondary concern. Through his political connections, Burr persuaded the New York state legislature to give the Manhattan Company a charter for a private water company that the water historian Gerald Koeppel calls a "remarkable entity . . . nothing like any company that existed in America." The state provided the Manhattan Company with a perpetual charter with rights of eminent domain over lands, rivers, and streams. Its charter required that within ten years it "furnish and continue a supply of pure and wholesome water sufficient for the use of all such citizens," but not to provide water to the city to fight fires. Most critically from a financial perspective, the charter permitted the company to use its surplus capital in any way it pleased—even to found a bank.[43]

The Manhattan Company proposed to use a steam pump to secure water from the Collect, a forty-eight-acre pond fed by an underground spring, rather than from the more distant Bronx River. Customers for Manhattan Company water, however, remained few. The company had a poor record of system maintenance, not repairing streets it had torn up to lay pipe and not repairing leaks. The quality of water from the Manhattan Company disintegrated as the city grew around it, with residents often using the Collect as a dumping ground. In the late 1830s, facing the inadequacies of the water supply provided by the Manhattan Company, the city constructed a system of cisterns and wells feeding a pumping station and a reservoir, but the water supply remained inadequate.[44]

In the early 1830s a massive fire and a cholera epidemic made clear the inadequacies of the city's water supply. Under the leadership of DeWitt Clinton Jr., a civil engineer and son of a former governor, the city proposed to shift entirely to a publicly supported water system, securing its supply from the distant Croton River. Water would be provided to the city by gravity flow through an aqueduct crossing the Harlem River on a high bridge and gathered in city reservoirs. In February 1833 the state legislature approved the appointment of water commissioners to supply the city with "Pure and Wholesome Water"[45] and in 1835 the city's voters approved the plan despite its cost.[46]

John B. Jervis, a noted civil engineer, directed construction of the aqueduct and water supply network.[47] The creation of the Croton System in 1842 was one of New York City's most important nineteenth-century infrastructure developments, including not only the aqueduct (which had a capacity of about ninety million gallons per day) but also reservoirs at 42nd Street and in Central Park.[48] While many New York residents did not have water piped into their homes, the city provided hydrants on street corners that provided broader access to Croton water for working-class residents. Without the enhanced water supply, the city would have lost its preeminence as America's leading city. As Croton water became available in the city, both public and private uses of water increased. Many New Yorkers installed water-using appliances such as sinks and toilets, their investments stimulated by a growing emphasis on the desirability of cleanliness and sanitation.[49] By 1850 New York had the highest level of water consumption per capita of any European or North American city, although there was a good deal of waste in the system.[50] The Croton Aqueduct and its reservoirs had created a new relationship between technology and nature in the landscape, linking the city with its hinterland through a technological network.[51]

Increased water consumption and urban population growth demonstrated the system's shortcoming, resulting in demands for its growth. A pattern was set for the city consistently to expand its quest for "clean" water in locations distant from its borders to supply its growing population. While the possibility of drawing the city's water supply from the Hudson River at its door was frequently raised, several factors resulted in its rejection. Most potent were the river's pollution, the costs of filtration and pumping stations, and the possibility of saltwater contamination. New Yorkers preferred "clean" water rather than "dirty water," however treated to remove its impurities.[52]

As the city expanded into watersheds farther and farther from its boundaries, it came into increasing conflict with the residents of the watersheds it was seeking to penetrate and exploit. The need to supply the city with more water raised major issues of the distribution of political and social power between the upstate rural watershed areas and New York City.[53] In the last decades of the nineteenth century, to meet these increasing demands for water, the city began construction of new aqueducts, dams, and reservoirs. Despite these additions, by 1911 the Croton System had reached its limits. The city's population had nearly doubled due to the arrival of hundreds of thousands of European immigrants, and its area had increased several fold with its consolidation in 1898 with Brooklyn, the East Bronx, most of Queens County, and Staten Island to form Greater New York. In addition, changes in the built environment and the adoption of new water-

PUMP ON GREENWICH STREET, BELOW CANAL

Fig. 9.2. W. A. Rogers, *Pump on Greenwich Street, below Canal*, New York, 1894. By this date most of the publicly available water in the city actually came from hydrants. Courtesy of the New York Public Library, http://digitalcollections.nypl.org/items/510d47e1–06f0 -a3d9-e040-e00a18064a99.

consuming devices had resulted in growing demands on supply. Increasingly the existing system of pumping stations and reservoirs to store and distribute the Croton waters became obsolete. New York obviously required new and larger water supplies, but major issues arose about what the source of the water should be and the entity that could most effectively supply it.[54]

In 1895 the New York State legislature granted the privately controlled Ramapo Water Company powers to acquire water rights throughout the state and to sell the water to varied municipalities. Privatization would have further reinforced the concept of water as a commodity. The company sought to capture control of New York City's future water supply beyond the Croton by purchasing water rights from upcountry residents, especially in the water-rich Catskill Mountain region north of the city. Strong opposition to Ramapo's plan developed on the part of both progressively minded political figures and the Merchants' Association of New York, a group of civic-minded businessmen with concerns over proper public policy. In their opinion water was too important a substance to turn over to private interests. In a classic case of the public good versus private interests, in 1901 the state legislature voted to repeal the Ramapo charter.[55]

UPSTATE DILEMMAS: CONFLICT AND COMPROMISE

The rejection of the Ramapo plan still left unsettled the issue of where New York was going to acquire its needed water supplies. In 1903 the city's water consultants reported that the upstate Catskill watershed, an elevated and heavily forested region, could fulfill New York's water needs and provide a tasteless, odorless, and colorless supply. A bacteriological laboratory established in the 1890s assured the public of its safety. In 1905 the state legislature created the Board of Water Supply (BWS). The board proceeded to plan and construct facilities to impound the waters of Esopus Creek to distribute the water throughout the city. The new system included the Ashokan Reservoir and the ninety-two-mile Catskill Aqueduct, completed in 1915. In 1928 the Catskill System was completed with construction of the Schoharie Reservoir and the Shandaken Tunnel. These infrastructures made a major impact on the Catskill landscape.[56] The decision to exploit distant rural water sources pitted New York City against upstate interests, as the city's need for water threatened to disrupt aspects of rural society. Two thousand residents, for instance, were displaced to make room for the Ashokan Reservoir, and other Catskill residents suffered dislocations in their daily activities. On the other hand, some argued that the exploitation of the water resources of the Catskills could provide economic benefits for that region, such as employment, and balance the costs of the disruptions.

The Catskill water system was an immense project, almost tripling the amount of water delivered daily to New York. By the 1920s, however, as the city's population grew, it became clear that even Catskill water was not sufficient to meet the city's future needs. The eyes of the BWS turned toward new sources, focusing on two tributaries of the interstate river, the Delaware, originating in New York State, for additional supplies. The states of New Jersey and Pennsylvania, however, also drew upon the water of the Delaware both for drinking water and to support recreational activities. Outraged at New York's plan, they appealed to the U.S. Supreme Court to protect their rights. Investigation by a court-appointed master ended up with a victory for New York—the city would be permitted to draw water from the Delaware River, although less than it had originally desired (440 million rather than 600 million gallons each day). The city's exploitation of new sources had again averted a water shortage by extending its environmental footprint even farther.[57]

Accessing the Delaware involved construction of a major reservoir at Cannonsville, New York, building several smaller reservoirs, and digging a forty-four-mile tunnel. These actions would have further disrupted the lives and activities of Catskill area residents, and opposition swelled to the proposal. An older but previously rejected alternative now surfaced: tapping into the Hudson River and using filtration to guarantee the water's quality. Even though this meant abandoning the long-standing principle of using the best-quality water obtainable, Hudson River proponents argued that building a filtration plant and pumping station would be considerably less costly than building the reservoir and tunnel, and it would not require the dislocation of rural populations that constructing the reservoirs would entail. Filtration would guarantee high-quality water for the city while in case of drought the Hudson River's huge flow would mitigate against any supply shortages.[58]

Engineers from the Board of Water Supply and politicians from New York City fought back vigorously, insisting that Catskill water was superior in quality to that of the Hudson, even if filtered. The opposition of New York City water officials was aided by a public perception that the river was badly polluted, a claim for which there was some reality. The BWS, political forces within the city, and economic interests tied to utilizing mountain supplies defended the city's water policy.

Accentuating this dispute, the controversy occurred during a long-term drought that highlighted New York's leaking infrastructure and failure to meter its water supplies to control consumption. As the historian David Soll notes, "The BWS engineers had a confident vision of themselves as the providers of pure water by masterminding the construction of complex dams and reservoirs," not by pumping dirty Hudson River water.[59] In the face of this formidable opposition, the advocates of using the Hudson River for the New York water supply retreated, and within several years their plans had been abandoned.

Construction of the Delaware System to join the Croton and Catskill Systems to provide water to New York City began in 1937, greatly aided by funding from New Deal public works programs.[60] The system was completed in various stages: the Delaware Aqueduct, 1944; the Rondout Reservoir, 1950; the Neversink Reservoir, 1954; the Pepacton Reservoir, 1955; and the Cannonsville Reservoir, 1964. But while the Delaware System was completed in 1967, it did not suffice to meet New York's water needs, as nature intervened with droughts which showed that new construction alone would not solve the city's appetite for water.[61]

In the period after 1967 financial stress, the rise of the environmental movement, and a focus on ecological principles challenged the city's water policy priorities. Because of financial stringency, the BWS had neglected the condition of the water infrastructure as well as environmental conditions in the upstate watersheds. A newly created city bureaucracy, the Department of Environmental Protection (DEP), assumed the functions of the BWS but did little to improve watershed conditions and ignored many of the interests of watershed residents.[62]

Conflict also developed over chlorine treatment of effluent from the watershed sewage treatment plants that had adverse effects on fish populations. Tension built up between the state and the city, as each maintained that it was protecting the public interest. Which would be paramount, the concerns of New York City water users or those of recreational river users in the watershed areas of the state?[63] Watershed sportsmen joined in a newly formed voluntary Catskill Waters organization to cooperate with the state Department of Environmental Conservation to pressure the legislature for regulations on the release policy at the dams. Confronted by its reduced power in the state capital, the city and the DEP were forced to accede to the legislation, as state environmental concerns changed the power balance.[64]

Watershed protection became a major public policy issue in the 1980s and early 1990s, driven by the need to meet the standards created by the strengthened federal Safe Drinking Water Act of 1986. As the city attempted to enforce stringent measures to protect water quality that would have adversely affected farming practices, resistance grew from Catskill farmers and communities. In the face of this opposition, the city embraced a green agenda that included policies to substantially reduce city water usage. Beginning in 1986 the city began to meter water use for the first time. In addition, it encouraged and subsidized water-conserving measures such as low-flow toilets and leak reduction, reducing pressure on the city-maintained sewage treatment plants. Breaking a historical trend, the city's water consumption fell sharply rather than increasing as it had done in the past.[65]

In 1995 the city announced that it had reached a Watershed Memorandum of Agreement (MOA) with the Catskill interests. Under the agreement, the city would reduce watershed pollution, maintain water quality, and support measures to maintain the region's economic viability. Over the succeeding years the city upgraded its five Catskill wastewater treatment plants and replaced thousands of privately owned leaking septic systems to protect watershed water quality. In another historical reversal, the city agreed not to acquire additional land in the Catskills unless owners were willing to sell and to permit recreational use of the land it did acquire. In a move toward maintaining cooperation, the MOA established a local development called the Catskill Watershed Corporation to work with local interests to protect the watershed.

Development in the Croton watershed produced a pollution load that compelled the city to begin filtering water from this region (about 10 percent of the city's supply) beginning in 2007.[66] To avoid the expense of filtering water from the Catskills, the MOA adopted a massive conservation plan to protect the watershed from pollution.[67] Under this approach the DEP purchased or protected through conservation easements over 52,609 hectares of land. The MOA and its measures toward water conservation marked the departure by the city from an approach that emphasized the construction of massive reservoirs and dams toward embrace of a "low-technology" strategy of watershed management.[68] This approach brought it into line with current environmental values as well as maintaining good relationships with its watershed neighbors. For the first time in the history of its water system, New York City had reduced rather than expanded its environmental footprint.

Currently the DEP is constructing the largest capital construction project in its history—a third water tunnel to supplement two existing tunnels constructed in 1917 and 1935. All tunnels originate at the Hillview Reservoir in Yonkers. Tunnel Number 1 supplies Manhattan Island. In the 1950s city officials became concerned that this tunnel, which had not been inspected since its opening in 1917, made the island vulnerable in the event of a breakdown. A new tunnel was authorized in 1954 and begun in 1970. Completion is planned for 2020. The tunnel will be more than sixty miles long and as much as five hundred feet below street level. It is predicted that it will cost over $6 billion, but such estimates always are uncertain, and construction has been halted several times because of a shortage of funds and political uncertainties.[69] As of 2016 twenty-four deaths had resulted from the tunnel construction, although a death has not occurred since 1997.

COMPARISONS AND CONCLUSIONS

What kinds of answers can be given to the questions posed at the beginning of this chapter? Has the idea of the "public good" been clearly defined during a lengthy period of continuing demographic and spatial expansion? Have public or private authorities best served the populations of the British capital and the Empire City? And how have London and New York coped with problems associated with an increasing per capita demand for water?

Throughout the period between 1800 and 2000 London witnessed ongoing debates about the relationship between the most important of human resources and the public good. Beginning in the mid-nineteenth century, and continuing with growing intensity until the early 1900s, urban health reformers—Sir John Simon, Sir Edwin Chadwick, William Farr at the General Register Office, and scientific specialists at the London County Council—repeatedly cast the supply debate in moral terms.

The clearest examples here were Farr's outraged diary-like comments during the East End cholera crisis of 1866, the first epidemic of the infection that elicited a quasi-legal attempt to find a water company "guilty before the bar of public opinion." (During the outbreaks of the 1850s companies responsible for the dis-

semination of infected—or as they were then described, "dirty"—supplies all too
easily slipped through an exceptionally weak regulatory net.) In Farr's view in
1866 the poorest members of the metropolitan population had been ruthlessly
exploited by a private concern that deprived its customers of the most basic of
human needs, which should be freely available at the point of delivery.[70] During
the final forty years of the century the same discourse was taken up and elabo-
rated by radicals who equated pure water supplies with a completely different
kind of self-governing municipal capital.

Surprisingly, there is strong evidence to suggest that in the second half of the
nineteenth century the metropolitan companies gradually began to deliver better
supplies than radical critics allowed. The evidence for the period between 1800
and 1870 is open to several different interpretations, but during the final thirty
years of the century the "typhoid" index—a comparison of London's cause-
specific death rate from the "autumn fever" with those in governmentally and
administratively reformed cities in the Midlands and North—indicated that the
inhabitants of the capital were probably drinking better water than their provincial counterparts.[71] It was also highly likely that epidemiological conditions were
better in London than places like Manchester, Liverpool, and Leeds.[72]

Root-and-branch municipalizers had long taken it as given that private concerns must deliver smaller volumes of dirty and more heavily infected supplies
than public boards and committees. Certainly the London water companies were
notoriously corrupt and awarded themselves unduly large profits and dividends,
but between 1870 and 1900 their increasingly scientifically and technically adept
engineers finally developed more effective means of selecting, storing, and filtering raw supplies. When the Metropolitan Water Board took over in 1903, it
continued this trend. The new body built on the progress that had already been
made. In the long period between the final third of the nineteenth century until
the abolition of the MWB in the early 1970s, the public-private divide may have
been of secondary importance.

Since the late 1980s a new kind of privatization has served London and
Londoners poorly. Thames Water has been anything but a reliable protector of
the capital's supply or of the public good. Of course private ownership in the
early twenty-first century is a quite different kind of animal from its nineteenth-
century predecessor. From the 1870s onward a small number of reforming critics
were already moving toward a more theorized definition of the "trade in water"
and using terminologies akin to those underlying what is now called the commodification of nature and the way in which it is exploited in the name of serving
vital human needs.[73] But by the early years of the new millennium a revolutionary
change had occurred: a quite different kind of economic and financial world than
that which had been in existence as recently as the 1970s had come into being.

The most important of human resources had taken on the status of electronically and instantaneously transferable units of exchange in fully globalized financial markets. The incessant changes of ownership and control, and the convoluted and debt-ridden corporate structure of Thames Water, reinforced the point.

Finally there is the issue of meeting the capital's ever-growing demand for larger per capita quantities of water. Throughout the nineteenth century the companies failed to keep pace with exceptionally rapid rates of demographic expansion. Not only that, they failed to serve many thousands of members of the metropolitan population. From the early twentieth century onward, the Metropolitan Water Board saw its major tasks as simplifying supply requirements, making supply universal and constant, and using new bacteriological expertise to ensure that quality kept pace with quantity. Seventy years later, the undercapitalized Thames Water Authority worked from a broadly similar script. However, from the 1970s onward increasing numbers of urban policy makers moved toward a realization that within a generation and a half, world cities in the economically highly developed world would begin to suffer their own variant of the kind of water stress routinely associated with daily life in less affluent societies. New ways of maximizing supply to meet London's exceptionally high levels of demand—reducing leakage rates, metering domestic supplies, reducing profligate demand, and gradually moving toward a less water-intensive urban culture—would need to be found.

As we have seen, since the early 1990s Thames Water's performance in these areas has been patchy to poor. Critics can only hope that increasing scientific, environmental, and public scrutiny will modify company performance. This is essential, not least because no political party in the post-Thatcher era has been able or willing to formulate anything remotely like a general model of deprivatization. Either the will has been lacking—this was the case throughout the Blair years between 1997 and 2007—or would-be reformers have been overwhelmed by the sheer scale and expense of what would amount to a national economic counterrevolution. For good or ill, the future belongs to Thames Water. Critics can only hope that the imminent reform of Ofwat will force every supplier of water and wastewater service to concentrate more intensively on the public good.

An additional task in the capital will be to increase the powers of the Mayor's Office and move toward that elusive nineteenth-century vision—a form of metropolitan government that allows Londoners to interrogate the inner workings of companies and agencies that play a central role in maintaining the quality of life of every member of the community. The water task is mountainously demanding, but it is closely linked to a cluster of other, non-water-related issues.

In contrast to London, New York has greater freedom in determining conditions relating to its water system in regard to source and distribution, but it does not have absolute freedom because of state government authority over aspects of city governance and often tense relationships with watershed regions from which it has drawn its supplies. In addition, because of the interstate nature of the Delaware River, the city faced limits on its authority. In the face of these constraints, the city has often bargained successfully to secure the policies it preferred, exchanging some privileges in its watershed regions in exchange for the right to enlarge its water system.

New York City takes great pride in the quality of its water, which is known as the industry "Gold Standard." Since the implementation of the MOA in 1995, the city has taken careful precautions to protect the quality of the source water derived from its watersheds. The water today is chlorinated to kill germs, fluoride is added to prevent cavities, and sodium hydroxide is used to lessen acidity. Aside from the recently completed filtration plant for the water from the New Croton Reservoir, 90 percent of the supply is not filtered.

Problems with pollution, however, still exist. The leading issue involves turbidity from sediment in the water, an issue engineers recognized as early as 1903. In 1998 environmental and fishing groups sued the city, claiming that sediment from the Schoharie Reservoir had made the water so muddy that it violated the Clean Water Act. The plaintiffs won their suit and the courts fined the city $5 million. To correct the problem, the city purchased thousands of additional acres of land to protect stream banks and to control development within the watershed. In 2006 the problem surfaced again, as heavy storms washed clay particles into the reservoirs. To clarify the water, the city began adding tons of alum per day to enable it to meet federal water quality standards. The addition of this chemical dismayed state environmental officials who oversaw the watershed, but the city feared that if it could not control turbidity, the Environmental Protection Agency (EPA) might require it to filter its water. The city continues to add alum.[74]

The recent case of lead poisoning in the water system of Flint, Michigan, and the revelations of similar issues involving lead pipes in other cities make clear the need for constant vigilance over the quality of water supplies. New York's reservoirs and distribution systems have had low levels of lead content, below risk standards set by the EPA in the Lead and Copper Rule of 1991. Still dangers exist from household tap water that has been contaminated by lead leached from service lines and soldering in pipes installed decades ago. The New York City Department of Environmental Protection has a program to reduce the amount of lead that dissolves into tap water. The city has also prohibited the installation of lead service lines since 1961, and in 1987 it banned the use of lead solder. The DEP provides free lead testing and monitors older homes with lead service lines or lead soldering in pipes. It also adds phosphoric acid to create a protective film on them to reduce corrosion of lead and other toxic metals.[75] New York tap water has had average lead levels below the EPA Action Level of 15 parts per billion except for 2010, although a significant percentage of samples had higher levels.[76] Concern over lead levels in the water supply requires careful watchfulness over water quality. In regard to biological risks, New York has not experienced a severe case of waterborne disease since the introduction of Croton water in the nineteenth century. However, outbreaks of chlorine-resistant cryptosporidium and giardia occurred throughout the nation in the 1980s and 1990s, and New York had scattered cases.[77] Aware of the possible risks, in 1993 the New York Department of Environmental Protection, the Department of Health, and the Mental Hygiene program launched a Waterborne Disease Risk Assessment Program that began tracking diarrheal illnesses and investigated the relationship of tap water consumption to gastrointestinal disease. Since the program began, the rates of cryptosporidium and giardia have steadily declined.[78] To provide added protection to drinking water quality, the city constructed the world's largest ultra-violet water treatment facility, thus providing an added layer of protection against pathogens and other microorganisms.[79]

Since making the decision to derive its water supply from an upcountry watershed and have public control of its water system, New York City has acted through regulatory actions, technology improvements, and enforcement of high standards to retain its reputation as having a premium water supply. While in the process of obtaining supplies to meet increasing demand, however, in the past New York had created friction with residents of its rural watershed areas and neighboring states. Through a process of arbitration and favorable court decisions, as well as adjusting its own consumption patterns, the city was able to reach an equilibrium both in providing sufficient water for its inhabitants' needs and maintaining peaceful relations with its neighbors. In taking these actions, New York City has secured its reputation as a leader among the world's metropolitan areas in the provision of clean and ample water for its citizens. Its record demonstrates that London will almost certainly have to wait a long time before being assured of a fairly priced supply delivered by a private company that has earned the trust of its consumers.

NOTES

Introduction: Environment and Daily Life in London, 1800–2000

1. There is now a large and contentious literature on Roman demographic history. For a detailed overview, see Walter Scheidel, "Roman Population Size: The Logic of the Debate," in *People, Land, and Politics: Demographic Developments and the Transformation of Roman Italy, 300 B.C.–A.D. 14*, ed. Luuk de Ligt and Simon Northwood (Leiden: Brill, 2008), 17–70. For further context, see Neville Morley, *Metropolis and Hinterland: The City of Rome and the Italian Economy, 200 B.C.–A.D. 200* (Cambridge: Cambridge University Press, 1996).

2. Norman Vance, *The Victorians and Ancient Rome* (Oxford: Blackwell, 1997).

3. The pioneering study of this topic is Saskia Sassen, *The Global City: New York, London, Tokyo* (Princeton, NJ: Princeton University Press, 1991). See also Sassen's edited collection, *Global Networks, Linked Cities* (London: Routledge, 2002). Historians of Rome and the Roman Empire now draw on the idea of globalization to emphasize the nodal and interconnected role played by immensely large urban cities in antiquity. See Martin Pitts and Miguel John Versluys, eds., *Globalisation and the Roman World: World History, Connectivity and Material Culture* (New York: Cambridge University Press, 2015).

4. See Joel A. Tarr, *The Search for the Ultimate Sink: Urban Pollution in Historical Perspective* (Akron, OH: University of Akron Press, 1996).

5. Martin V. Melosi, *The Sanitary City: Urban Infrastructure in America from Colonial Times to the Present* (Baltimore: Johns Hopkins University Press, 1999); Melosi, *Garbage in the Cities: Refuse, Reform, and the Environment, 1880–1980* (College Station: Texas A&M University Press, 1981).

6. William Cronon, *Nature's Metropolis: Chicago and the Great West* (New York: Norton, 1991). See also Cronon, "A Place for Stories: Nature, History, and Narrative," *Journal of American History* 78, no. 4 (1992): 1347–76.

7. See the seminal work by Donald Worster, "Transformations of the Earth: Toward an Agroecological Perspective in History," *Journal of American History* 76, no. 4 (1990): 1087–106. For "first" and "second" nature, see Cronon, *Nature's Metropolis*, 56. For compelling overviews of environmental history as a totality, see John R. McNeill, "Observations on the Nature and Culture of Environmental History," *History and Theory* 42, no. 4 (Dec. 2003): 5–43; Stephen Mosley, *The Environment in World History* (London: Routledge, 2010).

8. Douglas, *Cities*, 1; Martin V. Melosi, "The Place of the City in Environmental History," *Environmental History Review* 17, no. 1 (1993): 1–23.

9. Joel A. Tarr to Martin V. Melosi, 6 Sept. 1992, cited in Melosi, "Foreword," in Tarr, *Search for the Ultimate Sink*, xxii.

10. James Winter, *London's Teeming Streets, 1830–1914* (London: Routledge, 1993); Colin G. Pooley and Jean Turnbull, *Migration and Mobility in Britain since the Eighteenth Century* (London: UCL Press, 1998); Chris Otter, *The Victorian Eye: A Political History of Light and Vision in Britain, 1800–1910* (Chicago: University of Chicago Press, 2008). Lynda Nead's theorized wanderings round *Victorian Babylon: People, Streets and Images in Nineteenth-Century London* (New Haven, CT: Yale University Press, 2000) are essential reading for urban-environmental historians.

11. The "great nature debate" continues apace, both among philosophers and historians. See, from a vast literature, Kate Soper, *What Is Nature? Culture, Politics, and the Non-Human* (Oxford: Blackwell, 1995); Ted Steinberg, *Acts of God: The Unnatural History of Natural Disasters in America* (New York: Oxford University Press, 2006); Brian Roberts, Peter J. Atkins, and I. G. Simmons, *People, Land and Time: An Historical Introduction to the Relations between Landscape, Culture and Environment* (London: Arnold, 1998); James Winter, *Secure from Rash Assault: Sustaining the Victorian Environment* (Berkeley: University of California Press, 1999); Daniel Schneider, *Hybrid Nature: Sewage Treatment and the Contradictions of the Industrial Ecosystem* (Cambridge, MA: MIT Press, 2011).

12. S. Martin Gaskell, "Gardens for the Working Class: Victorian Practical Pleasure," *Victorian Studies* 23 (summer 1980): 479–501; Howard LeRoy Malchow, "Public Gardens and Social Action in Late Victorian London," *Victorian Studies* 29 (autumn 1985): 97–124; Peter Thorsheim, "Green Space and Class in Imperial London," in *The Nature of Cities: Culture, Landscape, and Urban Space*, ed. Andrew Isenberg (Rochester, NY: University of Rochester Press, 2006), 24–37. On the intersection of class and green space for urban residents in the United States, see Matthew W. Klingle, *Emerald City: An Environmental History of Seattle* (New Haven, CT: Yale University Press, 2007); Michael Rawson, *Eden on the Charles: The Making of Boston* (Cambridge, MA: Harvard University Press, 2010); Colin Fisher, *Urban Green: Nature, Recreation, and the Working Class in Industrial Chicago* (Chapel Hill: University of North Carolina Press, 2015).

13. See Peter J. Atkins, ed., *Animal Cities: Beastly Urban Histories* (Aldershot, UK: Ashgate, 2012); Hannah Velten, *Beastly London: A History of Animals in the City* (London: Reaktion Books, 2013).

14. The historiography is well and fully covered in Vanessa Taylor and Frank Trentmann, "Liquid Politics: Water and the Politics of Everyday Life in the Modern City," *Past and Present*, no. 211 (May 2011): 199–241; John Broich, *London: Water and the Making of the Modern City* (Pittsburgh: University of Pittsburgh Press, 2013); Emma M. Jones, *Parched City: A History of London's Public and Private Drinking Water* (Winchester, UK: Zero Books, 2013).

15. Alwyne Wheeler, *The Tidal Thames: The History of a River and Its Fishes* (London: Routledge and Kegan Paul, 1979); Leslie B. Wood, *The Restoration of the Tidal Thames* (Bristol, UK: Adam Hilger, 1982); Bill Luckin, *Pollution and Control: A Social History of the Thames in the Nineteenth Century* (Bristol, UK: Adam Hilger, 1986). See also Dale H. Porter, *The Thames Embankment: Environment, Technology, and Society in Victorian London* (Akron, OH: University of Akron Press, 1998); Stephen Halliday, *The Great Stink of London: Sir Joseph Bazalgette and the Cleansing of the Victorian Metropolis* (Stroud, UK: Sutton, 1999); Rosemary Ashton, *One Hot Summer: Dickens, Darwin, Disraeli, and the Great Stink of 1858* (New Haven, CT: Yale University Press, 2017). On the Lea, see Jim Clifford, *West Ham and the River Lea: A Social and Environmental History of London's Industrialized Marshland, 1839–1914* (Vancouver: UBC Press, 2017).

16. See William A. Cavert, *The Smoke of London: Energy and Environment in the Early Modern City* (Cambridge: Cambridge University Press, 2016); Christine L. Corton, *Fog: The Biography* (Cambridge, MA: Harvard University Press, 2015); Peter Thorsheim, *Inventing Pollution: Coal, Smoke, and Culture in Britain since 1800* (Athens, OH: University of Ohio Press, 2006).

17. There is no single volume overview of cholera in nineteenth-century Britain; however, see R. J. Morris, *Cholera, 1832: The Social Response to an Epidemic* (London: Croom Helm, 1976); Michael Durey, *The Return of the Plague: British Society and the Cholera, 1831–2* (Dublin: Gill and Macmillan, 1979); Gerry Kearns, "Cholera, Nuisances and Environmental Management in Islington, 1830–1855," in *Living and Dying in London*, ed. William F. Bynum and Roy Porter (London: Wellcome Institute for the History of Medicine, 1991), 94–125. For medico-social context, see the invaluable Christopher Hamlin, *Cholera: The Biography* (Oxford: Oxford University Press, 2009).

18. See in particular Anne Hardy, *The Epidemic Streets: Infectious Disease and the Rise of Preventive Medicine, 1856–1900* (Oxford: Clarendon Press, 1993). On infant mortality, see the pioneering Naomi Williams and Graham Mooney, "Infant Mortality in an 'Age of Great Cities': London and the English Provincial Cities Compared, c. 1840–1910," *Continuity and Change* 9, no. 2 (1994): 185–212; Robert Woods, *The Demography of Victorian England and Wales* (Cambridge: Cambridge University Press, 2000), 247–304; Eilidh Garrett et al., eds., *Infant Mortality: A Continuing Social Problem* (Aldershot, UK: Ashgate, 2007).

19. For global perspectives on urban-environmental change, see James H. Spencer, *Globalization and Urbanization: The Global Urban Ecosystem* (Lanham, MD: Rowman & Littlefield, 2014); Harold L. Platt, *Building the Urban Environment: Visions of the Organic City in the United States, Europe, and Latin America* (Philadelphia: Temple University Press, 2015); Marcello Di Paola, *Ethics and Politics of the Built Environment: Gardens of the Anthropocene* (Cham, Switzerland: Springer, 2017).

20. Jerry White, *London in the Nineteenth Century: "A Human Awful Wonder of God"* (London: Jonathan Cape, 2007), 172; White, *London in the Twentieth Century: A City and Its People* (London: Viking, 2001), 207.

21. O. F. G. Hogg, *The Royal Arsenal: Its Background, Origin and Subsequent History* (Oxford: Oxford University Press, 1963).

22. K. H. Hawkins, *A History of Bass Charrington* (Oxford: Oxford University Press, 1978).

23. Philippe Chalmin, *The Making of a Sugar Giant: Tate and Lyle, 1859–1989*, trans. Erica Long-Michalke (New York: Harwood Academic, 1990).

24. Louise Raw, *Striking a Light: The Bryant and May Matchwomen and Their Place in Labour History* (London: Continuum, 2009).

25. See White, *City and Its People*, 207.

26. The starting point is still the classic E. A. Wrigley, "A Simple Model of London's Importance in Changing English Society and Economy, 1650–1750," *Past and Present* 37, no. 1 (1967): 44–70. See also Jeremy Boulton, "London, 1540–1700," in *The Cambridge Urban History of Britain*, vol. 2, *1540–1840*, ed. Peter Clark (Cambridge: Cambridge University Press, 2000), 315–47.

27. Mayor and Assembly of London, "Better Infrastructure," www.london.gov.uk/what wedo/whatwedo/business-and-economy/better-infrastructure, accessed 16 Mar. 2017.

28. On contemporary size and scale, see Annemarie Schneider and Curtis E. Wood-

cock, "Compact, Dispersed, Fragmented, Extensive? A Comparison of Urban Growth in Twenty-five Global Cities using Remotely Sensed Data, Pattern Metrics and Census Information," *Urban Studies* 45, no. 3 (2008): 659–92.

29. J. A. Yelling, *Slums and Slum Clearance in Victorian London* (London: Allen & Unwin, 1986). Anthony S. Wohl set the agenda more than forty years ago in *The Eternal Slum: Housing and Social Policy in Victorian London* (London: Edward Arnold 1977), and in his *Endangered Lives: Public Health in Victorian Britain* (Cambridge, MA: Harvard University Press, 1983). See also Gareth Stedman Jones's seminal *Outcast London: A Study in the Relationship between Classes in Victorian Society* (Oxford: Clarendon Press, 1971); David R. Green, *From Artisans to Paupers: Economic Change and Poverty in London, 1790–1870* (Aldershot, UK: Scolar Press, 1995).

30. The best study is still F. M. L. Thompson, *The Rise of Respectable Society: A Social History of Victorian Britain, 1830–1900* (London: Fontana, 1988).

31. The best biography of the "sanitary dictator" is Christopher Hamlin, *Public Health and Social Justice in the Age of Chadwick: Britain, 1800–1854* (Cambridge: Cambridge University Press, 1998). But there is still much of value in S. E. Finer, *The Life and Times of Sir Edwin Chadwick* (London: Methuen, 1952); Anthony Brundage, *England's "Prussian Minister": Edwin Chadwick and the Politics of Government Growth, 1832–1854* (University Park: Pennsylvania State University Press, 1988).

32. On the optimistic dynamics of the filth–fertilizer interchange, see Schneider, *Hybrid Nature*; Jamie Benedickson, *The Culture of Flushing: A Social and Legal History of Sewage* (Vancouver: UBC Press, 2007); Erland Mårald, "'Everything Circulates': Agricultural Chemistry and Recycling Theories in the Second Half of the Nineteenth Century," *Environment and History* 8, no. 1 (Feb. 2002): 65–84. The economics of the Chadwickian ideal are examined in Nicholas Goddard, "'A Mine of Wealth': The Victorians and the Agricultural Value of Sewage," *Journal of Historical Geography* 22, no. 3 (July 1996): 274–90.

33. William Stanley Jevons, *The Coal Question: An Enquiry Concerning the Progress of the Nation* (London: Macmillan, 1865).

34. Bill Luckin, *Death and Survival in Urban Britain: Disease, Pollution and Environment. 1800–1950* (London: I. B. Tauris, 2015), 17, 125.

35. Luckin, *Death and Survival*, 145–49.

36. See the massively documented John Copeland Nagle, "The Idea of Pollution," *UC Davis Law Review* 43, no. 1 (Nov. 2009): 1–78. The backcloth here is Mary Douglas, *Purity and Danger: An Analysis of Concepts of Pollution and Taboo* (London: Routledge and Kegan Paul, 1966); Douglas, *Implicit Meanings: Selected Essays in Anthropology* (London: Routledge and Kegan Paul, 1975); Douglas (with Aaron Wildavsky), *Risk and Culture: An Essay on the Selection of Technological and Environmental Dangers* (Berkeley: University of California Press, 1982). For sociological contiguities with Douglas's approach, see Ulrich Beck, *Risk Society: Towards a New Modernity* (London: Sage, 1992); Beck, "World Risk Society as Cosmopolitan Society? Ecological Questions in a Framework of Manufactured Uncertainties," *Theory, Culture and Society* 13, no. 4 (1996): 1–32. On "self-abuse" and its influence on ideas of pollution, see Thomas Laqueur, *Solitary Sex: A Cultural History of Masturbation* (New York: Zone Books, 2003), esp. 169–77.

37. On John Martin and his utopian plans, see Mary L. Pendered, *John Martin, Painter: His Life and Times* (London: Hurst and Blackett, 1923), 196, 213, 303–4; Thomas Balston, *John Martin, 1789–1854: His Life and Works* (London: Duckworth, 1947), 122, 125–28.

38. See Peter Reed, *Acid Rain and the Rise of the Environmental Chemist in Nineteenth*

Century Britain: The Life and Work of Robert Angus Smith (Aldershot, UK: Ashgate, 2014); and the pioneering Roy M. MacLeod, "The Alkali Acts Administration, 1863–84: The Emergence of the Civil Scientist," *Victorian Studies* 9, no. 2 (Dec. 1965): 85–112.

39. The most important figure throughout the life of the commission was the innovative and distinguished chemist Sir Edward Frankland. On his life and times, see Colin A. Russell, *Edward Frankland: Chemistry, Controversy and Conspiracy in Victorian England* (Cambridge: Cambridge University Press, 1996); and for incisive context, Christopher Hamlin, *A Science of Impurity: Water Analysis in Nineteenth Century Britain* (Berkeley: University of California Press, 1990). See also Leslie Rosenthal, *The River Pollution Dilemma in Victorian England: Nuisance Law versus Economic Efficiency* (Aldershot, UK: Ashgate, 2014).

40. See Lee Jackson, *Dirty Old London: The Victorian Fight against Filth* (New Haven, CT: Yale University Press, 2014).

41. Evidence of John Gavin and R. Bowie, *Report by the General Board of Health on the Supply of Water to the Metropolis* (London: HMSO, 1850), vol. 21, qs. 724–31.

42. Luckin, *Pollution and Control*; Halliday, *Great Stink*; Ashton, *One Hot Summer*.

43. Joan Lock, *The Princess Alice Disaster* (London: Robert Hale, 2013).

44. British Parliamentary Papers [hereafter BPP], *Royal Commission on the Water Supply of the Metropolis 1828*, 9:61.

45. The best accounts remain Wood, *Restoration of the Tidal Thames*; Wheeler, *Tidal Thames*.

46. Luckin, *Pollution and Control*, 141–55.

47. See the extraordinarily predictive "The Thames: A Salmon River," *Spectator*, 11 Dec. 1897, 14.

48. Department for Environment, Food & Rural Affairs, *Review of the Thames Tideway Tunnel* (London: National Audit Office, 2017).

49. *Second Report of the Commissioners Appointed to Enquire into the Best Means of Preventing the Pollution of Rivers (River Lee)* (London: HMSO, 1867).

50. BPP, *Select Committee on Rivers Pollution (River Lee)*, 1886, vol. 11, qs. 846–62.

51. Sea Jung Ra, "River Lee Most Polluted River in the Country," East London Lines, Oct. 16, 2011, http://www.eastlondonlines.co.uk/2011/10/river-lee-most-polluted-river-in-the-country-2/.

52. Cavert, *Smoke of London*; Corton, *Fog*; Thorsheim, *Inventing Pollution*.

53. Mark Jenner, "The Politics of London Air: John Evelyn's *Fumifugium* and the Restoration," *Historical Journal* 38, no. 3 (1995): 535–51.

54. F. A. R[ollo] Russell, *London Fogs* (London: E. Stanford, 1880), 22.

55. This idea was prominent in each Russell London fogs of the author's ruminations on atmospheric pollution. For a particularly strident articulation, see Rollo Russell, *Atmosphere in Relation to Human Life and Health* (Washington, DC: Smithsonian Institution, 1896).

56. Henry T. Bernstein, "The Mysterious Disappearance of Edwardian London Fog," *London Journal* 1, no. 2 (1975): 189–206.

57. Carlos Flick, "The Movement for Smoke Abatement in 19th-Century Britain," *Technology and Culture* 21, no. 1 (Jan. 1980): 29–50.

58. Peter Thorsheim, "Interpreting the London Fog Disaster of 1952," in *Smoke and Mirrors: The Politics and Culture of Air Pollution*, ed. E. Melanie DuPuis (New York: New York University Press, 2004), 154–69.

59. Douglas, *Cities*, 88–109.

60. The phrase was coined by Bill Luckin in "Pollution in the City," in *The Cambridge Urban History of Britain*, vol. 3, *1840–1950*, ed. Martin Daunton (Cambridge: Cambridge University Press, 2000), 220–21. Several authors have questioned the validity and proposed chronology of a "refuse revolution." See Tim Cooper, "Challenging the 'Refuse Revolution': War, Waste and the Rediscovery of Recycling, 1900–50," *Historical Research* 81, no. 214 (2008): 710–31; Cooper, "Burying the 'Refuse Revolution': The Rise of Controlled Tipping in Britain, 1920–1960," *Environment and Planning A* 42, no. 5 (2010): 1033–48.

61. Asa Briggs, *Victorian Things* (Chicago: University of Chicago Press, 1989), 27. See also Matthew Gandy, *Recycling and the Politics of Urban Waste* (London: Earthscan, 1994).

62. J. C. Dawes, *Report of an Investigation into the Public Cleansing Service in the Administrative County of London* (London: HMSO, 1929); William A. Robson, *The Government and Misgovernment of London* (London: Allen and Unwin, 1939), 201–12.

63. Jonathan Prynn, "Recycling in London Has Fallen for the First Time," *Evening Standard*, 21 Nov. 2014.

64. See John Davis, *Reforming London: The London Government Problem, 1855–1900* (Oxford: Clarendon Press, 1988); Ken Young and Patricia L. Garside, *Metropolitan London: Politics and Urban Change, 1837–1981* (London: Edward Arnold, 1982); Richard Dennis, "Modern London" in *The Cambridge Urban History of Britain*, vol. 3, *1840–1950*, ed. Martin Daunton (Cambridge: Cambridge University Press, 2000), 95–132.

65. See Young and Garside, *Metropolitan London*; White, *London in the Nineteenth Century*.

66. The Metropolitan Board of Works remains under-documented. The best accounts are David Owen, *The Government of Victorian London, 1855–1889: The Metropolitan Board of Works, the Vestries, and the City Corporation* (Cambridge, MA: Belknap Press of Harvard University Press, 1982); Gloria C. Clifton, *Professionalism, Patronage and Public Service: The Staff of the Metropolitan Board of Works, 1856–1889* (London: Athlone, 1992).

67. On the LCC, see Young and Garside, *Metropolitan London*; Andrew Saint, ed., *Politics and the People of London: The London County Council, 1889–1965* (London: Hambleton Press, 1989); Susan D. Pennybacker, *A Vision for London, 1889–1914: Labour, Everyday Life and the LCC Experiment* (London: Routledge, 1995).

68. The best study remains Gwendoline M. Ayers, *England's First State Hospitals and the Metropolitan Asylums Board, 1867–1930* (London: Wellcome Institute for the History of Medicine, 1971).

69. Paths through the political and administrative jungle can be found in Michael Hebbert, "Governing the Capital," in *The Crisis of London*, ed. Andy Thornley (London: Routledge, 1992), 134–44; Michael Hebbert, *London: More by Fortune than Design* (Chichester, UK: John Wiley, 1998), 100–129; Tony Travers, *The Politics of London: Governing an Ungovernable City* (Basingstoke, UK: Palgrave Macmillan, 2004); White, *London in the Twentieth Century*, 355–404.

70. London's Pulse: Medical Officer of Health Reports, 1848–1972, https://wellcome library.org/moh/, accessed 13 Apr. 2018.

71. This guardedly optimistic view has been championed by Hardy, *Epidemic Streets*; Owen, *Government of Victorian London*; and A. Clinton and P. Murray in "Reassessing the Vestries: London Local Government, 1855–1900," in *Government and Institutions in the Post-1832 United Kingdom*, ed. Alan O'Day (Lewiston: NY: Edwin Mellen Press, 1995), 51–84.

72. See the proposed program in London Assembly, *Growing, Growing, Gone: Long-Term Sustainable Growth for London* (London: Greater London Authority, 2016), https://www.london.gov.uk/sites/default/files/growing_growing_gone_-_long-term_sustainable_growth_for_london_report.pdf.

73. John Berger, *Ways of Seeing* (Harmondsworth, UK: Penguin, 1972).

74. See James G. Hanley, "Parliament, Physicians, and Nuisances: The Demedicalization of Nuisance Law, 1831–1855," *Bulletin of the History of Medicine* 80, no. 4 (winter 2006): 702–32; Christopher Hamlin, "Sanitary Policing and the Local State, 1873–1874: A Statistical Study of English and Welsh Towns," *Social History of Medicine* 18, no. 1 (Apr. 2005): 39–61; Tom Crook, *Governing Systems: Modernity and the Making of Public Health in England, 1830–1910* (Oakland: University of California Press, 2016).

75. The term "Anthropocene" divides geologists and environmentalists. In opposition to environmentalists, geologists argue that there is no convincing evidence to support the view that from around the middle of the twentieth century, human exploitation and despoliation of nature became so intense that it marked the onset of a new stage or era in global history. See Joseph Stromberg, "What Is the Anthropocene and Are We in It?" *Smithsonian Magazine*, Jan. 2013, www.smithsonianmag.com/science-nature/what-is-the-anthropocene-and-are-we-in-it-1648014014. On late nineteenth-century discussions of humanity's impact on the global environment, see Thorsheim, *Inventing Pollution*, 32.

76. L. D. Schwarz, *London in the Age of Industrialization: Entrepreneurs, Labor Force, and Living Conditions, 1700–1850* (Cambridge: Cambridge University Press, 1992); John Landers, *Death and the Metropolis: Studies in the Demographic History of London, 1670–1830* (Cambridge: Cambridge University Press, 1993).

77. "Health of London in 1859," in *Annual Report of the Registrar General, 1859* (London: HMSO, 1860), xxxvii.

78. Those with the means to do so frequently asserted that travel to sunnier and warmer places was essential to restoring their health after being too long in London; see John Pemble, *The Mediterranean Passion: Victorians and Edwardians in the South* (Oxford: Clarendon Press, 1987).

79. Reginald Barbizon (later 12th Earl of Meath), "Health and Physique of Our City Populations," *Nineteenth Century* 10 (July 1881): 80–89; Barbizon, "Decay of Bodily Strength in Towns," *Nineteenth Century* 21 (May 1887): 673–76. See also Malchow, "Public Gardens and Social Action"; Thorsheim, "Green Space and Class."

1. Greater London's Rapid Growth, 1800–2000

1. Eurostat uses a broad definition of metropolitan London and includes the communities with significant commuting populations. "Database—Eurostat," http://ec.europa.eu/eurostat/web/metropolitan-regions/data/database, accessed 3 Aug. 2016. The Office of National Statistics has a more limited definition of the "Greater London Built-up Area" which added a little more than 1.6 million people to Greater London's population in the 2011 census. Geoportal—Office for National Statistics, https://geoportal.statistics.gov.uk/geoportal/catalog/main/home.page#BD_Built-up_areas_(E+W)_Mar_2011_Boundaries_(Generalised_Grid).zip, accessed 11 May 2016.

2. John Robert McNeill, *Something New under the Sun: An Environmental History of the Twentieth-Century World* (New York: W. W. Norton, 2000), 76–80, 269–95.

3. Beijing and Tokyo/Edo have long but oscillating populations that at times reached into the millions, and they provide other examples of long-term urban density. Rome and

Constantinople are two more early examples of cities that maintained very large populations over extended periods of time. Rome maintained a population in the millions between the second and fifth century, before experiencing a dramatic collapse. It reached one million again only in the early twentieth century.

4. Jerry White, *London in the Nineteenth Century* (London: Jonathan Cape, 2007); White, *London in the Twentieth Century* (London: Viking, 2001); John Marriott, *Beyond the Tower: A History of East London* (New Haven, CT: Yale University Press, 2011); Richard Dennis, "Modern London," in *The Cambridge Urban History of Britain*, vol. 3, *1840–1950*, ed. Martin Daunton (Cambridge: Cambridge University Press, 2000), 95–132.

5. Harold James Dyos, *Victorian Suburb: A Study of the Growth of Camberwell* (Leicester: University Press, 1961); John Marriott, "West Ham: London's Industrial Centre and Gateway to the World, I: Industrialization, 1840–1910," *London Journal* 13, no. 2 (1987): 121–42; Nick Draper, "Across the Bridges: Representations of Victorian South London," *London Journal* 29, no. 1 (2004): 25–43; Richard Dennis, *Cities in Modernity* (Cambridge: Cambridge University Press, 2008); Michael John Law, *The Experience of Suburban Modernity: How Private Transport Changed Interwar London* (Manchester: Manchester University Press, 2014); Simon T. Abernethy, "Opening up the Suburbs: Workmen's Trains in London 1860–1914," *Urban History* 42, no. 1 (Feb. 2015): 70–88; Bill Luckin, *Death and Survival in Urban Britain: Disease, Pollution and Environment, 1850–1950* (London: I. B. Tauris, 2015), 149–54; Jim Clifford, *West Ham and the River Lea: A Social and Environmental History of London's Industrialized Marshland, 1839–1914* (Vancouver: UBC Press, 2017).

6. Bill Luckin, *Pollution and Control: A Social History of the Thames in the Nineteenth Century* (Boston: A. Hilger, 1986); Peter Thorsheim, *Inventing Pollution: Coal, Smoke, and Culture in Britain since 1800* (Athens: Ohio University Press, 2006); John Broich, *London: Water and the Making of the Modern City* (Pittsburgh: University of Pittsburgh Press, 2013); Frank Trentmann and Vanessa Taylor, "Liquid Politics: Water and the Politics of Everyday Life in the Modern City," *Past & Present* 211, no. 1 (May 2011): 199–241; Andrea Tanner, "Dust-O! Rubbish in Victorian London, 1860–1900," *The London Journal* 31 (Nov. 2006): 157–78.

7. Exceptions include John Sheail, "Sewering the English Suburbs: An Inter-War Perspective," *Journal of Historical Geography* 19, no. 4 (Oct. 1993): 433–47; Nicholas Goddard, "Sanitate Crescamus: Water Supply, Sewage Disposal and Environmental Values in a Victorian Suburb," in *Resources of the City: Contributions to an Environmental History of Modern Europe*, ed. Dieter Schott, Bill Luckin, and Genevieve Massard-Guilbaud (Aldershot, UK: Ashgate, 2005), 132–48; Joseph Goddard, "Landscape and Ambience on the Urban Fringe: From Agricultural to Imagined Countryside," *Environment and History* 15 (Nov. 2009): 413–39; Hadrian Cook, "'An Unimportant River in the Neighbourhood of London': The Use and Abuse of the River Wandle," *The London Journal* 40, no. 3 (27 Oct. 2015): 225–43.

8. "London Brownfield Sites Review," London Datastore, http://data.london.gov.uk/dataset/london-brownfield-sites-review, accessed 10 May 2016; "Current and Historic Landfills," *DATA.GOV.UK Open Up Government*, https://data.gov.uk/data-request/current-and-historic-landfills, accessed 10 May 2016; Shanta Barley, "Toxic Waste Clean-up on Olympic Site Cost Taxpayers £12.7m," *The Guardian*, 12 Nov. 2010, http://www.theguardian.com/environment/2010/nov/12/toxic-waste-clean-up-olympic.

9. *London Sustainable Drainage Action Plan: Draft for Public Consultation* (London:

Greater London Authority, Oct. 2015), https://www.london.gov.uk/sites/default/files/lsdap_final.pdf.

10. White, *London in the Nineteenth Century*, 69–83.

11. Much of Inner London, from Chelsea to Stepney to Hackney began as suburbs on the edge of the city, but have lost most of their suburban characteristics.

12. Lynn Lees, "Metropolitan Types: London and Paris Compared," in *The Victorian City: Images and Realities*, ed. Harold James Dyos and Michael Wolff (London: Routledge, 1973), 1:413–28.

13. John Marriott, "Smokestack: The Industrial History of the Thames Gateway," in *London's Turning: Thames Gateway-Prospects and Legacy*, ed. Philip Cohen and Michael J. Rustin (London: Ashgate, 2008), 17–30.

14. "Territorial Distribution and Subdivision, 1861 Census of England and Wales, General Report; with Appendix of Tables," 1863, A Vision of Britain through Time, http://www.visionofbritain.org.uk/census/SRC_P/4/EW1861GEN; 74,816 acres equals 302.76961 square kilometers. Great Britain Historical GIS project at the University of Portsmouth, "London AdmC through time | Population Statistics | Area (Acres)," A Vision of Britain through Time, http://www.visionofbritain.org.uk/unit/10041790/cube/AREA_ACRES, accessed 3 Aug. 2016.

15. Historical maps provide further confirmation of the scale of rapid urbanization. Digitization projects over the past decade make large-scale historical maps significantly more useful for historical research. Researchers can explore the maps using zoom and pan functions and it is possible to stack numerous historical maps over modern satellite images in Google Earth's digital globe. The National Library of Scotland also provides an excellent web interface to explore a number of Ordnance Survey maps over satellite images; Vision of Britain provides its own series of maps, including the first Ordnance Surveys, which range from the start through to the middle of the nineteenth century. "Historical Maps," A Vision of Britain through Time, http://www.visionofbritain.org.uk/maps/#, accessed 8 Oct. 2010; "Ordnance Survey Maps," National Library of Scotland, http://maps.nls.uk/os/, accessed 3 Aug. 2016; Old Maps Online, http://www.oldmapsonline.org, accessed 3 Aug. 2016; "Georeferencing," The British Library, http://www.bl.uk/projects/georeferencing, accessed 3 Aug. 2016.

16. Digital versions of maps discussed in this chapter are online, and readers can view these high-resolution versions to see the detail discussed. Richard Horwood, *Plan of the Cities of London and Westminster, the Borough of Southwark, and Parts Adjoining, Shewing Every House*, 1795, The British Library, http://www.bl.uk/onlinegallery/onlineex/crace/p/007000000000005u00174000.html.

17. Benjamin Tees Davis, *London and Its Environs* (1841), The British Library, http://www.bl.uk/onlinegallery/onlineex/crace/l/007000000000007u00241000.html.

18. Davis, *London and Its Environs*.

19. "Seamless Layer, Ordnance Survey Maps, London, Five Feet to the Mile, 1893–1896," Explore Georeferenced Maps—National Library of Scotland, http://maps.nls.uk/geo/explore/#zoom=10&lat=51.4907&lon=-0.1330&layers=163&b=1, accessed 3 Aug. 2016.

20. William Mudge, "Ordnance Survey, Sheet 1," First Series (England and Wales, 1805), A Vision of Britain through Time, http://visionofbritain.org.uk/maps/sheet/first_edition/sheet1.

21. Henry Morley, "Londoners over the Border," *Household Words*, 12 Sept. 1857,

Dickens Journals Online, http://www.djo.org.uk/indexes/articles/londoners-over-the
-border.html; Mary Dobson, "Malaria in England: A Geographical and Historical Perspective," *Parassitologia* 36, no. 1–2 (1994): 35; Clifford, *West Ham and the River Lea*, 15–21,
54–57.

22. W. R. Powell, ed., "West Ham: Markets and Fairs, Marshes and Forest," in *A History of the County of Essex* (London: Victoria County History, 1973), 6:93–96, http://
www.british-history.ac.uk/report.aspx?compid=42757.

23. Clifford, *West Ham and the River Lea*, 14–36.

24. "Seamless Layer, Ordnance Survey Maps, London, Five Feet to the Mile, 1893–
1896."

25. Clifford, *West Ham and the River Lea*, 122–27; Glen O'Hara, *The Politics of Water in
Post-War Britain* (London: Palgrave Macmillan, 2017), 55–84.

26. Antony Taylor, "'Commons-Stealers,' 'Land-Grabbers' and 'Jerry-Builders': Space,
Popular Radicalism and the Politics of Public Access in London, 1848–1880," *International
Review of Social History* 40, no. 3 (Dec. 1995): 383–407, esp. 404–5.

27. Taylor, "'Commons-Stealers,'" 401–5.

28. Epping Forest was significantly larger on the first Ordnance Survey maps from
1805 when compared with Ordnance Surveys from the late nineteenth century or modern
satellite images: Mudge, "Ordnance Survey, Sheet 1."

29. Lees, "Metropolitan Types: London and Paris Compared," 417.

30. Great Britain Historical GIS Project at the University of Portsmouth, "Camber-
well RegD/PLPar through Time | Population Statistics | Total Population," A Vision of
Britain through Time, http://visionofbritain.org.uk/unit/10167450/cube/TOT_POP,
accessed 18 Feb. 2016; Great Britain Historical GIS Project at the University of Ports-
mouth, "Islington CP/Vest/AP through Time | Population Statistics | Total Population,"
A Vision of Britain through Time, http://visionofbritain.org.uk/unit/10020554/cube
/TOT_POP, accessed 3 Aug. 2016.

31. The first series of Five Feet to the Mile maps of London are not available online.
Researchers can access them through Digimap. The revised maps are available through
the National Library of Scotland. "Ordnance Survey Maps, London, Five Feet to the
Mile"; "Digimap Historic," http://digimap.edina.ac.uk/historic/, accessed 10 Nov. 2015;
"Seamless Layer, Ordnance Survey Maps, London, Five Feet to the Mile, 1893–1896."

32. Great Britain Historical GIS Project at the University of Portsmouth, "Eltham
St John the Baptist AP/CP through Time | Population Statistics | Total Population," A
Vision of Britain Through Time, http://visionofbritain.org.uk/unit/10040589/cube
/TOT_POP, accessed 3 Aug. 2016. The region is covered by the map sheet Kent VIII.NW
that was revised between 1893 and 1895. "OS Six Inch, 1888–1931," Explore Georeferenced
Maps—National Library of Scotland, http://maps.nls.uk/geo/explore/#zoom=15&lat
=51.4515&lon=0.0542&layers=176&b=1, accessed 3 Aug. 2016.

33. The sheets for this region include London LVI, LXX, LXIX and Middlesex XV, XIV, most of which were revised in the early 1890s, with a few later revisions
from 1912 (in which cases it is possible to switch to the Six Inch series to find the early
1890s surveys). "OS 25 Inch, 1890s–1920s," Explore Georeferenced Maps—National
Library of Scotland, http://maps.nls.uk/geo/explore/#zoom=13&lat=51.5096&lon=-0
.3596&layers=176&b=1, accessed 3 Aug. 2016.

34. Ealing's population grew from 14,000 in 1851 to 95,000 in 1901 and 311,000 in 1951.

"Historical Census Population," London Datastore, http://data.london.gov.uk/dataset
/historic-census-population, accessed 25 Apr. 2016.

35. The sheets for this region include London II.SW and Middlesex X.SE, X.NE,
and V.SW, which were revised in 1894. "OS Six Inch, 1888–1931," Explore Georeferenced Maps—National Library of Scotland, http://maps.nls.uk/geo/explore
/#zoom=12&lat=51.5867&lon=-0.3289&layers=171&b=1, accessed 3 Aug. 2016.

36. "London N.W., Surveyed: 1951–1955; OS One Inch 7th Series, 1955–1961,"
Explore Georeferenced Maps—National Library of Scotland, http://maps.nls.uk/geo
/explore/#zoom=12&lat=51.5938&lon=-0.3492&layers=11&b=1, accessed 3 Aug. 2016.

37. 1951: 1.26 million; 1961: 1.24 million; 1971: 1.23 million; 1981: 1.16 million; 1991:
1.11 million; 2001: 1.22 million. These figures were derived by adding the populations of
Hillingdon, Harrow, Brent, Ealing, and Hounslow in the "Historical Census Population."

38. "Historical Census Population."

39. "OS Six Inch, 1888–1913," Explore Georeferenced Maps—National Library of
Scotland, http://maps.nls.uk/geo/explore/#zoom=12&lat=51.5691&lon=0.1396&layers
=6&b=1, accessed 11 Sept. 2017.

40. "OS One Inch 7th series, 1955–61," Explore Georeferenced Maps—National
Library of Scotland, http://maps.nls.uk/geo/explore/#zoom=12&lat=51.5382&lon=0.11
38&layers=11&b=1, accessed 11 Sept. 2017.

41. Andrzej Olechnowicz, *Working-Class Housing in England between the Wars: The
Becontree Estate* (Oxford: Clarendon Press of Oxford University Press, 1997), 2.

42. "Historical Census Population."

43. Goddard, "Sanitate Crescamus."

44. "OS One Inch 7th series, 1955–61."

45. White, *London in the Nineteenth Century*, 67–89; White, *London in the Twentieth
Century*, 24–36.

46. Olechnowicz, *Working-Class Housing.*

47. White, *London in the Twentieth Century*, 36–60; John Sheail, *An Environmental History of Twentieth-Century Britain* (London: Palgrave, 2002).

48. White, *London in the Twentieth Century*, 428.

49. Croydon and West Ham were county boroughs, with independent control over
services like education and public health, but most other Outer London suburbs remain
urban districts under the jurisdiction of the Middlesex, Essex, Kent, or Surrey county
councils.

50. White, *London in the Twentieth Century*, 428–30.

51. Clifford, *West Ham and the River Lea*, 151.

52. Law, *Experience of Suburban Modernity*, 32.

53. Law, *Experience of Suburban Modernity*, 23, 214.

54. Law, *Experience of Suburban Modernity*, 80.

55. A. J. P. Taylor, *English History, 1914–1945* (Oxford: Oxford University Press, 1965),
304.

56. Law, *Experience of Suburban Modernity*, 89.

57. British Parliamentary Papers [hereafter BPP], *Report of the Committee on London
Roads*, 1958, Cmnd. 812, 3–4.

58. Department of Scientific and Industrial Research Road Research Laboratory,
Research on Road Traffic (London: HMSO, 1965), 245.

59. BPP, *London Transport Board: Annual Report and Accounts for the Year Ended 31 December 1965*, 24; BPP, *London Transport Board: Annual Report and Accounts for the Year Ended 31 December 1969*, 29.

60. "Traffic Flows, Borough," London Datastore, https://data.london.gov.uk/dataset /traffic-flows-borough, accessed 16 Nov. 2017.

61. Law, *Experience of Suburban Modernity*, 89–91.

62. White, *London in the Twentieth Century*, 32. Road transport emissions remain a major problem in London, even if they are getting better, with excessive levels of NO_2. Rosie Brooke and Katie King, "Updated Analysis of Air Pollution Exposure in London," report to the Greater London Authority, 20 Feb. 2017, https://www.london.gov.uk/sites /default/files/aether_updated_london_air_pollution_exposure_final_20-2-17.pdf.

63. Luckin, *Death and Survival in Urban Britain*, 118–40; Thorsheim, *Inventing Pollution*.

64. McNeill, *Something New under the Sun*, 66.

65. Peter Thorsheim, "The Corpse in the Garden: Burial, Health, and the Environment in Nineteenth-Century London," *Environmental History* 16, no. 1 (2011): 38–68.

66. Great Britain Historical GIS Project at the University of Portsmouth, "West Ham MB/CB through Time | Population Statistics | Total Population," A Vision of Britain through Time, http://www.visionofbritain.org.uk/unit/10025904/cube/TOT_POP, accessed 25 Apr. 2016.

67. Edward Goldie Howarth and Mona Wilson, *West Ham: A Study in Social and Industrial Problems; Being the Report of the Outer London Inquiry Committee* (London: J. M. Dent, 1907).

68. Law, *Experience of Suburban Modernity*, 4–6; Luckin, *Death and Survival in Urban Britain*, 149–54; White, *London in the Twentieth Century*, 34–37.

69. Abernethy argues a broad cross section of workers in Greater London moved to the suburbs between 1860 and 1914 and that the cheaper rent and improved environment offset the cost of commuting. "Opening up the Suburbs," 72.

70. Abernethy, "Opening up the Suburbs."

71. "Current and Historic Landfills"; Tanner, "Dust-O!," 157–78.

72. D. C. Gooddy et al., "Nitrogen Sources, Transport and Processing in Peri-urban Floodplains," *Science of the Total Environment* 494–95 (Oct. 2014): 28–38, 10.1016/j.scitotenv.2014.06.123; Tom Bawden, "Landfill Dumps across UK 'at Risk of Leaking Hazardous Chemicals,'" *Independent*, 21 Feb. 2016, http://www.independent.co.uk/environment /landfill-dumps-across-uk-at-risk-of-leaking-hazardous-chemicals-a6887956.html.

73. Geographic Information Systems database created by identifying all the industrial sites on the *Ordnance Survey London Town Plans*, 1st Revisions, Scale Five Feet to the Mile, Surveyed 1893–1895, Landmark Information Group (UK) TIFF geospatial data download using EDINA Historic Digimap Service 2013, http://edina.ac.uk/digimap. See my map in Leslie Tomory's chapter; and Clifford, *West Ham and the River Lea*, 26–36.

74. John Marriott, "'West Ham: London's Industrial Centre and Gateway to the World,' II: Stabilization and Decline 1910–1939," *London Journal* 14, no. 1 (May 1989): 43–58; White, *London in the Twentieth Century*, 188–90.

75. White, *London in the Twentieth Century*, 198.

76. White, *London in the Twentieth Century*, 189–90.

77. "London/TQ, 1:1,250/1:2,500, 1947–64," Explore Georeferenced Maps—National Library of Scotland, http://maps.nls.uk/geo/explore/#zoom=15&lat=51.4886&lon=-0 .0635&layers=173&b=1, accessed 11 Sept. 2017.

78. White, *London in the Twentieth Century*, 206.

79. Chris Rhodes, "Manufacturing: Statistics and Policy," Briefing Paper (London: House of Commons Library, 6 Aug. 2015), 6, http://www.parliament.uk/briefing-papers /sn01942.pdf.

80. "Mapped: How the UK Generates Its Electricity," Carbon Brief, 12 Oct. 2015, https://www.carbonbrief.org/mapped-how-the-uk-generates-its-electricity.

81. Greater London's 2 percent is a fraction of East Midlands, which has the largest industrial workforce at 12 percent. Rhodes, "Manufacturing: Statistics and Policy."

82. The Olympic Park and redevelopment north of King Cross are two examples of expensive redevelopment projects which have started to reduce the number of brown-fields since the database was created in 2009.

83. Lance Frazer, "Paving Paradise: The Peril of Impervious Surfaces," *Environmental Health Perspectives* 113, no. 7 (July 2005): 456–62; *London Sustainable Drainage Action Plan: Draft for Public Consultation*.

84. Local Government Board, P.M. Crosthwaite, *Rivers Lee and Stort Flooding* (London, 1920), identifier: 001111178, British Library, 4–11; Clifford, *West Ham and the River Lea*, 122–27.

85. *London Sustainable Drainage Action Plan: Draft for Public Consultation*.

86. Clifford, *West Ham and the River Lea*, 62–70.

87. White, *London in the Twentieth Century*, 42–60.

88. Google, Inc., Google Earth, https://www.google.com/earth/, accessed 3 Aug. 2016.

89. "Database—Eurostat."

90. *"London's Environment Revealed: State of the Environment Report for London* (London: Greater London Authority, Environment Agency, Natural England and the Forestry Commission, 2011, updated 2013), 22, https://data.london.gov.uk/dataset/state -environment-report-london.

91. *London Sustainable Drainage Action Plan: Draft for Public Consultation*, 11.

92. This would be in addition to the billions of pounds already allocated to the Thames Tideway and Lee tunnels, which will prevent dumping mixed storm water and sewage into the Thames and Lea. Tideway, "The Tunnel—Tideway | Reconnecting London with the River Thames," Tideway, http://www.tideway.london, accessed 3 Oct. 2016; "Lee Tunnel—London Tideway Improvements," Thames Water, http://www.thameswater .co.uk/about-us/10113.htm, accessed 19 Jan. 2015.

93. The mayor of London's website provides an overview of major environmental projects and objectives. "Environment," Mayor of London—London Assembly, https:// www.london.gov.uk/what-we-do/environment, accessed 10 May 2016.

2. Imagining the Metropolitan Environment in the Modern Period

1. John Davis, *Reforming London: The London Government Problem, 1855–1900* (Oxford: Clarendon Press, 1988), chap. 1. These are central issues for the authors of chapters on London in the *Cambridge Urban History of Britain* (hereafter *CUH*). See Leonard Schwarz, "London, 1700–1840," in *CUH*, vol. 2, *1700–1840*, ed. Peter Clark (Cambridge: Cambridge University Press, 2000), 641–71; Richard Dennis, "Modern London," in *CUH*, vol. 3, *1840–1950*, ed. Martin Daunton (Cambridge: Cambridge University Press, 2001), 95–132.

2. William Wordsworth, *The Prelude, with a Selection from the Shorter Poems, the Son-

nets, *The Recluse, and The Excursion, and Three Essays on the Art of Poetry*, ed. Carlos Baker (New York: Holt, Rinehart, and Winston, 1954), 181.

3. Schwarz, "London, 1700–1840," 670.

4. David R. Green, "Distance to Work in Victorian London: A Case Study of Henry Poole, Bespoke Tailors," *Business History* 30 (1988): 179–93; Colon G. Pooley and Jean Turnbell, *Migration and Mobility in Britain since the Eighteenth Century* (London: UCL Press, 1998), 190. They find an average of 4.1 km in the period 1750–1879 and 11.6 km from 1880 to 1994. My thanks to Bill Luckin for these references.

5. Alison O'Byrne, "The Art of Walking in London: Representing Urban Pedestrianism in the Early Nineteenth Century," *Romanticism* 14 (2008): 94–107.

6. Dennis, "Modern London," 120; Lynda Nead, *Victorian Babylon: People, Streets, and Images in Nineteenth-Century London* (New Haven, CT: Yale University Press, 2000), 62–67; James Winter, *London's Teeming Streets: 1830–1914* (London: Routledge, 1993).

7. Henry Mayhew, *London Labour and the London Poor*, 4 vols. (1861–1862; rpt. New York: Dover, 1968), 2:142–45.

8. Mayhew, *London Labour*, 2:144. The sort of urban sensory experience I am outlining here is well explored by Chris Otter with regard to urban light: *The Victorian Eye: A Political History of Light and Vision in Britain, 1800–1910* (Chicago: University of Chicago Press, 2008), 62–98.

9. Mayhew, *London Labour*, 1:53–55; Gareth Stedman Jones, *Outcast London: A Study in the Relationship between Classes in Victorian Society* (London: Peregrine-Pelican, 1976), 33–51, 91–92; George Orwell, "Hop Picking Diary," https://hoppicking.wordpress.com/page/2/.

10. Anthony Wohl, *The Eternal Slum: Housing and Social Policy in Victorian London* (London: Edward Arnold, 1977).

11. Charles Poulson, *Victoria Park: A Study in the History of East London* (London: Stepney Books, 1976), 42.

12. R. S. R. Fitter, *London's Natural History* (London: Collins, 1945).

13. Carole Rawcliffe, *Urban Bodies: Communal Health in Late Medieval English Towns and Cities* (Woodbridge, Suffolk: Boydell Press, 2013); Mary Douglas, "Environments at Risk," in *Science in Context*, ed. Barry Barnes and David Edge (Cambridge, MA: MIT Press, 1982), 260–75.

14. Schwarz, "London, 1700–1840," 643, 659; Frederick H. Spencer, *Municipal Origins: An Account of English Private Bill Legislation Relating to Local Government, 1740–1835; with a Chapter on Private Bill Procedure* (London: Constable and Co., 1911).

15. Sidney Webb and Beatrice Webb, *English Local Government from the Revolution to the Municipal Corporations Act: Statutory Authorities for Special Purposes* (London: Longmans, Green, 1922), 1–88.

16. Schwarz, "London, 1700–1840," 647. London parishes like St. Pancras and St. Marylebone were larger than most European cities. Francis Sheppard, "St. Leonard, Shoreditch," in David Owen, *The Government of Victorian London, 1855–1889: The Metropolitan Board of Works, the Vestries, and the City Corporation*, ed. Roy MacLeod, with contributions by David Reeder, Donald Olsen, and Francis Sheppard (Cambridge, MA: Belknap Press of Harvard University Press, 1982), 326–27.

17. Dennis, "Modern London," 96, 103.

18. Davis, *Reforming London*, 3–7; Bill Luckin, "The Metropolitan and the Municipal:

The Politics of Health and Environment, 1860–1920," in *Death and Survival in Urban Britain* (London: I. B. Tauris, 2015), 69–89.

19. *A History of the County of Middlesex. City of Westminster,* part 1, *Victoria County History,* ed. Patricia E. C. Croot, with Alan Thacker and Elizabeth Williamson (London: Institute for Historical Research, 2009), 13:39–41.

20. V. D. Lipman, *Local Government Areas, 1834–1945* (Oxford: Blackwell, 1949).

21. Joseph Ritson, *A Digest of the Proceedings of the Court Leet of the Manor and Liberty of Savoy, Parcel of the Duchy of Lancaster, in the County of Middlesex, from the Year 1682 to the Present Time* (London, 1789).

22. Compare Spencer, *Municipal Origins*; Paul Langford, *Public Life and the Propertied Englishman, 1689–1798* (Oxford: Clarendon Press, 1991).

23. Owen, *Government of Victorian London,* 33. Compare Schwarz, "London, 1700–1840," 643, 659.

24. Christopher Hamlin, "Nuisances and Community in Mid-Victorian England: The Attractions of Inspection," *Social History* 38 (2013): 346–79; Otter, *Victorian Eye,* 99–134; Tom Crook, "Sanitary Inspection and the Public Sphere in Late Victorian and Edwardian Britain: A Case Study in Liberal Governance," *Social History* 32 (2007): 369–93; and Crook, *Governing Systems: Modernity and the Making of Public Health in England, 1830–1910* (Berkeley: University of California Press, 2016).

25. St. George's Hanover Square Paving Committee Minute Book, 1829, Westminster Archives, C1003–4.

26. Mansion House Council on the Dwellings of the Poor, *The London Health Laws: A Manual of the Law affecting the Housing and Sanitary Condition of Londoners with Special Attention to the Dwellings of the Poor* (London: Cassell and Co., 1897), 4.

27. In fact, Londoners were remarkable mobile. See Schwarz, "London, 1700–1840," 654; Dennis, "Modern London," 117.

28. Nuisances Complaint Book, St. George's in the East, Vestry, 7 May, 26 Aug., 28 Oct. 1859, Bancroft Library, STE 132.

29. Tower Hamlets Board of Works, Petitions, Bancroft Library, #8; Poulson, *Victoria Park,* 80–83.

30. Nuisances Complaint Book, St. George's in the East, 8 June, 12 Aug. 1856.

31. Dennis, "Modern London," 109.

32. Ian Maclachlan, "A Bloody Offal Nuisance: The Persistence of Private Slaughter-Houses in Nineteenth-Century London," *Urban History* 34 (2007): 227–54.

33. Petitions, #9, 1 July 1856, Tower Hamlets Board of Works, Bancroft Library, TH 8652.

34. Christopher Hamlin, "Edwin Chadwick and the Engineers, 1842–1854: Systems and Anti-Systems in the Pipe-and-Brick Sewers War," *Technology and Culture* 33 (1992): 680–709.

35. Annmarie Adams, *Architecture in the Family Way: Doctors, Houses, and Women, 1870–1900* (Montreal: McGill-Queen's University Press, 1996).

36. *Florence Nightingale on Public Health Care,* ed. Lynn McDonald, vol. 6, *The Collected Works of Florence Nightingale,* ed. Lynn McDonald, 13 vols. (Waterloo, Ont.: Wilfrid Laurier University Press, 2004), 560–64.

37. J. Parry Laws, "Report to the Main Drainage Committee of the LCC on Sewer Air Investigations," London Metropolitan Archives, LCC Main Drainage Committee, Presented Papers, vol. 19, 7 Dec. 1893.

38. For the union of urban (and particularly underground) space and disease transmissibility, see Roger Cooter, "Anticontagionism and History's Medical Record," in *The Problem of Medical Knowledge: Examining the Social Construction of Medicine*, ed. Peter Wright and Andrew Treacher (Edinburgh: Edinburgh University Press, 1982), 87–108; Rosalind Williams, *Notes on the Underground: An Essay on Technology, Society, and the Imagination* (Cambridge, MA: MIT Press, 1990); and Donald Reid, *Paris Sewers and Sewermen: Realities and Representations* (Cambridge, MA: Harvard University Press, 1991).

39. It would be naive to assume this was conflict-free, as Susan Pennybacker reminds us: *A Vision for London, 1889–1914: Labour, Everyday Life and the LCC Experiment* (London: Routledge, 1995), chap. 3.

40. Compare Graeme Davison, "The City as a Natural System: Theories of Urban Sociology in Early Nineteenth-Century Britain," in *The Pursuit of Urban History*, ed. Derek Fraser and Anthony Sutcliffe (London: Edward Arnold, 1983), 349–70; Pat Garside, "West End, East End," in *Metropolis, 1890–1940*, ed. Anthony Sutcliffe (Chicago: University of Chicago Press, 1984), 221–58.

41. David Englander, "Comparisons and Contrasts: Henry Mayhew and Charles Booth as Social Investigators," in Englander and Rosemary O'Day, *Retrieved Riches: Social Investigation in Britain, 1840–1914* (Aldershot, UK: Scolar Press, 1995), 105–42.

42. Peter C. Gould, *Early Green Politics: Back to Nature, Back to the Land, and Socialism in Britain, 1880–1900* (New York: St. Martin's Press, 1988); Peter Thorsheim, *Inventing Pollution: Coal, Smoke, and Culture in Britain since 1800* (Athens: Ohio University Press, 2006); Bill Luckin, "Unending Debate: Town, Country and the Construction of the Rural in England, 1870–2000," in *Death and Survival in Urban Britain* (London: I. B. Tauris, 2015), 141–54.

43. T. R. Malthus, *An Essay on the Principle of Population; or, A View of Its Past and Present Effects on Human Happiness; With an Inquiry into Our Prospects Respecting the Future Removal or Mitigation of the Evils Which It Occasions*, 1803 version with the variora of 1806, 1807, 1817, and 1826, ed. Patricia James, 2 vols. (Cambridge: Cambridge University Press, 1989), 1:301.

44. Thorsheim, *Inventing Pollution*; Peter Brimblecombe, *The Big Smoke: A History of Air Pollution in London since Medieval Times* (London: Methuen, 1987).

45. George Dodd, *The Food of London: The Chief Varieties, Sources of Supply, Probable Quantities, Modes of Arrival, Processes of Manufactures, Suspected Adulteration, and Machinery of Distribution of the Food for Community of Two Millions and a Half* (London: Longman, Brown, Green, and Longmans, 1856), 2–7.

46. James G. Hanley, *Healthy Boundaries: Property, Law, and Public Health in England and Wales, 1815–1872* (Rochester, NY: University of Rochester Press, 2016); David Sunderland, "'A Monument to Defective Administration'? The London Commissions of Sewers in the Early Nineteenth Century," *Urban History* 26, no. 3 (Dec. 1999): 349–72.

47. Dale Porter, *The Thames Embankment: Environment, Technology, and Society in Victorian London* (Akron, OH: University of Akron Press, 1998).

48. F. O. Ward and Edwin Chadwick, *Circulation or Stagnation, Being a Translation of a Paper by F.O. Ward Read at the Sanitary Congress Held at Brussels in 1856 in the Arterial and Venous System for the Sanitation of Towns, with a Statement of the Progress Made for Its Completion since Then by Sir Edwin Chadwick, Formerly Chief Executive Officer of the First General Board of Health* (London: Cassell, 1889); Christopher Hamlin, *Public Health and*

Social Justice in the Age of Chadwick: Britain, 1800–1854 (Cambridge: Cambridge University Press, 1998).

49. Gwilym Gibbon and Reginald Bell, *History of the L.C.C., 1889–1939* (London: MacMillan, 1939), 434–36; Christopher Hamlin, "William Dibdin and the Idea of Biological Sewage Treatment," *Technology and Culture* 29 (1988): 189–218.

50. On the water, see Asok Mukhopadhyay, *Politics of Water Supply: The Case of Victorian London* (Calcutta: World Press, 1981); and John Broich, *London: Water and the Making of the Modern City* (Pittsburgh: University of Pittsburgh Press, 2013). On calculations, see Hamlin, "Edwin Chadwick and the Engineers."

51. Bill Luckin, *Pollution and Control: A Social History of the Thames in the Nineteenth Century* (Bristol, UK: Adam Hilger, 1986).

52. T. J. Nelson, *An Incredible Story, Told in a Letter, to the Rt. Hon. Earl of Beaconsfield, Prime Minister* (London: Jas Truscott, 1879), in Christopher Hamlin, *Sanitary Reform in the Provinces*, vol. 2, *Sanitary Reform in Victorian Britain*, ed. Michelle Allen-Emerson (London: Pickering and Chatto, 2012), 431–45.

53. Gibbon and Bell, *L.C.C.*, 390–93; Andrzej Olechnowicz, *Working-Class Housing in England between the Wars: The Becontree Estate* (Oxford: Clarendon Press, 1997).

54. Christopher Hamlin, "Sewage: Waste or Resource," *Environment* 22, no. 8 (1980): 16–20, 38–42; William Crookes, "The Economy of Nitrogen," *Quarterly Journal of Science*, n.s. 8 (1878): 145–66; Frederick Charles Krepp, *The Sewage Question: Being a General Review of All Systems and Methods Hitherto Employed in Various Cities for Draining Cities and Utilising Sewage* (London: Longmans, Green, 1867).

55. Bernard Becker, *Scientific London* (New York: D. Appleton, 1875), 332.

56. Keith H. Vignoles, *Charles Blacker Vignoles: Romantic Engineer* (Cambridge: Cambridge University Press, 1982).

57. Becker, *Scientific London*, 129–31.

58. Angus McLaren, "Contraception and the Working Classes: The Social Ideology of the English Birth Control Movement in Its Early Years," *Comparative Studies in Society and History* 18 (1976): 236–51.

59. Gregg Mitman, *The State of Nature: Ecology, Community, and American Social Thought, 1900–1950* (Chicago: University of Chicago Press, 1992); William Cronon, *Nature's Metropolis: Chicago and the Great West* (New York: W. W. Norton, 1991).

60. Fitter, *London's Natural History*, 1.

61. I. F. Clarke, *Voices Prophesying War, 1763–1984* (Oxford: Oxford University Press, 1966).

62. Henry Howorth, "The Most Recent Changes of Level and Their Teaching: The Rapid Collapse of Some Districts at the Close of the Mammoth Age," *Geological Magazine*, series 4, no. 1 (1894): 404–13; Vincent L. Gaffney et al., *Europe's Lost World: The Rediscovery of Doggerland*, Research Report (Council for British Archaeology), no. 160 (York: Council for British Archeology, 2009).

63. Megan Lane, "The Moment Britain Became an Island," BBC News, 15 Feb. 2011, http://www.bbc.com/news/magazine-12244964.

64. William Crookes, "Address of the President before the British Association for the Advancement of Science, Bristol, 1898," *Science*, n.s. 8 (1898): 561–75.

65. "Failing Ocean Current Raises Fears of Mini Ice Age," *New Scientist*, 30 Nov. 2005; https://www.newscientist.com/article/dn8398-failing-ocean-current-raises-fears-of-mini

-ice-age/; Steve Connor, "The Gulf Steam Is Slowing Down Faster than Ever, Scientists Say," *Independent*, 23 Mar. 2015; http://www.independent.co.uk/environment/gulf-stream-is-slowing-down-faster-than-ever-scientists-say-10128700.html.

66. James C. McKusick, *Green Writing Romanticism and Ecology*, 2nd ed. (New York: Palgrave Macmillan, 2010), 95–111; I. F. Clarke, *The Tale of the Future, from the Beginning to the Present Day; a Check-List of Those Satires, Ideal States, Imaginary Wars and Invasions, Political Warnings and Forecasts, Interplanetary Voyages and Scientific Romances—All Located in an Imaginary Future Period—That Have Been Published in the United Kingdom between 1644 and 1960* (London: Library Association, 1961); Bill Luckin, "'The Heart and Home of Horror': The Great London Fogs of the Late Nineteenth Century," in *Death and Survival in Urban Britain* (London: I. B. Tauris, 2015), 118–40.

67. Edward Bickersteth, *Works* (New York: Appleton, 1832), 363; Elizabeth Stone, *God's Acre, or, Historical Notices Relating to Churchyards* (London: Parker, 1858), 133.

68. James Thomson, *The City of Dreadful Night* (Yellow Springs, OH: Kahoe and Spieth, 1926), viii, stanzas 10–13.

69. Garside, "West End, East End," 234–36; Luckin, "Unending Debate."

70. "Heathrow Third Runway," *The Guardian*, 1 July 2015, http://www.theguardian.com/environment/heathrow-third-runway; "Teddington Action Group against Increased Flight Noise," Teddington Action Group, http://www.teddingtonactiongroup.com/, both accessed 11 Oct. 2015.

3. Death and the Environment in London, 1800–2000

1. Leonard D. Schwarz, *London in the Age of Industrialisation: Entrepreneurs, Labour Force and Living Conditions, 1700–1850* (Cambridge: Cambridge University Press, 1992), table 5.5, 134. See also John Landers, *Death and the Metropolis: Studies in the Demographic History of London, 1670–1830* (Cambridge: Cambridge University Press, 1993).

2. For black spots in healthier districts, see the chapter 8 in this volume by Bill Luckin and Andrea Tanner.

3. Charles Mason, "Scavenging: Disposal of Refuse," *Journal of the Sanitary Institute* 26 (1895): 464–81, 476.

4. Medical Officer's Annual Report (hereafter MOAR), London County Council (LCC), 1964, 4.

5. Sean Boyle and Richard Hamblin, *The Health Economy of London* (London: King's Fund, 1997), 11.

6. Standard mortality rates are deaths given per thousand living; standard mortality ratios compare "the actual number of deaths in an area with the expected number given its demographic profile, if it had the same death rates as" the reference population of England and Wales. See Boyle and Hamblin, *Health Economy*, 5.

7. William Wordsworth, "Lines Written upon Westminster Bridge" (1802), *Times*, 2 Jan. 1855, cited in Lee Jackson, *Dirty Old London: The Victorian Fight against Filth* (New Haven, CT: Yale University Press, 2015), 212.

8. Stephen Halliday, "Death and Miasma in Victorian London: An Obstinate Belief," *British Medical Journal* (2001): 1469–71.

9. For the pre-nineteenth-century history of London smoke, see Peter Brimblecombe, *The Big Smoke: A History of Air Pollution in London since Medieval Times* (London: Methuen, 1987), 1–86, 90.

10. Henry T. Bernstein, "The Mysterious Disappearance of Edwardian London Fog," *London Journal* 1 (1975): 189–206, 192.

11. Charles Dickens, *Bleak House* (1853; London: Penguin Books, 1974), 49.

12. MOAR, St George Southwark (1873–1874), 18; MOAR, Hampstead (1867), 64, cited in Anne Hardy, *The Epidemic Streets: Infectious Disease and the Rise of Preventive Medicine* (Oxford: Oxford University Press, 1993), 236.

13. MOAR, St James's Westminster (1858), 15; (1863), 45, cited in Hardy, *Epidemic Streets*, 241.

14. Bill Luckin, "'The Heart and Home of Horror': The Great London Fogs of the Later Nineteenth Century," in *Death and Survival in Urban Britain* (London: I. B. Tauris, 2015), 121. For a cultural history of London fog, see Christine L. Corton, *London Fog: The Biography* (Cambridge, MA: Belknap Press of Harvard University Press, 2015).

15. Rollo Russell, *London Fogs* (London: Edward Stanford, 1880), 27.

16. Russell, *Fogs*, 22–24; "Fogs," annotation, *Lancet* 1 (1880): 665–66, 665.

17. Luckin, "Heart and Home," 122.

18. Luckin, "Heart and Home," 122.

19. "Fogs," 666.

20. Russell, *Fogs*, 26.

21. Bernstein, "Mysterious Disappearance," 206.

22. W. D. P. Logan, "Mortality in the London Fog Incident, 1952," *Lancet* 1 (1953): 336–38, 338; Christopher Klein, "The Great Smog of 1952," History Channel, 6 Dec. 2012, www.history.com/news/the-killer-fog-that-blanketed-london-60-years-ago.

23. MOAR, LCC, 1960, 49.

24. MOAR, LCC, 1962, 15. See also J. A. Scott, "The London Fog of 1962," *Medical Officer* 109 (1975): 250–52.

25. Rohan Naik, "Silent Killer: In London, Air Pollution Has Become a Matter of Life and Death," *Pacific Standard*, 6 Sept. 2018, https://psmag.com/environment/air-pollution-is-killing-london.

26. H. Lyon Thompson, "The Collection and Disposal of House and Trade Refuse," *Journal of the Royal Sanitary Institute* 32 (1911): 57–61, 57. Dust holes were fixed brick or wooden bunkers, located in basements, back yards or gardens. See Jackson, *Dirty Old London*, 7; see also Andrea Tanner, "Dust-Oh! Rubbish in Victorian London, 1860–1900," *London Journal* 31, no. 2 (2006): 157–78.

27. William Hamer, "Nuisance from Flies," MOAR, LCC, 1907, appendix 2, 7.

28. F. M. L. Thompson, *Victorian England: The Horse-Drawn Society* (London: Bedford College, 1970).

29. W. Eassie, "Collection and Disposal of House Refuse," *Transactions of the Sanitary Institute* 6 (1883–1884): 221–29, 227.

30. Thompson, *Horse-Drawn Society*, 10; Nigel Morgan, "Infant Mortality, Flies and Horses in Later-Nineteenth-Century Towns: A Case Study of Preston," *Continuity and Change* 17 (2002): 97–132.

31. MOAR, LCC, 1909, 75.

32. Hamer, "Nuisance from Flies," 9. For Niven's views, see Morgan, "Infant Mortality."

33. George S. Graham-Smith, "The Relation of the Decline in the Number of Horse-Drawn Vehicles, and Consequently of the Urban Breeding Grounds of Flies, to the Fall

in Summer Diarrhoea Death Rate," *Journal of Hygiene* 29 (1929–1930): 122–38; Graham-Smith, "Further Observations on the Relation of the Decline in the Number of Horse-Drawn Vehicles to the Fall in Summer Diarrhoea Death-Rate," *Journal of Hygiene* 39 (1939): 558–62. For a fuller discussion of this issue, see Anne Hardy, *Salmonella Infections, Networks of Knowledge, and Public Health in Britain, 1880–1975* (Oxford: Oxford University Press, 2015), 71–77.

34. "The Trend of Infant Mortality," Notes and Comments, *Medical Officer* 54 (1935): 149.

35. On the history of smoking, see Matthew Hilton, *Smoking in British Popular Culture, 1800–2000: Popular Pleasures* (Manchester: Manchester University Press, 2000); Rosemary Elliott, *Women Smoking since 1890* (London: Routledge, 2008).

36. MOAR, Shoreditch, 1921, 28; MOAR, Hackney, 1965, 7

37. Boyle and Hamblin, *Health Economy*, map 3, 13. Heart disease and strokes, also known to be associated with smoking, and air pollution more generally, did not replicate this pattern. All London boroughs in 1989–1994 had SMRs for heart disease below one hundred, and for stroke only Croydon had an SMR above one hundred: maps 4, 5, 15.

38. For the dangers of domestic appliances, which are unquantifiable, see Department of the Environment, *The Health of the Nation: The Environment and Health*, Consultative Document, 1997, 45. In the 1990s lead was the pollutant of concern in gas-driven car engines; by 2010 diesel fuel had become the concern.

39. Peter Brimblecombe and Robert L. Maynard, eds., *The Urban Atmosphere and Its Effects* (London: Imperial College Press, 2001), 1:14–15.

40. For these water courses and others, see London's Lost Rivers, www.londonslostrivers.com, accessed 19 Mar. 2016; Tom Bolton, *London's Lost Rivers* (London: Random House, 2011).

41. Bill Luckin, *Pollution and Control: A Social History of the Thames in the Nineteenth Century* (Bristol, UK: Adam Hilger, 1986), 12–13.

42. British Parliamentary Papers [hereafter BPP], *Report of the Commissioners on the State of the Supply of Water in the Metropolis*, 1828, (267), ix, 104.

43. Anne Hardy, "Water and the Search for Public Health in London in the 18th and 19th Centuries," *Medical History* 24 (1984): 250–82, 253, 271–72.

44. Charles Creighton, *A History of Epidemics in Britain* (Cambridge: Cambridge University Press, 1891), 2:199–200, 217.

45. Hardy, *Epidemic Streets*, 152–53.

46. Hardy, *Epidemic Streets*, 153.

47. These developments are discussed in Luckin, *Pollution and Control*, 35–49.

48. Healthy carriers are individuals who have had typhoid and recovered, but who continue to harbor the bacteria in their bile duct and to excrete them in urine and feces. These bacteria may infect other people in due course through contaminated food or drink.

49. Ernest Hart, *Waterborne Typhoid* (London: Smith Elder, 1897).

50. Ernest Hart, *Report on the Influence of Milk in Spreading Zymotic Disease* (London: Smith Elder, 1897), 19–24. See also Luckin, *Pollution and Control*, 125–26.

51. See Hardy, *Epidemic Streets*, figs. 6.1, 6.3.

52. MOAR, LCC, 1892, 22; 1902, 58.

53. MOAR, LCC, 1895, 35–36.

54. For this effort, see Anne Hardy, "Cholera, Quarantine and the English Preventive System," *Medical History* 37 (1993): 250–69; Krista Maglen, *The English System: Quarantine, Immigration and the Making of a Port Sanitary Zone* (Manchester: Manchester University Press, 2014).

55. See the discussion in Luckin, *Pollution and Control*, 69–96.

56. BPP, *[Royal] Commissioners Appointed to Inquire into the Best Means of Preventing the Pollution of Rivers, Sixth Report: Domestic Water Supply of Great Britain*, 1874, C. 1112, xxxiii, 472, cited in Luckin, *Pollution and Control*, 77.

57. Central Board of Health, *Lancet* (31 Mar. 1832): 938.

58. Central Board of Health, *Lancet* (31 Mar. 1832): 938.

59. W. P. Bain, "The Cholera at West Ham," *Lancet* 2 (1857): 476; Dr. Elliott, "Cholera at West Ham," *Lancet* 1 (1858): 152

60. Medical News, "Cholera in Sweden," *Lancet* 2 (1858): 363; "Epidemics at Large," Medical Annotations, *Lancet* 2 (1858): 660.

61. Elizabeth Odling, *Memoir of the Late Alfred Smee, F.R.S. by His Daughter* (London: George Bell and Sons, 1878), 73–74.

62. Royston Lambert, *Sir John Simon and English Sanitary Administration* (Bristol, UK: McGibbon and Kee, 1963), 435–36. See also *Lancet* 2 (1871): 227, 326.

63. For the politics and progress of London water improvement after 1860, see Luckin, *Pollution and Control*, 141–55; Christopher Hamlin, *What Becomes of Pollution? Adversary Science and the Controversy on the Self-Pollution of Rivers in Britain, 1750–1914* (New York: Garland, 1987).

64. John Hassan, *The Seaside, Health and Environment in England since 1800* (Aldershot, UK: Ashgate, 2003), 43–46, 49–51.

65. Hardy, *Salmonella Infections*, 46.

66. Hardy, *Salmonella Infections*, 47.

67. MOAR, Newington, 1900, 27–28.

68. MOAR, Local Government Board, PP, 1914, xxxix, 47.

69. MOAR, Local Government Board, PP, 1914, xxxix, 47.

70. In Fulham in 1901 ninety-one hospitalized cases of enteric disease had a 10 percent death rate; forty-three cases treated at home resulted in a 25 percent fatality rate: MOAR, Fulham, 1901, 40.

71. J. T. C. Nash, "Shellfish and Their Relation to Disease, More Particularly Typhoid Fever," *Journal of State Medicine* 11 (1903): 710–26, 716.

72. MOAR, LCC, 1902, 59.

73. MOAR, LCC, 1902, 725.

74. MOAR, Southwark, 1900, section 3: "Special Report on an Outbreak of Enteric Fever," 22–23.

75. MOAR, LCC, 1902, 61.

76. MOAR, LCC, 1903, appendix 1: "Report by the Medical Officer Presenting the Report by Dr Hamer on the Prevention of Enteric Fever in London at the Close of 1903," 2.

77. MOAR, LCC, 1903, appendix 1, 3. See also Hamer, in continuation of this appendix, 8–10.

78. William Hamer in discussion following Harold J. Kerr, "Refuse Disposal in Relation to the Enteric Group of Diseases," *Proceedings of the Royal Society of Medicine* 17 (1924): 33–46, 43.

79. MOAR, LCC, 1920, 1. See also MOAR, LCC, 1919, 19–20.

80. Hardy, *Epidemic Streets*, 142–43; and Hardy, "Cholera, Quarantine."

81. Anne Hardy, "Cholera in London" (unpublished manuscript, 1990), 37.

82. Charles Murchison, "Contributions to the Etiology of Continued Fever," *Medico-Chirurgical Transactions* 41 (1858): 219–306, 229. Murchison's source was Dr. Bateson [*sic*], *On Contagious Fevers* (London, 1818), untraced.

83. Murchison, "Contributions," 229.

84. Murchison, "Contributions," 251.

85. MOAR, LCC, 1892, 10.

86. MOAR, LCC, 1920, 2.

87. MOAR, LCC, 1920, 12.

88. Charles Booth, *Life and Labour of the People in London*, 2nd series, *Industry* (London: Macmillan, 1903), 5:96.

89. Booth, *Life*, 2:103–7; 3:77, 318–19; 4:266, 285. "Phossy jaw" is phosphorus necrosis of the jaw, commonly seen in the women who worked in the matchstick industry in the nineteenth and early twentieth centuries. Phosphorus was a key component of Victorian matches.

90. Booth, *Life*, 4:285–86.

91. John Spear, "Anthrax in London," Local Government Board, *Twelfth Annual Report*, PP 1882–83, Medical Officer's Supplement for 1882, 98–131; Rosemary Wall, *Bacteria in Britain, 1880–1939* (London: Pickering and Chatto, 2013), 95–123.

92. Neil Pemberton and Michael Worboys, *Mad Dogs and Englishmen: Rabies in Britain, 1830–2000* (Basingstoke, UK: Palgrave Macmillan, 2007), 52, 70–71, 80, 108, 128, 134.

93. MOAR, LCC, 1935, 7.

94. MOAR, LCC, 1925, 5–7.

95. MOAR, LCC, 1913, 203.

96. MOAR, LCC, 1925, 7–8.

97. MOAR, LCC, 1925, 8. This event more or less coincided in time with the diminishing fly incidence after 1900.

98. For the impact of the Registrar's decisions, see MOAR, LCC, 1945, 4, 6.

99. MOAR, LCC, 1945, 6.

100. "Health of London in Wartime," editorial, *Medical Officer* 75 (1945): 37. The worst year was 1940 with 7,973 deaths.

101. W. Allen Daley and R. Benjamin, "Tuberculosis in London in Wartime," *British Medical Journal* 2 (1942): 417–20, 417.

102. Daley and Benjamin, "Tuberculosis," 419, 420.

103. MOAR, LCC, 1945, 7, 10, 11.

104. "The London County Council," editorial, *Medical Officer* 83 (1950): 41.

105. "The London County Council," 41. For debates about how London should be governed in this period, see Ken Young, "London Government 1920–1986: Ideal and Reality," *London Journal* 20, no. 1 (2001): 57–68.

106. MOAR, Shoreditch, 1951, 4.

107. MOAR, Shoreditch, 1960, 20.

108. MOAR, Hackney, 1973, 3.

109. See Huw Francis, "Epilogue," in *Recalling the Medical Officer of Health: Writings by Sidney Chave*, ed. Michael Warren and Huw Francis (London: King Edward's Hospital Fund for London, 1987), 147–48.

110. Like Herbert Morrison, Scott regarded the London Government Act of 1964 as mistaken; see "John Alexander Scott," *Medical Officer* 113 (1965): 181.

111. London tuberculosis deaths per 1,000 population stood at 0.06 in 1964: MOAR, LCC, 1964, 8.

112. MOAR, LCC, 1964, 8; lung as principal cancer site, 9.

113. MOAR, LCC, 1962, 12.

114. MOAR, LCC, 1960, 13.

115. Smoking bans did not take effect in Britain until 2006.

116. Boyle and Hamblin, *Health Economy*, 5.

117. Boyle and Hamblin, *Health Economy*, map 1, 12.

118. Boyle and Hamblin, *Health Economy*, 12.

119. Boyle and Hamblin, *Health Economy*, map 2, 14. For the impact of various air pollutants, see Department of the Environment (hereafter DES), *The Health of the Nation: The Environment and Health Consultative Document* (London: HMSO, 1999), 41.

120. DES, *Health*, 49.

121. J. C. H. Miles et al., *Indicative Atlas of Radon in England and Wales* (Chilton, UK: Health Protection Agency, 2007), 14, https://www.ukradon.org/cms/assets/gfx/content/resource_2686cs3a0844cee4.pdf.

122. Mark McCarthy and Jake Ferguson, *Environment and Health in London* (London: King's Fund, 1999).

123. McCarthy and Ferguson, *Environment*, 8.

124. McCarthy and Ferguson, *Environment*, 14.

125. McCarthy and Ferguson, *Environment*, 17, 19. The boom in bicycling came in the 2000s.

126. McCarthy and Ferguson, *Environment*, 21, 30.

127. McCarthy and Ferguson, *Environment*, 34.

128. Steven Cummins, "Improving Health in Cities: The Challenge of Our Urban Environment," Inaugural Lecture, London School of Hygiene and Tropical Medicine, 17 Nov. 2015.

129. These infections were: smallpox, measles, scarlet fever, diphtheria, whooping cough, "fever," and diarrhea.

130. MOAR, LCC, 1895, 14.

131. MOAR, LCC, 1895, 14.

132. MOAR, LCC, 1902, Report of the Public Health Committee submitting the Report of the Medical Officer, iii.

133. MOAR, LCC, 1902, 16.

134. Bridges and Balloons, 17 Aug. 2016, https://bridgesandballoons.com-villages-london.

4. London and Early Environmentalism in Britain, 1770–1870

I wish to acknowledge the assistance of Sarah Ferguson, Carolyn Day, Sarah Hamilton, Joseph Stubenrauch, the editors, and two anonymous reviewers in helping me to improve this chapter.

1. Sverker Sörlin and Paul Warde, "Making the Environmental Historical—An Introduction," in *Nature's End: History and the Environment*, ed. Sverker Sörlin and Paul Warde (Basingstoke, UK: Palgrave Macmillan, 2009), 1–19; Stephen Bocking, "Environmentalism," in *The Cambridge History of Science*, vol. 6, *The Modern Biological and Earth Sciences*,

ed. Peter J. Bowler and John V. Pickstone (Cambridge: Cambridge University Press, 2009), 602–21.

2. Clarence J. Glacken, *Traces on the Rhodian Shore* (Berkeley: University of California Press, 1967).

3. Glacken, *Traces*, vii; Charles E. Rosenberg, "Epilogue: *Airs, Waters, Places*: A Status Report," *Bulletin of the History of Medicine* 86 (2012): 661–70.

4. Glacken, *Traces*, 549–50; Sörlin and Warde, "Making the Environmental Historical," 3–4; Bocking, "Environmentalism," 602–3; Linda Nash, *Inescapable Ecologies: A History of Environment, Disease, and Knowledge* (Berkeley: University of California Press, 2006), 1; James Winter, *Secure from Rash Assault: Sustaining the Victorian Environment* (Berkeley: University of California Press, 1999), 19; Bill Luckin, "Pollution in the City," in *The Cambridge Urban History of Britain*, vol. 3, *1840–1950*, ed. Martin Daunton (Cambridge: Cambridge University Press, 2000), 208; Vicky Albritton and Fredrik Albritton Jonsson, *Green Victorians: The Simple Life in John Ruskin's Lake District* (Chicago: University of Chicago Press, 2016), 9–11.

5. Walter Beinart and Lotte Hughes, *Environment and Empire* (Oxford: Oxford University Press, 2007); Albritton and Albritton Jonsson, *Green Victorians*; Luckin, "Pollution in the City," 207–28; and Luckin, *Pollution and Control: A Social History of the Thames in the Nineteenth Century* (Bristol, UK: Adam Hilger, 1986); Winter, *Secure from Rash Assault*; Harriet Ritvo, *The Animal Estate: The English and Other Creatures in the Victorian Era* (Cambridge, MA: Harvard University Press, 1987), chaps. 5 and 6; and Ritvo, *The Dawn of Green: Manchester, Thirlmere, and Modern Environmentalism* (Chicago: University of Chicago Press, 2009); Peter Thorsheim, "Green Space and Class in Imperial London," in *The Nature of Cities*, ed. Andrew C. Isenberg (Rochester, NY: University of Rochester Press, 2006), 24–37; Nicholas Daly, *The Demographic Imagination and the Nineteenth-Century City* (Cambridge: Cambridge University Press, 2015), 161–88.

6. Beinart and Hughes, *Environment and Empire*, chaps. 4, 7, and 12; Albritton and Albritton Jonsson, *Green Victorians*; Ritvo, *Dawn of Green*; Richard H. Grove, *Green Imperialism: Colonial Expansion, Tropical Island Edens, and the Origins of Environmentalism, 1600–1860* (Cambridge: Cambridge University Press, 1995); Peter Thorsheim, *Inventing Pollution: Coal, Smoke, and Culture in Britain since 1800* (Athens: Ohio University Press, 2006); Fredrik Albritton Jonsson, *Enlightenment's Frontier: The Scottish Highlands and the Origins of Environmentalism* (New Haven, CT: Yale University Press, 2013).

7. Winter, *Secure from Rash Assault*, 19; Vladimir Jankovic, *Confronting the Climate: British Airs and the Making of Environmental Medicine* (Basingstoke, UK: Palgrave Macmillan, 2010), 2, 9–10, 36.

8. Glacken, *Traces*, 621; Jankovic, *Confronting the Climate*, 4–5; Rosenberg, "Epilogue," 662–63.

9. Jankovic, *Confronting the Climate*, 2, 9–10; Roy Porter, *The Greatest Benefit to Mankind: A Medical History of Humanity* (New York: W. W. Norton, 1998), 302, 643–44; George Stocking Jr., *Victorian Anthropology* (New York: Free Press, 1987), 14.

10. Jankovic, *Confronting the Climate*; Nash, *Inescapable Ecologies*; Rosenberg, "Epilogue."

11. Nash, *Inescapable Ecologies*, 5.

12. John Hogg, *London as It Is* (1837; New York: Garland Publishing, 1985), xiii–xiv, xvii, xix–xx.

13. "Asiatic Cholera in Southwark," *Times*, 14 Sept. 1853, 10A. A "knacker's yard" was a business engaged in slaughtering diseased or elderly horses, and processing them for their hides and meat.

14. "Cholera in Southwark."

15. "Cholera in Southwark."

16. Glacken, *Traces*, 429, 460, 501, 552, 563; Jankovic, *Confronting the Climate*; Mark Harrison, *Climates and Constitutions: Health, Race, Environment and British Imperialism in India, 1600–1850* (Oxford: Oxford University Press, 1999); Alain Corbin, *The Foul and the Fragrant: Odor and the French Social Imagination* (Cambridge, MA: Harvard University Press, 1988); James C. Riley, *The Eighteenth-Century Campaign to Avoid Disease* (New York: St. Martin's Press, 1987).

17. Jankovic, *Confronting the Climate*; Nash, *Inescapable Ecologies*, chap. 1; Gregg Mitman, "In Search of Health: Landscape and Disease in American Environmental History," *Environmental History* 10 (Apr. 2005): 154–55.

18. "Cholera in Southwark."

19. John Charles Hall, "The Cholera," *Times*, 13 Sept. 1853, 12A.

20. John Conolly, *The Working Man's Companion: The Physician*, vol. 1, *The Cholera* (London: Charles Knight, 1832), 9, 99.

21. Conolly, *Working Man's Companion*, 1:9, 24, 26, 31, 40, 41, 57, 70, 73, 74, 88, 94, 95, 105, 110, 138, 145, 149, 156, 157, 158, 172, 175, 179, 182, 194, 202, 204, (Asiatic) 49, 126.

22. Bill Luckin, *Death and Survival in Urban Britain: Disease, Pollution and Environment, 1800–1950* (London: I. B. Tauris, 2015), 56–68, 56; Michael Worboys, *Spreading Germs: Disease Theories and Medical Practice in Britain, 1865–1900* (Cambridge: Cambridge University Press, 2000), 35–42, 113–17; Michael Zeheter, *Epidemics, Empires, and Environments: Cholera in Madras and Quebec City, 1818–1910* (Pittsburgh: University of Pittsburgh Press, 2015).

23. Zeheter, *Epidemics, Empires, and Environments*, 7. For an account of contemporary disputes regarding cholera's causes and infectiousness, see Christopher Hamlin, *Cholera: The Biography* (Oxford: Oxford University Press, 2009), esp. chap. 4; and Margaret Pelling, *Cholera, Fever and English Medicine, 1825–1865* (Oxford: Oxford University Press, 1978).

24. "Cholera in Southwark"; Sylvia N. Tesh, "Miasma and 'Social Factors' in Disease Causality," *Journal of Health, Politics, Policy and Law* 20, no. 4 (1995): 1010–11.

25. "Cholera in Southwark."

26. Jankovic, *Confronting the Climate*, 59, 94–95.

27. "The Cholera," *Times*, 15 Sept. 1853, 6C.

28. Hall, "Cholera."

29. "circumstance, n.," *Oxford English Dictionary Online* (hereafter *OED*) (Oxford: Oxford University Press, 2016), https://www.oed.com/view/Entry/33377?rskey=LxRl9q&result=1&isAdvanced=false; Jankovic, *Confronting the Climate*, 9, 34.

30. "Cholera in Southwark."

31. Thomas Southwood Smith, *A Treatise on Fever* (London: Longman, 1830), 348–49; Christopher Hamlin, "Predisposing Causes and Public Health in Early Nineteenth-Century Medical Thought," *Social History of Medicine* 5, no. 1 (1992): 62–69; and Hamlin, *Public Health and Social Justice in the Age of Chadwick: Britain, 1800–1854* (Cambridge: Cambridge University Press, 1998); Tesh, "Miasma and 'Social Factors'"; John V. Pick-

stone, "Dearth, Dirt, and Fever Epidemics: Rewriting the History of British 'Public Health,' 1780–1850," in *Epidemics and Ideas: Essays on the Historical Perception of Pestilence*, ed. Terrance Ranger and Paul Slack (Cambridge: Cambridge University Press, 1992), 125–48.

32. Jankovic, *Confronting the Climate*, 26–34; Hamlin, "Predisposing Causes," 43–70.

33. Thomas Bateman, *Reports of the Diseases of London* (London: Longman, 1819), 82, 236, 250.

34. Gregg Mitman, *Breathing Space: How Allergies Shape Our Lives and Landscapes* (New Haven, CT: Yale University Press, 2007), 12–14.

35. Thomas Bartlett, *Consumption: Its Causes, Prevention, and Cure* (London: Hippolyte Balliere, 1855), 146–49.

36. Bartlett, *Consumption*, 148–49; "M'Cormac and Bartlett on Consumption," *Dublin Quarterly Journal of Medical Science* 21, no. 41 (1856): 177; Jankovic, *Confronting the Climate*, 119–20.

37. James Carter, *Memoirs of a Working Man* (London: Charles Knight, 1845), 230–31; Luckin, "Pollution in the City," 209; and Luckin, *Death and Survival*, 121–23, 129–30.

38. Katherine Byrne, *Tuberculosis and the Victorian Literary Imagination* (Cambridge: Cambridge University Press, 2011), 16; Helen Bynum, *Spitting Blood: The History of Tuberculosis* (Oxford: Oxford University Press, 2012), chap. 3.

39. Byrne, *Tuberculosis*, 13, 26; Jankovic, *Confronting the Climate*; Hamlin, "Predisposing Causes"; and Hamlin, *Public Health and Social Justice*.

40. Hamlin, *Public Health and Social Justice*, 62–63; Bynum, *Spitting Blood*, 61.

41. Hamlin, "Predisposing Causes"; Jankovic, *Confronting the Climate*, 26–34; Tesh, "Miasma and 'Social Factors'"; Pickstone, "Dearth, Dirt, and Fever."

42. Charles E. Rosenberg, *Explaining Epidemics and Other Studies in the History of Medicine* (Cambridge: Cambridge University Press, 1992), 77; James Johnson, *A Change of Air, or The Pursuit of Health* (London: S. Highly and T. and G. Underwood, 1831), i.

43. Hector Gavin, *Unhealthiness of London and the Necessity for Remedial Measures* (1847; New York: Garland, 1985), 65.

44. "Death from Asiatic Cholera, Adjourned Coroner's Inquest," *Times*, 27 Aug. 1853, 10F.

45. "Cholera in Southwark."

46. Hamlin, "Predisposing Causes," 51–59; Jankovic, *Confronting the Climate*, 15–16; Nash, *Inescapable Ecologies*, 27–28, 56–68; Corbin, *Foul and the Fragrant*, 11–21.

47. Jankovic, *Confronting the Climate*, 141, 149; Harrison, *Climates and Constitutions*; Zeheter, *Epidemics, Empires, and Environments*.

48. Jankovic, *Confronting the Climate*, 121, 126; Mitman, *Breathing Space*, 14; Beinart and Hughes, *Environment and Empire*, 35–36; Harrison, *Climates and Constitutions*, 111–47; E. M. Collingham, *Imperial Bodies: The Physical Experience of the Raj, c. 1800–1947* (Cambridge: Polity Press, 2001), 83–88; Dane Kennedy, *The Magic Mountains: Hill Stations and the British Raj* (Berkeley: University of California Press, 1996).

49. Jankovic, *Confronting the Climate*, 46–54, 59, 94–96, 116.

50. Charles Dickens, *Dombey and Son* (1848; London: Penguin, 2002), 523.

51. "unwholesome, *adj.*," *OED*.

52. Gavin, *Unhealthiness of London*, 39–40.

53. Victor Bailey, *"This Rash Act": Suicide across the Life Cycle in the Victorian City* (Stanford, CA: Stanford University Press, 1998), 66–69.

54. Jankovic, *Confronting the Climate*, 48–49.

55. James Devlin, "The Model Lodging-Houses, and the Working Classes," in *Meliora; or, Better Times to Come*, ed. Viscount Ingestre (1853; London: Frank Cass, 1971), 2:166.

56. Sidney Godolphin Osborne, "Immortal Sewage," in *Meliora*, 2:7.

57. Anon., "Leaves from the Lives and Opinions of Working Men. Second Series," reprinted in *Meliora*, 2:115.

58. Thomas Shillitoe, *Journal of the Life, Labours, and Travels of Thomas Shillitoe, in the Service of the Gospel of Jesus Christ*, ed. A. R. B. (London: Harvey and Darton, 1839), 1:8–9.

59. Shillitoe, *Journal*, 1:v; D. Bruce Hindmarsh, *The Evangelical Conversion Narrative: Spiritual Autobiography in Early Modern England* (Oxford: Oxford University Press, 2005), 6–8; David Vincent, *Bread, Knowledge and Freedom: A Study in Nineteenth-Century Working Class Autobiography* (London: Methuen, 1981), 14–19.

60. Shillitoe, *Journal*, 1:1–4.

61. Shillitoe, *Journal*, 1:1–5.

62. Jankovic, *Confronting the Climate*, 6; Rosenberg, *Explaining Epidemics*, 74–85; Luckin, *Death and Survival*, 125–26.

63. Anon., "Student Life in London," *Medical Times and Gazette*, 24 Dec. 1853, 658–59.

64. Rosenberg, *Explaining Epidemics*, 77; Hamlin, "Predisposing Causes," 55–56.

65. Gavin, *Unhealthiness of London*, 65–66.

66. Gavin, *Unhealthiness of London*, 66; James Ranald Martin, *The Influence of Tropical Climates on European Constitutions* (London: John Churchill, 1856), 138; James Johnson, *The Influence of Tropical Climates on European Constitutions* (Portsmouth, UK: Motley and Harrison, 1818), 446–47.

67. Johnson, *Change of Air*, 2–4; Jankovic, *Confronting the Climate*, 88, 119–22.

68. Hogg, *London as It Is*, xii–xvii.

69. Hogg, *London as It Is*, 91–92, 101, 114, 133–37, 151–52, 157–61, 311–12.

70. "Review of John Hogg, *London as It Is*," *Monthly Review* 3, no. 1 (Sept. 1837): 69.

71. Jankovic, *Confronting the Climate*, 6, 42–43.

72. William Cowper, *The Task* (1785), in *The Poems of William Cowper*, vol. 2, ed. John D. Baird and Charles Ryskamp (Oxford: Oxford University Press, 1995), bk. 1, line 749; Lynda Nead, *Victorian Babylon: People, Streets, and Images in Nineteenth-Century London* (New Haven, CT: Yale University Press, 2000), 3–4.

73. Hogg, *London as It Is*, chap. 3.

74. Hogg, *London as It Is*, 181–82; Hogg's italics.

75. Gavin, *Unhealthiness of London*, 40, 65.

76. George A. Walker, *Gatherings from Graveyards: Particularly Those of London* (London: Longmans, 1839), 9.

77. Jankovic, *Confronting the Climate*, 12, 36–38, 64–65; Thorsheim, *Inventing Pollution*, 10–18.

78. Thomas Miller, *Picturesque Sketches of London: Past and Present* (London: National Illustrated Library, 1852), 230.

79. Jankovic, *Confronting the Climate*, 88–90.

80. "London," *Chambers's Journal*, 29 July 1843, 221–22.

81. Johnson, *Change of Air*, 1–2; "A Looking-Glass for London No. XVIII," *Penny Magazine* 6, no. 328 (1837): 260–61; Christopher Ferguson, *An Artisan Intellectual: James Carter and the Rise of Modern Britain, 1792–1853* (Baton Rouge: Louisiana State University Press, 2016), chap. 3; Thomas De Quincey, "The Nation of London" (1834), in *The*

Collected Writings of Thomas De Quincey, ed. David Masson (London: A. and C. Black, 1896), 1:181.

82. Christopher J. Ferguson, "Inventing the Modern City: Urban Culture and Ideas in Britain, 1780–1880" (PhD diss., Indiana University, 2008), 5–7.

83. Johnson, *A Change of Air*, i.

84. Hogg, *London as It Is*, 32.

85. Raymond Williams, *The Country and the City* (Oxford: Oxford University Press, 1973).

86. Thorsheim, *Inventing Pollution*, 28–30, 111–17; Christine Corton, *London Fog: The Biography* (Cambridge, MA: Belknap Press of Harvard University Press, 2015), 17–25.

87. Dr. James Ranald Martin quoted in *The Second Report of the Commissioners for Inquiring into the State of Large Towns and Populous Districts* (London: HMSO, 1845), 298.

88. Hamlin, *Public Health and Social Justice*; Pickstone, "Dearth, Dirt and Fever."

89. "Cholera in Southwark."

90. "Cholera in Southwark"; Luckin, "Pollution in the City," 211; Hamlin, *Public Health and Social Justice*.

91. Luckin, "Pollution in the City," 213; Ferguson, *Inventing the Modern City*, 175–77.

92. Asa Briggs, *Victorian Cities* (1963; Berkeley: University of California Press, 1993), 22.

93. Editorial, *The Builder*, 19 Sept. 1846, 445.

94. John Snow, *On the Mode and Communication of Cholera* (London: John Churchill, 1849), 8–9, 11.

95. Snow, *Mode of Communication of Cholera* (London: John Churchill, 1855), 76–81, 38–51, 38.

96. Snow, *Mode of Communication of Cholera*, 57.

97. Luckin, *Death and Survival*, 56–68; Worboys, *Spreading Germs*; Peter Baldwin, *Contagion and the State in Europe, 1830–1930* (Cambridge: Cambridge University Press, 1999), 123–243. For two accounts celebrating Snow as a pioneering medical theorist, see Steven Johnson, *The Ghost Map: The Story of London's Most Terrifying Epidemic—and How It Changed Science, Cities, and the Modern World* (New York: Riverhead, 2006); and Sandra Hempel, *The Strange Case of the Broad Street Pump: John Snow and the Mystery of Cholera* (Berkeley: University of California Press, 2007).

98. Nash, *Inescapable Ecologies*, 6; Worboys, *Spreading Germs*; Mitman, *Breathing Space*, 8; Christopher Hamlin, "Providence and Putrefaction: Victorian Sanitarians and the Natural Theology of Health and Disease," in *Energy and Entropy: Science and Culture in Victorian Britain*, ed. Patrick Brantlinger (Bloomington: Indiana University Press, 1989), 93–123.

99. Mitman, *Breathing Space*, 8; Mitman, "In Search of Health," 195.

100. Luckin, *Death and Survival*; Baldwin, *Contagion and the State*; Anne Hardy, *The Epidemic Streets: Infectious Disease and the Rise of Preventive Medicine, 1856–1900* (Oxford: Clarendon Press, 1993).

101. Luckin, "Pollution in the City," 209, 227.

102. Briggs, *Victorian Cities*, chap. 8.

103. Gareth Stedman Jones, *Outcast London: A Study in the Relationship between the Classes in Victorian Society* (Oxford: Clarendon Press, 1971).

104. Judith R. Walkowitz, *City of Dreadful Delight: Narratives of Sexual Danger in Late-*

Victorian London (Chicago: University of Chicago Press, 1992); Jonathan Schneer, *London 1900: The Imperial Metropolis* (New Haven, CT: Yale University Press, 1999).

105. Glacken, *Traces*, 549–50; Stocking, *Victorian Anthropology*, 14; Luckin, "Pollution in the City," 224; and Luckin, "Revisiting the Idea of Degeneration in Urban Britain, 1830–1900," *Urban History* 32, no. 2 (2006): 234–52.

106. Mitman, *Breathing Space*, xii, 8.

107. Bill Luckin, "The Shaping of a Public Environmental Sphere in Late Nineteenth-Century London," in *Medicine, Health and the Public Sphere in Britain, 1600–2000*, ed. Steve Sturdy (London: Routledge, 2002), 224–40; Luckin, *Death and Survival*, 132; Thorsheim, *Inventing Pollution*, 48–56; Corton, *London Fog*, 91–92.

108. Robert Colls, *Identity of England* (Oxford: Oxford University Press, 2002), 207.

109. Seth Koven, *Slumming: Sexual and Social Politics in Victorian London* (Princeton, NJ: Princeton University Press, 2004), 94–103; A Country Parishioner, "Our Child Visitors from London," *Spectator*, 15 Sept. 1888, 1259; Thorsheim, *Inventing Pollution*, 63–67.

110. Sanderson quoted in Sonya O. Rose, *Which People's War? National Identity and Citizenship in Britain, 1939–1945* (Oxford: Oxford University Press, 2003), 210.

111. Rose, *Which People's War?*, 210–12.

112. Nash, *Inescapable Ecologies*, 5; Rosenberg, "Epilogue," 668–70.

113. Colls, *Identity of England*, 235–36.

5. Green Space in London

1. Julian Hunt, "London's Sustainability: An Overview," in *London's Environment: Prospects for a Sustainable World City*, ed. Julian Hunt (London: Imperial College Press, 2005), 8.

2. Susan Lasdun, *The English Park: Royal, Private and Public* (New York: Vendome Press, 1992), 150.

3. Henry W. Lawrence, "The Greening of the Squares of London: Transformation of Urban Landscapes and Ideals," *Annals of the Association of American Geographers* 83, no. 1 (1993): 90–118; Jeremy Burchardt, *Paradise Lost: Rural Idyll and Social Change in England since 1800* (London: I. B. Tauris, 2002), 46; Aya Sakai, "'Re-Assessing' London's Squares: The Development of Preservation Policy, 1880–1931," *Town Planning Review* 82, no. 6 (2011): 615–37.

4. Quoted in Lasdun, *English Park*, 130.

5. Burchardt, *Paradise Lost*, 53–54.

6. Lasdun, *English Park*, 149.

7. Chris Cook and John Stevenson, *The Longman Handbook of Modern British History, 1714–2001* (London: Longman, 2001), 78–81.

8. James H. Winter, *London's Teeming Streets, 1830–1914* (London: Routledge, 1993), 165.

9. Lasdun, *English Park*, 128.

10. Lasdun, *English Park*, 128; David A. Reeder, "The Social Construction of Green Space in London prior to the Second World War," in *The European City and Green Space: London, Stockholm, Helsinki and St Petersburg, 1850–2000*, ed. Peter Clark (Aldershot, UK: Ashgate, 2005), 50.

11. Lasdun, *English Park*, 190.

12. Antony Taylor, "'Commons Stealers,' 'Land-Grabbers' and 'Jerry-Builders': Space,

Popular Radicalism and the Politics of Public Access in London, 1848–1880," *International Review of Social History* 40 (1995): 385–86.

13. Lasdun, *English Park*, 185.

14. Jerry White, *London in the Nineteenth Century: "A Human Awful Wonder of God"* (London: Jonathan Cape, 2007), 262, 370, 432; John Wigley, *The Rise and Fall of the Victorian Sunday* (Manchester: Manchester University Press, 1980), 68–69.

15. Taylor, "'Commons Stealers,'" 402.

16. Lasdun, *English Park*, 160; Burchardt, *Paradise Lost*, 56.

17. Taylor, "'Commons Stealers,'" 391, 399.

18. "Parks without Railings," *Manchester Courier*, 26 Sept. 1913, Metropolitan Public Gardens Association (hereafter MPGA) cuttings collection, Guildhall Library, London; White, *London in the Nineteenth Century*, 372–73.

19. Gareth Stedman Jones, *Outcast London: A Study in the Relationship between Classes in Victorian Society* (London: Verso, 2013), 241–42, 291–92.

20. Nan H. Dreher, "The Virtuous and the Verminous: Turn-of-the-Century Moral Panics in London's Public Parks," *Albion* 29, no. 2 (Mar. 1997): 246–67, 260, 264.

21. "Threatened Beauty Spots," *Globe*, 27 June 1916, MPGA cuttings collection, Guildhall Library, London.

22. David Edward Owen, *The Government of Victorian London, 1855–1889: The Metropolitan Board of Works, the Vestries, and the City Corporation* (Cambridge, MA: Belknap Press of Harvard University Press, 1982), 150; Matti O. Hannikainen, *The Greening of London, 1920–2000* (Aldershot, UK: Ashgate, 2016), 34–35. Half a century later private donors raised over £160,000 to help its successor, the London County Council, purchase 131 acres of Kenwood, adjacent to Hampstead Heath. The amount of land that was open to the public expanded further when Lord Iveagh donated Kenwood House and 75 acres of land surrounding it to the LCC in the mid-1920s.

23. White, *London in the Nineteenth Century*, 95, 469.

24. Reeder, "The Social Construction," 41.

25. Burchardt, *Paradise Lost*, 47–48. Londoners' penchant for referring to green space as the lungs of the city dates to the 1820s, if not earlier. See Winter, *London's Teeming Streets*, 153.

26. S. Martin Gaskell, "Gardens for the Working Class: Victorian Practical Pleasure," *Victorian Studies* 23 (summer 1980): 479–501; Howard LeRoy Malchow, "Public Gardens and Social Action in Late Victorian London," *Victorian Studies* 29 (autumn 1985): 97–124; Peter Thorsheim, "Green Space and Class in Imperial London," in *The Nature of Cities: Culture, Landscape, and Urban Space*, ed. Andrew Isenberg (Rochester, NY: University of Rochester Press, 2006), 24–37; Robyn Mary Curtis, "English Women and the Late Nineteenth Century Open Space Movement" (PhD diss., Australian National University, 2016).

27. Alun Howkins, *Reshaping Rural England: A Social History, 1850–1925* (London: HarperCollins Academic, 1991), 229. In 1899 the Commons Preservation Society merged with the National Footpaths Preservation Society (founded in 1884) to form the Commons and Footpaths Preservation Society. Today the group, which recently celebrated its sesquicentennial, is known as the Open Spaces Society.

28. Lord Eversley, *Commons, Forests and Footpaths* (London: Cassell, 1910), 2; John Ranlett, "'Checking Nature's Desecration': Late-Victorian Environmental Organization," *Victorian Studies* 26, no. 2 (1983): 197–222.

29. "The Kyrle Society," *Woman's Gazette*, June 1878, 87; Mary Logan, *Guide to the Italian Pictures at Hampton Court, with Short Studies of the Artists*, Kyrle Pamphlets—No. 2 (London: A. D. Innes, 1894). For an excellent recent study that sheds new light on the Hills and other female environmental reformers, see Curtis, "English Women."

30. Octavia Hill, "The Future of Our Commons," *Fortnightly Review*, Nov. 1877, 640–41.

31. Winter, *London's Teeming Streets*, 170.

32. David A. Reeder, "London and Green Space, 1850–2000: An Introduction," in *The European City and Green Space: London, Stockholm, Helsinki and St Petersburg, 1850–2000*, ed. Peter Clark (Aldershot, UK: Ashgate, 2005), 36.

33. Alun Howkins, *The Death of Rural England: A Social History of the Countryside since 1900* (Abingdon, UK: Taylor and Francis, 2003), 105.

34. Raphael Samuel, *Island Stories: Unravelling Britain, Theatres of Memory*, vol. 2 (London: Verso, 1998).

35. Patrick Joyce, *The Rule of Freedom: Liberalism and the Modern City* (London: Verso, 2003), 214.

36. Gerry Kearns, "Biology, Class and the Urban Penalty," in *Urbanising Britain: Essays on Class and Community in the Nineteenth Century*, ed. Gerry Kearns and Charles W. J. Withers (Cambridge: Cambridge University Press, 1991), 12–30; Anne Hardy, *The Epidemic Streets: Infectious Disease and the Rise of Preventive Medicine, 1856–1900* (Oxford: Clarendon Press, 1993), 238.

37. Bill Luckin, "Pollution in the City," in *The Cambridge Urban History of Britain*, vol. 3, *1840–1950*, ed. Martin Daunton (Cambridge: Cambridge University Press, 2000), 207–28; Peter Thorsheim, *Inventing Pollution: Coal, Smoke, and Culture since 1800* (Athens: Ohio University Press, 2006); Lee Jackson, *Dirty Old London: The Victorian Fight against Filth* (New Haven, CT: Yale University Press, 2014).

38. Christopher Hamlin, "The City as a Chemical System? The Chemist as Urban Environmental Professional in France and Britain, 1780–1880," *Journal of Urban History* 33, no. 5 (2007): 702–28; Michelle Elizabeth Allen, *Cleansing the City: Sanitary Geographies in Victorian London* (Athens: Ohio University Press, 2008); Clare Hickman, "'To Brighten the Aspect of Our Streets and Increase the Health and Enjoyment of Our City': The National Health Society and Urban Green Space in Late-Nineteenth Century London," *Landscape and Urban Planning* 118 (2013): 112–19.

39. Dale H. Porter, *The Thames Embankment: Environment, Technology, and Society in Victorian London* (Akron, OH: University of Akron Press, 1998); White, *London in the Nineteenth Century*, 61; Ian Douglas, *Cities: An Environmental History* (London: I. B. Tauris, 2013), 260.

40. "A Word for the Surrey Side," *Times*, 21 Jan. 1914, MPGA cuttings collection, Guildhall Library, London. Webb's dream of pedestrian access along the South Bank did not became a reality until much later, when the Silver Jubilee Walkway opened in 1977. See Philip Howard, "Pedestrian Trail Opens New Thameside Vistas to Jubilant Londoners," *Times*, 9 June 1977, 2.

41. "Proceedings of the Health Section," *Sanitary Record*, n.s. 1 (20 Oct. 1879): 141.

42. John A. Burton, *The Naturalist in London* (Newton Abbot, UK: David & Charles, 1974), 31; Thorsheim, *Inventing Pollution*, 34–35, 64; Paul A. Elliott, *British Urban Trees: A Social and Cultural History, ca. 1800–1914* (Winwick, UK: White Horse Press, 2016), chap. 7.

43. Robert Angus Smith, *A Centenary of Science in Manchester* (London: Taylor and Francis, 1883), 62.

44. Burton, *Naturalist in London*, 32.

45. J. O. Springhall, "Lord Meath, Youth, and Empire," *Journal of Contemporary History* 5 (1970): 97–111; F. H. A. Aalen, "Lord Meath, City Improvement, and Social Imperialism," *Planning Perspectives* 4 (1989): 127–52; Joyce Bellamy, "The Metropolitan Public Gardens Association," *London Gardener, or the Gardener's Intelligencer* 9 (2003): 29–35.

46. MPGA, *Report for the Year 1904*, 30, Guildhall Library, London.

47. Lord Meath, "The London County Council and Open Spaces," *New Review*, Dec. 1892, 705.

48. Lord Meath, "Public Playgrounds for Children," *Nineteenth Century*, Aug. 1893, 268.

49. Peter Thorsheim, "The Corpse in the Garden: Burial, Health, and the Environment in Nineteenth-Century London," *Environmental History* 16, no. 1 (2011): 38–68; Tim Brown, "The Making of Urban 'Healtheries': The Transformation of Cemeteries and Burial Grounds in Late-Victorian East London," *Journal of Historical Geography* 42 (2013): 12–23.

50. Meath, "London County Council," 701–7, 705.

51. "Playing Fields for London," *Times*, 6 Mar. 1890, 8; Editorial, *Times*, 6 Mar. 1890, 9. See also H. W. deB. Peters, *The London Playing Fields Society: Centenary History, 1890 to 1990* (Brentford: The Society, 1990).

52. Dreher, "Virtuous and the Verminous," 254.

53. On the prevalence of such ideas internationally during the late nineteenth and early twentieth centuries, see J. Edward Chamberlin and Sander L. Gilman, eds., *Degeneration: The Dark Side of Progress* (New York: Columbia University Press, 1985); Daniel Pick, *Faces of Degeneration: A European Disorder, c. 1848–c. 1918* (Cambridge: Cambridge University Press, 1989). For a specifically British focus, see Bill Luckin, "Revisiting the Idea of Degeneration in Urban Britain, 1830–1900," *Urban History* 33, no. 2 (2006): 234–52; Ina Zweiniger-Bargielowska, *Managing the Body: Beauty, Health, and Fitness in Britain, 1880–1939* (New York: Oxford University Press, 2010), esp. chap. 1; James J. Harris, "Body Politics: Public Health and Politics in Britain, 1885–1922" (PhD diss., Ohio State University, 2017).

54. T. C. Horsfall, discussing Basil Holmes, "Open Spaces, Gardens, and Recreation Grounds," *Transactions of the Town Planning Conference, London, 10–15 October 1910*, 494. On the remarkable life and influence of this reformer, see Michael Harrison, "Thomas Coglan Horsfall and 'the Example of Germany,'" *Planning Perspectives* 6, no. 3 (1991): 297–314; Harold L. Platt, *Shock Cities: The Environmental Transformation and Reform of Manchester and Chicago* (Chicago: University of Chicago Press, 2005).

55. Helena Beaufoy, "Order out of Chaos: The London Society and the Planning of London, 1912–1920," *Planning Perspectives* 12, no. 2 (1997): 135–64.

56. Hannikainen, *Greening of London*, 25.

57. Hannikainen, *Greening of London*, 35, 55.

58. Hannikainen, *Greening of London*, 24; Marco Amati and Makoto Yokohari, "The Establishment of the London Greenbelt: Reaching Consensus over Purchasing Land," *Journal of Planning History* 6, no. 4 (2007): 314.

59. "Sunday Recreation," *Daily Telegraph*, 19 Apr. 1934, clipping in London Metropolitan Archives, CL/PK/1/24; Hannikainen, *Greening of London*, 58–59.

60. "Games on Sundays," 9 May 1934, London Metropolitan Archives, CL/PK/1/24.

61. L. J. Phillips to the LCC, 29 June 1934, London Metropolitan Archives, CL/PK/1/24.

62. Deputations on the Subject of Sunday Competition Games, 29 June 1934, London Metropolitan Archives, CL/PK/1/24.

63. "Heathman," letter to the editor, *Hampstead and Highgate Express*, 22 Sept. 1939.

64. MPGA, *Report for the Year 1939*, 13, Guildhall Library, London; Thorsheim, "Corpse in the Garden," 61.

65. Report of the Parks Committee, LCC, Minutes, 21 Apr. 1942, and 20 June 1944, London Metropolitan Archives. On the history of allotment gardening, see Burchardt, *Paradise Lost*, 50–52.

66. Corporation of London Public Relations Office, *A Living Environment* (London, 2001).

67. "The Firemen's Farm in the Heart of the City of London," *Illustrated London News*, 19 Aug. 1944, 217.

68. F. E. Carter to Chief Administrative Officer, Regional Headquarters, London Civil Defence Region, 29 Jan. 1942, London Metropolitan Archives, LC/C.E./WAR/02/104.

69. A. J. H. Clayton to CO/RF/R.H.Q., 8 Aug. 1941, London Metropolitan Archives, LC/C.E./C/WAR/02/104; Hannikainen, *Greening of London*, 149; Peter Thorsheim, *Waste into Weapons: Recycling in Britain during the Second World War* (New York: Cambridge University Press, 2015), 175.

70. Thorsheim, *Waste into Weapons*.

71. Hannikainen, *Greening of London*, 131–32, 154.

72. "Amenities of London Squares," *Country Life*, 25 Sept. 1942, MPGA cuttings collection, Guildhall Library, London.

73. "Playing Fields as Allotments," *Times*, 24 May 1940, MPGA cuttings collection, Guildhall Library, London.

74. MPGA, *Report for the Year 1940*, 6.

75. "Greater London's Green Spaces," *Architects' Journal*, 2 Oct. 1941, MPGA cuttings collection, Guildhall Library, London; Hannikainen, *Greening of London*, 135.

76. H. H. Martin to the LCC, 5 Aug. 1942, London Metropolitan Archives, CL/PK/1/24.

77. Report of the Parks Committee, LCC, Minutes, 20 Oct 1942, London Metropolitan Archives.

78. Anne R. Vernon to the LCC, 23 May 1943, London Metropolitan Archives, CL/PK/1/24.

79. Report of the Parks Committee, LCC, Minutes, 2 Nov 1943, London Metropolitan Archives.

80. E. O. Hoppé, *Rural London in Pictures* (London: Odhams, 1951), 11.

81. "Wild Flowers in the City," *Times*, 1 Sept. 1942; "Nature Makes Her Own Garden in a Blitzed Site," *Illustrated London News*, 23 June 1945, 678–79.

82. Burton, *Naturalist in London*, 23.

83. MPGA, *Report for the Year 1940*, 7.

84. Gerald Dix, "Patrick Abercrombie, 1879–1957," in *Pioneers in British Planning*, ed. Gordon E. Cherry (London: Architectural Press, 1981), 110.

85. LCC, Minutes, 13 Apr. 1943, 84–85, London Metropolitan Archives; J. H. Forshaw and Patrick Abercrombie, *County of London Plan* (London: Macmillan, 1944).

86. Patrick Abercrombie, *Greater London Plan, 1944* (London: HMSO, 1945).

87. Forshaw and Abercrombie, *County of London Plan*, 2–3.

88. Forshaw and Abercrombie, *County of London Plan*, 1, 3–4.

89. Forshaw and Abercrombie, *County of London Plan*, 10, 36, 39. Fabiano Lemes de Oliveira, "Green Wedges: Origins and Development in Britain," *Planning Perspectives* 29, no. 3 (2014): 357–79.

90. John M. Eyler, *Victorian Social Medicine: The Ideas and Methods of William Farr* (Baltimore: Johns Hopkins University Press, 1979).

91. Mervyn Miller, "Raymond Unwin (1860–1940)," in *Pioneers of British Planning*, ed. Gordon Cherry, 72–102, (London: Architectural Press, 1981); Burchardt, *Paradise Lost*, 163.

92. Hannikainen, *Greening of London*, 109, 124, 150.

93. William J. Bull, "The Best Memorial to Queen Victoria: A Green Girdle around London," *Sphere*, 4 May 1901, 128–29; Lord Meath, "The Green Girdle round London," *Sphere*, 20 July 1901, 64.

94. Patrick Joseph Murray, "The Council for the Preservation of Rural England, Suburbia and the Politics of Preservation," *Prose Studies* 32, no. 1 (Apr. 2010): 25–37; Amati and Yokohari, "Establishment of the London Greenbelt," 311–37, esp. 316.

95. "Airport at Stations," *Daily Mail*, 10 June 1942, in MPGA cuttings, Guildhall Library.

96. Camilla Ween, "London, England: A Global and Sustainable Capital City," in *Green Cities of Europe: Global Lessons on Green Urbanism*, ed. Timothy Beatley (Washington, DC: Island Press, 2012), 182, 211.

97. Amati and Yokohari, "Establishment of the London Greenbelt," 314–16.

98. Amati and Yokohari, "Establishment of the London Greenbelt," 317–18, 330. Arguments about such trade-offs have long been part of the discussion; see Green Belt Working Group, *The Improvement of London's Green Belt* (London: Standing Conference on London and South East Regional Planning, 1976); Martin J. Elson, Caroline Steenberg, and Nicola Mendham, *Green Belts and Affordable Housing: Can We Have Both?* (Bristol, UK: Policy Press, 1996).

99. David Matless, *Landscape and Englishness* (London: Reaktion Books, 1998), 35.

100. Patricia L. Garside, "Politics, Ideology, and the Issue of Open Space in London, 1939–2000," in *The European City and Green Space: London, Stockholm, Helsinki and St Petersburg, 1850–2000*, ed. Peter Clark (Aldershot, UK: Ashgate, 2005), 93.

101. Bill Luckin, "Unending Debate: Town, Country and the Construction of the Rural in England, 1870–2000," in *Death and Survival in Urban Britain* (London: I. B. Tauris, 2015), 141–54.

102. Luckin, "Unending Debate," 147–48.

103. On the ability of parks to cool the city, see Hunt, "London's Sustainability," 8. On particulate pollution, see Paul Henderson, "Biodiversity and the Urban Environment: Benefits, Trends and Opportunities," in Hunt, *London's Environment*, 126.

104. Hannikainen, *Greening of London*, 188; Richard Reynolds, *On Guerilla Gardening: A Handbook for Gardening without Boundaries* (New York: Bloomsbury, 2008).

105. Hannikainen, *Greening of London*, 189–90; Thorsheim, "Corpse in the Garden."

106. Reeder, "London and Green Space," 40; "A Guide to the Green Chain Walk," South London Club, https://www.southlondonclub.co.uk/blog/2017/9/22/a-guide-to-the-green-chain-walk, accessed 28 July 2019.

107. Hannikainen, *Greening of London*, 180.

108. Thorsheim, *Inventing Pollution*, 142, 158.

109. Taryn J. P. Nixon, "Foundations of a World City—London's Historic Environment and Future," in Hunt, *London's Environment*, 42; Ween, "London," 183.

110. Burton, *Naturalist in London*, 19.

111. Hannikainen, *Greening of London*, 49–50.

112. For the building owner's perspective, see "Welcome to London's Highest Garden," https://skygarden.london/sky-garden, accessed 28 July 2019; for a critique published upon its opening, see "Critics Hit the Roof Garden," GardenDrum, last modified 18 Jan. 2015, https://gardendrum.com/2015/01/18/critics-hit-the-roof-garden/.

113. Gary Grant, "Extensive Green Roofs in London," *Urban Habitats* 4, no. 1 (2006): 52, 57; D. B. Rowe, "Green Roofs as a Means of Pollution Abatement," *Environmental Pollution* 159, no. 8–9 (2011): 2100–10.

114. Sustainability has become an influential concept among organizations large and small, from the United Nations to business firms and local authorities. In 2002 Mayor Ken Livingstone established the London Sustainable Development Commission, a body which has been instrumental in helping policy makers to consider the long view. See London Assembly, "About the London Sustainable Development Commission," https://www.london.gov.uk/about-us/organisations-we-work/london-sustainable -development-commission/who-we-are/about-lsdc, accessed 28 July 2019. The scholarly literature on this topic is immense. See esp. Mike Jenks and Colin Jones, eds., *Dimensions of the Sustainable City* (Dordrecht, The Netherlands: Springer, 2010); Paul Warde, "The Invention of Sustainability," *Modern Intellectual History* 8, no. 1 (Apr. 2011): 153–70; Ingrid Leman-Stefanovic and Stephen B. Scharper, *The Natural City: Re-Envisioning the Built Environment* (Toronto: University of Toronto Press, 2012); Christopher W. Wells, "Green Cities, the Search for Sustainability, and Urban Environmental History," *Journal of Urban History* 40, no. 3 (2014): 613–20; and Rebecca Leigh Rutt and Natalie Marie Gulsrud, "Green Justice in the City: A New Agenda for Urban Green Space Research in Europe," *Urban Forestry and Urban Greening* 19 (Sept. 2016): 123–27.

6. Moving East

1. For contemporary concerns, see Peter Thorsheim, *Inventing Pollution: Coal, Smoke, and Culture in Britain since 1800* (Athens: Ohio University Press, 2006); Bill Luckin, "Pollution in the City," in *Cambridge Urban History of Britain*, vol. 3, *1840–1950*, ed. M. J. Daunton (Cambridge: Cambridge University Press, 2000): 207–28; Lee Jackson, *Dirty Old London: The Victorian Fight against Filth* (New Haven, CT: Yale University Press, 2014).

2. A. E. Dingle, "'The Monster Nuisance of All': Landowners, Alkali Manufacturers, and Air Pollution, 1828–64," *Economic History Review* 35 (1982): 529–48; Peter Reed, "Robert Angus Smith and the Alkali Inspectorate," in *The Chemical Industry in Europe, 1850–1914: Industrial Growth, Pollution, and Professionalization*, ed. Ernst Homburg, Anthony S. Travis, and Harm G. Schröter (Dordrecht, Netherlands: Kluwer Academic, 1998), 149–64; Reed, "The Alkali Inspectorate, 1874–1906: Pressure for Wider and Tighter Pollution Regulation," *Ambix* 59 (2012): 131–51.

3. L. D. Schwarz, *London in the Age of Industrialisation: Entrepreneurs, Labour Force, and Living Conditions, 1700–1850* (Cambridge: Cambridge University Press, 1992), 241–63. See also Joyce M. Bellamy, "Occupational Statistics in the Nineteenth Century," in *The Census and Social Structure: An Interpretative Guide to Nineteenth Century Censuses*

for England and Wales, ed. Richard Lawton (London: F. Cass, 1978), 165–78; Guy Routh and Charles Booth, *Occupations of the People of Great Britain, 1801–1981* (Basingstoke, UK: Macmillan, 1987), 1–18.

4. Richard Dennis, "Modern London," in *Cambridge Urban History of Britain*, 3:121–22. See the following articles, all in *London Journal* 21 (1996): Martin J. Daunton, "Industry in London: Revisions and Reflections," 1–8; Paul Johnson, "Economic Development and Industrial Dynamism in Victorian London," 27–37; David Green, "The Nineteenth-Century Metropolitan Economy: A Revisionist Interpretation," 9–26.

5. Peter Hall, *The Industries of London since 1861* (London: Hutchinson University Library, 1962), 21.

6. Michael Ball and David Sunderland, *An Economic History of London, 1800–1914* (London: Routledge, 2001), 294, 317.

7. Dennis, "Modern London," 124; Anthony S. Wohl, *Endangered Lives: Public Health in Victorian Britain* (Cambridge, MA: Harvard University Press, 1983), 220.

8. Ball and Sunderland, *Economic History*, 316–17.

9. John Marriott, *Beyond the Tower: A History of East London* (New Haven, CT: Yale University Press, 2011).

10. Ball and Sunderland, *Economic History*, 316.

11. Peter J. Atkins, "Animal Wastes and Nuisances," in *Animal Cities: Beastly Urban Histories*, ed. Peter J. Atkins (Farnham, UK: Ashgate, 2012), 19–52, 30–31; David Owen et al., *The Government of Victorian London, 1855–1889: The Metropolitan Board of Works, the Vestries, and the City Corporation* (Cambridge, MA: Harvard University Press, 1982), 153–54.

12. John A. Tully, *Silvertown: The Lost Story of a Strike That Shook London and Helped Launch the Modern Labor Movement* (New York: Monthly Review Press, 2014), 64–82. On Thames pollution, see Bill Luckin, *Pollution and Control: A Social History of the Thames in the Nineteenth Century* (Bristol, UK: Adam Hilger, 1986), chap. 1.

13. Dennis, "Modern London," 109.

14. *Report of the Royal Commission on Noxious Vapours*, British Parliamentary Papers (hereafter BPP), 1878, C. (2d series) 2159, hereafter RNV, 308.

15. Ball and Sunderland, *Economic History*, 316–17.

16. Second Report of the Commissioners Appointed to Inquire into the Best Means of Preventing the Pollution of Rivers (River Lee), BPP, 1867, C. (1st series) 3835, xiii.

17. "The River Thames," *Engineering*, 14 Aug. 1874, 125.

18. Tully, *Silvertown*, 68.

19. Wohl, *Endangered Lives*, 215; RNV, 305.

20. Ben Pontin, "The Common Law Clean Up of the 'Workshop of the World': More Realism about Nuisance Law's Historic Environmental Achievements," *Journal of Law and Society* 40 (2013): 173–98.

21. On the development of pollution control and administration, see Tom Crook, *Governing Systems: Modernity and the Making of Public Health in England, 1830–1910* (Oakland: University of California Press, 2016), chap. 4; Christopher Hamlin, "Nuisances and Community in Mid-Victorian England: The Attractions of Inspection," *Social History* 38, no. 3 (2013): 346–79; and Hamlin, "Public Sphere to Public Health: The Transformation of 'Nuisance,'" in *Medicine, Health, and the Public Sphere in Britain, 1600–2000*, ed. Steve Sturdy (New York: Routledge, 2002), 346–79; James G. Hanley, *Healthy Boundaries: Property, Law, and Public Health in England and Wales, 1815–1872* (Rochester, NY: University of Rochester Press, 2016).

22. Wohl, *Endangered Lives*, 179.

23. Wohl, *Endangered Lives*, 195; Joseph Robinson, *Sanitary Inspectors' Practical Guide* (London: Shaw & Sons, 1884).

24. Reed, "Alkali Inspectorate"; Dingle, "'Monster Nuisance of All'"; Reed, "Robert Angus Smith and the Alkali Inspectorate."

25. Peter Reed, *Acid Rain and the Rise of the Environmental Chemist in Nineteenth-Century Britain: Science, Technology and Culture, 1700–1945.* (Farnham, UK: Ashgate, 2014), 157–59.

26. Jerry White, *London in the Nineteenth Century: "A Human Awful Wonder of God"* (London: Vintage, 2008), chap. 15; Owen et al., *Government of Victorian London*, chap. 1.

27. Gloria Clifton, *Professionalism, Patronage and Public Service in Victorian London: The Staff of the Metropolitan Board of Works, 1856–1889* (London: Athlone Press, 1992), chap. 13.

28. Dennis, "Modern London," 101.

29. John Simon, *Reports Relating to the Sanitary Condition of the City of London* (London: John W. Parker, 1854), 24.

30. Ian MacLachlan, "A Bloody Offal Nuisance: The Persistence of Private Slaughter-Houses in Nineteenth-Century London," *Urban History* 34 (2007): 227–54, 228–29; Peter J. Atkins, "The Urban Blood and Guts Economy," in Atkins, *Animal Cities*, 77–106, 82–84.

31. MacLachlan, "Bloody Offal Nuisance," 237–38.

32. Simon, *Reports Relating to the Sanitary Condition*, 24.

33. *Smithfield and the Slaughter-Houses: A Letter to the Right Honorable Viscount Morpeth* (London: Smith Elder, 1847), 13.

34. *Annual Report of the Medical Officer of Health*, County of London (hereafter ARLCC) (1894), 45; ARLCC (1896), 53.

35. Daunton, "Industry in London," 3–4; Alfred Spencer, "On the Supervision of Offensive Trades in the Metropolis," *Transactions of the Society of Medical Officers of Health, Session, 1884–5* (1885): 22–43, 26; Caroline M. Barron, *London in the Later Middle Ages: Government and People, 1200–1500* (Oxford: Oxford University Press, 2004), 264.

36. Atkins, "Animal Wastes and Nuisances," 28, citing 57 Geo. III, c. 29.

37. Edwin Chadwick, *Report on the Sanitary Condition of the Labouring Population of Great Britain* (London: Clowes, 1842).

38. Select Committee on The Health of Towns, PP (11), (1840), 165, cited in MacLachlan, "Bloody Offal Nuisance," 238.

39. Christopher Hamlin, *Public Health and Social Justice in the Age of Chadwick: Britain, 1800–1854* (Cambridge: Cambridge University Press, 1998).

40. Metropolitan Buildings Act (1844), 7 & 8 Vict., c. 84, clauses 55–57. See also Spencer, "Supervision of Offensive Trades," 23–24.

41. Alexander Wynter Blyth, *A Manual of Public Health* (London: Macmillan, 1890), 248.

42. Atkins, "Animal Wastes and Nuisances," 29.

43. *Report from the Select Committee of the House of Lords on Injury from Noxious Vapour*, BPP (14), (1862), 238; Metropolis Building Act (1855), 18 & 19 Vict., c. 122

44. *Report from the Select Committee on Noxious Businesses*, BPP (284), (1873), iv; Slaughterhouses etc. Metropolis Act (1874), 37 & 38 Vict., c. 67; Spencer, "Supervision of Offensive Trades," 24–25.

45. Wohl, *Endangered Lives*, 179–80.

46. *Report from Select Committee on Noxious Businesses* (1873), x, 434; Simon, *Reports Relating to the Sanitary Condition*, 25.

47. *Report from Select Committee on Noxious Businesses* (1873), xvii; Atkins, "Animal Wastes and Nuisances," 31; Metropolis (Local Management) Act (1855), 18 & 19 Vict., c. 120.

48. Atkins, "Blood and Guts Economy," 100.

49. Dubruntfaut, "Manufacture of Beet Root Sugar in France," *Farmer's Register* 5 (1 Nov. 1837): 403; Charles Kingzett et al., "Albumin of Commerce," *Pharmaceutical Journal and Transactions* 8 (27 Sept. 1877): 253–54. Edward Ballard, "Report by Dr. Ballard on the Effluvium Nuisances Arising in Connexion with Various Manufacturing and Other Branches of Industry," in *Sixth Annual Report of the Local Government Board, 1876–77, Supplement, Containing the Report of the Medical Officer for 1876* (London: George E. Eyer, 1877), 145–46, 213.

50. Atkins, "Blood and Guts Economy," 102.

51. James Halkett, "On the Adulteration of Bone Dust," *Quarterly Journal of Agriculture* 11 (1840): 177–78; *Report from the Select Committee of the Health of Towns*, BPP (28), (1840), 58; Ballard, "Effluvium Nuisances," 224–36; Spencer, "Supervision of Offensive Trades," 27–28.

52. *Report from the Select Committee on the Public Health Bill and Nuisances Removal Amendment Bill*, BPP (13), (1855), 4.

53. Ballard, "Effluvium Nuisances," 164–67.

54. Atkins, "Blood and Guts Economy," 96.

55. Spencer, "Supervision of Offensive Trades," 31.

56. Atkins, "Blood and Guts Economy," 90–98.

57. Ballard, "Effluvium Nuisances," 168–80.

58. Ballard, "Effluvium Nuisances," 180–85; Blyth, *Manual of Public Health*.

59. Atkins, "Blood and Guts Economy," 98; Blyth, *Manual of Public Health*, 284.

60. Ballard, "Effluvium Nuisances," 146, 189–92. The other stomachs had a different consistency, not suited for food.

61. Spencer, "Supervision of Offensive Trades," 28.

62. Slaughterhouses & c. (Metropolis) Act (1874), c. 65; Atkins, "Animal Wastes and Nuisances," 32; bylaws listed in Blyth, *Manual of Public Health*, 248–70.

63. Blyth, *Manual of Public Health*, 265–66.

64. ARLCC (1894), 45; ARLCC (1896), 53.

65. The Public Health (London) Act (1891), 54 & 55 Vict., c. 76.

66. ARLCC (1893), 45.

67. ARLCC (1894), 46.

68. MacLachlan, "Bloody Offal Nuisance," 247; *London Statistics 1907–8: Statistics of the Administrative County of London, and of the Public Services Carried on Therein* (London: London County Council, 1908), 18:110; P. L. Simmonds, *Waste Products and Undeveloped Substances; A Synopsis of Progress Made in Their Economic Utilisation during the Last Quarter of a Century at Home and Abroad* (London: R. Hardwicke, 1873), 29–30; Atkins, "Blood and Guts Economy," 104; Spencer, "Supervision of Offensive Trades," 25.

69. "West Ham: Local Government and Public Services," in *A History of the County of Essex*, ed. W. R. Powell (London: Institute of Historical Research, 1973), 96–112.

70. Henry Morley, "Londoners over the Border," *Household Words*, 12 Sept. 1857, 241.

71. "West Ham: Local Government and Public Services."

72. See, for example, the glue shop bylaw discussed in Blyth, *Manual of Public Health*, 284–86; for disinfectants in tanneries, see 282; for building standards, see 250ff.; for tall chimneys, see 282.

73. Blyth, *Manual of Public Health*, 284; Spencer, "Supervision of Offensive Trades," 31.

74. Reed, " Alkali Inspectorate," 134–35.

75. Wohl, *Endangered Lives*, 230; for salt, cement, manure, nitric acid, ammonia, chlorine, and gas, see Alkali &c. Works Regulation Act (1881), 44 & 45 Vict., c. 37.

76. Ballard, "Effluvium Nuisances," 272–76.

77. Spencer, "Supervision of Offensive Trades," 30, 32.

78. *29th Annual Report on Alkali, &c. Works by the Chief Inspector* (London: HMSO, 1893), 1–2, 101,

79. Ballard, "Effluvium Nuisances," 242–47; Spencer, "Supervision of Offensive Trades," 29–30.

80. P. L. Cottrell, "Resolving the Sewage Question: Metropolis Sewage and Essex Reclamation Company, 1865–81," in *Cities of Ideas: Civil Society and Urban Governance in Britain, 1800–2000: Essays in Honour of David Reeder*, ed. Robert Colls, Richard Rodger, and David A. Reeder (Aldershot, UK: Ashgate, 2004), 67–95, 69–74.

81. Joseph Bazalgette and Henry Letheby, "Report on an Inspection of Manure and Chemical Works in the Neighbourhood of the Northern and Southern Outfalls. Ordered to Be Printed May 19th 1865," in *Minutes of Proceedings of the Metropolitan Board of Works* (Jan.–June 1865): 607–9.

82. *Journal of Gas Lighting, Water Supply, & Sanitary Improvement*, 8 Aug. 1865, 611; Bazalgette and Letheby, "Report on an Inspection of Manure and Chemical Works," 607–9.

83. Ballard, "Effluvium Nuisances," 258; *Report on the Lower Thames Nuisance* (Medical Department of the Local Government Board, 1873). On Ballard, see G. H. Brown, "Edward Ballard," in *Lives of the Fellows*, ed. William Munk (Royal College of Physicians, 1897).

84. RNV, 327.

85. Simon, *Reports Relating to the Sanitary Condition*, 136.

86. Peter Brimblecombe, *The Big Smoke: A History of Air Pollution in London since Medieval Times* (New York: Methuen, 1987), 98.

87. Thorsheim, *Inventing Pollution*.

88. Simon, *Reports Relating to the Sanitary Condition*, 184–87.

89. Brimblecombe, *Big Smoke*, 101–3.

90. Smoke Nuisance Abatement (Metropolis) Act (1853), 16 & 17 Vict., c. 128; Amendment (1856), 19 & 20 Vict., c. 107.

91. B. W. Clapp, *An Environmental History of Britain since the Industrial Revolution* (London: Longman, 1994), 33–34; *Smoke Consuming Furnaces—Returns*, BPP (550), (1861).

92. Wohl, *Endangered Lives*, 220.

93. RNV, 307.

94. Wohl, *Endangered Lives*, 223.

95. RNV, 315.

96. ARLCC (1906), 61.

97. Mark Jenner, "The Politics of London Air: John Evelyn's *Fumifugium* and the Restoration," *The Historical Journal* 38 (1995): 535–51; Brimblecombe, *Big Smoke*, chaps. 2–3.

98. Wohl, *Endangered Lives*, 212, 220–21; Brimblecombe, *Big Smoke*, chap. 6.

99. Brimblecombe, *Big Smoke*, 109, 113, 163–65; Thorsheim, *Inventing Pollution*, 55, 94, 113–15, 131.

100. *Parliamentary Debates, Fourth Series* (1906), 23 May 1906, 157:1257.

101. W. Keld Whytehead, *The City Smoke Prevention Act, with Suggestions on the Use of Smoke-Consuming Furnaces* (London: J. Weale, 1851); David Brownlie, "John George Bodmer: His Life and Work, Particularly in Relation to the Evolution of Mechanical Stoking," *Transactions of the Newcomen Society* 6 (1925): 86–110; Carlos Flick, "The Movement for Smoke Abatement in 19th-Century Britain," *Technology and Culture* 21 (1980): 29–50.

102. *Smoke Consuming Furnaces—Returns*.

103. Brimblecombe, *Big Smoke*, chap. 8; Thorsheim, *Inventing Pollution*, chap. 11.

104. Goad Fire Insurance Plans, British Library, www.bl.uk/onlinegallery/onlineex/firemaps/fireinsurancemaps.html.

105. Leslie Tomory, "The Environmental History of the Early British Gas Industry, 1812–1830," *Environmental History* 17 (2012): 29–54; *Report of the Commissioners Appointed by His Majesty to Inquire into the State of the Supply of Water in the Metropolis*, BPP (IX), (1828).

106. *Report of the Commissioners Appointed by His Majesty to Inquire into the State of the Supply of Water in the Metropolis*, 42, 67–74, 98, 101–2; "Extracts from the Public Newspapers," *The Cottager's Monthly Visitor* 7 (1827): 526. See also Luckin, *Pollution and Control*; Christopher Hamlin, *A Science of Impurity: Water Analysis in Nineteenth Century Britain* (Berkeley: University of California Press, 1990).

107. Gasworks Clauses Act (1847), 10 Vict., c. 15, 21–23.

108. *Lighting and Watching of Parishes in England and Wales* (1830), 11 Geo. IV, c. 27; Lighting and Watching Act (1833), 3 & 4 Will. IV, c. 90.

109. Luckin, *Pollution and Control*, 163–72.

110. Thomas Bartlett Simpson, *Gas-Works: The Evils Inseparable from Their Existence in Populous Places* (London: W. Freeman, 1866), 44–52.

111. Lewis Thompson, *The Chemistry of Gas Lighting: A Collection of Fragments from Vols. II and III of "The Journal of Gas Lighting"* (London: Journal of Gas Lighting, 1860), chap. 2; Wohl, *Endangered Lives*, 230.

112. Stirling Everard, *The History of the Gas Light and Coke Company, 1812–1949* (London: Benn, 1949), 181–82.

113. Christopher Hamlin, "Letheby, Henry (1816–1876)," in *Oxford Dictionary of National Biography*, ed. H. C. G. Matthew, Brian Harrison, and Lawrence Goldman (Oxford: Oxford University Press, 2004).

114. "City of London Commission of Sewers, Tuesday Sept. 23. The City of London Gas-works," *Journal of Gas Lighting*, 30 Sept. 1856, 540; Simpson, *Gas-Works*, 40–43.

115. Everard, *History of the Gas Light*, 237, 242–43.

116. *Gas Journal*, 20 Nov. 1877, 790–97, 827–33; *Sulphur Compounds in Gas: Report of the Proceedings before a Committee of the House of Commons on the Crystal Palace District Gas and the Gaslight & Coke Company Bills* (London: W. B. King, 1877), 38, 101, 105–9; British Association of Gas Managers, *Report of Proceedings, Thirteenth Annual Meeting* (1876), 69.

117. *Sulphur Compounds in Gas*, 24.

118. RNV, 24–25.

119. "Nuisance from Sulphuric Acid Fumes," *Sanitary Record*, 17 Aug. 1877, 113; RNV, 316, 319.

120. "Nuisance from Chemical Works," *Sanitary Record*, 13 Dec. 1878, 381.

121. Ball and Sunderland, *Economic History*, 312–13.

122. Ball and Sunderland, *Economic History*, 312–13.

123. Ball and Sunderland, *Economic History*, 313–15.

124. George Rosen, *A History of Public Health* (1952; Baltimore: Johns Hopkins University Press, 2015), 245–50; V. Long, *The Rise and Fall of the Healthy Factory: The Politics of Industrial Health in Britain, 1914–60* (London: Palgrave MacMillan, 2010), 56–61; Reed, *Acid Rain*, 155–57.

125. "The Home of Doulton Ware," *Brick and Clay Record* 6 (1897): 311–16.

126. Clapp, *Environmental History of Britain*, 26.

127. "Lambeth District Board of Work. Thursday, May 29. Alleged Nuisance at the London Gas-works," *Gas Journal*, 9 June 1857, 294.

128. "The Home of Doulton Ware," 312–13.

129. "The Ventilation of the Houses of Parliament," *Architect*, 4 Oct. 1884, 215.

130. "The Smoke Question: The Lambeth Potteries and Westminster Abbey," *British Clayworker*, Sept. 1900, 210–11, and Aug. 1914, 134.

131. Spencer, "Supervision of Offensive Trades," 34–38, 41–42; Ballard, "Effluvium Nuisances," 58–60.

132. ARLCC (1894), 45–46.

133. "Nuisance from Asphalte [*sic*]," *Sanitary Record*, 26 Oct. 1877, 271.

134. Stephen Mosley, *The Chimney of the World: A History of Smoke Pollution in Victorian and Edwardian Manchester* (London: Routledge, 2013), 180–83.

135. Bill Luckin, "The Shaping of a Public Environmental Sphere in Late Nineteenth-Century London" in *Medicine, Health, and the Public Sphere in Britain, 1600–2000*, ed. Steve Sturdy (New York: Routledge, 2002), 224–40.

136. Thorsheim, *Inventing Pollution*, chap. 3.

137. Simon, *Reports Relating to the Sanitary Condition*, 27.

138. Reed, "Alkali Inspectorate," 149; Reed, *Acid Rain*, 157–59.

7. Water and Its Meanings in London, 1800-1914

The author would like to thank the following for their helpful comments: the editors of this volume, Carry van Lieshout, Frank Trentmann, and two anonymous reviewers.

1. Ivan Illich, *H₂o and the Waters of Forgetfulness* (London: Marion Boyars, 1986), 24–25, 76.

2. Abel Wolman, "The Metabolism of Cities," *Scientific American* 213, no. 3 (1965): 179–90; Maria Kaika and Erik Swyngedouw, "The Urbanization of Nature: Great Promises, Impasse, and New Beginnings," in *The New Blackwell Companion to the City*, ed. Gary Bridge and Sophie Watson (2000; Oxford: Blackwell, 2011), 567–80; Karen Bakker, *An Uncooperative Commodity: Privatizing Water in England and Wales* (Oxford: Oxford University Press, 2003), 20; Jamie Linton, *What Is Water? The History of a Modern Abstraction* (Vancouver: University of British Columbia Press, 2010), 148–61; William Cronon, *Nature's Metropolis: Chicago and the Great West* (New York: W.W. Norton, 1991); Joel A. Tarr, *The Search for the Ultimate Sink: Urban Pollution in Historical Perspective* (Akron, OH: University of Akron Press, 1996).

3. Erik Swyngedouw, "The Political Economy and Political Ecology of the Hydro-Social Cycle," *Journal of Contemporary Water Research & Education* 142 (2009): 56–60.

4. Thomas Osborne, "Security and Vitality: Drains, Liberalism and Power in the Nine-

teenth Century," in *Foucault and Political Reason: Liberalism, Neo-Liberalism, and Rationalities of Government*, ed. Andrew Barry, Thomas Osborne, and Nikolas Rose (Chicago: University of Chicago Press, 1996), 114; Bakker, *Uncooperative Commodity*, 20; Karen Bakker, "From Archipelago to Network: Urbanization and Water Privatization in the South," *Geographical Journal* 169, no. 4 (2003): 328–41; Matthew Gandy, "Vicissitudes of Urban Nature: Transitions and Transformations at a Global Scale," *Radical History Review* 107 (2010): 180–81; Maria Kaika, *City of Flows: Modernity, Nature and the City* (New York: Routledge, 2004).

5. For technology's scripted and unscripted uses, see Madeline Akrich, "The Description of Technical Objects," in *Shaping Technology / Building Society: Studies in Sociotechnical Change*, ed. Wiebe E. Bijker and John Law (Cambridge, MA: MIT Press, 1992), 205–24.

6. Carry van Lieshout, "London's Changing Waterscapes: The Management of Water in Eighteenth-Century London" (PhD diss., University of London, 2012), 194–96, https://kclpure.kcl.ac.uk/portal/files/32139633/2013_Van_Lieshout_Carry_0430811_ ethesis.pdf.

7. Karen Bakker and Gavin Bridge, "Material Worlds? Resource Geographies and the 'Matter of Nature,'" *Progress in Human Geography* 30, no. 1 (2006): 18.

8. Tony Allan, *Virtual Water: Tackling the Threat to Our Planet's Most Precious Resource* (London: I. B. Taurus, 2011); Jim Clifford, "The River Lea in West Ham: A River's Role in Shaping Industrialization on the Eastern Edge of Nineteenth-Century London," in *Urban Rivers: Remaking Rivers, Cities, and Space in Europe and North America*, ed. Stéphane Castonguay and Matthew Evenden (Pittsburgh: University of Pittsburgh Press, 2012), 34–56; *Parliamentary Debates*, 2nd series (1825), 12:992–93.

9. Anne Hardy, "Parish Pump to Private Pipes: London's Water Supply in the Nineteenth Century," in *Living and Dying in London*, ed. W. F. Bynum and Roy Porter, *Medical History*, suppl. no. 11 (1991): 83–84; Margaret Pelling, "Contagion/Germ Theory/Specificity," in *Companion Encyclopaedia of the History of Medicine*, ed. W. F. Bynum and Roy Porter (London: Routledge, 1993), 1:310.

10. Bill Luckin, "The Metropolitan and the Municipal: The Politics of Health and Environment in London, 1860–1920," in *Cities of Ideas: Governance and Citizenship in Urban Britain*, ed. Robert Colls and Richard Rodger (Aldershot, UK: Ashgate, 2004), 53.

11. John Graham-Leigh, *London's Water Wars: The Competition for London's Water Supply in the Nineteenth Century* (London: Francis Boutle, 2000).

12. Metropolis Water Act (1902), 2 Edw. 7, c. 41.

13. For early industrial consumers and firefighting, see Leslie Tomory, *The History of the London Water Industry, 1580–1820* (Baltimore: John Hopkins University Press, 2017), 197–201, 209–12; van Lieshout, "London's Changing Waterscapes." For wells, see Joseph Prestwich, *A Geological Inquiry Respecting the Water-bearing Strata of the Country around London, with Reference especially to the Water Supply of the Metropolis, and including some Remarks on Springs* (London: John Van Voorst, 1851), 55, 67, 235.

14. *Report by the General Board of Health on the Supply of Water to the Metropolis*, British Parliamentary Papers (hereafter BPP) 1850, C. (1st series) 1218, 15; *Report by the General Board of Health on the Supply of Water to the Metropolis*, Appendix I, *Returns to Queries Addressed to Metropolitan Water Companies*, BPP 1850, C. (1st series) 1281, 4.

15. *Royal Commission for Inquiring into State of Large Towns and Populous Districts,*

First Report, Minutes of Evidence, BPP 1844, C. (1st series) 572, qs. 5874–75; Hardy, "Parish Pump," 78; interview with Mrs. Malins, Evening News, 21 Sept. 1908, Islington Local History Centre: Cuttings Box, L5.7, typescript.

16. Joseph Hillier, "Implementation without Control: The Role of the Private Water Companies in establishing Constant Water in Nineteenth-Century London," Urban History 41, no. 2 (2014): 228–46.

17. London's population recorded in the 1801 census was 958,863. This "inner ring" population had expanded to 4,211,056 by 1891 (LCC's "municipal London," 121 sq. mi.). Greater London's 1891 population was 5,633,332 (Metropolitan Police District, 701 sq. mi.). See Royal Commission on the Water Supply of the Metropolis [hereafter Balfour Commission], Minutes of Evidence, BPP 1893–1894, XL pt 1, C. (2nd series) 7172-I, qs. 3051–60; Balfour Commission, Appendixes, XL pt 2, C. (2nd series) 7172-II, appendix C, tables 1, 2; Stephen Inwood, A History of London (London: Macmillan, 1998), 411.

18. Metropolitan Water Board [hereafter MWB], London's Water Supply, 1903–1953 (London: Staples, 1953), 43.

19. Rosemary Weinstein, "New Urban Demands in Early Modern London," in Bynum and Porter, Living and Dying in London, 30.

20. John Wright, The Dolphin: or, Grand Junction Nuisance, Proving that Seven Thousand Families in Westminster and Its Suburbs Are Supplied with Water in a State Offensive to the Sight ... and Destructive to Health (London: T. Butcher, 1827).

21. Metropolis Water Act (1852), 15 & 16 Vict., c. 84; Anne Hardy, "Water and the Search for Public Health in London in the Eighteenth and Nineteenth Centuries," Medical History 28 (1984): 265–66.

22. Bill Luckin, Pollution and Control: A Social History of the Thames in the Nineteenth Century (Bristol, UK: Adam Hilger, 1986), 15; and for the politics of cholera, see chapter 4 in Pollution and Control.

23. Report on the Cholera Epidemic of 1866 in England: Supplement to the Twenty-Ninth Annual Report of the Registrar-General of Births, Marriages and Deaths, BPP 1868, C. (1st series) 4072, xxxi (London deaths from 27 May to 3 Nov. 1854), xxxix.

24. Report on the Cholera Epidemic of 1866, xiii, xxxii.

25. Report on the Cholera Epidemic of 1866, xv–xx.

26. "The East London Water Supply," East London Observer, 29 Sept. 1866, 2; "Memorial to the Honourable the Board of Trade," in Report by Captain Tyler to Board of Trade on Quantity and Quality of Water Supplied by East London Waterworks Company, BPP 1867, no. 339, 37–38.

27. Report on the Cholera Epidemic of 1866, xlv.

28. Luckin, Pollution and Control, 80–81, 89–95; Christopher Hamlin, A Science of Impurity: Water Analysis in Nineteenth-Century Britain (Bristol, UK: Adam Hilger, 1990), 191ff.

29. Margaret Pelling, Cholera, Fever and English Medicine: 1825–1865 (Oxford: Oxford University Press, 1978); Anne Hardy, The Epidemic Streets: Infectious Disease and the Rise of Preventative Medicine 1856–1900 (Oxford: Clarendon Press, 1993); Luckin, Pollution and Control; Bill Luckin, "Evaluating the Sanitary Revolution: Typhus and Typhoid in London, 1851–1900," in Urban Disease and Mortality in Nineteenth Century England, ed. Robert Woods and John Hugh Woodward (London: Batsford Academic and Educational, 1984); Christopher Hamlin, Public Health and Social Justice in the Age of Chadwick (Cambridge: Cambridge University Press, 1998).

30. Luckin, *Pollution and Control*, 3–4. Christopher Hamlin, "State Medicine in Great Britain," in *The History of Public Health and the Modern State*, ed. Dorothy Porter (Amsterdam: Rodopi, 1994), 142–44.

31. Christopher Hamlin, "'Waters' or 'Water'? Master Narratives in Water History and Their Implications for Contemporary Water Policy," *Water Policy* 2, no. 4–5 (2000): 313–25.

32. Illich, H_2O, 76; Linton, *What Is Water?*; Graeme Wynn, "Foreword," in Linton, *What Is Water?*, xi.

33. Dale H. Porter, *The Thames Embankment: Environment, Technology, and Society in Victorian London* (Akron, OH: University of Akron Press, 1998), 16; Luckin, *Pollution and Control*, 180–81.

34. Hanna Steyne, "Stinking Foreshore to Tree Lined Avenue: Investigating the Riverine Lives Impacted by the Construction of the Thames Embankments in Victorian London," *Papers from the Institute of Archaeology* 23, no. 1 (2013): 1–11, http://www.pia-journal.co.uk/articles/10.5334/pia.429/; Stephen Oliver, "Fantasies in Granite: The Thames Embankments as a Boundary to the River," *Literary London: Interdisciplinary Studies in the Representation of London* 5, no. 1 (2007), http://literarylondon.org/the-literary-london-journal/archive-of-the-literary-london-journal/issue-5-1/fantasies-in-granite-the-thames-embankments-as-a-boundary-to-the-river/. On water's enclosures, see also Veronica Strang, *The Meaning of Water* (Oxford: Berg, 2004).

35. Thames Conservancy, *The Thames Conservancy, 1857–1957* (London: Thames Conservancy, 1957); Carol Rose, "The Comedy of the Commons: Custom, Commerce, and Inherently Public Property," in *Property and Persuasion: Essays on the History, Theory, and Rhetoric of Ownership* (Boulder, CO: Westview Press, 1994), 105–62; Bakker, *Uncooperative Commodity*, chap. 2; Joshua Getzler, *A History of Water Rights at Common Law* (Oxford: Oxford University Press, 2006), 268–327.

36. G. J. Shaw-Lefevre, "The London Water Supply," *Nineteenth Century* 44 (1898): 987–88, 990.

37. *Royal Commission on Water Supply, 1868–69: Report*, BPP, XXXIII, C. (1st series) 4169, 165; Hamlin, "'Waters' or 'Water'?"; Illich, H_2o, 7; Kaika, *City of Flows*, 32.

38. Kaika, *City of Flows*, 37, 30.

39. Vanessa Taylor and Frank Trentmann, "Liquid Politics: Water and the Politics of Everyday Life in the Modern City," *Past and Present* 211 (2011): 211.

40. van Lieshout, "London's Changing Waterscapes," 194–95; Mark Jenner, "From Conduit Community to Commercial Network? Water in London, 1500–1725," in *Londinopolis: Essays in the Cultural and Social History of Early Modern London*, ed. Paul Griffiths and Mark Jenner (Manchester: Manchester University Press, 2000), 250.

41. van Lieshout, "London's Changing Waterscapes," 57–64, 269; Garrett Hardin, "The Tragedy of the Commons," *Science* 162, no. 3859 (13 Dec. 1968): 1243–48. Martin V. Melosi, "Path Dependence and Urban History: Is a Marriage Possible?" in *Resources of the City: Contributions to an Environmental History of Modern Europe*, ed. Dieter Schott, Bill Luckin, and Genevieve Massard-Guilbaud (Aldershot, UK: Ashgate, 2005), 262–74.

42. *Minutes of Evidence taken before the Select Committee on the Supply of Water to the Metropolis*, BPP 1821, no. 706, 71; van Lieshout, "London's Changing Waterscapes," 213–26; Frank Trentmann and Vanessa Taylor, "From User to Consumer: Water Politics in Nineteenth-Century London," in *The Making of the Consumer*, ed. Frank Trentmann (Oxford: Berg, 2006), 56.

43. Charles Kingsley, "The Air-Mothers" (1869), in *Sanitary and Social Lectures* (London: Macmillan, 1880), 153, 156–57.

44. Arthur Shadwell, *The London Water Supply* (London: Longmans, Green, and Co., 1899), 12–13 (emphases in original); Trentmann and Taylor, "From User to Consumer," 69. For these leagues, see Taylor and Trentmann, "Liquid Politics."

45. Martin Daunton, "The Material Politics of Natural Monopoly: Consuming Gas in Victorian Britain," in *The Politics of Consumption*, ed. Martin Daunton and Matthew Hilton (Oxford: Berg, 2001), 72, 77, 80, 88. On the regulations' limitations, see Robert Millward, "The Emergence of Gas and Water Monopolies in Nineteenth-Century Britain: Contested Markets and Public Control," in *New Perspectives on the Late Victorian Economy*, ed. James Foreman-Peck (Cambridge: Cambridge University Press, 1991), 96–124. See also Gas Works Clauses Act (1847), 10 Vict., c. 15; and Waterworks Clauses Act (1847), 10 & 11 Vict., c. 17.

46. Daunton, "Material Politics," 76, 88. See also Chris Otter, "Making Liberalism Durable: Vision and Civility in the Late Victorian City," *Social History* 27, no. 1 (2002): 1–15; Chris Otter, *The Victorian Eye: A Political History of Light and Vision in Britain, 1800–1910* (Chicago: University of Chicago Press, 2008).

47. On Theakston's work for the East London Waterworks Co., see Public Monument & Sculpture Association, https://pmsa.org.uk/pmsa-database/2891/, accessed 29 June 2018. On Father Thames, classical forebears, and other sacred associations, see Peter Ackroyd, *Thames: Sacred River* (2007; London: Vintage, 2008), 24, passim; Pamela Odih, *Watersheds in Marxist Ecofeminism* (Newcastle, UK: Cambridge Scholars, 2014); M@, "Who Is Old Father Thames," *Londonist* (blog), 2017, https://londonist.com/2015/07/who-was-old-father-thames.

48. "Dirty Father Thames," *Punch*, 7 Oct. 1848; "Faraday Giving His Card to Father Thames," *Punch*, 21 July 1855; "Father Thames Introducing His Offspring to the Fair City of London," *Punch*, 3 July 1858; "How Dirty Old Father Thames Was Whitewashed," *Punch*, 31 July 1858; "The London Bathing Season," *Punch*, 18 June 1859.

49. Patrick Joyce, *The Rule of Freedom: Liberalism and the Modern City* (London: Verso, 2003); Tom Crook, *Governing Systems: Modernity and the Making of Public Health in England, 1830–1910* (Oakland: University of California Press, 2016), 264–65, passim.

50. Edwin Chadwick, "Head to Foot Washing," *Journal of the Society of Arts* (17 Aug. 1877): 885; Charles Booth's London, BOOTH/B/350: Notebook, 39: Interview with W. Weston, Superintendent of the . . . Bethnal Green Division, 4 Jan. 1898, http://booth.lse.ac.uk/notebooks/b350#?cv=20&c=0&m=0&s=0&z=-640.6982%2C-239.1096%2C2770.3978%2C1647.7778; P. Thompson and T. Lummis, *Family Life and Work Experience before 1918, 1870–1973*, 7th ed., UK Data Service, 2009, https://beta.ukdataservice.ac.uk/datacatalogue/doi/?id=2000#!#1, interview 365.

51. Charles Kingsley, "The Tree of Knowledge" (1874), in *Sanitary and Social Lectures*, 178.

52. Tom Crook, "'Schools for the Moral Training of the People': Public Baths, Liberalism and the Promotion of Cleanliness in Victorian Britain," *European Review of History/Revue européenne d'histoire* 13, no. 1 (2006): 23, 37–39; Crook, "Power, Privacy and Pleasure: Liberalism and the Modern Cubicle," *Cultural Studies* 21, no. 4–5 (2007): 564.

53. Thompson and Lummis, *Family Life and Work Experience*, interview 404.

54. Vanessa Taylor, "Brewers, Temperance and the Nineteenth-Century Drinking Fountain Movement" (PhD diss., University of London, 2006).

55. Gilbert (1903), quoted in "The Shaftesbury Memorial Fountain," in *Survey of London*, vols. 31 and 32, *St James Westminster*, Part 2, ed. F. H. W. Sheppard (London: Athlone Press for the LCC, 1963), 101–10, British History Online, http://www.british-history.ac.uk/survey-london/vols31–2/pt2/pp101–110.

56. London Metropolitan Archives (hereafter LMA): ACC/3168/001: MDFCTA Minutes, 7 Nov. 1862; ACC/3168/002: MDFCTA Minutes, 17 June 1868; ACC/3168/003: MDFCTA Minutes: 6 July 1896; 5 Oct. 1887. ACC/3168/004: MDFCTA Minutes: 30 May 1899; 3 Nov. 1903; Geoffrey Finlayson, *Citizen, State and Social Welfare in Britain, 1830–1990* (Oxford: Clarendon Press, 1994), 6n.

57. Taylor and Trentmann, "Liquid Politics," 226; Hillier, "Implementation without Control," 244–46.

58. Hackney Archives: J/Z 1: [Col. Ducat and Dr F. W. Barry] *Inquiry directed by the Local Government Board into the Causes of the Failure of the East London Water Supply in the Summer of 1895* (London, 1895), 215; (I. A. Crookenden, Secretary, "The Great Drought, 1895: Supply of Water to the East End of London by the East London Waterworks Company: Statement of Facts" [14 Aug. 1895]). See also *Balfour Commission*, C. (2nd series) 7172; *Royal Commission on Water Supply within the Limits of the Metropolitan Water Companies*, BPP 1900, *Minutes of Evidence*, Vol. I , Cd. 45; *Royal Commission on Water Supply*, *Minutes of Evidence*, Vol. II, Cd. 198 [Llandaff Commission].

59. Millward, "Emergence of Gas and Water Monopolies," 96. On party political approaches to water reform in this period, see John Broich, *London: Water and the Making of the Modern City* (Pittsburgh: University of Pittsburgh Press, 2013). For market failure, see Bakker, *Uncooperative Commodity*, 19–20.

60. Taylor and Trentmann, "Liquid Politics," 232, 234.

61. MWB, *London's Water Supply*, 26–29.

62. Though see Kingsley, "Air-Mothers," 152–53.

63. "The Water Supply of London," *Times*, 19 July 1892, 8.

64. Distinct kinds of "waters" from distant sources were considered in *Royal Commission on Water Supply*, 1868–69, 167–68. See also on mineral qualities, Hamlin, "'Waters' or 'Water'?"

65. B. F. C. Costelloe, "London v. the Water Companies," *Contemporary Review* 67 (June 1895): 812.

66. Shaw-Lefevre, "London Water Supply," 987–88, 990. Asok Mukhopadhyay, "The Politics of London Water," *The London Journal* 1, no. 2 (1975): 207–25; John Sheail, "Underground Water Abstraction: Indirect Effects of Urbanization on the Countryside," *Journal of Historical Geography* 8, no. 4 (1982): 395–408; Vanessa Taylor, "Watershed Democracy or Ecological Hinterland? London and the Thames River Basin, 1857–1989," in *Rivers Lost—Rivers Regained*, ed. Dietrich Schott, Martin Knoll, and Uwe Lübken (Pittsburgh: University of Pittsburgh Press, 2017), 63–81.

67. MWB, *London's Water Supply*, 100.

68. Martin Daunton, "Public Place and Private Space: The Victorian City and the Working-Class Household," in *The Pursuit of Urban History*, ed. Derek Fraser and Anthony Sutcliffe (London: Edward Arnold, 1983), 215, 232; Osborne, "Security and Vitality," 115; Patrick Joyce, *The Rule of Freedom: Liberalism and the Modern City* (London: Verso, 2003), 12, 66, 69, 74; compare Taylor and Trentmann, "Liquid Politics," 213–14, 240–41.

69. Hillier, "Implementation without Control," 245–46.

70. Taylor and Trentmann, "Liquid Politics." For construction of demand, see, e.g., Elizabeth Shove, *Comfort, Cleanliness and Convenience: The Sociology of Normality* (Oxford: Berg, 2003).

71. *Balfour Commission,* C. (2nd series) 7172-I, qs. 890–908, 2995–3045; *Balfour Commission,* C. (2nd series) 7172-II, appendix A.9, table 1.

72. *Balfour Commission,* C. (2nd series) 7172-I, qs. 886–89; Taylor and Trentmann, "Liquid Politics," 208–13. On waste, see Hillier, "Implementation without Control."

73. "Water for Trade Purposes," *The Star,* 27 Mar. 1895. This cited an unnamed Private Act No. 117 for the penalty on children.

74. Thompson and Lummis, *Family Life and Work Experience,* interview 125.

75. Thompson and Lummis, *Family Life and Work Experience,* interview 365. See also Ruth Schwartz Cowan, *More Work for Mother: The Ironies of Household Technology from the Open Hearth to the Microwave* (New York: Basic Books, 1983); Joanna Bourke, "Housewifery in Working-Class England 1860–1914," *Past and Present* 143 (1994): 167–97.

76. Mrs. I. Beeton, *Mrs Beeton's Every-Day Cookery and Housekeeping Book* (1865; London: Bracken Books, 1984), v; Illich, H_2O, 1–2.

77. Beeton, *Mrs Beeton's Every-Day Cookery,* v. See also B. W. Richardson, "Woman as a Sanitary Reformer," *Report of the Fourth Congress of the Sanitary Institute of Great Britain* (London: Office of the Institute, 1880), 2:185–202, 196.

78. Karen Harvey, *The Little Republic: Masculinity and Domestic Authority in Eighteenth-Century Britain* (Oxford: Oxford University Press, 2012), 38–39; Beeton, *Mrs Beeton's Every-Day Cookery,* i.

79. Beeton, *Mrs Beeton's Every-Day Cookery,* v; emphasis in original.

80. *Balfour Commission,* C. (2nd series) 7172-I, qs. 882–83; *Return, as Regards Each Water Company in Metropolis, of Name of Parish Where Supply is Constant, and Where Intermittent,* BPP 1895, no. 459, 5; Taylor and Trentmann, "Liquid Politics," 205.

81. *Cost of Living of the Working Classes: Report of an Enquiry by the Board of Trade into Working Class Rents, Housing and Retail Prices, together with the Standard Rates of Wages Prevailing in Certain Occupations in the Principal Industrial Towns of the United Kingdom,* BPP 1908, Cd. 3864, 44, 54.

82. Thompson and Lummis, *Family Life and Work Experience,* interview numbers 365 and 006.

83. For example, LCC Medical Officer of Health Shirley Forster Murphy, *Balfour Commission,* C. (2nd series) 7172-II, appendix C. 18; Luckin, *Pollution and Control,* 129–34. For poverty studies from the 1880s, see, e.g., Finlayson, *Citizen, State and Social Welfare,* 108–15.

84. Margery Spring Rice, *Working-Class Wives: Their Health and Conditions* (Harmondsworth, UK: Pelican Books, 1939), 100, 136.

85. William Robson, *The Government and Misgovernment of London* (London: George Allen & Unwin, 1939), 116; *Water Undertakings (England and Wales) Return,* BPP 1914, no. 395, 30.

86. For waterscapes, see n. 9; Marina Moskowitz, "Backyards and Beyond: Landscapes and History," in *History and Material Culture: A Student's Guide to Approaching Alternative Sources,* ed. Karen Harvey (London: Routledge, 2009), 67–84.

87. Illich, H_2O, 7; Linton, *What Is Water?,* 4.

88. See n. 7. On baths, see *Balfour Commission,* C. (2nd series) 7172-I], q. 3235.

89. Luckin, *Pollution and Control*, 132–33.

90. Leslie B. Wood, *The Restoration of the Tidal Thames* (Bristol, UK: Adam Hilger, 1982), 53. On concern about declining fish stocks, see Alwyne Wheeler, *The Tidal Thames: The History of a River and Its Fishes* (London: Routledge, Kegan & Paul, 1979), 19–83; Vanessa Taylor, "Whose River? London and the Thames Estuary, 1960–2014," *The London Journal* 40, no. 3 (2015): 244–71. For an account of engagement with ecosystems in Victorian London, see Agnes Kneitz, "Polluting Thames, Declining City: London as an Ecosystem in Charles Dickens' *Our Mutual Friend*," in Schott, Knoll, and Lübken, *Rivers Lost—Rivers Regained*, 216–34. For campaigning by the Thames Preservation League (1883) and others, see, e.g., Paul Readman, *Storied Ground: Landscape and the Shaping of English National Identity* (Cambridge: Cambridge University Press 2018), chap. 6.

91. Joel A. Tarr, "The Separate vs. Combined Sewer Problem: A Case Study in Urban Technology Design Choice," *Journal of Urban History* 5, no. 3 (1979): 308–39; "Thames Water," Tideway, https://www.tideway.london/, accessed 25 May 2018.

8. "A Once Rural Place"

1. The best account is still John Davis, *Reforming London: The London Government Problem 1855–1900* (Oxford: Oxford University Press, 1988).

2. David Owen, *The Government of Victorian London 1855–1889: The Metropolitan Board of Works, the Vestries and the City Corporation* (Cambridge, MA: Belknap Press of Harvard University Press, 1982); H. J. Dyos, *Victorian Suburb: A Study of the Growth of Camberwell* (Leicester, UK: Leicester University Press, 1961); A. Clinton and P. Murray, "Reassessing the Vestries: London Local Government 1855–1900," in *Government and Institutions in the Post-1832 United Kingdom*, ed. Alan O'Day (Lewiston, N.Y.: Edwin Mellen Press, 1995), 51–84; and Anne Hardy, *The Epidemic Streets: Infectious Disease and the Rise of Preventive Medicine 1856–1900* (Oxford: Clarendon Press, 1993).

3. Geoffrey Best, *Mid-Victorian Britain 1851–75* (London: Weidenfeld and Nicolson, 1971), 11. See also the classic Adna Ferrin Weber, *The Growth of Cities in the Nineteenth Century: A Study in Statistics* (London: Macmillan, 1899), 40–56.

4. *Annual and Decennial Reports of the Registrar-General*, British Parliamentary Papers, 1838–1920; *Census Reports for Great Britain*, 1801–1921, http://www.visionofbritain.org.uk/census/all_censuses.

5. Juliet Davis, "The Making and Remaking of Hackney Wick, 1870–2014: From Urban Edgeland to Olympic Fringe," *Planning Perspectives* 31, no. 3 (2016): 425–57.

6. Daniel Defoe, *A Tour thro' the Whole Island of Great Britain, Divided into Circuits or Journies* (London: J. M. Dent, 1927), cited in Millicent Rose, *The East End of London* (London: Cresset Press, 1951), 123. See also William Robinson, *The Histories and Antiquities of the Parish of Hackney, in the County of Middlesex* (London: J. B. Nichols, 1842–1843); Charles Booth, *Life and Labour of the People in London*, Third Series, *Religious Influences* (London: Macmillan, 1902), 74.

7. See G. E. Mitton, *Hackney and Stoke Newington*, ed. Walter Besant (London: Adam and Charles Black, 1908); George Grocott, *Hackney Fifty Years Ago: Some Reminiscences* (London: Potter, 1915); *Twentieth Annual Report of the Hackney Board of Works, 1875–6* (London: Hackney Board of Works, 1856–1899), 24.

8. Charles Booth, "Condition and Occupations of the People of East London and Hackney, 1887," *Journal of the Royal Statistical Society* 51, no. 2 (1888): 276–339.

9. Booth, *Life and Labour*, 74.

10. Metropolitan Borough of Hackney, *Report of the Distress Committee 1909*, 7.

11. See on these related issues Gareth Stedman Jones, *Outcast London: A Study in the Relationship between Classes in Victorian London* (Oxford: Clarendon Press, 1971), and David R. Green, *From Artisans to Paupers: Economic Change and Poverty in London 1780– 1870* (Aldershot, UK: Scolar Press, 1995).

12. Stedman Jones, *Outcast London*.

13. Edward Hart, "Mortality Statistics of Healthy and Unhealthy Districts of London," *Sanitary Record* 6 (1879): 57.

14. David R. Green, *Pauper Capital: London and the Poor Law, 1790–1870* (Aldershot, UK: Ashgate, 2010).

15. On Edward Frankland, see Christopher Hamlin, *A Science of Impurity: Water Analysis in Nineteenth-Century Britain* (Berkeley: University of California Press, 1990); Hamlin, "Edward Frankland's Early Career as London's Official Water Analyst: The Context of 'Previous Sewage Contamination,'" *Bulletin of the History of Medicine* 56, no. 1 (1982): 56–76. Note Tripe's position in *Annual Report of the Medical Officer of Health, Hackney, 1871* (London: Hackney Board of Works, 1856–1899), 30–31.

16. Emma M. Jones, *Parched City: A History of London's Public and Private Drinking Water* (Winchester, UK: Zero Books, 2013), 105–21.

17. For outlines of an astonishingly complex issue, see Michael Hebbert, "Governing the Capital," in *The Crisis of London*, ed. Andy Thornley (London: Routledge, 1992), 134–44; Tony Travers, *The Politics of London: Governing an Ungovernable City* (Basingstoke, UK: Palgrave Macmillan, 2004).

18. *Annual Reports by the Medical Officer of Health on the Sanitary District of Hackney* (London: Hackney Board of Works, 1856–1899; Metropolitan Borough of Hackney, 1900–1910). For an appreciative obituary, see "John William Tripe M.D.," *British Medical Journal* 1 (30 Apr. 1892): 941. On Tripe's successor, see "John King Warry" in *Alumni Cantabrigienses: A Biographical List of All Known Students*, ed. John Venn (Cambridge: Cambridge University Press, 1953), 3:310.

19. On Charles Booth, see T. S. Simey and Margaret Simey, *Charles Booth Social Scientist* (London: Oxford University Press, 1960); Rosemary O'Day and David Englander, *Mr Charles Booth's Inquiry: Life and Labour of the People of London Reconsidered* (London: Hambledon, 1993); and David Englander, *Poverty and Poor Law Reform: From Chadwick to Booth, 1834–1914* (London: Routledge, 2013). See also Lawrence Goldman, *Science, Reform and Politics in Victorian Britain: The Social Science Association, 1857–1886* (Cambridge: Cambridge University Press, 2004).

20. We can get to the heart of Tripe's view of the water theory and much else in John W. Tripe, *Report on the Cholera Epidemic of 1866 within Hackney District* (London: Hackney District Board of Works, 1866); and *Report of the Sanitary Committee on the Cholera Epidemic and the Preliminary Arrangements for Carrying out the Sanitary Act 1866* (London: Hackney District Board of Works, 1866).

21. For overviews of infection theories during our period, see Margaret Pelling, *Cholera, Fever and English Medicine, 1825–1865* (Oxford: Oxford University Press, 1978); Michael Worboys, *Spreading Germs: Disease Theories and Medical Practice in Britain 1865– 1900* (Cambridge: Cambridge University Press, 2000); and Christopher Hamlin, *Cholera: The Biography* (Oxford: Oxford University Press, 2009).

22. *Annual Report of the Medical Officer of Health, Hackney, 1873*, 20; and *Twenty Fourth Annual Report of the Hackney Board of Works, 1879–80*, 10.

23. This was a ubiquitous aspect of the water debate. See, for example, *Annual Report of the Medical Officer of Health, Hackney, 1873,* 20; *Twenty Fourth Annual Report of the Hackney Board of Works, 1879–80,* 10.

24. *Annual Report of the Medical Officer of Health, Hackney, 1882,* 18–21.

25. On this issue, see the comments in *Annual Report of the Medical Officer of Health, Hackney, 1882,* 18–21.

26. On the long-term development of London's water supply, the best synoptic overview is still Anne Hardy, "Water and the Search for Public Health in London in the Eighteenth and Nineteenth Centuries," *Medical History* 28, no. 3 (July 1984): 250–82. On late nineteenth-century water shortages, see Vanessa Taylor, Heather Chappells, Will Medd, and Frank Trentmann, "Drought Is Normal: The Sociotechnical Evolution of Drought and Water Demand in England and Wales," *Journal of Historical Geography* 35, no. 3 (July 2009): 568–91; and Vanessa Taylor and Frank Trentmann, "Liquid Politics: Water and the Politics of Everyday Life in the Modern City," *Past and Present* 221, no. 1 (May 2011): 189–241.

27. John King Warry returned to this issue nearly every year in the 1890s. See *Annual Report of the Medical Officer of Health, Hackney, 1895,* 42–49; and *Annual of the Medical Officer of Health, Hackney, 1898,* 43–49. See also *Hackney Vestry Second Annual Report, 1895–6,* (London: Hackney Board of Works, 1895–1896), 3–4.

28. *Annual Report of Hackney Metropolitan Council, 1907* (London: Metropolitan Borough of Hackney, 1907), 55.

29. *Annual Report of the Medical Officer of Health, Hackney, 1920,* 30.

30. *Thirty Sixth Annual Report of Hackney District Board, 1891,* 32.

31. *Second Report of the Commissioners Appointed to Inquire into the Best Means of Preventing the Pollution of Rivers Commission (River Lee Inquiry)* (London: George Eyre and William Spottiswoode, 1867).

32. *Annual Report of the Medical Officer of Health, Hackney, 1874,* 21.

33. *Annual Report of Hackney District Board, 1885–6,* 5; *Annual Report of the Medical Officer of Health, Hackney, 1885,* 36.

34. *Annual Report of the Medical Officer of Health, Hackney, 1889,* 61–3; *Annual Report of the Medical Officer of Health, Hackney, 1897,* Appendix A, "Conference of Delegates upon the Pollution of the River Lea," 76–92.

35. *Annual Report of the Medical Officer of Health, Hackney, 1905,* 67.

36. See the comments of Major Archibald Church, *Hansard Parliamentary Debates* (House of Commons), 25 July 1929, vol. 230, cols. 1485–86.

37. Leo Hickman, "Journey along the Lee," *The Guardian,* 9 Oct. 2009, https://www .theguardian.com/environment/2009/oct/09/river-lee-polluted-source. For historical context, see Jim Clifford, *West Ham and the River Lea: A Social and Economic History of London's Industrialized Marshland 1839–1914* (Vancouver: UBC Press, 2017).

38. On the clash between administrative boundaries and the elusiveness of patterns of pollution, see Bill Luckin, *Death and Survival in Urban Britain: Disease, Pollution and Environment, 1800–1950* (London: I. B. Tauris, 2015), 94–95.

39. The unending story of smoke in London can be pieced together from W. H. Te Brake, "Air Pollution and Fuel Crises in Preindustrial London, 1250–1650," *Technology and Culture* 16, no. 3 (1975): 337–59; William A. Cavert, *The Smoke of London: Energy and Environment in the Early Modern City* (Cambridge: Cambridge University Press, 2017); Christine L. Corton, *London Fog: The Biography* (Cambridge, MA: Harvard University

Press, 2015); Peter Thorsheim, *Inventing Pollution: Coal, Smoke, and Culture in Britain since 1800* (Athens: University of Ohio Press, 2006); and Thorsheim, "Interpreting the London Fog Disaster of 1952," in *Smoke and Mirrors: The Politics and Culture of Air Pollution*, ed. E. Melanie Dupuis (New York: New York University Press, 2004), 154–69.

40. *Annual Report of the Medical Officer of Health, Hackney, 1866*, 10; and Tripe, *Report on the Cholera Epidemic.*

41. *Annual Report of the Medical Officer of Health, Hackney, 1880*, 54.

42. *Annual Report on the Sanitary Condition, Hackney, 1899*, 25.

43. Meteorological Office, *London Fog Inquiry, 1901–2: Report to the Meteorological Council of Smoke* (London: HMSO, 1903).

44. The crucial starting point here is still Roy M. Macleod, "The Alkali Acts Administration, 1863–84: The Emergence of the Civil Scientist," *Victorian Studies* 9, no. 2 (Dec. 1965): 85–112. But see also Peter Reed, *Acid Rain and the Rise of the Environmental Chemist in Nineteenth-Century Britain: The Life and Work of Robert Angus Smith* (Farnham, UK: Ashgate, 2016).

45. Conditions during that slightly earlier period are graphically described in "The Fog," *Medical Times and Gazette* 2 (1873): 697; and "The Fog," *Lancet* 1 (1874): 27–28; and A. Parker, "Air Pollution Research and Control in Britain," *American Journal of Public Health* 47 (1957): 563.

46. In Manchester the clearing of the skies during the Depression reinforced a long-cherished belief that smoke betokened high levels of employment. See Stephen Mosley, *The Chimney of the World: A History of Smoke Pollution in Victorian and Edwardian Manchester* (Cambridge: White Horse Press, 2001).

47. W. H. Hamer, *Annual Report of the Council for 1914*, vol. 3, *Public Health* (London: London County Council, 1915), 3:40.

48. London housing and the London housing crisis, which never goes away, has generated a distinguished literature. See the seminal and recently reissued Anthony S. Wohl, *The Eternal Slum: Housing and Social Policy in Victorian London* (London: Routledge, 1977); David Englander, *Landlord and Tenant in Urban Britain, 1838–1918* (Oxford: Clarendon Press, 1983); and J. A. Yelling, *Slums and Slum Clearance in Victorian London* (London: Allen & Unwin, 1986).

49. John Benn claimed that its earliest members were "full of great schemes mostly framed to secure a millennium for London by return of post"—quoted in Ken Young and Patricia L. Garside, *Metropolitan London: Politics and Urban Change, 1837–1981* (London: Edward Arnold, 1982), 60. See also John Davis, "The Progressive Council," in *Politics and the People of London: The London County Council, 1889–1965*, ed. Andrew Saint (London: Hambledon, 1989), 27–29, 60.

50. John Burnett, *A Social History of Housing, 1815–1985* (London: Methuen, 1986), 145.

51. Michelle Allen, *Cleansing the City: Sanitary Geographies in Victorian London* (Athens: Ohio University Press, 2008), 116–24.

52. H. J. Dyos, quoted in Burnett, *Social History of Housing*, 146.

53. Davis, "Progressive Council," 42–44.

54. For context, see Susan Juliet Laurence, "The Politics of Housing in Hackney, 1880–1914" (PhD diss., London School of Economics, 1987).

55. Booth, *Life and Labour*, 78.

56. "Report on the Housing of the Working Classes in Hackney," in *Annual Report of the Medical Officer of Health, Hackney, 1901*, 64.

57. "Report on the Housing," 71. Today, many Londoners are forced to devote a considerably higher proportion of their income to rent than was the case a century ago.

58. "Petition from the Social Democratic Party," in *Annual Report of Hackney Metropolitan Borough, 1910*, 137–42.

59. *Report of the Medical Officer of Health Hackney, 1875*, 22. See also *Report of the Medical Officer of Health, Hackney, 1867*, 17, and *Report of the Medical Officer of Health Hackney, 1868*, 21.

60. Stedman Jones, *Outcast London*, 192.

61. See Tim Cooper, "Challenging the 'Refuse Revolution': War, Waste and the Rediscovery of Recycling, 1900–1950," *Historical Research* 81, no. 214 (2008): 710–31; Cooper, "Recycling Modernity: Waste and Environmental History," *History Compass* 8, no. 9 (2010): 1114–25. On London, see Andrea Tanner, "Dust-O! Rubbish in Victorian London, 1860–1900," *London Journal* 31, no. 2 (2006): 157–78.

62. C. F. Young, *Report of the Medical Officer on the Collection and Disposal of House Refuse by London Sanitary Authorities*, London County Council, paper no. 207, 22 Oct. 1894.

63. *Annual Report of Hackney District Board 1866*, 5, and *Annual Report 1867*, 4.

64. *Annual Report of the Medical Officer of Health, Hackney, 1878*, 27.

65. *Annual Report of the Medical Officer of Health, Hackney, 1897*, 60.

66. *Annual Report of the Medical Officer of Health, Hackney, 1881*, 25.

67. *Annual Report of the Medical Officer of Health, Hackney, 1902*, 67. See also W. Francis Goodrich, *Refuse Disposal and Power Production* (London: Archibald Constable, 1904).

68. William A. Robson, *The Government and Misgovernment of London* (London: Allen and Unwin, 1939), 227–28; J. C. Dawes, *Report of an Investigation into the Public Cleansing Service in the Administrative County of London* (London: HMSO, 1929).

69. Michel Foucault, *Power/Knowledge: Selected Interviews and Other Writings 1972–1977*, ed. and trans. by Colin Gordon (London: Pantheon, 1980).

70. *Annual Report of the Medical Officer of Health, Hackney, 1895*, 49–54.

71. *Annual Report of the Medical Officer of Health, Hackney, 1895*, 49–54.

72. This situation had not been remedied by the mid-1930s. See William Alexander Robson, *The World's Greatest Metropolis: Planning and Government in Greater London* (Pittsburgh: University of Pittsburgh Press, 1963), 227–28.

73. See Harry Edwin Haward, *The London County Council from Within: Forty Years' Official Recollections* (London: Chapman and Hall, 1932), 358.

74. For clarification, see Graham Mooney and Andrea Tanner, "Infant Mortality, a Spatial Problem: Notting Dale Special Area in George Newman's London," in *Infant Mortality: A Continuing Social Problem*, ed. E. Garrett et al. (Aldershot, UK: Ashgate, 2007), 79–98.

75. Hector Gavin, *Sanitary Ramblings, Being Sketches and Illustrations of Bethnal Green: A Type of the Condition of the Metropolis and Other Large Towns* (London: John Churchill, 1848).

76. For methodological analysis of this issue, see Graham Mooney, Bill Luckin, and Andrea Tanner, "Patient Pathways: Solving the Problem of Institutional Mortality during the Later Nineteenth Century," *Social History of Medicine* 12, no. 2 (1999): 227–69.

77. *Annual Report of the Medical Officer of Health, Hackney, 1873*, 13.

78. *Annual Report of the Medical Officer of Health, Southwark, the Vestry of St George the Martyr* (London: Vestry of St George the Martyr, Southwark, 1895), 33.

79. See Jan Marsh, *Back to the Land: The Pastoral Impulse in England 1880–1914* (London: Quartet Books, 1982); Peter Gould, *Early Green Politics: Back to Nature, Back to the Land, and Socialism in Britain, 1880–1900* (Brighton, UK: Harvester, 1988); and Dennis Hardy, *Alternative Communities in Nineteenth Century England* (London: Longman, 1979).

80. *Annual Report of the Medical Officer of Health, Southwark, 1895*, 34–35.

81. *Medical Officer of Health Report, Southwark Vestry of the Parish of St. George the Martyr, 1905* (London: Vestry of St George the Martyr, Southwark, 1905), 33.

82. *Medical Officer of Health Report, Southwark, 1905*, 33.

83. *Medical Officer of Health Report, Southwark, 1905*, 33.

84. *Report of the Sanitary Condition of the Hackney District for the Year 1913* (London: Hackney District Board of Works, 1913), 18.

9. Water for the Multitudes

1. Matthew Gandy, *Concrete and Clay: Reworking Nature in New York City* (Cambridge, MA: MIT Press, 2002), 22.

2. Ian Douglas, *Cities: An Environmental History* (London: I. B. Tauris, 2013), 119.

3. Tony Travers, *The Politics of London: Governing an Ungovernable City* (Basingstoke, UK: Palgrave Macmillan, 2003), 79.

4. Bill Luckin, *Pollution and Control: A Social History of the Thames in the Nineteenth Century* (Bristol, UK: Adam Hilger, 1986), 12.

5. Jerry White, *London in the Nineteenth Century: A Human Awful Wonder of God* (London: Vintage, 2007), 50.

6. White, *London in the Nineteenth Century*, 54.

7. Emma M. Jones, *Parched City: A History of London's Public and Private Drinking Water* (London: Zero, 2012), 96–102; Frank Trentmann and Vanessa Taylor, "Water Politics in Nineteenth Century London," in *The Making of the Consumer: Knowledge, Power and Identity*, ed. Frank Trentmann (Oxford: Berg, 2006), 63–64, 73.

8. Anne Hardy, "Water and the Search for Public Health in London in the Eighteenth and Nineteenth Centuries," *Medical History* 28 (1984): 250–84; and Hardy, "Parish Pump to Private Pipes: London's Water Supply in the Nineteenth Century," in *Living and Dying in London: Medical History Supplement 11*, ed. W. F. Bynum and Roy Porter (London: Wellcome Institute, 1991), 77–81.

9. World Health Organization, *The Diagnosis, Treatment and Prevention of Typhoid Fever* (Geneva: WHO, 2003).

10. E. H. Greenhow, "Proceedings in Reference to the Diarrheal Districts of England," in British Parliamentary Papers [hereafter BPP], *Second Report of the Medical Officer to the Privy Council*, 1860, C.2736, 362. On viral variants of the disease, which were almost certainly circulating in nineteenth- and early twentieth-century Britain, and which are now massively destructive killers in the developing world, see Marvin S. Krober et al., "Bacterial and Viral Pathogens Causing Fever in Infants Less Than 3 Months Old," *JAMA Pediatrics* 139 (1985): 889–92. Both in the past and present flies have also played a central role in spreading the infection. See Anne Hardy's perceptive remarks on this issue in chapter 3 of this volume.

11. *Report of the Medical Council in Relation to the Cholera Epidemic of 1854* (London: HMSO, 1855), 6; William Farr, "The Cholera Epidemic of 1853–4," in BPP, *Seventeenth Annual Report of the Registrar-General* (London: HMSO, 1856), 74–108.

12. Christopher Hamlin, *A Science of Impurity: Water Analysis in Nineteenth Century*

Britain (Berkeley: University of California Press, 1990); Michael Worboys, *Spreading Germs: Disease Theories and Medical Practice in Britain, 1865–1900* (Cambridge: Cambridge University Press, 2000).

13. Christopher Hamlin, "Edward Frankland's Career as London's Official Water Examiner 1865–1876: The Context of 'Previous Sewage Contamination,'" *Bulletin of the History of Medicine* 56 (1982): 56–76.

14. Luckin, *Pollution and Control*, 48–49.

15. Stephen Halliday, *The Great Stink of London: Sir Joseph Bazalgette and the Cleansing of the Victorian Metropolis* (Stroud: Sutton, 1998).

16. Luckin, *Pollution and Control*, 72–73.

17. BPP, *Royal Commission on the Metropolitan Sewage Discharge, First Report*, 1880, vol. 40, appendix O.

18. Luckin, *Pollution and Control*, 141–57.

19. John Davis, *Reforming London: The London Government Problem, 1855–1900* (Oxford: Clarendon Press, 1988); Jerry White, *London in the Twentieth Century: A City and Its People* (London: Vintage, 2001), 355–403; Travers, *Politics of London*.

20. BPP, *Royal Commission Appointed to Inquire into the Water Supply of the Metropolis, Report and Minutes of Evidence*, 1893–1894, C.7172, 40:16.

21. Emma M. Jones, *Parched City: A History of London's Public and Private Drinking Water* (Winchester, UK: Zero Books, 2013), 105–59; John Broich, *Water and the Making of the Modern City* (Pittsburgh: University of Pittsburgh Press, 2013), 59–60, 152–54.

22. Hardy, "Water and the Search for Public Health," 91–93.

23. Fred Pearce, *Watershed: The Water Crisis in Britain: Society, Technology and Science* (London: Junction Books, 1982), 127–49; David Kinnersley, *Troubled Water: Rivers, Politics and Pollution* (London: Hilary Shipman, 1988), 92–105.

24. John Hassan, *A History of Water in Modern England and Wales* (Manchester: Manchester University Press, 1998), 162.

25. Harold Macmillan used this famous phrase in his first speech to the House of Lords as Lord Stockton. See "Stockton Attacks Thatcher Policies," *Times*, 9 Nov. 1985. On privatization and water privatization, see Richard Vinen, *Thatcher's Britain: The Politics and Social Upheaval of the 1980s* (London: Simon and Schuster, 2009), 192–203: David Parker, The *Official History of Privatisation*, vol. 2, *Popular Capitalism, 1987–1997* (London: Routledge, 2012), 246–49.

26. Defra, *The Development of the Water Industry in England and Wales* (London: HMSO, 2006), 19.

27. "Who Really Owns the London Water?" Blue Gold, 31 Jan. 2012, https://water finance.wordpress.com/2012/01/31/who-really-owns-the-london-water/; John Allen and Michael Pryke, "Financializing Household Water: Thames, Water, MEIF and 'Ring-Fenced' Politics," *Journal of Regions, Economy and Society* 6 (2013): 419–39.

28. Karen J. Bakker, "Neoliberalizing Nature? Market Environmentalism in Water Supply in England and Wales," in *Neoliberal Environments: False Promises and Unnatural Consequences*, ed. Nik Heynen et al. (London: Routledge, 2008), 101–13; Karen J. Bakker, *An Uncooperative Commodity: Privatizing Water in England and Wales* (Oxford: Oxford University Press, 2003).

29. Manuel Schiffler, *Water, Politics and Money: A Reality Check on Privatization* (London: Springer, 2015), 66–69, 75–77.

30. Press Association, "Thames Water Profits Up 29.5 Percent but Household Bills Set

to Increase," *The Guardian*, 5 June 2015; Alex Brummer, "Sewer Rats? The Greedy Foreign Owners of Our Water Firms Squeeze Customers Dry; Thames Water Avoiding Tax Is the Final Insult," *Daily Mail*, 11 June 2013.

31. Rachel Rickard Straus, "Millions Could Face Water Bill Hike as Thames Water Asks Permission to Squeeze an Extra £29 from Every Customer," 13 Aug. 2013, https:// www.thisismoney.co.uk/money/bills/article-2389783/Thames-Water-asks-permission -squeeze-extra-29-customer.html.

32. Pearce, "Water Industry"; Aditya Chakrabarty, "Thames Water: The Drip, Drip, Drip of Discontent," *The Guardian*, 15 June 2014.

33. Mayor of London, *Securing London's Water Future: The Mayor's Water Strategy* (London: Greater London Authority, 2011), 34, https://www.london.gov.uk/sites/default /files/gla_migrate_files_destination/water-strategy-oct11.pdf.

34. Will Hutton, "Thames Water: A Private Equity Plaything That Takes Us for Fools," *The Guardian*, 11 Nov. 2012.

35. "What Is the Point of a Regulator if Water Companies Can Overcharge Customers 1.2bn?" *Independent*, 12 Jan. 2016.

36. UK House of Commons, Public Account Committee, *Economic Regulation of the Water Sector Report*, 2015, http://www.parliament.uk/business/committees-a-z/commons -select/public-accounts-committee/news/parliament-2015/economic-regulation-of -water-sector-rep/.

37. Emma Glanfield, "How the New £4 Billion Super Sewer Will Stop London Returning to the Days of the Great Stink . . . but Will Increase Bills by £80," *Daily Tele- graph*, 8 Sept. 2014.

38. Jennifer Rankin, "'Super Sewer' in London and South-East Could Add £80 to Water Bills," *The Guardian*, 12 Sept. 2014.

39. Ian Griffith, "Planned London Super Sewer Branded Waste of Time and Taxpayer Money," *The Guardian*, 27 Nov. 2014.

40. "Thames Water Price Bid Criticized by Consumer Body," BBC News, 12 Aug. 2013, http://www.bbc.co. uk/news/business-236663406; Emily Gosden, "Water Bills to Rise by £80 as London Super Sewer Approved," *Independent*, 18 Jan. 2016.

41. Department for Environment, Food & Rural Affairs, "Thames Tideway Tunnel Gets Go Ahead," 12 Sept. 2014, http://www.gov.uk/government /news/thames/tideway -tunnel-gets-go-ahead; Hutton, "Thames Water."

42. Gerard T. Koeppel, *Water for Gotham: A History* (Princeton, NJ: Princeton Uni- versity Press, 2000), 25–27, 57–59.

43. Koeppel, *Water for Gotham*, 75–82; Martin Melosi, *The Sanitary City: Urban Infra- structure in America from Colonial Times to the Present* (Baltimore: Johns Hopkins Univer- sity Press, 2000), 36–37.

44. Koeppel, *Water for Gotham*, 102–38; Diane Galusha, *Liquid Assets: A History of New York City's Water System* (Fleischmanns, NY: Purple Mountain Press, 1999, 2002), 13–15.

45. Koeppel, *Water for Gotham*, 150–55.

46. Koeppel, *Water for Gotham*, 167–72; Melosi, *Sanitary City*, 83–84.

47. Koeppel, *Water for Gotham*, 185–217.

48. New York City, Department of Environmental Protection, "History of New York City's Water Supply System," accessed 22 Aug. 2019, https://www1.nyc.gov/site/dep/ water/history-of-new-york-citys-drinking-water.page; Galusha, *Liquid Assets*, 19–32.

49. Gandy, *Concrete and Clay*, 38; Suellen Hoy, *Chasing Dirt: The American Pursuit of Cleanliness* (New York: Oxford, 1996).

50. Edward Wegmann, *The Water Supply of the City of New York, 1658–1895* (New York: Wiley, 1896), 64, 81.

51. Gandy, *Concrete and Clay*, 34–37; Maria Kaika, *City of Flows: Modernity, Nature, and the City* (New York: Routledge, 2005), 25–28.

52. Kaika, *City of Flows*, 54. For Kaika, "bad" water was "nonprocessed," but the advocates for using Hudson River water would have processed (filtered) it.

53. David Soll, *The Empire of Water: An Environmental and Political History of the New York City Water Supply* (Ithaca, NY: Cornell University Press, 2013), 35.

54. Gandy, *Concrete and Clay*, 41.

55. Melosi, *Sanitary City*, 121.

56. DEP, "History of New York City's Water Supply System"; Galusha, *Liquid Assets*, 89–112; Melosi, *The Sanitary City*, 126–27.

57. Soll, *Empire of Water*, 105–7; Galusha, *Liquid Assets*, 167–77.

58. Soll, *Empire of Water*, 105–7; Galusha, *Liquid Assets*, 178–85.

59. Soll, *Empire of Water*, 124.

60. Soll, *Empire of Water*, 128–29.

61. Gandy, *Concrete and Clay*, 48–51.

62. Soll, *Empire of Water*, 105–7.

63. Soll, *Empire of Water*, 143.

64. Soll, *Empire of Water*, 143–47.

65. Soll, *Empire of Water*, 159–65.

66. David W. Dunlap, "As a Plant Nears Completion, Croton Water Flows Again to New York City," *New York Times*, 8 May 2015. Conditions in the Croton watershed had not necessarily been pristine in the first decades of its existence. See, for instance, Timothy Matlack Cheesman, "Report of a Recent Sanitary Inspection of One of the Sources of the Croton Water Supply," *Transactions of the New York Academy of Medicine* 10 (1893): 194.

67. Soll, *Empire of Water*, 188, 194–95.

68. Soll, *Empire of Water*, 73, 181; "New York City Water Supply System," Wikipedia, https://en.wikipedia.org/wiki/New_York_City_water_supply_system.

69. "New York City Water Tunnel No. 3," Wikipedia, https://en.wikipedia.org/wiki/New_York_City_Water_Tunnel_No_3. Tunnel No. 2 still operates and connects to Tunnel No. 1. When Tunnel No. 3 is completed, it will be closed for inspection.

70. BPP, *Report on the Cholera Epidemic of 1866 in England: Supplement to the Twenty-Ninth Annual Report of the Registrar-General*, 1868, C. 4070 (1st series), vol. 37, 191 passim.

71. BPP, *Royal Commission Appointed to Inquire into the Water Supply of the Metropolis, Report and Minutes of Evidence*, 1893–1894, C.7172, vol. 40, ii, appendix G.1, table 2.

72. Bill Luckin, "The Metropolitan and the Municipal: The Politics of Health and Environment, 1860–1920," in *Cities of Ideas: Essays in Honour of David Reeder*, ed. Robert Colls and Richard Rodger (Aldershot, UK: Ashgate, 2004), 46–66.

73. Diana Liverman, "Who Governs at What Scale and at What Price? Geography, Environmental Governance and the Commodification of Nature," *Annals of the Association of American Geographers* 94 (2004): 734–38.

74. Anthony DePalma, "New York's Water Supply May Need Filtering," *New York Times*, 20 July 2006; Sarah Laskow, "Stirring Trouble," *Politico*, 6 Apr. 2015, http://www.capitalnewyork.com/article/city-hall/2015/04/8564883/stirring-trouble; Riverkeeper,

"Threats to NYC's Tap Water," 22 May 2013, http://www.riverkeeper.org/campaigns /safeguard/threats-to-nycs-tap-water/.

It is now recognized that suspended sediments often transport pollutants such as phosphorus, oil, and grease.

75. New York City, DEP, "Lead in Household Plumbing FAQs," accessed 22 Aug. 2019, https://www1.nyc.gov/site/dep/water/lead-in-household-plumbing-faq.page; New York State, Department of Environmental Conservation, "Facts about the NYC Watershed," accessed 22 Aug. 2019, http://www.dec.ny.gov/lands/58524.html. These pages are no longer available.

76. Eric Roy, "Lead in Drinking Water: Chemistry, Policy, New York City Case Study," 3 Feb. 2016, http://www.hydroviv.com/water-smarts/lead-in-drinking-water101-chemistry-policy-new-york-city-case-study; Sheila Kaplan, "Toxic Taps: Lead Is Still the Problem," Investigative Reporting Workshop, 8 Aug. 2012, http://investigativereporting workshop.org/investigations/toxic-taps/story/toxic-taps-lead-is-still-the-problem/.

77. Gary S. Logsdon, "How Waterborne Disease Outbreaks Relate to Treatment Failures," Association of Environmental Engineering & Science Professors, 2006, http:// www.aeespfoundation.org/sites/default/files/pdf/AEESP_CS_3.pdf.

A major outbreak of cryptosporidium occurred in the city of Milwaukee in 1993, involving over four hundred thousand people.

78. New York City, DEP, *Waterborne Disease Risk Assessment Program*, 2018, https:// www.google.com/search?client=firefox-b-1-d&channel=tus&q=New+York+City%2C +DEP%2C+Waterborne+Disease+Risk+Assessment+Program%2C+http%3A%2F%2F www.nyc.gov%2Fhtml%2Fdep%2Fhtml%2Fdrinking_water%2Fwdrap.shtml.

79. Sarah Crean, "New York City Constructs World's Largest Ultra-Violet Water Treatment Facility," *New York Environment Report*, 15 Nov. 2013, http://www.nyenvironment report.com/new-york-city-constructs-worlds-largest-ultra-violet/.

INDEX

Abercrombie, Patrick, 125–26
Aberdeen and Temair, 2nd Marquis of (George Gordon), 121
Abu Dhabi Investment Fund, 200
Act for Better Paving, Improving and Regulating the Streets of the Metropolis (1817), 139
agricultural land, 23, 30, 43
air pollution: from automobiles, 37, 74–75, 84; and coal fires, 37, 84; and early environmentalist thinking, 105, 109; and flies, 73–74; and fogs, 9–10, 70–72, 105; and gas purification, 150; and green space, 128; in Hackney, 183–84; mental health and, 107; from smoking, 74–75, 84; vegetation and, 118
airports, 67
air quality: domestic, 71, 96; and early environmentalist thought, 105; and environmental deterioration, 70; and environmental law, 136; fogs as focus of, 71; urban, nineteenth century, 117
air raids. *See* Blitz, the
alcohol (drinking), 80, 96, 99–100, 109, 192
Alkali Acts, 136, 143, 149, 151, 152, 154, 184
alkali industry, 132, 143, 150
Alkali Inspectorate, 8, 118, 136, 143
allergies, 94, 109
Amati, Marco, 128
ammonia production, 151, 154
animals: bombed-out sites and, 124; and green arteries, 118; naturalists and, 49; and outdoor leisure, 49; processing of, 55, 137–43; and study of urban-environmental history, 5
animals (types of): birds, 49, 122; cattle and cows, 28, 71, 138, 141; dogs, 48, 75, 81, 140; eels, 197; fish, 9, 61, 78–79, 148, 172, 197, 208; horses, 26, 53, 73, 74, 138, 139, 168; pigs, 55, 122; sheep, 138, 140, 141; waterfowl, 43
Anthropocene, 14, 65, 67
Anthropological Society, 63
Anti-Water Monopoly Association, 164–65
Ashokan Reservoir, 206
Association for Jewish Youth, 121
Atkins, Peter, 138

atmospheric pollution. *See* air pollution
Attlee, Clement, 34
automobiles: and green space after Second World War, 125; ownership of in interwar years, 36; pollution related to motor vehicles and 72, 74, 75, 84, 85; and population dispersal, 37; traffic from motor vehicles and, 36–37, 120

Bacon, John, 166
Balfour Commission, 171
Ballard, Edward, 144
Barking, 32, 33, 57, 61, 85, 135, 143
Bartlett, Thomas, 94–95
Bateman, Thomas, 94
Bateson, Charles, 71
baths, public, 167–68
Battersea ammonia works, 151
Battersea Park, 115, 124
Bazalgette, Joseph, 60, 61, 117, 143–44, 198
Beckton Gasworks, 32, 135, 151
Beckton Park, 129
Becontree Housing Estate, 33, 34, 63
Beeton, Isabella, 172
Belloc, Hilaire, 59
Bermondsey, 26, 30, 48, 77, 133, 140–41, 159
Bevington's Manure Works, 144
Bickersteth, Edward, 67
Binnie, Chris, 202
Black Deep, 61, 156
Blake, William, 14, 46
Blitz, the, 82, 124, 125
blood boilers, 139–40, 141
blood driers, 139–40, 141
Board of Water Supply (BWS), 206, 207–8
Bodmer, Johann Georg (John George), 148
bone boilers, 139, 140, 141, 142
Booth, Charles, 58, 78, 80, 108, 178, 181, 186
boroughs, 11, 14, 25, 35, 83, 180–81, 184–85
Brabazon, Reginald. *See* Meath, 12th Earl of
Brent, River, 27, 40
brewers, 133, 159
brewing, 6, 132